Gregg Typing/Series Seven

TYPING 1

GENERAL COURSE

ALAN C. LLOYD, Ph.D.
Director of Career Advancement, The Olsten Corporation, Westbury, New York

FRED E. WINGER, Ed.D.
Former Professor of Office Administration and Business Education, Oregon State University, Corvallis, Oregon

JACK E. JOHNSON, Ph.D.
Professor, Department of Office Administration/Business Education, East Texas State University, Commerce, Texas

REBECCA A. HALL
Department Chairperson for Business and Office Education, Centerville High School, Centerville, Ohio

PHYLLIS C. MORRISON, Ph.D.
Professor of Business and Business Education, Robert Morris College, Coraopolis, Pennsylvania

JOHN L. ROWE, Ed.D.
Late Chairperson of Business and Vocational Education, University of North Dakota, Grand Forks, North Dakota

GREGG DIVISION/McGRAW-HILL BOOK COMPANY

New York   Atlanta   Dallas   St. Louis   San Francisco   Auckland   Bogotá   Guatemala
Hamburg   Johannesburg   Lisbon   London   Madrid   Mexico   Montreal   New Delhi
Panama   Paris   San Juan   São Paulo   Singapore   Sydney   Tokyo   Toronto

Sponsoring Editors / Joseph Tinervia, Barbara N. Oakley
Editing Supervisors / Matthew Fung, Scott Kurtz, Gloria Schlein
Design Supervisors / Caryl Valerie Spinka, Sheila Granda
Production Supervisors / Frank Bellantoni, Laurence Charnow

Text Designer / Michaelis/Carpelis Design Associates, Inc.
Cover Designer / Studios South
Text Photographs / Martin L. Bough, Corporate Studios Communications, Inc.
Text Illustrators / Helen Miner, Jon Weiman
Technical Studio / Burmar Technical Corp.

The equipment shown in the photographs on pages 3, 65, 128, and 189 was
provided through the courtesy of J. P. Egan Co., IBM, The Mead Corporation,
Olivetti Corporation, Royal Business Machines, Inc., and SCM Corporation.
The form used on page 225 reprinted with the permission of, and available from,
Julius Blumberg, Inc., New York, New York 10013.

Library of Congress Cataloging in Publication Data

Main entry under title:

Typing 1, general course.

    (Gregg typing, series seven)
    Includes index.
    1. Typewriting—Study and teaching (Secondary)
I. Lloyd, Alan C.   II. Series.
Z49.T9557   652.3   81-15640
ISBN 0-07-038281-6   AACR2

Gregg Typing, Series Seven
Typing 1, General Course

   7 8 9 0 JHJH 8 9 8 7 6 5·

ISBN 0-07-038281-6

PREFACE

Series Seven is an exciting all-new edition of the famous *Gregg Typing* programs. Developed with the needs of students and teachers in mind, *Series Seven* offers all the text and workbook materials needed for a comprehensive, modern typewriting program. It also offers many exciting features that make *Series Seven* an effective instructional system.

PARTS OF THE PROGRAM

Designed to meet the needs of one-semester, one-year, or two-year courses of instruction, *Series Seven* offers a variety of student's textbooks and workbooks, as well as a special Teacher's Edition for each student's text:

Typing 1, General Course. The first-year *Gregg Typing* book offers 150 lessons of instruction. The first 75 lessons (one semester) are devoted to learning the keyboard and typing for personal use.

Typing 2, Advanced Course. The second-year *Gregg Typing* text includes a useful, comprehensive Reference Section for students. It also includes, of course, Lessons 151 through 300 of the *Gregg Typing* program.

Typing, Complete Course. Specially designed for the two-year program of instruction, the *Complete Course* text offers all 300 lessons from *Typing 1* and *Typing 2* in one binding.

Teacher's Editions. The three separate Teacher's Editions—one for each of the student's texts—include all the pages in the corresponding student's texts plus annotations intended only for the teacher. Each Teacher's Edition also includes a separate section of teaching methodology, as well as lesson-by-lesson teaching notes for all the lessons in that text.

Learning Guides and Working Papers. Four workbooks—one for each 75 lessons of instruction—provide not only the stationery and forms needed for all text jobs and in-baskets but also a variety of reinforcement and enrichment exercises correlated to the text copy and to the LABs (Language Arts for Business).

Instructional Recordings. The *Keyboard Presentation Tapes for Gregg Typing* are cassettes correlated to the textbook keyboard lessons in *Typing 1, General Course,* and in *Typing, Complete Course.*

Transparencies and Transparency Masters. These additional teaching tools are available to enhance the classroom presentation.

Resource Manual and Key. A complete key to all text jobs and projects (both in pica and in elite) is given in the *Resource Manual and Key.*

FEATURES OF GREGG TYPING, SERIES SEVEN

The *Series Seven* program incorporates many time-tested features from past editions of *Gregg Typing*; at the same time, it introduces innovative new features that both students and teachers will welcome. For example:

Diagnostic Exercises. Many timings utilize the Pretest/Practice/Posttest routine, which allows each student to diagnose areas in which additional skill development is needed. After taking a Pretest, students practice according to their specific needs (as diagnosed from the Pretest). After the Practice session, students take a Posttest, which enables them to see how the Practice session improved their skill.

Skill-Building Routines. In addition to the Pretest/Practice/Posttest routine, a variety of other skill-building routines are provided in the program. These routines help maintain student interest while developing the basic keyboarding skill.

Clinics. The Clinic that appears every sixth lesson is intended to strengthen skill development. Many of the Clinics use diagnostic routines.

Language Arts for Business (LABs). Concise, easy-to-understand LABs help students to review the basic uses of punctuation, capitalization, and abbreviations and to avoid the most common errors in using plurals, contractions, possessives, and so on. Students reinforce and apply the LAB rules as they type sentences and production assignments.

Cyclical Approach. In *Series Seven*, concepts are taught once and recycled several times, with each cycle building on the previous one and becoming progressively more complex. Each cycle is a "level," equal to half a semester. Thus the full two-year program includes eight levels—four per year.

Competency Checks. At the conclusion of each level of work, a Competency Check provides both the student and the teacher with an opportunity to check the student's level of performance. These Competency Checks may be used as informal or formal evaluations.

Tests. In the *Resource Manual and Key* are eight additional Competency Checks parallel to those in the text. These may be reproduced for classroom use as formal tests.

Information Processing. Word processing and data processing terminology and special applications are integrated into the text. Students, for example, format (and later fill in) form letters, type from simulated dictated copy, and prepare a procedures manual for a word processing center.

Decision-Making Exercises. To simulate real-life business experience, the *Series Seven* program includes many exercises that require students to make realistic "on-the-job" decisions. The complexity of the decisions to be made increases as students progress through the program.

Various Input Modes. Students will format letters, memos, and so on, from various input modes—for example, from unarranged copy, from handwritten copy, from rough draft, and from incomplete information.

The *Series Seven* program greatly reflects the comments, suggestions, and recommendations we received from many teachers, graduate students, and students throughout the country. We sincerely appreciate their contributions to the effectiveness of this publication. We especially thank all the teachers who participated in group sessions to discuss their needs and their students' needs, the teachers who reviewed the manuscripts that were developed as a result of the group sessions, the students who tested all our materials, and of course, the researchers who are continually helping to improve the teaching of typing. All have been instrumental in the development of *Series Seven*.

The Authors

CONTENTS

INTRODUCTION   Glossary of Terms **viii** / The Typewriter **x** / Getting Ready to Type **xii**

**LEVEL 1
KEYBOARDING**

GOAL: 30/3'/5e

UNIT 1 Keyboarding—The Alphabet

1 Home Keys: A, S, D, F, J, K, L, and Semicolon • Space Bar • Carriage or Carrier Return 2
2 Keys: H, E, and O 5
3 Keys: M, R, and I 6
4 Keys: T, N, and C • Figuring Speed 8
5 Keys: Right Shift, V, and Period • Punctuation Spacing • Counting Errors • Proofreading 10
6 Clinic: Skill Drive 12

UNIT 2 Keyboarding—The Alphabet

7 Keys: W, Comma, and G 13
8 Keys: B, U, and Left Shift 15
9 Keys: P, Q, and Colon 16
10 Keys: Hyphen, Z, and Diagonal • Punctuation Spacing 18
11 Keys: Y, X, and Question Mark 20
12 Clinic: Skill Drive 21

UNIT 3 Formatting—Basic Techniques and Procedures

13 Tab Stops • Indenting for Paragraphs • Typing All-Capital Letters 22

14 Formatting: Horizontal Centering • Job: Centering 24
15 Formatting: Block Centering • Job: Block Centering 26
16 Counting Lines • Formatting: Vertical Centering • Jobs: Advertisements 27
17 Formatting: Spread Centering • Formatting Announcements • Jobs: Announcements 30
18 Clinic: Technique Drive 31

UNIT 4 Keyboarding—The Numbers

19 Keys: 1, 2, and 3 • Formatting Enumerations • Jobs: Enumerations 32
20 Keys: 4, 5, and 6 • Jobs: Enumerations 34
21 Keys: 7, 8, and 9 • Formatting Poems • Jobs: Poems 36
22 Keys: 0, ½, and ¼ • Selecting an Appropriate Format • Jobs: Displays 38
23 Constructing Fractions • Typing Mixed Numbers • Formatting Recipes • Jobs: Recipes 40
24 Clinic: Number Drive 42

UNIT 5 Keyboarding—The Symbols

25 Keys: #, $, %, and & 43

26 Keys: (,), ', and " • Construct an Exclamation Point • Quotation Marks With Other Punctuation 45
27 Keys: __, *, ¢, and @ 47
28 Keys: !, =, and + • Phrases • Constructed Characters 49
29 Review of Symbol Keys • Jobs: Announcement, Enumeration 51
30 Clinic: Speed Drive 53

UNIT 6 Adjusting and Correcting—Techniques

31 Correcting Errors (Erasing, Tape, Fluid) • Jobs: Informal Notes 54
32 Correcting Errors (Squeezing and Spreading Characters) • Jobs: Informal Notes 55
33 Right Margin Bell • Making Line-Ending Decisions • Jobs: Informal Notes 57
34 Formatting Postal Card Messages • Job: Postal Card Form Messages • Aligning • Job: Fill-In Messages 58
35 Typing on Ruled Lines • Formatting Fill-Ins on Ruled Lines • Job: Ruled Fill-Ins on Reply Cards 60
36 Review 61
37 Competency Check 63

**LEVEL 2
FORMATTING FOR PERSONAL USE**

GOAL: 35/3'/5e

UNIT 7 Preparing for Production Typing

38 Rules of Word Division • Jobs: Dividing Words 66
39 More Rules of Word Division • Jobs: Word Division 68
40 LAB 1: Capitalization • Proofreaders' Marks • Jobs: Rough-Draft Paragraph and Enumeration 69
41 Jobs: Handwritten Draft; Rough-Draft Enumerations 71
42 Formatting an Outline • Jobs: Outlines 73
43 Clinic: Speed Drive 75

UNIT 8 Formatting One-Page Reports

44 Formatting a One-Page Report • Jobs: Reports 76
45 Formatting Side Headings in Reports • Jobs: Reports With Side Headings 78
46 LAB 2: Capitalization • Formatting Paragraph Headings in Reports • Jobs: Report With Headings 80
47 Formatting Run-In References • Jobs: Reports With Run-In References 81
48 Formatting References and Enumerations in a Report • Job: Report With Enumeration and References 83

49 Clinic: Accuracy Drive 86

UNIT 9 Formatting Letters

50 Formatting Personal-Business Letters in Modified-Block Style • Jobs: Personal-Business Letter 87
51 Job: Personal-Business Letter • Formatting Small Envelopes • Job: Addressing Small Envelopes 89
52 LAB 3: Number Style • Jobs: Personal-Business Letters 90
53 Formatting Business Letters in Modified-Block Style • Jobs: Business Letters 92
54 Formatting Enclosure Notations • Job: Business Letter • Formatting Large Envelopes • Job: Addressing Large Envelopes 94
55 Clinic: Speed Drive 96

UNIT 10 Formatting Tables

56 Formatting Tables • Jobs: Multicolumn Tables 97
57 Formatting Subtitles in Tables • Numbers in Columns • Jobs: Tables With Subtitles 99
58 LAB 4: Number Style • Formatting Blocked Column Headings • Jobs: Tables With Blocked Headings 101

59 Formatting Short Centered Column Headings • Jobs: Tables With Short Column Headings 102
60 Formatting Long Centered Column Headings • Jobs: Tables With Long Column Headings 103
61 Clinic: Number Drive 106

UNIT 11 Formatting Business Forms

62 Formatting Memos • Jobs: Memorandums 106
63 Jobs: Memorandums 109
64 LAB 5: Commas in Series • Formatting Forms • Jobs: Membership Applications; Transportation Requests 110
65 Formatting Display Forms • Jobs: Certificates; Membership Cards 112
66 Formatting Invoices • Jobs: Invoices 113
67 Clinic: Symbol Drive 115

UNIT 12 Formatting Long Reports

68 Formatting Long Reports • Job: Long Report 117
69/ LAB 6: Introductory *If, As,* and *When* Clauses • Formatting Text References and Footnotes • Job: Report With Footnotes 119
70

UNIT 12
(Continued)
71 Formatting Endnotes, a **122** Bibliography, and Cover

Page • Jobs: Endnotes, Bibliography, Cover
72 Formatting Bound Reports **124** • Job: Bound Report

73/ Review **125**
74
75 Competency Check **127**

UNIT 13   Keyboarding Skills Review
76 Skill Drive (5') **129**
77 Skill Drive (5') **131**
78 LAB 7: Commas in Compound Sentences • Skill Drive (5') **132**
79 Skill Drive (5') **133**
80 Technique Review • Skill Drive (5') **135**
81 Clinic: Techniques **136**

UNIT 14   Basic Formatting Review
82 Tabulator Review • Production Word Count • Centering Review **138**
83 Formatting Reports Review • Job: Long Report **139**
84 LAB 8: Commas Between Adjectives • Formatting Letters Review • Job: Letter **141**
85 Formatting Tables Review • Jobs: Multicolumn Tables **143**
86 Formatting Forms Review • Jobs: Memo; Invoice **144**
87 Clinic: Accuracy Drive **146**

UNIT 15   Formatting Reports
88 Formatting Minutes of a Meeting • Job: Minutes **148**
89 Formatting Magazine Articles • Jobs: Magazine Article; Minutes **150**
90 LAB 9: Commas After Introductory Words and **152**

Phrases • Formatting Resolutions • Jobs: Resolutions
91 Formatting Tables in Reports • Job: Two-Page Report With a Table **154**
92 Formatting an Itinerary • Job: Itinerary **155**
93 Clinic: Accuracy Drive **157**

UNIT 16   Formatting Tables
94 Formatting Ruled Tables • Job: Ruled Table **158**
95 Formatting Two-Line Column Headings • Jobs: Three-Column Tables **160**
96 LAB 10: Commas for Nonessential Elements • Formatting Tables With Leaders • Jobs: Two-Column Tables With Leaders **161**
97 Formatting Financial Statements • Jobs: Balance Sheet; Income Statement **163**
98 Jobs: Ruled Table With Leaders; Five-Column Table **165**
99 Clinic: Skill Drive **167**

UNIT 17   Formatting Letters
100 Letter-Placement Guide • Job: Letter **168**
101 Formatting an Attention Line • Formatting a Subject Line • Jobs: Letters **169**
102 LAB 11: Commas With Appositives • Formatting **171**

Letters With Indented Paragraphs • Formatting Letters in Block Style • Jobs: Letters
103 Formatting *cc* Notations **172** and *bcc* Notations • Assembling a Carbon Pack • Jobs: Letters
104 Formatting a Postscript • **174** Job: Letter
105 Clinic: Technique Drive **176**

UNIT 18   Formatting Business Forms
106 Formatting Credit Memorandums • Jobs: Credit Memorandums **178**
107 Formatting Purchase Requisitions and Purchase Orders • Jobs: Purchase Requisition; Purchase Orders **180**
108 LAB 12: Semicolons in Compound Sentences • Formatting Statements of Account • Jobs: Statements of Account **181**
109 Formatting Alphabetic File Cards • Jobs: File Cards; Table • Formatting Mailing Labels • Job: Mailing Labels **183**
110 Formatting Postal Card Addresses • Job: Postal Cards **184**
111 Review **186**
112 Competency Check **187**

**LEVEL 3
BASIC BUSINESS
FORMATTING**

GOAL: 38/5'/5e

UNIT 19   Formatting Reports
113/ Job: Business Report **190**
114
115 LAB 13: Exclamation Points • Formatting Legal Papers • Jobs: Power of Attorney; Bill of Sale **193**
116 Jobs: Will; Resolution **195**
117 Job: Legal Contract **197**
118 Clinic: Number Drive **199**

UNIT 20   Formatting Tables
119 Jobs: Ruled Tables **200**
120 Formatting Tables With Footnotes • Formatting Decimals in Table Columns • Jobs: Tables **202**
121/ LAB 14: Question Marks **204**
122 • Formatting Source Notes in Tables • Jobs: Display Tables With Leaders
123 Job: Leadered Display **206**
124 Clinic: Accuracy Drive **208**

UNIT 21   Formatting Letters
125/ Jobs: Letters • Formatting **209**
126 Enumerations in Letters • Jobs: Letters

127/ LAB 15: Quotation Marks **213**
128 • Formatting a Table Within a Letter • Jobs: Letters With a Table, *BCC* Notation, and Postscript
129 Formatting Letters on Baronial and Monarch Stationery • Jobs: Letters **216**
130 Clinic: Speed Drive **218**

UNIT 22   Formatting Business Forms
131/ Jobs: Purchase Requisitions; Purchase Orders **219**
132
133 LAB 16: Quotation Marks With Other Punctuation; Jobs: Business Invoice; Credit Memorandum **221**
134 Formatting Geographic File Cards • Jobs: File Cards; Ruled Table **223**
135 Formatting Legal Fill-In Forms • Job: Bill of Sale **224**
136 Review **225**

UNIT 23   Language Arts Review
137 Capitalization Review • Job: Letter **227**

138 Numbers Review • Jobs: Letters **229**
139 Comma Review • Jobs: Memorandums **231**
140 Comma Review • Semicolons Review • Jobs: Memorandums **233**
141 Exclamation Point, Question Mark, and Quotation Marks Review • Job: Report **235**
142 Clinic: Skill Drive **237**

UNIT 24   Applying for a Job
143– Formatting Résumés • **238**
147 Jobs: Résumés • Formatting and Composing Letters of Application • Jobs: Letters of Application • Filling Out Application Forms • Job: Application Forms • Composing Follow-Up Letters • Job: Follow-Up Letter
148 Language Arts Review **246**
149/ Competency Check **248**
150

**LEVEL 4
BUSINESS
FORMATTING**

GOAL: 40/5'/5e

SUPPLEMENTARY MATERIAL

Tables **S1** / Letters **S5** / Business Forms **S8** / Reports **S8** / Metric Supplement **S12** / Composition Exercises **S13** / Simulation: Callahan Publishing Company Conference **S17**

INDEX

Keys Introduced

A	3	5	35
B	15	6	35
C	8	7	36
D	3	8	37
E	5	9	37
F	3	0	38
G	14	½	39
H	5	¼	39
I	7	#	43
J	3	$	43
K	3	%	44
L	3	&	44
M	6	(	45
N	8	)	45
O	5	*	47
P	17	¢	48
Q	17	@	48
R	7	;	3
S	3	.	11
T	8	,	13
U	15	:	17
V	10	-	18
W	13	/	19
X	20	?	20
Y	20	+	49
Z	18	=	49
1	33	!	49
2	33	—	47
3	33	"	46
4	35	'	45

Others

Lock, 24; shift keys, 10, 15; constructed characters, 50

Drills

A–Z alphabet, 157–158, 209
1–0 numbers, 199
Symbols, 51, 132

Account, statements of, 182
Address block, 88, 180
Addresses
  on alphabetic file cards, 183
  dividing at end of line, 68
  on geographic file cards, 223
  inside (see Inside addresses)
  mailing, 90, 95
  on mailing labels, 184
  on postal cards, 185
  return, 87, 88, 90, 95
  state abbreviations in, 88
Adjectives
  commas between, 141, 233
  proper, capitalizing, 228
Alignment
  of decimals in columns, 100, 203
  with guide words, 59
  of numbers in columns, 100, 203
Apostrophe, space with, 45
Appositives, commas with, 171, 233
Attention line in letters, 169–170

Balance sheets, 164
Baronial stationery, 217
Bibliographies, 123
Bill of sale, 194
Blind carbon copy (bcc), 174
Body (message)
  of informal note, 55
  of memo, 107
  in letters, 87, 88
  in postal cards, 58
  of report, 76, 77, 117, 118
  words in, as letter-placement guide, 169
Book titles, underscoring, 82, 92
By-lines, 76, 150

Capitalization, 69, 80, 228
Capitals
  all-capital letters, 24
  initial cap, 80
  typing, 10, 15
Carbon copy (cc) notation, 173
  blind (bcc), 174
Carbon packs, 141, 173
Carbon paper, 141
Carriage or carrier return, 3, 32
Centering
  block, 26
  horizontal, 25, 36
  spread, 31
  vertical, 29, 36
Cents symbol (¢), 48, 50
Certificates, 112
Characters
  constructed, 50
  special (element machines), 50
Clauses
  independent, 132, 234
  introductory, 119, 232
Closing
  in business letter, 92, 93
  in informal note, 55
  in personal-business letter, 87, 88

Colons, space after, 19
Column headings in tables, 101, 102, 104, 160
Columns
  in business forms, 113, 114
  in tables (see Tables, columns in)
Commas, 232, 233 (see also Clauses)
  between adjectives, 141
  with appositives, 171
  in compound sentences, 132
  after introductory words or phrases, 152, 233
  for nonessential elements, 161
  in series, 110
  space after, 19
Complimentary closing (see Closing)
Compound words, dividing at end of line, 68
Constructed characters, 50
Constructed fractions, 40
Continuation pages
  for legal papers, 194, 419
  for reports, 117, 118
Contracts, legal, 198
Correcting errors, 54–56
Cover page for reports, 124
Credit memorandums, 179

Dates
  dividing at end of line, 68
  in informal notes, 55
  in letters, 87, 88, 92, 93, 169, 217
  month/year, 121
  in postal card messages, 59
Decimals in table columns, 203
Diagonal (slash), spacing before and after, 19
Diagonal key in constructing fractions, 40
Dollar sign ($)
  in invoices, 114
  space with, 43

Enclosure notations, 94
Endnotes, 123 (see also Bibliographies, References)
Enumerations, 34
  in letters, 211
  in reports, 84, 85
  titles in, 34
Envelopes
  large, 95, 96
  mailing and return addresses, 90
  small, 90
  special directions on, 95
Equals sign (=), 50
  space with, 49
Erasers, typewriter, 54
Errors (see also Typing techniques)
  correcting, 54–56
  counting, 11
Exclamation point (or mark), 46, 193, 236
  with quotation marks, 221

File cards
  alphabetic, 183
  geographic, 223
Financial statements, 164
Footnotes
  in reports, 120–121
  in tables, 203
Forms, 106–115, 178–185, 219–225 (see also specific types of forms, for example, Purchase orders)
  columns in, 113, 114
  display, 112
  guide words on, 113
  legal fill-in, 225
  ruled, 111
Fractions, 39, 40 (see also Numbers)

Guide words
  alignment with, 59
  on forms, 113
  in memos, 107

Headings
  in bibliographies, 123
  in business letters, 92
  column, in tables, 101, 102, 104, 160
  for endnotes, 123
  in invoices, 113
  in memos, 107
  in personal-business letters, 87, 88
  in reports
    paragraph, 80, 81
    side, 78, 118
Home keys, 2–4
Hyphens, space before and after, 18 (see also Word division)

ibid., 84
Inches, symbol for, 117
Income statements, 164
Independent clauses, 132
Initials, typist's, 92, 93
Inside addresses
  on baronial stationery, 217
  on letters, 87, 88
  on monarch stationery, 217
  number of lines from date, 169
Invoices, 113–115
Itineraries, 156

Job application letters, 241, 242, 245–246
Job application forms, 243–244
Jobs, applying for, 238–246

Key line in tables, 97, 100

Labels, mailing, 184
Leaders in tables, 162
Legal contracts, 198
Legal documents (see names of legal documents, for example, Power of attorney)
Legal fill-in forms, 225
Legal papers, 194
Legal typing, 186
Letter-placement guide, 169
Letterhead, 92, 93

Timings

Words	SI	Minutes	Page
84	1.09	3	44
84	1.12	3	48
84	1.13	3	52
84	1.13	3	53
90	1.11	3	54
90	1.13	3	56
90	1.14	3	57
90	1.16	3	58
90	1.20	3	60
90	1.20	3	62
90	1.20	3	63
96	1.23	3	66
96	1.25	3	68
96	1.26	3	71
96	1.26	3	73
96	1.26	3	78
96	1.26	3*	84
102	1.24	3	89
102	1.26	3	94
102	1.26	3*	96
102	1.26	3*	99
102	1.28	3*	104
105	1.27	3	107
105	1.29	3	113
105	1.29	3	116
105	1.30	3*	120
105	1.30	3	124
105	1.30	3	127
175	1.38	5	130
175	1.39	5	133
175	1.39	5	134
175	1.39	5	136
175	1.39	5*	138
175	1.39	5	142
175	1.38	5*	145
175	1.40	5*	147
175	1.37	5	148
185	1.36	5*	152
175	1.35	5	158
185	1.39	5	162
185	1.40	5	166
190	1.38	5*	175
190	1.39	5*	178
190	1.42	5	182
190	1.39	5*	185
190	1.44	5	188
195	1.30	5	191
195	1.33	5	197
195	1.36	5	200
195	1.37	5*	201
195	1.37	5*	204
195	1.39	5*	207
195	1.39	5*	208
200	1.32	5	210
200	1.34	5	213
200	1.37	5	217
200	1.38	5	219
200	1.39	5	220
200	1.41	5	222
200	1.41	5	224
200	1.41	5	227
200	1.47	5	232
200	1.47	5	235
200	1.48	5	247
200	1.48	5	249

* Pretest/Practice/Posttest.

Letters, 87–96, 168–175, 209–218 (see also parts of letters, for example, Body; Return addresses; Salutation)
  on baronial and monarch stationery, 217
  block-style, 172
  business, 92, 93
  carbon packs, 173
  enumerations in, 211
  folding, 90, 96
  with indented paragraphs, 171
  job application, 241, 242, 245–246
  line length in, 169
  modified-block style, 87, 92, 93
  personal-business, 87, 88
  tables within, 214
Lists (see Enumerations)

Magazine articles, 82, 150
Magazine titles, underscoring, 82, 92
Mailing address on envelopes, 90, 95
Mailing labels, 184
Meetings
  announcements of, 31
  minutes of, 149
Memorandums, 107, 108
  credit, 179
Message (see Body)
Minutes of meetings, 149
Monarch stationery, 217

Names
  on alphabetic file cards, 183
  dividing at end of line, 68
  on mailing labels, 184
  writer's, in letters, 87, 88
Notes, informal, 55
Nouns, capitalizing, 69, 228
Number style, 90
Number symbol (#), 43
Numbers, 229, 230 (see also Fractions)
  aligning in columns, 100, 203
  dividing at end of line, 68
  mixed, 40, 229
  as street names, 101, 230
  in time, 101, 230

Opening in letters, 87, 88, 92
Organizational chart, 444
Outlines, 73–74

Paper (see also Stationery)
  A4, 28, 87
  lines on a page, 28
  quality of, 140
  standard-size, 87
  standard length of, 28
  turned lengthwise, 102
Paragraphs
  indented, letters with, 171
  indenting for, 24
Parentheses
  in mathematical equations, 51
  space with, 45
Percent sign (%), space with, 44
Periods, spacing with, 11, 19 (see also Leaders in tables)
Plus sign (+), space with, 49

Poems, 37, 38
Postal cards, 58–59, 185
Postscript (PS), 175
Pounds, # as symbol for, 43
Power of attorney, 194
Production typing, 66–74
Production word count (PWC), 139
Proofreaders' marks, 70
Proofreading using paper bail, 12
Punctuation (see specific marks of punctuation, for example, Commas)
Purchase orders, 181
Purchase requisitions, 180
PWC (production word count), 139

Question marks, 204, 236
  with quotation marks, 221
  space after, 20
Quotation marks, 46, 213, 236
  for magazine article titles, 82
  with other punctuation, 221

Recipes, 41
References, 82, 84, 120 (see also Bibliographies; Endnotes; Footnotes)
Reports, 148–156
  bound, 125
  continuation pages, 117
  cover page for, 124
  enumerations in, 84, 85
  footnotes in, 120–121
  long, 117–125
  one-page, 76–85
  paragraph headings in, 80, 81
  run-in references in, 82
  side headings in, 78, 118
  tables in, 154
Resolutions (statements of opinion or fact), 153
Résumés, 238–240
Return addresses, 87, 88, 90, 95
Roman numerals, 50, 73, 74
Ruled lines, typing on, 60, 61
Ruled tables, 159

Sale, bill of, 194
Salutation (greeting)
  in informal note, 55
  in letters, 87, 88
  in postal card messages, 58
Semicolons, 19, 181, 234
Sentences, compound
  commas in, 132
  semicolons in, 181, 234
SI (syllabic intensity), 22
Signatures
  in informal notes, 55
  on letters, 87, 169
  on postal card messages, 58
Space bar, 2
Spacing, vertical, 28
Speed, figuring, 9, 17, 47
Spreading and squeezing to make corrections, 55–56
State name abbreviations, 88
Statements of account, 182
Stationery (see also Paper)
  baronial and monarch, 217
  letterhead, 92, 93

Street names, numbers as, 101, 230
Subject line in letters, 170
Subtitles
  in reports, 76, 77
  in tables, 100
Syllabic intensity (SI), 22
Syllables, dividing words by, 67, 68

Tab stops, 23
Tables, 97–105, 200–208
  column headings in, 101, 102, 104, 160
  columns in
    aligning decimals in, 165
    aligning numbers in, 100
    determining width of, 97–98
    with words and numbers, 159
  with footnotes, 203
  horizontal formatting of body, 97–98
  key line in, 97, 100
  with leaders, 162
  within letters, 214
  numbers in, 100, 202
  in reports, 154
  ruled, 159
  source notes for, 206
  subtitles in, 100
Tabulator, 23
Time, expressing, 101, 230
Typewriter erasers, 54
Typewriter ribbon, 140
Typewriters
  care of, 140
  carriage or carrier return, 3, 32
  element, special characters on, 50
Typing techniques
  correcting and adjusting, 54–61
  eyes on copy, 7, 32
  increasing accuracy, 185
  increasing speed, 21, 147
  position of feet, 16
  position of hands, 22
  posture, 9, 174
  recording errors, 17
  space bar, 2
  top row reaches, 33
Typists' initials in letters, 92, 93

Underscoring, 47
  of book and magazine titles, 82

Vertical spacing, 28

Wills (legal documents), 195
Word division, 67, 68
  line-ending decisions, 57, 58
Words a minute (wam), 9, 17
Writer's (return) address, 87, 88, 90, 95
Writer's initials in memos, 107
Writer's name
  in letters, 87, 88, 92, 93
  in magazine articles, 150

Z rule, 225
ZIP Code, space preceding, 88, 90, 95, 185

INTRODUCTION

The *Series Seven* program has been specially designed to help you develop your typewriting skills through a carefully planned, step-by-step process. To be sure that you understand the terms, the procedures, and the directions used throughout this book, as well as the operation of the machine you are using, be sure to read this introduction and refer to it whenever you have any question or problem.

GLOSSARY OF TERMS

The special terms and symbols used throughout this text are very easy to understand. Read the following glossary to be sure you know the meaning of the terms and symbols, and refer to the glossary whenever necessary.

GOAL STATEMENTS

Skill Goal. At the beginning of every unit, a skill goal is given—the goal you are aiming to achieve by the end of that unit. For example, the skill goal *To type 35/5'/5e* means "to type 35 words a minute for 5 minutes with 5 or fewer errors."

Production Goal. At the beginning of every lesson, one or more production goals are given for that lesson; for example, "To format a report from handwritten copy." Production goals alert you to the kinds of activities that you will type in each lesson.

FORMATTING INSTRUCTIONS

Formatting means arranging a document according to a specific set of rules.

A number of formatting terms and symbols are used to help you clearly understand the directions for completing each activity in *Series Seven*. The most commonly used terms and symbols and their meanings are given below.

Single spacing (or *double* or *triple spacing*) tells you how to set your typewriter for that particular lesson.

40-, 50-, 60-, or 70-Space line tells you the specific line length to use.

60P/70E indicates a 60-space line for typewriters with pica (P) type, a 70-space line for typewriters with elite (E) type.

5-Space tab tells you precisely where to set your tab stops for a particular lesson—in this case, 5 spaces from the left margin.

Arrows in production work are used as follows:

→ This arrow is used in some tables to show you the vertical center of your work.

↓ 3 Arrows with numbers tell you how many lines down the next line should be typed—in this case, 3 lines.

Standard format will be stated in the directions for letters, tables, and so on, once you have learned the standard format for these kinds of jobs. To refresh your memory of the standard format, page numbers are often provided; for example, "Standard format (see page 209)."

Body 120 words tells you there are 120 words in the body of a letter. Knowing the approximate length of a letter will help you to adapt the standard format to position the letter on the page. Thus the number of words in the body of the letter is given to help guide you.

Workbook 86 indicates that a form or a letterhead for that specific job is provided in the *Learning Guides and Working Papers* workbook. If no workbook page is cited, then you are to use plain paper.

SKILL-BUILDING ROUTINES

Typewriting is a skill, and a skill is best developed through directed practice. *Series Seven* provides a variety of effective skill-building routines to improve the speed and the accuracy of your typing, including the following:

A variety of **Pretest/Practice/Posttest** routines is offered—all designed to improve either speed or accuracy through a proven, step-by-step procedure. First the *Pretest* (a 2-, 3-, or 5-minute timing) helps you identify your speed or accuracy needs. Having identified your needs, you then do the *Practice* exercises—a variety of intensive improvement drills. After you have completed the *Practice* exercises, you take a *Posttest*. Because the Posttest is identical to the Pretest, the Posttest measures your improvement.

12-Second timings are routines in which you take a series of short timings to boost speed or accuracy.

30-Second timings are slightly longer routines in which you take a series of short timings.

"OK" timings help you build accuracy on alphabetic copy (that is, copy that includes all 26 letters of the alphabet). You take three 30-second timings on the copy to see how many error-free copies you can type.

SCALES AND INDEXES

Series Seven uses a variety of scales and indexes designed to help you (1) measure quickly—with little counting—how many words you have typed, (2) analyze whether you should practice speed drills or accuracy drills, and (3) identify the relative difficulty of the copy you are typing.

Word Count Scales. You get credit for typing a "word" whenever you advance 5 spaces. Thus when you have typed a 60-space line, you have typed 12 words. To save you time, word counts that appear at the right of a timing tell you the cumulative number of words you have typed at the end of each completed line.

The scale shown at the right, for example, is used with timings that have 12 words a line. In production work, the scale at the right also gives you stroking credit for using the tabulator, for centering, and for other nonstroking movements.

12
24
36
48
60

To quickly determine the words typed for *in*complete lines, use the scale that appears below each timing:

| 1 | 2 | 3 | 4 | 5 | 6 | 7 | 8 | 9 | 10 | 11 | 12

This scale quickly indicates the number of words typed. Just align the last word typed with the number on the scale.

When you take a 3- or 5-minute timing, use the speed markers (the small numbers above the copy) to quickly find your words-a-minute speed.

This special scale appears with 12-Second Timings:

25   30   35   40   45   50   55   60

It converts your typing speed during a 12-second timing into words-a-minute.

Practice Guide. In certain skill-building routines, you will use the following chart to find the drill lines you should type:

Pretest errors	0-1	2-3	4-5	6+
Drill lines	29-33	28-32	27-31	26-30

For example, if you made only 1 error in the Pretest, then the guide directs you to complete "Drill lines 29–33"; if you made 3 errors, you should complete "Drill lines 28–32"; and so on.

Syllabic Intensity (SI) Index. To indicate the relative difficulty of copy, syllabic intensity (SI) is often listed. The SI number is computed by dividing the number of actual words in the copy into the total number of syllables of all words. Thus 1.00 indicates copy that has one syllable per word; 1.50 indicates copy that has an average of one and a half syllables a word; and so on. The higher the number, the more difficult the copy.

LABs

Effective typewriting requires a knowledge of at least the basics of grammar, punctuation, and style. The *Series Seven* program provides Language Arts for Business (LABs) that offer concise, practical reviews and application exercises on punctuation, capitalization, and number use, for example. Thus you may review the most common language arts principles *as you type* sentences and production activities.

Before you start to type, take a few minutes to get to know the names, locations, and uses of the main parts of your typewriter. First, note whether you are using an electric or a manual machine. If you have an electric, decide whether you have a typebar machine similar to the one illustrated below or an element machine similar to the one shown on the next page. Now refer to the proper illustration as you take these steps for learning each machine part listed and described below and on the next page.

1. Read the description of the machine part.

2. Look at the drawing and note the location of the part.

3. Find the part on your machine—but do not operate it until instructed to do so. (The location of some parts varies from one make of machine to another.) If you cannot find a part quickly, ask your teacher or a classmate to help you find it.

BACKSPACE KEY. Moves the carriage or carrier backward one space at a time.

CARRIAGE (typebar only). Movable part of the machine that allows the typewriter to print across the page.

CARRIAGE RELEASE (typebar only). Frees the carriage so you can move it by hand.

CARRIAGE RETURN (typebar only). A lever (manual) or key (electric) used for returning carriage to left margin and advancing the paper for start of next line.

CARRIER (element only). Movable part of the machine that allows the typewriter to print across the page.

CARRIER RETURN (element only). Used for returning carrier to left margin and advancing the paper for start of next line.

ELEMENT (element only). Ball-like device that contains all the letters and symbols.

EXPRESS KEY (found on many element machines). Moves the carrier rapidly to the left without line spacing.

LINE SPACE SELECTOR. Controls space between lines of typing.

MARGIN RELEASE. Temporarily unlocks the margin.

MARGIN SCALE. Guides setting the margins (sometimes called *Carriage-Position Scale*).

MAIN PARTS OF A TYPEBAR MACHINE

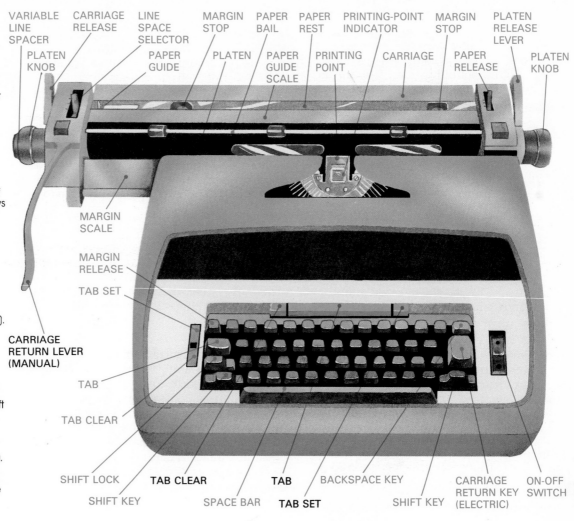

MAIN PARTS OF AN ELEMENT MACHINE

MARGIN STOPS. Key or lever used to block off side margins.

ON-OFF SWITCH (electric only). Controls motor power.

PAPER BAIL. Holds paper against the platen.

PAPER GUIDE. Blade against which paper is placed when paper is inserted.

PAPER RELEASE. Loosens paper for straightening or removing.

PLATEN. Large roller around which paper is rolled.

PLATEN KNOBS. Used to turn paper into the machine.

PLATEN RELEASE LEVER. Allows a temporary change in the line of writing.

PRINTING POINT. The place where the typebar or the element strikes the paper.

PRINTING POINT INDICATOR. Shows the position on the margin scale where the machine is ready to print.

SHIFT KEY. Positions the typebar or the element so that a capital letter can be typed.

SHIFT LOCK KEY. Permits typing a series of all-capital letters.

SPACE BAR. Used for spacing between characters or words.

TAB/TABULATOR. Moves the carriage/ carrier freely to preset points.

TAB CLEAR. Used to remove tab stops one at a time.

TAB SET. Positions tab stops.

VARIABLE LINE SPACER. Permanently changes the line of writing.

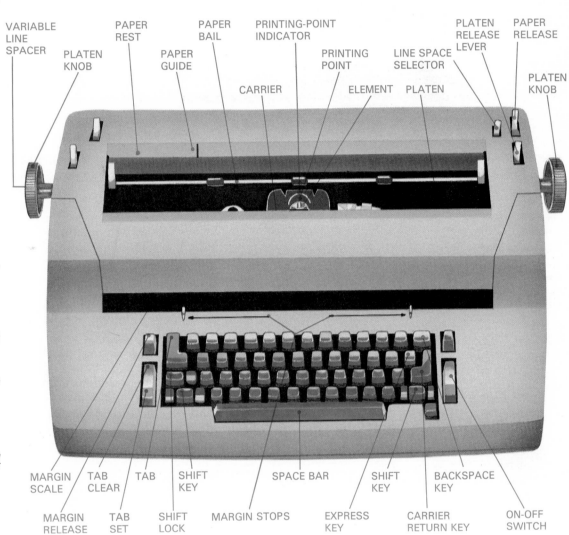

TYPE SIZES

10 pitch--pica
12 pitch--elite

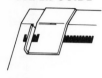

Typewriters are usually equipped with one of two sizes of type: pica or elite.

Pica type (also called *10 pitch*) is larger than elite. Pica prints 10 letters to an inch (25.4 mm). Elite type (called *12 pitch*) prints 12 letters to an inch (25.4 mm).

The width of standard paper is 8 ½ inches (216 mm), which is equal to 85 spaces of pica type or 102 spaces of elite type. Thus the center of standard paper is 42 on pica machines and 51 on elite machines, usually written 42P/51E.

CENTERING POINT

PAPER GUIDE

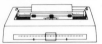

PLATEN CENTER

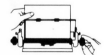

Three common methods for selecting a centering point are explained below. Each requires you to set the paper guide differently.

1. Set the paper guide at 0 and insert a sheet of paper. If you are using a pica machine, your centering point will be 42. If you are using an elite machine, your centering point will be 51. Therefore, if you use 42P/51E as the centering point, be sure to set your paper guide at 0 before you insert the paper.

2. The second method is to use 50 (or some other common centering point) as the centering point for any machine, pica or elite. Follow these steps to determine where the paper guide belongs:

   a. Pull the paper bail forward or up.
   b. Move the paper guide as far to the left as it can go.
   c. Set the carriage or carrier at 50 (or the centering point of your choice).
   d. Mark the center of the top of a sheet of paper by creasing it.
   e. Insert the creased sheet: hold it in your left hand, place it behind the

   platen, and draw the paper into the machine by turning the platen knob with your right hand.
   f. Engage the paper release to loosen the paper; then slide the paper left or right until the center crease is at the printing point—the point where the printing occurs. Then return the paper release to its original position.
   g. Slide the paper guide to the right until its blade edge is snugly against the sheet of paper.

Note on the margin scale exactly where you have set the paper guide. Now you will be able to confirm or correct the position of the paper guide very easily and quickly. Do so each time you begin typing.

3. Another method is to use the center of the platen as the centering point. (The center is usually marked by a small dot on the margin scale.) Depending on the length of the platen, the center may be 55P/66E or 65P/78E. Follow the same steps given in method 2 above to determine where the paper guide belongs.

PAPER HANDLING

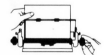

Practice this routine several times:

1. Confirm the paper guide setting.
2. Pull the paper bail forward or up.
3. With your left hand, place the paper behind the platen and against the paper guide; use your right hand to turn the right platen knob to draw in the paper. Advance the paper until about a third of the front is visible.
4. Check that the paper is straight by aligning the left edges of the front and the back against the paper guide. If they do not align, loosen the paper (by engaging the paper release) and straighten it.

5. Place the paper bail back against the paper. Adjust the rollers on the bail so that they are spread evenly across the paper.
6. Turn the right-hand platen knob until only ¼ inch or so of the paper shows above the bail. Now the paper is in the correct position for the opening drill of each lesson.
7. To remove the paper, draw the bail forward or up. Then engage the paper release (right hand) as you silently draw out the sheet of paper (left hand). Finally, return the paper release to its normal position.

FORMATTING

Formatting a document means arranging it according to a specific set of rules (or, sometimes, according to your own preference). Deciding on margins and line spacings is part of formatting.

MARGIN PLANNING

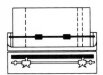

Margins at the left and right sides of a typed page are controlled by margin stops that limit the line of typing. To plan the left and right margin settings:

Left Margin. Subtract half the desired line from the center. For example, for a 40-space line, subtract 20 from the centering point you are using.

Right Margin. Add half the desired line length to the center. Then add 5 extra spaces (an allowance for line-ending adjustments).

Some sample margin settings appear in the next column.

Margin settings using 50 as the center:

Line Length	Pica	Elite
40-space line	30–75	30–75
50-space line	25–80	25–80
60-space line	20–85	20–85

Margin settings using 42P/51E as the center:

Line Length	Pica	Elite
40-space line	22–67	31–76
50-space line	17–72	26–81
60-space line	12–77	21–86

MARGIN SETTING

SPRING SET

HOOK ON

Spring-Set Machines. Some typewriters have a margin set key at each end of the carriage. For the *left margin*: (1) press the left margin set key, (2) move the carriage to the desired scale point, and (3) release the set key. For the *right margin*: (1) press the right margin set key, (2) move the carriage to the desired scale point, and (3) release the set key.

Hand-Set Machines. Many typewriters (including most element machines and most portables) have hand-set levers, not margin set keys. Each lever is moved separately by hand: (1) press down, or push in, the lever, (2) slide the stop right or left to the desired scale point, and (3) release the lever.

Hook-On Machines. Some typewriters have margin set keys on the keyboard. For the *left margin*: (1) move the carriage to the left margin, (2) hook onto the left margin stop by holding down the margin set key, (3) move the carriage to the desired scale point, and (4) release the set key. For the *right margin*: (1) move the carriage to the right margin, (2) hook onto the right margin stop by holding down the set key, (3) move the carriage to the desired point, and (4) release the set key.

LINE SPACING

The blank space between lines is controlled by the line space selector. Set it at *1* for single spacing, which provides no blank space between typed lines, and at *2* for double spacing, which provides 1 blank line between lines. Many machines also have 1½ spacing, 2½ spacing, and/or triple spacing.

Line Space Selector

Set at 1	Set at 2
single	double
single	
single	double
single	
single	double

WORK STATION ARRANGEMENT

Organizing the work station around the typewriter helps you complete your assignments more efficiently. For most typewriters and desk styles, the most efficient way to organize a typewriting work station is to:

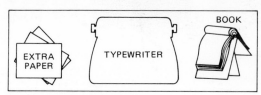

1. Place the typewriter near the center of the desk, even with the front of the desk.
2. Place supplies to one side of the typewriter.
3. Place materials to be typed on the opposite side of your supplies.
4. Store away all other items that are not being used.

If you are using a manual typewriter, arrange your work station as shown in the illustration above. Place the materials to be typed to your right, otherwise your vision will be blocked during carriage returns. On electric machines, the return of the carriage or carrier will not block your vision, so you may arrange the materials to be typed at your left or your right, depending on the desk style or whether you are left-handed or right-handed.

TYPEWRITING POSTURE

Your accuracy and speed in operating the typewriter will be affected by your posture.

Use appropriate posture from the first day so that you can learn to type well. Sit like the typist in the illustration:

Head erect and facing the book, which is tilted to reduce reflected light on the paper.
Back straight with body leaning forward slightly; shoulders level.
Body a handspan from the machine, centered opposite the J key.
Feet apart, firmly braced on the floor, one foot ahead of the other.
Fingers curved so that only the tips touch the keys.
Palms up slightly, off the front of the machine so that the fingers are free to move as you type.

LEVEL 1

KEYBOARDING

4. Vacating or abandoning the building.

If one or more of these events take
place, Harris Industries may exercise one
of ③ options: (1) it may terminate our
right to posession of the office space,
(2) it may terminate the lease, or (3) it
may declare the entire balance remaining of the
lease to be immediately due and payable,
and may take legal action to recover and
collect the balance.

TAX AND UTILITY ADJUSTMENT

We are required to pay all real property taxes and assessments that are levied
against the building, and Harris industries will pay all utilities (electricity, water, sewage). We are required to
pay any proportionate shares of any
increase in taxes for the ①1st year the
building is assessed or for the calendar
year in which the term of the lease commenced, whichever is later.

We are also required to pay
a proportionate share of any
increase in utilities payable
by Harris Industries. Our proportionate share shall be
a fraction of the total
number of square feet contained in the building.
In addition, we shall make
payments of all taxes and
assessments levied against
our furniture, equipment,
supplies, fixtures, and other
personal property located
in the building.

DAMAGE BY FIRE OR THE ELEMENTS

If the building is totally
destroyed by fire, tornado, or
other casualty, or if the building
is so damaged that repairs
cannot be completed within
90 days after the date of such
damage, we may give written
notice within 15 days that this
agreement is terminated. If
the agreement is not terminated, Harris Industries is obligated to reconstruct the building
to substantially the same condition in which it was immediately prior to the casualty.

ALTERATIONS AND IMPROVEMENTS

We are not permitted to make any
alterations, additions, or improvements to
the office space without the prior written
consent of Harris Industries. All alterations that we do make, shall become
the property of Harris industries whether
of a temporary or permanent nature.
no # We are permitted, however, to submit
a request in writing to remove temporary
alterations from the building when we
vacate the premises provided that the removal
of the alterations does not create permanent
damage to the building

HARRIS BUILDING

RENT SCHEDULE

Floor	Square Feet	Rent/Sq Ft
1	10,308	$11.25
2	12,286	10.00
3	11,375	10.25
4	10,395	11.05
5	11,620	10.15

The typewriter keyboard is now part of many, many different pieces of equipment. In the office, workers at all levels use the keyboard to type letters and memos, to input information into a computer or to retrieve data from the computer, to send electronic communications across the country or around the world, to reproduce copy quickly, and to perform any number of other tasks. In the home, men and women use the keyboard to input and calculate data on "personal" computers or to play electronic games. In schools, students use the keyboard to prepare reports, to solve problems, and to take tests.

Thus the term *keyboarding* is used to describe the process of inputting data by means of a keyboard. Keyboarding is a very valuable skill, and it is the skill you will concentrate on developing in Level 1.

In Level 1 you will . . .

1. Demonstrate which fingers control each key on the keyboard and each part of the typewriter.

2. Condition your fingers to control the keyboard at a useful level of operation.

3. Use your typewriter to produce very short written communications.

LESSON 1

UNIT 1 KEYBOARDING—THE ALPHABET

UNIT GOAL
16 WORDS A MINUTE

GOAL
- To type the home keys, use the space bar, and return the carriage or carrier with eyes on copy.

FORMAT
- Single spacing 40-space line

HOME KEY POSITION

The dark keys shown with white letters in the keyboard chart are the home keys.

Left Hand. Place your fingertips on the **A S D** and **F** keys.
Right Hand. Place your fingertips on **J K L** and **;** keys.

Curve your fingers so that only their tips lightly touch the keys. Your fingers are named for the home keys on which they rest: A finger, S finger, D finger, and so on, ending with Sem finger for the little finger on the ; key.

SPACE BAR

You will strike the space bar with the thumb of your writing hand—the right thumb if you are right-handed, the left thumb if you are left-handed. Whichever thumb you use should be poised above the middle of the space bar. The other thumb is not used; hold it close to its adjacent forefinger.

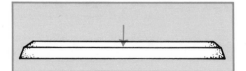

Strike center of space bar with thumb.

Now practice using the space bar with the right or left thumb.

Space once [*tap the space bar once*] . . . twice [*tap the space bar twice*] . . . once . . . once . . . twice . . . once . . . twice . . . once . . . twice . . . twice . . . once . . . once. . . . **Repeat.**

SERVICES

Harris has agreed, at its own expense, to furnish us with:

1. Electricity for routine lighting and the operation of general office machines such as typewriters, dictating equipment, and desk model adding machines.
2. Heat and air conditioning during usual business hours.
3. Elevator service.
4. Lighting replacement for standard lights.
5. Window washing with reasonable frequency.
6. Daily janitorial services.
7. Water.

Typist: ss with ds between items.

OFFICE SPACE USE *(Typist: This entire section should be placed after the RENT section)*

The office space that we are renting from Harris Industries shall be used for business or professional office purposes and for no other purpose without the prior written consent of Harris Industries. This office space may not be used for the purpose of retail sales. We are not permitted to do anything that is prohibited by any standard form of fire insurance policy. Since other tenants will also be in the building, we are not permitted to do anything that would obstruct or interfere with the rights of these tenants. If Harris or its customers cause damage to the building, however, we must pay for the cost of repairs.

SIGNS AND ADVERTISING

Without the prior written consent of Harris Industries, we shall not be ~~allowed the~~ permitted to paint or display any signs, placard, ~~lettering~~, or advertising material of any kind on or near the exterior of the building ~~we occupy~~.

Default

The following events may consitute a defalt of our agreement:

5] 1. Failure to pay rental.

    2. Failure to abide by the agree-
4] ments or conditions of the lease.

    3. Bankrupcy.

(Continued on next page)

CARRIAGE OR CARRIER RETURN

Manual Machine. Place the left forefinger and the next two fingers against the return lever. Flip the lever with a toss of the wrist to return the carriage to the margin, and return the hand to home key position.

Electric Machine. Extend the Sem finger to the adjacent return key. Lightly press the return key causing the carriage or carrier to return automatically, and return the finger to home key position.

Now practice using the carriage or carrier return.

> Space once ... twice ... once ... twice. ... Ready to return [*move hand to return lever or finger to return key*]. Return! [*Return the carriage or carrier.*] ... Home! [*Place fingers on home keys.*] ...   Repeat.

STROKING PRACTICE

Practice the F and J and space strokes shown in the drill below. If you are using a manual machine, experiment to see how hard you must tap the keys to get them to print evenly. Type each line once. After completing a set of lines, return the carriage or carrier twice.

Left forefinger, spacing thumb.   f f f   f f f   f f   f f   f   f   f f   f f   f   f   Return.

Right forefinger, spacing thumb.   j j j   j j j   j j   j j   j   j   j j   j j   j   j   Return twice.

  KEYS

Use forefingers.

Type each line once.

1   f f f   j j j   f f f   j j j   f f f   j j j   f f   j j   f f   j j   f   j   Return.
2   f f f   j j j   f f f   j j j   f f f   j j j   f f   j j   f f   j j   f   j   Return twice.

 KEYS

Use second fingers.

Type each line once.

3   d d d   k k k   d d d   k k k   d d d   k k k   d d   k k   d d   k k   d   k
4   d d d   k k k   d d d   k k k   d d d   k k k   d d   k k   d d   k k   d   k

 KEYS

Use third fingers.

Type each line once.

5   s s s   l l l   s s s   l l l   s s s   l l l   s s   l l   s s   l l   s   l
6   s s s   l l l   s s s   l l l   s s s   l l l   s s   l l   s s   l l   s   l

  KEYS

Use fourth fingers.

Type each line once.

7   a a a   ; ; ;   a a a   ; ; ;   a a a   ; ; ;   a a   ; ;   a a   ; ;   a   ;
8   a a a   ; ; ;   a a a   ; ; ;   a a a   ; ; ;   a a   ; ;   a a   ; ;   a   ;

JOB D-4. FILE CARDS

It is your responsibility to maintain a card file on all speakers. Type a file card (or slip of 5- by 3-inch paper) for each of the names in the table you received from Correspondent R. Type the speaker's name on line 2, 4 spaces from the left edge; leave 1 blank line; then tab-indent the other lines 3 spaces, like this:

```
Dotson, Betty Lou

   862 Emerson Street
   Austin, TX 78722

   Tel. No. 512-555-8200
```

JOB D-5. INTEROFFICE MEMORANDUM

The District Manager wants all the Louisiana sales and training representatives to attend the conference. Send a memo to these company representatives, informing them of the dates and location of the conference and who the opening session speaker is going to be. Supply an appropriate subject for your memorandum.

JOB D-6. REPORT

Type the report below and on pages S23–S24 whenever you are not sending information to or receiving information from Correspondent R. You are completing the report for the District Manager, and he prefers a side-bound, double-spaced style. You should complete a cover-title page for your report. The first three lines of the report title (as they appear in the report below) should be centered horizontally. Your name and the current date should be typed at the bottom of the cover page. Make a carbon copy of the report for your files.

```
              SUMMARY OF LEASE AGREEMENT
                     Harris
                  Callahan Building
                   District Office

                   (Current date)
                    new Harris
      The specifications for the Callahan Building in Baton Rouge, Lou-
isiana, have been established, and the lease agreement was drawn on
June 10, 19--.  A summary of the major stipulations of this lease is
presented in the following Report.

      RENT
5|  We have agreed to pay the sum of $2,500 rental on or before the first
                                          each and
    day of the month and on or before the first day of every successive
    calendar month thereafter for the full term of the lease.  The monthly
    rental fee of $1,500 is to be paid to Harris Industries, 2576 Florida
    Boulevard, Baton Rouge, LA 70802.
```

The rent schedule is provided below. (Typist: Get table at the end of the report and insert it here — center it horizontally and use single spacing.)

(Continued on next page)

CHECKPOINT

Type each character and space with a quick, sharp stroke.

Type lines 9–10 once. Then repeat lines 3, 5, and 7 or repeat the Checkpoint at a faster rate.

9 ff jj dd kk ss ll aa ;; f j d k s l a ;

10 ff jj dd kk ss ll aa ;; f j d k s l a ;

PRETEST

Type lines 11–12 at least once keeping your eyes on the copy.

11 fad fad ask ask lad lad dad dad sad sad   Return.

12 as; as; fall fall alas alas flask flask   Return twice.

HOME KEY WORD BUILDING

When you have completed a set of lines (13–14, 15–16, and so on), return the carriage or carrier an extra time.

Type lines 13–24 once.

13 fff aaa ddd fad fad aaa sss kkk ask ask

14 fff aaa ddd fad fad aaa sss kkk ask ask

15 aaa lll lll all all sss aaa ddd sad sad

16 aaa lll lll all all sss aaa ddd sad sad

17 lll aaa ddd lad lad aaa ddd ddd add add

18 lll aaa ddd lad lad aaa ddd ddd add add

19 ddd aaa ddd dad dad aaa sss ;;; as; as;

20 ddd aaa ddd dad dad aaa sss ;;; as; as;

21 a al ala alas alas; f fa fal fall falls

22 a al ala alas alas; f fa fal fall falls

23 l la las lass lass; f fl fla flas flask

24 l la las lass lass; f fl fla flas flask

POSTTEST

Type lines 25–26 at least once keeping your eyes on the copy. Note your improvement.

25 fad fad ask ask lad lad dad dad sad sad

26 as; as; fall fall alas alas flask flask

At the End of a Typewriting Session

Remove paper using paper release.

Center carriage or carrier.

Turn machine off if electric.

Cover machine at end of last period.

You will be receiving information from your partner to use in the preparation of letters, tables, reports, and other related correspondence. You will also be working on a report that is to be prepared for the Regional Manager. The report begins on page S22. Your work on this report must be delayed, however, when you either receive correspondence from your partner or send correspondence to your partner. You may work on the report whenever your Regional Office correspondence is not pending. Now begin your work by following the instructions for Job D-1 below.

JOB D-1. LETTER

You have been aware for about a month now that a national conference is going to be held in your district. Your District Manager, Mr. Matthew G. Preston, wants the letter below to be sent to the Regional Manager, Ms. Diane E. Foster, asking for the names of potential speakers for the conference.

Dear Diane:

Through the years we have kept on file a list of all the speakers who have participated in our regional conferences. This has been an extremely valuable aid to us in planning our program and for identifying the topics for the various sessions.

→ I would be interested in any of the speakers who have addressed any of our previous district meetings as well as those who have participated in other regional meetings. Would you please send me a copy of the master list of speakers that is filed in your office.

Yours sincerely, [Type my name and title]

JOB D-2. FOUR-COLUMN TABLE

When you receive a request from Correspondent R for recommendations on a site location for the conference, prepare the table immediately. Use the information in the next column to complete the table on the various site locations. Make a carbon copy for your files, and send the original to Correspondent R.

Type an appropriate title for the table—something that pertains to Correspondent R's request. Type the name of the company and the current date as subtitles to your table.

Note that the final column will contain items that are abbreviated. The first item in the final column will pertain to an overall rating, the second item in the final column will pertain to the price range, and the final item will give the number of units in the motel/hotel. These items are footnoted 1, 2, and 3; the footnotes should appear below the table with the following descriptions:

[1]G (Good), VG (Very Good), S (Superior).

[2]M (Medium Price Range), H (High Price Range), VH (Very High Price Range).

[3]Number of units in the hotel/motel.

Best Western-East
13552 Chef Menteur
   Highway
(504) 555-1700
VG[1], M[2], 85[3]

Bourbon Orleans
   Ramada Hotel
717 Orleans St.
(504) 555-5251
VG, H, 225

Delta Towers Hotel
1732 Canal St.
(504) 555-7741
G, H, 200

Fountain Bay Club
   Hotel
4040 Tulane Ave.
(504) 555-6111
VG, H, 410

Fairmont Hotel
University Place
(504) 555-7111
S, VH, 800

The Grand Hotel
1500 Canal St.
(504) 555-4471
G, H, 700

JOB D-3. LETTER

You will receive information on the conference speakers from Correspondent R. When you do, compose a letter to the Regional Office informing them of your choice for an opening session speaker on July 26. This speaker would also be needed to lead a round-table discussion on the 28th. Make your choice based on the availability dates listed in the table, and send your letter to Correspondent R. If your choice is between two people, select the speaker living closest to the conference site.

LESSON 2

GOAL
- To control H, E, and O keys by touch.

FORMAT
- Single spacing   40-space line

KEYBOARDING REVIEW

Type each line twice.

1 ff jj dd kk ss ll aa ;; f j d k s l a ;
2 asks asks fall fall lads lads lass lass

SPACE BAR

 H KEY

Use J finger.

Type each line twice.

3 jjj jhj hhh jjj jhj hhh jjj jhj hhh jhj
4 jhj ash ash jhj had had jhj has has jhj
5 jhj; a lad has; a lass has; add a half;

 E KEY

Use D finger.

Type each line twice.

6 ddd ded eee ddd ded eee ddd ded eee ded
7 ded she she ded led led ded he; he; ded
8 ded; he led; she led; he sees; she sees

 O KEY

Use L finger.

Type each line twice.

9   lll lol ooo lll lol ooo lll lol ooo lol
10 lol hoe hoe lol ode ode lol foe foe lol
11 lol old ode; oak hoe; sod fed; old foe;

CHECKPOINT

Eyes on copy while typing Checkpoint.

Type lines 12–13 once. Then repeat lines 3, 6, and 9 or repeat the Checkpoint at a faster rate.

12 she sells jade flakes; he sells old oak
13 she sells jade flakes; he sells old oak

PRETEST

Type lines 14–15 at least once keeping your eyes on the copy.

14 half dead hold sash jell look lake seed
15 half dead hold sash jell look lake seed

SIGNS AND ADVERTISING

Without the prior written consent of Cooper Industries, we shall not be permitted to paint or display any signs, placard, lettering, or advertising material of any kind on or near the exterior of the building.

DEFAULT

The following events may constitute a default of our agreement:

ss with ds between items
1. Failure to pay rental.
2. Failure to abide by the agreements or conditions of the lease.
3. Bankruptcy.
4. Vacating or abandoning the building.

If one or more of these events take place, Cooper Industries may exercise one of three options: (1) it may terminate our right to possession of the office space, (2) it may terminate the lease, or (3) it may declare the entire remaining balance of the lease to be immediately due and payable and may take legal action to recover it.

TAX AND UTILITY ADJUSTMENT

We are required to pay all real property taxes and assessments that are levied against the building, and Cooper Industries will pay all utilities (electricity, water, sewage). We are required to pay any proportionate shares of any increase in taxes for the first year the building is assessed or for the calendar year in which the term of the lease commenced, whichever is later.

We are also required to pay a proportionate share of any increase in utilities payable by Cooper Industries. Our "proportionate" share shall be a fraction of the total number of square feet contained in the building. In addition, we shall make payments of all taxes and assesments levied against our furniture, equipment, supplies, fixtures, and other personal property located in the building.

Typist: Insert this table at the end of the RENT section.

CALLAHAN BUILDING
RENT SCHEDULE

Floor	Square Feet	Rent/Sq Ft
1	18,308	$11.75
2	20,286	10.50
3	19,375	10.75
4	18,395	11.55
5	19,620	10.65

GENERAL INSTRUCTIONS

D You are Correspondent D in the District Office of Callahan Publishing Company, and your partner (another classmate) is Correspondent R in the Regional Office of the same company. The District Office is located at 1910 Perkins Road, Baton Rouge, LA 70808; the Regional Office address is Callahan Building, 3606 Mockingbird Lane, Dallas, TX 75205.

The student you team up with in this simulation should have about the same typing skills as you have. Your correspondence begins on page S21; your partner's work begins at the large R on page S17.

PRACTICE

When You Repeat a Line

Speed up on the second typing.

Make second typing smoother too.

Leave a blank line after second typing (return carriage or carrier twice).

Type each line twice.

16 half half hall hall hale hale hole hole
17 dead dead deal deal heal heal head head
18 hold hold sold sold fold fold folk folk
19 sash sash dash dash lash lash hash hash
20 jell jell sell sell self self elf; elf;
21 look look hook hook hood hood hoof hoof
22 lake lake fake fake fade fade jade jade
23 seed seed deed deed feed feed heed heed

POSTTEST

Type lines 14–15 at least once keeping your eyes on the copy. Note your improvement.

LESSON 3

GOAL
- To control M, R, and I keys by touch.

FORMAT
- Single spacing   40-space line

KEYBOARDING REVIEW

Type each line twice.

1 asdf jkl; heo; asdf jkl; heo; asdf jkl;
2 fake fake lose lose jade jade held held

 KEY

Use J finger.

Type each line twice.

3 jjj jmj mmm jjj jmj mmm jjj jmj mmm jmj
4 jmj me; me; jmj mom mom jmj ham ham jmj
5 jmj; fold a hem; make a jam; less fame;

RENT

We have agreed to pay the sum of $2,000 *rental* on or before the first day of the month and on or before the first day of each and every successive ~~calendar~~ month there after for the full term of the ~~current~~ lease. The monthly rental fee of $2,000 is to be paid to Cooper Industries, 5540 Forest Lane, Dallas, ~~Texas~~ TX 75230. *The rent schedule appears below. (Typist: Get table at the end of the report & insert it here — Center it horiz.)*

USE OF OFFICE SPACE

The office space that we are renting from Cooper Industries shall be used for business or professional office purposes and for no other purpose without the prior written consent of Cooper Industries. This office space may not be used for the purpose of retail sales. We are not permitted to do anything that is prohibited by any standard form of fire insurance policy. Since other tenants will also be in the building, we are not permitted to do anything that would obstruct or interfere with the rights of these tenants.

Cooper Industries Services *(Typist: Place this section after REPAIR AND MAINTENANCE)*

Cooper has agreed, at its own expense, to furnish us with:

1. Electricity for routine lighting and the operation of general office machines such as typewriters, dictating equipment, and desk model adding machines.
2. Heat and air conditioning during ~~usual business hours.~~
3. Elevator service.
4. Lighting replacement for *standard* lights.
5. Window washing *with reasonable frequency.*

6. Daily janitorial services.
7. water.

REPAIR AND MAINTENANCE

Cooper Industries shall make necessary repairs of damage to the building corridors, lobby, and equipment used to provide the services referred to below. If Callahan or its customers cause damage to the building, however, we must pay for the cost of repairs.

ALTERATIONS AND IMPROVEMENTS

All alterations that we do make, whether of a temporary or permanent nature, shall become the property of Cooper Industries. We are not permitted to make alterations, additions, or improvements to the office space without the prior written consent of Cooper Industries.

No ¶ We are permitted, however, to submit a request in writing to remove temporary alterations from the building when we vacate the premises, *provided that the removal of the alterations does not create permanent damage to any part of the building.*

DAMAGE BY FIRE OR THE Elements

If the building is totally destroyed by fire, tornado, or other caualty, or if the building is so damaged that repairs cannot be completed within ~~ninety~~ *90* days after the date of such damage, we may give written notice with in 15 days that this agreement is terminated. If the agreement is not terminated, Cooper Industries is obligated to reconstruct the building substantially to the same condition in which it was *immediately* prior to the casualty.

(Continued on next page)

SPACE BAR

R KEY

Use F finger.

Type each line twice.

6 fff frf rrr fff frf rrr fff frf rrr frf
7 frf for for frf far far frf err err frf
8 frf; from me; for her marks; more jars;

I KEY

Use K finger.

Type each line twice.

9   kkk kik iii kkk kik iii kkk kik iii kik
10 kik lid lid kik dim dim kik rim rim kik
11 kik; dear sir; for his risk; if she is;

CHECKPOINT

Type lines 12–13 once. Then repeat lines 3, 6, and 9 or repeat the Checkpoint at a faster rate.

12 her dark oak desk lid is a joke; he has
13 added a rare look from some old red oak

PRETEST

Type lines 14–15 at least once keeping your eyes on the copy.

14 mare hire elms foal lame dark aide jars
15 mare hire elms foal lame dark aide jars

PRACTICE

Eyes on Copy

It will be easier to keep your eyes on the copy if you:

Understand how the line is arranged.

Review the chart for key positions.

Maintain an even pace.

Resist looking up.

16 mare mare mere mere mire mire more more
17 hire hire fire fire dire dire sire sire
18 elms elms alms alms arms arms aims aims
19 foal foal loam loam foam foam roam roam
20 lame lame dame dame fame fame same same
21 dark dark dare dare dale dale sale sale
22 jars jars jams jams jade jade joke joke

POSTTEST

Type lines 14–15 at least once keeping your eyes on the copy. Note your improvement.

If Correspondent D has not yet asked you for a list of potential speakers, prepare it now. Use the information below to complete your table. Make a carbon copy for your files, and send the original to Correspondent D when you receive the request to do so.

John Griffin
5432 Tyler Avenue
Jacksonville, FL 32205
(904) 555-0067
Availability: 7/27–7/28[a]

Betty Lou Dotson
862 Emerson Street
Austin, TX 78722
(512) 555-8200
Availability: 7/29–7/30

Kathy Sanchez
3875 Hawthorne Drive
Mobile, AL 36609
(205) 555-3489
Availability: 7/26–7/27

Robert T. Watson
220 Forest Avenue
Biloxi, MS 39530
(601) 555-7293
Availability: 7/30[c]

Paula Coulter
564 Olive Street
Decatur, GA 30030
(404) 555-3847
Availability: 7/26–7/30[b]

Frank Tennison
1504 Mendez Drive
New Orleans, LA 70122
(504) 555-8320
Availability: 7/26–7/30

JOB R-3. LETTER

When you receive the recommended-site-locations table from Correspondent D, compose a letter to the District Manager. In your letter you should make your final recommendation for the conference site location. Use the following criteria to determine which site would be the best choice: (1) you need at least 175 rooms for your conference, (2) you should select the best price range, (3) you should select the hotel/motel with the best rating. cc: Gen. Mgr.

JOB R-4. FILE CARDS

You should keep a file on all conference site locations for future reference. Prepare a file card (or slip of 5-by 3-inch paper) for each of the hotels/motels in the table you received from Correspondent D. Type the name on line 2, 4 spaces from the left edge; leave 1 blank line; then tab-indent the other lines 3 spaces, like this:

```
    Fairmont Hotel

       University Place
       New Orleans, LA 70122

       Tel. No. 504-555-7111
```

JOB R-5. INTEROFFICE MEMORANDUM

Send a memo to all district managers, informing them of the dates and location of the conference. Also tell them who the opening session speaker is going to be. (Correspondent D will provide this information.) Supply an appropriate subject for your memorandum.

JOB R-6. REPORT

Type the report below and on pages S19–S20 whenever you are not sending information to or receiving information from Correspondent D. You are completing the report for the Regional Manager, and she prefers a side-bound, double-spaced style. You should complete a cover-title page for your report. The first three lines of the report title (as they appear in the report below) should be centered horizontally. Your name and the current date should be typed at the bottom of the cover page. Make a carbon copy of the report for your files.

SUMMARY OF LEASE AGREEMENT

Callahan Building
Regional Office

(Current date)

The specifications for the new Callahan Building in Dallas, Texas, have been established, and the lease agreement was drawn on May 10, 19--. A summary of the major stipulations of that lease is presented in this report.

(Continued on next page)

LESSON 4

GOALS
- To control T, N, and C keys by touch.
- To figure speed using the speed scales.

FORMAT
- Single spacing   40-space line

KEYBOARDING REVIEW

Type each line twice.

1 asdf jkl; heo; mri; asdf jkl; heo; mri;
2 safe safe herd herd joke joke mild mild

SPACE BAR

T KEY

Use F finger.

Type each line twice.

3 fff ftf ttt fff ftf ttt fff ftf ttt ftf
4 ftf kit kit ftf ate ate ftf toe toe ftf
5 ftf; it is the; to the; for the; at it;

N KEY

Use J finger.

Type each line twice.

6 jjj jnj nnn jjj jnj nnn jjj jnj nnn jnj
7 jnj ten ten jnj and and jnj net net jnj
8 jnj; for the; in an effort; of an honor

C KEY

Use D finger.

Type each line twice.

9 ddd dcd ccc ddd dcd ccc ddd dcd ccc dcd
10 dcd can can dcd ace ace dcd arc arc dcd
11 dcd; on a deck; in each car; cannot act

CHECKPOINT

Type lines 12–13 once. Then repeat lines 3, 6, and 9 or repeat the Checkpoint at a faster rate.

12 there is a carton of jade on this dock;
13 mail a file card to the nearest stores;

CALLAHAN CONFERENCE SIMULATION
A Simulation for Two

GENERAL INSTRUCTIONS

This simulation involves two persons—one who works in the Regional Office of Callahan Publishing Company and one who works in the District Office of the same company. The Regional Office address is Callahan Building, 3606 Mockingbird Lane, Dallas, TX 75205. The District Office is located at 1910 Perkins Road, Baton Rouge, LA 70808. The General Manager (your teacher) is located in the Callahan Building in Dallas.

Team up with a District Office Correspondent (another student) who has about the same typing skills as you have. The Regional Office correspondence begins at the large *R* below; the District Office correspondence begins at the large *D* on page S20.

R During this simulation you will be working on a report for the Regional Manager in St. Louis. The report begins on page S18. Your work on this report will be interrupted occasionally so that you can prepare and send correspondence to your partner. Work with your partner must have priority—complete these activities immediately, even if it means that your typing on the report will be temporarily delayed. Now start with Job R-1 below.

JOB R-1. LETTER

The Regional Manager, Ms. Diane E. Foster, has asked you to type the letter below, which she drafted on her way to work. Make all the corrections that she has indicated. The letter is being sent to Mr. Matthew G. Preston, District Manager.

Dear Matt:

As you know, next summer we are going to hold a regional conference in New Orleans from July 26 through July 30. The facilities we have had at our disposal at other conferences in the past ten years have been excellent.

We want to continue this fine tradition at next year's meeting. Therefore, would you please research the possible site locations and send me your recommendations by the first

(Continued in next column)

of next month. I'm sure you remember the meetings at San Antonio, Birmingham, and Little Rock.

Cordially yours, [Type my name and title]

JOB R-2. FOUR-COLUMN TABLE

When you receive a request from Correspondent D for a list of possible speakers, prepare the table immediately. Use the information below and on the next page to complete your table. Make a carbon copy for your files, and send the original to Correspondent D.

Type an appropriate title for the table—something that pertains to Correspondent D's request. Type the name of the company and the current date as subtitles to your table.

Note the three footnotes (shown as *a*, *b*, and *c*) after the availability dates. The notes at the bottom of the table should read as follows:

[a]Will not be available until after 6 p.m. on the 27th.

[b]Must depart for Jacksonville at 3 p.m. on the 30th.

[c]Will be available all day on the 30th.

1. **If you type for 1 minute:** Find out how many "average" words you type in the time allowed. Every 5 strokes (letters and spaces) counts as 1 average word. Thus a 40-stroke line is 8 words long; two such lines, 16 words; and so on.

2. **For an incomplete line,** use the scale (below line 15 on this page); the number above which you stop is your word count for that incomplete line. **Example:** If you type lines 14 and 15 (see below) and start over, getting as far as the word *sink* in line 14, you have typed 16 + 1 = 17 words.

3. **If you type for more than 1 minute:** To find out your 1-minute rate, you will need to divide the word total by the number of minutes you typed. **Example:** 37 words in 2 minutes would be 37 ÷ 2 = 18½ = 19 wam (words a minute). Count a fraction as a whole word.

4. **If you type for less than 1 minute:** To find out your 1-minute rate, you will have to multiply the total number of words typed because you typed for less than 1 minute. If you type for 30 seconds, you will have to multiply by 2 (2 × 30 = 60 or 1 minute). If you type for 12 seconds, you will have to multiply by 5 (5 × 12 = 60—1 minute). **Example:** 9 words in 30 seconds would be 9 × 2 = 18 wam.

PRETEST

Type lines 14–15 at least once keeping your eyes on the copy.

14 sink cane tone then tick jots etch rain   8
15 sink cane tone then tick jots etch rain   16
     | 1 | 2 | 3 | 4 | 5 | 6 | 7 | 8

PRACTICE

Check Your Posture

Feet—apart, on floor.

Back—erect, leaning forward.

Hands—close together, fingers curved, low.

Eyes—focused on book.

Type each line twice.

16 sink sink rink rink link link kink kink
17 cane cane came came cake cake care care
18 tone tone done done lone lone none none
19 then then than than thin thin this this
20 tick tick lick lick sick sick kick kick
21 jots jots lots lots lets lets jets jets
22 held held herd herd hard hard hand hand
23 rain rain raid raid said said sail sail

POSTTEST

Type lines 14–15 at least once keeping your eyes on the copy. Note your improvement.

SENTENCE COMPOSITION (Continued)

10. What are you going to do when you finish high school?

11. Why do some people dislike going to a dentist?

12. What were some of the hardships faced by the pioneers?

13. What is significant about July 4, 1776?

14. Why do we celebrate Thanksgiving?

15. What is the equator?

PARAGRAPH COMPOSITION

Use a paragraph of at least three complete sentences to answer each of the questions below. Use a clean sheet of paper, start on line 10 from the top, and type on a 50-space line. *Keep your eyes on your copy and concentrate on the words as you type.*

1. Where would you like to spend your next vacation and why?

2. Name your favorite season of the year, and tell why you prefer that time of year.

3. Describe what the world will be like in the year 2050.

4. What career do you want to pursue and why?

5. In what state would you like to live the rest of your life and why?

LESSON 5

GOALS
- To control the right shift key, V, and period keys by touch.
- To recognize typographical errors in copy and count them.
- To use the paper bail as an aid for locating copy errors.

FORMAT
- Single spacing   40-space line

KEYBOARDING REVIEW

Type each line twice.

1. `asdf jkl; jh de lo jm fr ki ft jn dc ;;`

2. `cash free dine jolt milk iron trim star`

RIGHT SHIFT KEY

Use Sem finger.

Use the right shift key to capitalize letters typed with the left hand. To make the reach easier, curl the second and third fingers of your right hand as you complete the following three-step sequence:

1. **Cap!** Keeping J finger in home position, extend Sem finger to press the right shift key and hold it down firmly.
2. **Strike!** [or the name of the letter to be capitalized]. While the shift is still depressed, use the left hand to strike the letter that is to be capitalized.
3. **Home!** Release the shift key, and return all fingers to home position.

For a capital A, for example, you would think "Cap!" as you press the right shift, "A!" as you strike the letter, and "Home!" as all fingers snap back to home position.

Type each line twice.

3. `;;; C;; C;; ;;; S;; S;; ;;; T;; T;; ;;;`

4. `;;; Cal Cal ;;; Sam Sam ;;; Ted Ted ;;;`

5. `;;; Ada Ada ;;; Rae Rae ;;; Dee Dee ;;;`

V KEY

Use F finger.

Type each line twice.

6. `fff fvf vvv fff fvf vvv fff fvf vvv fvf`

7. `fvf vie vie fvf via via fvf eve eve fvf`

8. `fvf; via a van; move over; vie for love`

PHRASE COMPOSITION (Continued)

3. What is the name of your school newspaper or local newspaper?
4. What is your favorite television program?
5. What is your favorite record?
6. Name a book that you enjoyed reading.
7. What city and country would you like to visit?
8. Who is your favorite sports personality?
9. Who is the President of the United States?
10. Name two large cities in the United States.
11. Name two large states in the United States.
12. Name a past president of the United States.
13. Give the last names of two of your teachers.
14. Name two jobs you would enjoy doing.
15. Name two popular soft drinks.

SENTENCE COMPOSITION

Answer each of the following questions by typing a complete sentence of six or more words. (Each sentence must have a subject and a predicate.) Use a clean sheet of paper, start on line 10 from the top, and type on a 50-space line. *Keep your eyes on your copy and concentrate on each sentence as you type.*

Example Question:
When do the leaves start to fall?

Example Response:
In my state, the leaves start to fall in September.

1. What is the most difficult thing about a foreign language?
2. Why do we have taxes?
3. Why do we have insurance?
4. How is typewriting going to help you?
5. What have you learned from any one of your courses in school this year?
6. Why did you enroll in typewriting?
7. What kind of person would you like to have as a friend?
8. What are some of your assets?
9. What is the purpose of a space bar on a typewriter?

(Continued on next page)

. KEY

Use L finger.

Type each line twice.

9 lll l.l ... lll l.l ... lll l.l ... lll
10 l.l Sr. Sr. l.l Fr. Fr. l.l Dr. Dr. l.l
11 vs. ea. Co. St. Rd. Ave. div. ctn. std.

PUNCTUATION

Space twice after a period at the end of a sentence. Do not space at the end of a line.

Space once after a period that follows an abbreviation and after a semicolon.

Type each line twice.

12 Roll the dimes. There are five stacks.
13 See Ann at the door. She has the food.

Type each line twice.

14 Dr. S. Romer called; he read the lines.
15 Elm St. is ahead; East Ave. veers left.

CHECKPOINT

Type lines 16–17 once. Then repeat lines 3, 6, and 9 or repeat the Checkpoint at a faster rate.

16 Dr. Sara is on call; she asked Anne for 8
17 five half liters of cold milk in a jar. 16
   | 1 | 2 | 3 | 4 | 5 | 6 | 7 | 8

COUNTING ERRORS

Workbook 6.

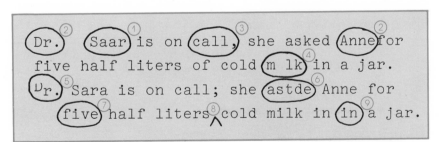

1. Circle any word in which there is an error.

2. Count a word as an error if the spacing after it is incorrect.

3. Count a word as an error if the punctuation after it is incorrect.

4. Count a word as an error if it contains a letter so light that you can't read it.

5. Count a word as an error if it contains a raised capital letter.

6. Count only 1 error against 1 word, no matter how many errors it may contain.

7. Count each failure to follow directions in spacing, indenting, and so on, as an error.

8. Count each word that is omitted as an error.

9. Count each word that is repeated incorrectly as an error.

NUMBER COMPOSITION

Use *only one number* to answer each of the following questions. Use a clean sheet of paper, start on line 10 from the top, and type on a 50-space line. *Keep your eyes on your copy and concentrate on each answer as you type.*

Example Question:
How many days are there in December?

Example Response:
31

1. How many letters are there in the alphabet?
2. How many states are there in the United States?
3. How many brothers do you have?
4. How many sisters do you have?
5. What is the current year?
6. How old are you?
7. How many different teachers do you have this year?
8. How many months in a year?
9. How many days in a week?
10. How many letters in your first name?
11. How many letters in your last name?
12. How many years have you been going to school?
13. How many movies did you see last month?
14. How many cents in a dollar?
15. How many years in a century?

PHRASE COMPOSITION

Use a phrase of two or three words to respond to each of the following. Use a clean sheet of paper, start on line 10 from the top, and type on a 50-space line. *Keep your eyes on your copy and concentrate on each answer as you type.*

Example Question:
Where would you like to live?

Example Response:
In Colorado

1. What are your school colors?
2. Who is your best friend?

(Continued on next page)

PROOFREAD USING THE PAPER BAIL

When you proofread copy, you are looking mainly for typographical errors (incorrect characters or spaces). Proofreading your typewritten copy accurately is as important as typing it accurately in the first place. Using your paper bail like a ruler to guide your eyes line by line across the page will help you proofread accurately.

LESSON 6

CLINIC

GOALS
- To analyze key control and complete special drills to strengthen control.
- To type 16 words a minute for 1 minute.

FORMAT
- Single spacing   40-space line

PRETEST

Take two 1-minute timings on lines 1–3 to determine your typing rate. Figure your speed and count your errors.

```
1  keel dose fell seat fool sale veer tone   8
2  fall dear mail reed coil jest dead race   16
3  tee; heal amt. Todd keel dose fell seat   24
   |  1  |  2  |  3  |  4  |  5  |  6  |  7  |  8
```

PRACTICE

Type lines 4–15 four times. Then proofread and circle errors. Repeat words or lines in which you made errors.

If You Omit Spaces, as in the Example Above, Then:

Check that your palms do not touch the machine.

Think "Space" for each space bar stroke.

Type calmly, evenly— not hastily or hurriedly.

Check that thumb is only ¼ inch above space bar.

Workbook 7–10.

```
4   keel keel feel feel heel heel reel reel
5   dose dose nose nose rose rose lose lose
6   fell fell tell tell sell sell jell jell
7   seat seat feat feat heat heat meat meat

8   fool fool food food mood mood hood hood
9   sale sale male male tale tale dale dale
10  veer veer jeer jeer seer seer deer deer
11  tone tone done done lone lone cone cone

12  fall fall mall mall tall tall hall hall
13  dear dear hear hear fear fear near near
14  mail mail sail sail jail jail rail rail
15  reed reed need need deed deed heed heed
```
(Continued on next page)

COMPOSITION EXERCISES

In this course you learned how to format typewritten letters, reports, and tables. But you also need to acquire the skill of composing copy at the typewriter. Then when you have developed your composition skills, you will be able to create projects in your own words and display each project in one of the various formats you learned in this course.

The following section is designed to strengthen your composition skills. The jobs in this section are arranged from simple to complex, starting with a one-word response and concluding with an entire-paragraph response.

Follow the directions and examples given for each stage of composition as you compose your answers to each of the questions. Single-space each response, but double-space between responses.

ONE-WORD COMPOSITION

Use *only one word* whenever possible to answer each of the following questions. Use a clean sheet of paper, start on line 10 from the top, and type on a 50-space line. *Keep your eyes on your copy and concentrate on each answer as you type.*

Example Question:
    What is your favorite color?

Example Response:
    Blue

1.   What is your favorite sport?

2.   What color eyes do you have?

3.   What vegetable do you like best?

4.   What color is your hair?

5.   What is your favorite fruit?

6.   What is your favorite class?

7.   What is your favorite hobby?

8.   What is your favorite make of automobile?

9.   What is your favorite season of the year?

10.   What is the last name of your favorite actor?

11.   What is the last name of your favorite actress?

12.   What is your favorite month?

13.   What is your favorite day of the week?

14.   In what month is your birthday?

15.   Name one of the oceans.

PRACTICE (Continued)

Type lines 16–23 four times. Then proofread and circle errors. Repeat words or lines in which you made errors.

16 coil coil soil soil toil toil foil foil
17 jest jest vest vest nest nest rest rest
18 dead dead head head lead lead read read
19 race race lace lace face face mace mace

20 tee; tee; teen teen seen seen see; see;
21 heal heal veal veal meal meal real real
22 amt. amt. dis. dis. std. std. ins. ins.
23 Todd Todd Sara Sara Vera Vera Cass Cass

POSTTEST

Take two 1-minute timings on lines 1–3. Figure your speed and count your errors. Note your improvement.

LESSON 7

UNIT 2 KEYBOARDING—THE ALPHABET

GOAL
- To control W, comma, and G keys by touch.

FORMAT
- Single spacing   40-space line

* 20 words a minute for 2 minutes with 4 errors or less.

KEYBOARDING REVIEW

Type each line twice.

1 jest fail sake not; mist card Rev. chin
2 Rick loves that fame; Val did not join.

SPACE BAR

 W KEY

Use S finger.

Type each line twice.

3 sss sws www sss sws www sss sws www sws
4 sws hew hew sws own own sws war war sws
5 sws; white swans swim; sow winter wheat

, KEY

Use K finger.
Space once after a comma.

Type each line twice.

6 kkk k,k ,,, kkk k,k ,,, kkk k,k ,,, k,k
7 k,k it, it, k,k an, an, k,k or, or, k,k
8 k,k; if it is, as soon as, two or three

The conversion to a metric system of measurement in this country is slowly taking place in business and industry; therefore, in the office environment you may need to learn certain style rules for typing. Read each metric rule presented below. For each rule, type the group of four drill lines once. Repeat the lines or take a series of 1-minute timings.

Rule 1. A lowercase letter is used to spell a metric term or abbreviation except for (1) a metric term that begins a sentence, (2) the word *Celsius*, and (3) the abbreviation *L*, for liter or liters.

1 Kilometers, centimeters, and millimeters measure distances. 12
2 The big jar holds exactly 7.1 liters; that can, 9.7 liters. 12
3 The carton of butter we bought yesterday weighed 454 grams. 12
4 The Celsius thermometer read 26 degrees; it was a nice day. 12
| 1 | 2 | 3 | 4 | 5 | 6 | 7 | 8 | 9 | 10 | 11 | 12

Rule 2. The singular and the plural forms of metric abbreviations are the same.

5 Only 1 L of fluid is left; she already used more than 50 L. 12
6 The box contains 12 g of powder, but you must mix only 1 g. 12
7 Each granule weighs 1 dg (decigram); the jar is over 16 dg. 12
8 One particle is 1 mm long; the others are about 10 mm long. 12
| 1 | 2 | 3 | 4 | 5 | 6 | 7 | 8 | 9 | 10 | 11 | 12

Rule 3. A blank space is used in place of the comma to separate sets of three digits.

9 In metrics we must type 1,000,000 grams as 1 000 000 grams. 12
10 She obtained these results: 0.293 847 mL and 0.567 340 mL. 12
11 The ship weighed nearly 20 000 kg; the canoe weighed 20 kg. 12
12 The distance from the earth to the moon is over 358 770 km. 12
| 1 | 2 | 3 | 4 | 5 | 6 | 7 | 8 | 9 | 10 | 11 | 12

Rule 4. A period is not used after a metric abbreviation, except at the end of a sentence.

13 They lost 150 mL, 225 mL, 350 mL, and 425 mL in four weeks. 12
14 One boxer weighed 67 kg; the opponent weighed nearly 69 kg. 12
15 The measurements were off by nearly 5 cm, 14 cm, and 25 cm. 12
16 One of my friends lost 10 kg; the other gained about 12 kg. 12
| 1 | 2 | 3 | 4 | 5 | 6 | 7 | 8 | 9 | 10 | 11 | 12

Rule 5. Figures (and words) are used with metric terms and abbreviations (unless the reference is obviously general and nontechnical).

17 We drove 500 kilometers today and 400 kilometers yesterday. 12
18 Make a mixture by adding 1.3 g of powder to 1.5 L of water. 12
19 The length of the paper is 215 mm, and the width is 280 mm. 12
20 The specifications require strips exactly 2.5 mm in length. 12
| 1 | 2 | 3 | 4 | 5 | 6 | 7 | 8 | 9 | 10 | 11 | 12

SPACE BAR

G KEY

Use F finger.

Type each line twice.

9 fff fgf ggg fff fgf ggg fff fgf ggg fgf
10 fgf egg egg fgf leg leg fgf get get fgf
11 fgf; give a dog, saw a log, sing a song

CHECKPOINT

Type lines 12–14 once. Then repeat lines 3, 6, and 9 or take two 2-minute timings on the Checkpoint.

12 While we watched, the first team jogged 8
13 to the front of the field. The win was 16
14 two in a row; the team likes victories. 24

| 1 | 2 | 3 | 4 | 5 | 6 | 7 | 8

PRETEST

Take two 1-minute timings on line 15, and determine your speed by using the faster rate.

15 king scow well gown elk, crew mow, sag,

| 1 | 2 | 3 | 4 | 5 | 6 | 7 | 8

PRACTICE

Type each line twice.

16 king king sing sing wing wing ring ring
17 scow scow stow stow show show snow snow
18 well well welt welt went went west west
19 gown gown town town tows tows toes toes

20 elk, elk, ilk, ilk, irk, irk, ink, ink,
21 crew crew grew grew grow grow glow glow
22 mow, mow, how, how, hot, hot, not, not,
23 sag, sag, wag, wag, rag, rag, gag, gag,

POSTTEST

Take two 1-minute timings on line 15, and determine your speed by using the faster rate. Note your improvement.

C O N T R A C T   5

     THIS CONTRACT, made and concluded this eighth day of   19

September, by and between the firm of Harter & Heath Inc., of   31

1396 Sierra Avenue, Santa Fe, New Mexico, party of the first   43

part, and Mr. Sherwin E. Forrest, 107 Dahlia Drive, Garden Grove, 57

California, party of the second part.   64

     ARTICLE 1. The said party of the second part covenants   77

and agrees to and with the party of the first part to furnish his 90

services to the said party of the first part as special demon-   102

strator and representative for the period of one year, or twelve   115

calendar months, beginning July 1, 19--, and expiring June 30,   128

19--; and the said party of the second part covenants and agrees   141

to perform faithfully all duties incident to such employment.   153

     ARTICLE 2. The said party of the first part covenants   165

and agrees to pay the said party of the second part, for the   177

same, the sum of nine thousand six hundred dollars ($9,600) in   190

twelve equal installments of eight hundred dollars ($800) each.   203

     IN WITNESS WHEREOF, the parties to this contract have   215

hereunto set their hands and seals, the day and year first above   228

written.   230

Party of the First Part: Party of the Second Part: 242

_____   _____ 256
R. W. Abernathy, Vice President   Sherwin E. Forrest   269

_____   _____ 283
Witness to Signature   Witness to Signature   294

LESSON 8

GOAL
- To control B, U, and left shift keys by touch.

FORMAT
- Single spacing   40-space line

KEYBOARDING REVIEW

Type each line twice.

1 wick foal corn them jive logo dim, wags
2 Coco gave me jewels; Frank mailed them.

KEY

Use F finger.

Type each line twice.

3 fff fbf bbb fff fbf bbb fff fbf bbb fbf
4 fbf bag bag fbf rob rob fbf ebb ebb fbf
5 fbf, a bent bin, a big bag, a back bend

KEY

Use J finger.

Type each line twice.

6 jjj juj uuu jjj juj uuu jjj juj uuu juj
7 juj jug jug juj flu flu juj urn urn juj
8 juj; jumbo jet, jungle bugs, just a job

LEFT SHIFT KEY

Use A finger.

Use the left shift key to capitalize letters typed with the right hand. To make the reach easier, curl the second and third fingers of your left hand as you complete the following three-step sequence:

1. **Cap!** Keeping F finger in home position, extend A finger to press the left shift key and hold it down firmly.

2. **Strike!** While the shift key is still depressed, use the right hand to strike the letter that is to be capitalized.

3. **Home!** Release the shift key, and return all fingers to home position.

Type each line twice.

9   aaa Jaa Jaa aaa Kaa Kaa aaa Laa Laa aaa
10 aaa Joe Joe aaa Kim Kim aaa Lee Lee aaa
11 Otis Iris Nita Mark Uris Hans Jose Kebo

REPORT 3
One-page report, with footnotes.

THE ART OF LISTENING
By [*Your name*]

Good listening requires certain responsibilities from all of us, as we shall see in the following paragraphs.

RESPONSIBILITIES OF THE LISTENER

To become an effective listener, we have to prepare for the task. "Choose whenever possible a position that allows you to see his or her gestures and clearly hear the tone of voice . . . ."[1] You should sit up straight and look directly at the speaker.

Leonard suggests an excellent idea for improving listening. He believes that

> one good way of eliminating this obstacle to effective listening is to occupy your excess thinking time usefully. Think about the presentation itself. Every now and then, summarize what the speaker has said.[2]

RESULTS OF GOOD LISTENING

If you improve your listening techniques, you will develop a positive attitude, you will improve your interest level, and you will improve your decision-making abilities.

---

[1]Herta A. Murphy and Charles E. Peck, Effective Business Communications, 3d ed., McGraw-Hill Book Company, New York, 1980, p. 679.

[2]Donald J. Leonard, Shurter's Communication in Business, 4th ed., McGraw-Hill Book Company, New York, 1979, p. 415.

REPORT 4
Legal typing: Resolution.

RESOLUTION

WHEREAS Janice Renée Carlton will retire from the presidency of The Business Club of Wayne High School upon her forthcoming graduation from this institution; and

WHEREAS she has devoted all her skill and much of her time to the development, expansion, and services of the Club, to the end that under her leadership the Club has grown both in its contribution to and in its prestige in the said Wayne High School; and

WHEREAS she has proved herself a generous leader, a warm and kindly person, and an associate much endowed with the ability to inspire others. therefore be it

RESOLVED, that the officers and members of The Business Club truly compliment and commend her for her devotion to them in their behalf and do express their deep gratitude to

JANICE RENÉE CARLTON

CHECKPOINT

Type lines 12–14 once. Then repeat lines 3, 6, and 9 or take two 2-minute timings on the Checkpoint.

12 Sharing a new car with friends is great   8
13 fun. Just look at that engine; hear it   16
14 hum. Drive with a flair, but use care.   24

   | 1 | 2 | 3 | 4 | 5 | 6 | 7 | 8

PRETEST

Take two 1-minute timings on line 15, and determine your speed by using the faster rate.

15 beef junk bout sun, blot vast gist bran

   | 1 | 2 | 3 | 4 | 5 | 6 | 7 | 8

PRACTICE

Check Your Feet.
They Should Be:

In front of the chair.

Firmly on the floor, square, flat.

Apart, with 6 or 7 inches between the ankles.

One foot a little ahead of the other.

Type each line twice.

16 beef been bean bead beak beam beat bear
17 junk dunk bunk bulk hulk hunk sunk sulk
18 bout boat boot bolt bold boll doll dole
19 sun, nun, run, bun, gun, gum, hum, sum,
20 blot blob blow blew bled bred brad bran
21 vast vest jest lest best west nest rest
22 gist list mist must gust dust rust just
23 bran brad bred brew brow crow crew craw

POSTTEST

Take two 1-minute timings on line 15, and determine your speed by using the faster rate. Note your improvement.

LESSON 9

GOAL
- To control P, Q, and colon keys by touch.

FORMAT
- Single spacing   40-space line

KEYBOARDING REVIEW

Type each line twice.

1 blue java brag mold silk when face club
2 Cora waved flags, but Jama went hiking.

REPORT 1
(Continued)

New Business
Ms. Quinn then introduced the need for
planning a campaign to let job applicants
know of the new openings in our office. It
will be studied further at our next meeting.
Respectfully Submitted,

Bob Dawson, Secretary

REPORT 2
One-page.

FEASABILITY OF A FOUR-DAY CLASS WEEK

By (Your name)

There is a trend in the *business* community twoard a 4-day work week.
The idea of a shorter workweek is filtering in to the educational
community. There is ~~certainly~~ *definitely* a need for Alternatives to the
present system of 5 days, which is ~~very~~ becoming costly for all involved.

SELECTION OF THE PARTICIPANTS

The researcher chose to *de*limit the sample to two separate categories: (1) Faculty, Staff, and Students who live on campus; and
(2) commuting students who live off ~~the~~ campus.

PURPOSE OF THE STUDY

It was the purpose of the study to identify University
opinions of a 4-day class week.

FINDINGS OF THE STUDY

One of the major findings of the study was *that* 55% of those surveyed wished to keep the ~~present~~ 5-day class week. The majority
of those with this opinion were Students. Comuter students, *however,* wanted
to try the 4-day class week; and Faculty and Staff were *also* of this
opinion. ~~also~~

The most popular option for a four-day class week is for
classes to be conducted on Monday through Thursday, with Friday
~~being~~ reserved as a day when Students could ~~obtain~~ *recieve* counseling or
advisement from the faculty.

 KEY

Use Sem finger.

Type each line twice.

3   ;;; ;p; ppp ;;; ;p; ppp ;;; ;p; ppp ;p;

4   ;p; pen pen ;p; nap nap ;p; ape ape ;p;

5   ;p; a pen pal, a pale page, a proud pup

Q KEY

Use A finger.

Type each line twice.

6   aaa aqa qqq aaa aqa qqq aaa aqa qqq aqa

7   aqa quo quo aqa que que aqa qui qui aqa

8   aqa quiet quip, quick quote, aqua quilt

: KEY

Use Sem finger and left shift key.

Space twice after a colon.

Type each line twice.

9   ;;; ;:; ::: ;;; ;:; ::: ;;; ;:; ::: ;:;

10   Ms. Lia: Mr. Kwi: Dr. Que: Mrs. Boe:

11   Dear Ms. Jo: Dear Mr. Mai: Dear Jeri:

CHECKPOINT

To figure rate for 1 minute, divide by 2 the total number of words typed for 2 minutes.

Errors, however, are not divided but recorded as a total for the entire timing.

Type lines 12–14 once. Then repeat lines 3, 6, and 9 or take two 2-minute timings on the Checkpoint.

12   TV lets us view the top news as it pops   8

13   up around the globe; an item takes life   16

14   with the clever quip of the journalist.   24
     | 1 | 2 | 3 | 4 | 5 | 6 | 7 | 8

PRETEST

Take two 1-minute timings on line 15, and determine your speed by using the faster rate.

15   pace quit prep quad ping shop que; quod
     | 1 | 2 | 3 | 4 | 5 | 6 | 7 | 8

PRACTICE

Type each line twice.

16   pace pack park part pare page pane pale

17   quit quip quiet quill quick quirk quire

(Continued on next page)

MEMORANDUM

(Date) December 4, 19--/(To) 16

J. D. Hill/Personnel Director/ 23

(From) Matthew S. Sanchez/Training 32

director/(Subject) Part-Time Workers 42

Cooper High School has just recently 49

informed me that they will be sending 57

2 young people to us for the next 6 to 66

8 weeks. as you recall, we agreed to 74

provide some practicle workexperience 82

for the (education office) students at 89

Cooper. 91

The students will be with us from 100

9/12 (daily). Could you have some one 107

from your office meet with them to 114

inform them of our personnel policies?/ 122

MSS/(Your initials) 127

FILL-IN POSTAL CARD MESSAGES

Use the copy below to prepare three postal card form messages. Then use the data below the message to complete the missing information.

[*Current date*]

Dear [*Type name of policyholder*]
 [*Type policy number*]:

Our records show that your last policy review was held on [*Type in date of review*].

To be sure that your policy remains up to date, call our office at 555-8376 to schedule another policy review.

Adam Rivers
Agent

Alex Gresham	Margaret Davis	Pauline Sanchez
Policy 083-47	Policy 072-36	Policy 045-38
Review Date:	Review Date:	Review Date:
6/17/80	7/23/79	4/3/81

REPORT 1
Minutes of a meeting.

Personnel Committee 12

MINUTES OF THE SPECIAL MEETING 32

[*Today's Date*] 46

ATTENDANCE 49

A special meeting of the Personnel Committee was 61

held in the office of Ms. Quinn, who presided at 71

the meeting. The session began at two o'clock and 81

adjourned at four. All members were there except Alan 92

Schmidt, who was represented by Helen Sampson. 101

UNFINISHED BUSINESS 109

The secretary read the minutes of the last monthly 120

Conference, and they were approved with one small change 131

that was noted. 134

Mr. Stern reported on the survey of ages of company 147

employees; a copy of the survey is attached to and be! 160

comes part of these minutes. 166

(*Continued on next page*)

PRACTICE
(Continued)

18 prep peep jeep weep beep seep step stop
19 quad aqua quack quail quake quart qualm
20 ping pint pins pink pine pike pile pipe
21 shop chop crop prop plop flop slop slow
22 que; ques quest queen quell queue queer
23 quod quot quota quoth quoit quote quori

POSTTEST

Take two 1-minute timings on line 15, and determine your speed by using the faster rate. Note your improvement.

LESSON 10

GOALS
- To control hyphen, Z, and diagonal keys by touch.
- To use correct spacing with the semicolon, colon, period, comma, hyphen, dash, and diagonal.

FORMAT
- Single spacing   40-space line

KEYBOARDING REVIEW

Type each line twice.

1 left best dome quip wave jogs chin bake
2 Meg saved her worn black quilt for Pam.

SPACE BAR

 KEY

Use Sem finger.
Do not space before or after hyphens.

Type each line twice.

3 ;;; ;p- ;-; --- ;;; ;p- ;-; --- ;p- ;-;
4 ;p- ;-; self-made ;p- ;-; one-third ;-;
5 ;p- ;-; part-time ;p- ;-; one-fifth ;-;

 KEY

Use A finger.

Type each line twice.

6 aaa aza zzz aaa aza zzz aaa aza zzz aza
7 aza zip zip aza zap zap aza zed zed aza
8 aza, to zig, to zag, to zing, to seize,

LETTER 7

Business letter with *bcc* and enclosure notations. Block format. Body 119 words.

[*Today's date*] / Ms. Annette Rudd / Business 13
Teacher / Tulsa Technical High School / 2370 21
Yale Avenue, S. / Tulsa, OK 74114 / Dear Ms. 31
Rudd: / Thank you for writing us and asking 39
whether we might have a person from our 47
office come to speak to the students in your 56
office procedures class. 62

Mr. Jeffrey Scott, a member of our personnel 72
staff, will plan to join you at 9 a.m. on Tuesday, 83
December 13. He will speak to your students 92
on "What a Temporary Position Can Do for 100
You," and his presentation will last about 45 109
minutes. A copy of his handout is enclosed for 119
you to review. 122

Mr. Scott has had considerable office expe- 131
rience, and he has worked for Tulsa Tempo- 139
raries for the past five years. I am sure you 149
will enjoy his enthusiastic and professional 158
presentation on temporary employment in the 167
Tulsa area. / Very truly yours, / John R. Blake 180
/ Personnel Manager / [*Your initials*] / Enclo- 185
sure / bcc: Karen Turner 191

BANK PROGRAMMER OPENING

5 We have a position for a senior programmer and bank analyst for our Blue Hill Office. The salary is open. At least five years' experience in banking or programming is required. You may choose your own hardware. If you are interested, please write to 5

DATA SOFTWARE CO.
124 BLAINE DRIVE
AUGUSTA, ME 04330

Please run the ad for one week. / Sincerely, / Grace T. West / Director of Personnel / [your initials]

LETTER 8

Business letter with display. Standard format with indented paragraphs. Body 102 words.

[Today's date] / Mr. Jerry Lydell / Ads Department / Blue Hill News / Blue Hill, ME 04614 / Dear Mr. Lydell:

We wish to place in your paper the following ad for a bank programmer. Please arrange the ad in two columns, 3 inches deep, in the same format that you used for our records clerk ad two weeks ago.

LETTER 9

Business letter. Standard format. Body 55 words.

(Today's date) / Ms. Ineź T. Williams / 12
Busïness Department / Central High 19
School / Grand Forks, ND 58210 / Dear Ms. 27
Williams: 30

We were delighted to hear that 5 38
of your part-time cooperative educa- 43
tion students will be working on a 52
basis for our company starting Feb. 60
10. Please have your students report 68
to the personnel office, Building A, 76
on the 3d floor at our University Ave. 84
location. Their work assignments will 92
be made at that time. / Sincerely, / J. D. 106
Hill / Personnel Director 113

KEY

Use Sem finger.

Do not space before or after a diagonal.

Type each line twice.

9 ;;; ;/; /// ;;; ;/; /// ;;; ;/; /// ;/;

10 ;/; his/her ;/; her/him ;/; us/them ;/;

11 to/from slow/fast fall/winter Mar./Apr.

CHECKPOINT

Type lines 12–14 once. Then repeat lines 3 and 6 (page 18) and 9 or take two 2-minute timings on the Checkpoint.

12 Our teams would not quit because of the   8

13 size and voice of their pep club crowd.   16

14 Their jumps and tricks brought the win.   24

PUNCTUATION SPACING

Space once after a semicolon.

Space twice after a colon.

Space twice after a period at the end of a sentence.

Space once after a period used with some initials and titles.

Do not space after a period used with degrees or with letters in a group.

Type lines 15–24 once. Note the spacing before and after each punctuation mark.

15 The dance looks nice; it shows balance.

16 The skit was tops; it was so organized.

17 Two courses are open: science and art.

18 Three members went: Ann, Lee, and Joe.

19 Send it to me. I can print it so fast.

20 The skirt is plaid. It matches a suit.

21 Ms. Kebo asked Dr. T. S. Laos to speak.

22 Mr. and Mrs. Lark were honored at noon.

23 She earned her Ph.D. from Oregon State.

24 The U.S.A. and the U.S.S.R. were there.

Type lines 25–32 once. Again, note the spacing before and after each punctuation mark.

Space once after a comma.

Do not space before or after a hyphen.

Do not space before or after a dash (two hyphens).

Do not space before or after a diagonal.

25 When Jean called me, I was not at home.

26 Send them red, white, and green copies.

27 The up-to-date calendar was so helpful.

28 His mother-in-law is the new president.

29 That machine--the black one--is broken.

30 The office gives good service--on time.

31 The fall/winter catalog has new colors.

32 The on/off button is on the right side.

LETTER 4

Business letter. Standard format. Body 97 words.

[*Today's date*] / Mr. Raymond Monroe / 122   13
North Cover Street / Bedford, PA 15522 / Dear   22
Mr. Monroe: 25

Thank you for your letter and your com-   33
ments about the article on the rock concerts.   43
It is nice to hear from the many people who   52
are looking forward to a fantastic summer of   61
rock concerts.   64

A complete schedule of all our summer   72
concerts is going to appear in the March issue   82
of <u>Views of Our Youth</u>. You will be happy to   98
see that we are planning a concert in Pitts-   107
burgh on August 18.   111

The person in charge of the Pittsburgh con-   120
cert is Ms. Glenda Hart. You can write to her   130
at 1021 McClure Street, Munhall, PA 15120.   138

Cordially yours, / Marie Preston, Editor /   153
[*Your initials*]   155

schedule. We would like to   105
plan a meet with you on   110
November 15 or 18. Would you   116
be interested in a meet on   121
either of these two dates?   127
¶ We can arrange to meet either   134
in the afternoon or during the   140
evening. Because of the distance   147
between our schools, an   152
evening meet might be   156
more convenient for us.   161
¶ Please let me hear from you   168
soon. / Very truly yours, / Conrad   178
Simpson / Athletic Manager /   183
[*your initials*] / cc: League Office   189

LETTER 5

Business letter with subject line and *cc* notation. Block format. Body 115 words.

[*Today's date*] / Athletic Department /   12
Springs High School / 1800 Keystone   19
Road / Sand Springs, OK 74063 /   24
Ladies and Gentlemen: / Subject: 33
Gymnastics Competition   38

¶ We have recently learned that   45
Springs High School is planning   51
to start a gymnastics squad   57
for next fall's competition. We   63
are members of the gymnastics   69
Conference, and we are pleased   76
to welcome you to our league.   82
¶ As a first-year member,   88
you are probably in the mid-   93
dle of planning your competition   100

LETTER 6

Business letter with subject line and postscript. Standard format. Body 73 words.

(Today's date) / Ms. Roberta Matson /   12
American Testing Agency / 160 E. Kellog   20
Blvd. / St. Paul, Mn 55101 / Dear Ms.   29
Matson: / Subject: Typing Tests   36

Last week you mentioned that your   44
agency has been developing an employment test for   54
office typists. I would like to learn more   63
about the test. ¶ We have for many years   72
used 5- and 10-minute tests for all our appli-   81
cants. However, we have found that there is little   91
correlation between an applicant's perfor-   99
mance on the test and performance on   107
the job. ¶ I hope that you will write to tell   117
us about your test. / Sincerely, / Roberta   131
Hendricks / Personnel Department / PS I'm   142
enclosing a stamped envelope for writ-   149
ing me about your testing program.   156

LESSON 11

GOAL
- To control Y, X, and question mark keys by touch.

FORMAT
- Single spacing   40-space line

KEYBOARDING REVIEW

Type each line twice.

1 deft lack vase more haze wing quip jibe
2 Zipp made quick jet flights over Nawbi.

SPACE BAR

 Y KEY

Use J finger.

Type each line twice.

3 jjj jyj yyy jjj jyj yyy jjj jyj yyy jyj
4 jyj yip yip jyj aye aye jyj joy joy jyj
5 jyj; yard of yarn, yield a yawn, a Yule

X KEY

Use S finger.

Type each line twice.

6 sss sxs xxx sss sxs xxx sss sxs xxx sxs
7 sxs vex vex sxs mix mix sxs wax wax sxs
8 sxs; next taxi, sixty Texans, lax taxes

 ? KEY

Use Sem finger and left shift key.

Space twice after a question mark.

Type each line twice.

9 ;;; ;/; ;/? ;?; ;;; ;/; ;/? ;?; ;/; ;?;
10 ;/; ;?; now? now? ;?; how? how? ;?;
11 who? when? where? what? why? next?

CHECKPOINT

Type lines 12–14 once. Then repeat lines 3, 6, and 9 or take two 2-minute timings on the Checkpoint.

12 Grab your camera; fix the lens. Take a   8
13 quick shot. Go to the zoo. Wait for a   16
14 move or a jump. Ready? Get that shot.   24

  | 1 | 2 | 3 | 4 | 5 | 6 | 7 | 8

LETTER 2

Personal-business letter. Standard format. Body 117 words.

304 West Geneva Road /Wheaton, — 7
IL 60187/ [Today's date]/Mr. — 19
R.C. Hargrove, Manager /The — 24
Stardust Manor Hotel /46 — 29
Franklin Street /Baltimore, MD — 35
21225 /Dear Mr. Hargrove: — 41
  Last week I had the — 46
privilege of staying at the — 52
Stardust Manor. I was — 56
somewhat in a hurry — 60
when I left because I had — 66
a plane to catch the — 70
morning of my departure. — 75
In my haste, I did not — 80
look closely at my bill. — 85
Upon arriving home, how- — 89
ever, I found an error — 94
in the charges to my room. — 100
  The bill includes three — 105
long-distance phone calls — 111
to New York City, for a total — 117
of $13.25. I did not make — 122
these calls and do not know — 128
the names of the parties — 133
called. Would you please — 138
look into this matter — 142
and refund me the $13.25. — 148

My apologies for not — 153
finding the error in my — 158
bill until this late date. — 163
Yours truly, /Stacy Maxton — 174

LETTER 3

Personal-business letter with enclosure and postscript notations. Standard format. Body 111 words.

1726 Lee Street/Flint, Mi 48560/ — 7
(Today's date)/R. B. Wards Inc./ — 20
1100 Griswold Avenue/Detroit, MI 48226/ — 28
Gentlemen: — 31
  On September 12 I purchased an — 38
electric iron, Model gT-246A, from — 45
your Griswold store. the price of the — 53
iron is $43.50. When I found out that — 61
the iron did not work, I sent it back — 69
immediately to you asking that my acount be — 75
credited for $34.50. On my October 15 — 84
statement, I noticed that my account — 92
had not been credited and that I had been — 100
charged for that iron. The same was — 107
true in my Nov. 15 statement. — 114
  Please take care of this matter — 122
& see that the correction is reflected — 130
in my Dec. statement. I have enclosed — 138
all correspondence on this trans- — 145
action, including a copy of my reciept — 153
of purchase./Cordially,/Edgar Mills/ — 167
Enclosures/PS: My account number is 88- — 177
345-909. — 179

PRETEST

Take two 1-minute timings on line 15, and determine your speed by using the faster rate.

15 play zany yoke pays zest yews jazz tax?
　　| 1 | 2 | 3 | 4 | 5 | 6 | 7 | 8

PRACTICE

Type each line twice.

To Type Faster
Read copy before typing it.
Aim for smoothness in stroking.

16 play flay clay slay shay stay sway away
17 zany maze daze doze hazy lazy hazy haze
18 yoke yolk your you, year yea, yet, yes?
19 pays nays mays jays hays days cays bays

20 zest sizes oversize full-size half-size
21 yews yaws yams yaps yaks yard yarn yawn
22 jazz nuzzle muzzle puzzle dazzle razzle
23 tax? taxi? text? next? flex? flax?

POSTTEST

Take two 1-minute timings on line 15, and determine your speed by using the faster rate. Note your improvement.

LESSON 12

CLINIC

GOALS
- To strengthen reaches on third, home, and bottom rows.
- To type 20 words a minute for 2 minutes with 4 errors or less.

FORMAT
- Single spacing   40-space line

PRETEST

Take a 1-minute timing on each line.

Third row　　1 They will type quiet quips from a page.　8
Home row　　2 Jed had asked for the glass in a flash.　8
Bottom row　3 Zach, move that ax back into that cave.　8
　　　　　　　　| 1 | 2 | 3 | 4 | 5 | 6 | 7 | 8

PRACTICE

Type lines 4–8 twice. Then proofread and circle errors.

4 rook work lurk dirk kirk keep kelp kilt
5 full foul fowl file fire four fort fore
6 jolt jets joke just jerk jugs jowl jaws
7 tort were quit quip tour prep pour were
8 your type true pert pipe wipe ripe prop

(Continued on next page)

TABLE 9
Three-column, with leaders.

Pryor's Service Center

BALANCE SHEET

October 31, 19--

```
ASSETS
     Cash ............................... $5,025.00
     Accounts Receivable .................  1,200.00
     Furniture ...........................  3,050.00
          Total Assets ...................            $9,275.00

LIABILITIES
     Accounts Payable .................... $1,050.00
     Mortgage Payable ....................  2,275.00
          Total Liabilities ..............            $3,325.00

EQUITY
     Dolores Pryor, Capital .............. $2,670.00
     Net Income ..........................  3,280.00
          Total Equity ...................             5,950.00
          Total Liabilities and Equity               $9,275.00
```

LETTERS

LETTER 1

Personal-business letter. Standard format. Body 81 words.

122 North Cover Street / Bedford, PA 15522 9
November 22, 19-- / Ms. Marie Preston, Editor 23
Views of Our Youth / 133 West Barnes Street 31
New York, NY 10038 / Dear Ms. Preston: 39

In a recent issue of <u>Views of Our Youth</u> I 56
read a fine article about the rock concerts that 66
are being planned for the coming summer 74
season. 75

Would it be possible to obtain additional 85
details about the concerts? My friends and I 94
would like to know if you are planning a 102
concert in the Pittsburgh area, since that one 112
would be closest for us. 117

Please let me know as soon as possible about 127
any anticipated concert dates in the Pittsburgh 136
area. 138

Sincerely yours, / Raymond Monroe 152

Check Your Hands

Palms are low but do not touch the machine.

Hands are flat and level across their backs.

The thumb is above the center of the space bar.

Hands are so close you could lock the thumbs.

All fingers are curved so that you type on the tips.

Type lines 9–13 twice. Then proofread and circle errors.

```
 9  wade jade fade fads gads dads lads lass
10  hash mash cash wash rash gash lash dash
11  gall fall hall hale kale sale dale gale
12  skid slid sled fled flag slag shag shad
13  drag lark lake khan fast load glad clad
```

Type lines 14–18 twice. Then proofread and circle errors.

```
14  pan, tan, man, fan, ran, van, ban, can,
15  bend bind mine mice mace calm acme came
16  move cove cave nave vain vein vine vane
17  nabs cabs cubs cobs cons conk cone cane
18  mix, fix, nix, ace, size daze maxe viz.
```

Repeat the group of lines that was the most difficult.

POSTTEST

Take a 1-minute timing on each of lines 1–3. Note your improvement.

2-MINUTE TIMINGS

SI means "syllabic intensity—the average number of syllables per word." A paragraph with all one-syllable words would have an SI of 1.00.

Take two 2-minute timings on lines 19–23. Use your paper bail to proofread your copy. Circle your errors and figure your score on each timing.

```
19  By the time you have typed the lines in     8
20  these first twelve lessons, you will be    16
21  able to type faster than you can write.    24
22  Relax.  You can adjust the machine, and    32
23  you can zoom through your work quickly.    40
    |  1  |  2  |  3  |  4  |  5  |  6  |  7  |  8    SI 1.16
```

LESSON 13

UNIT 3 FORMATTING—BASIC TECHNIQUES AND PROCEDURES

UNIT GOAL
24/2'/4e

GOALS
- To use the shift lock to type all capitals.
- To use three tabular keys to set a tab, to clear a tab, and to indent a new paragraph.

FORMAT
- Single spacing   50-space line

KEYBOARDING SKILLS

Type each line twice.

Words
Speed
Accuracy

```
1  aqua wish face join milk cozy play sobs over text
2  The girls may make a profit if they sing for Dot.
3  Just pack my box with five dozen quilts and rugs.
```

TABLE 7
Four-column, with rules, Totals line, and footnote.

EMPLOYEE VACATION AND SPENDING HABITS

(Summer, 19--)

Vacation Site	Number of Employees	Percent of Employees	Average Daily Expenses
Metropolitan City	24	27	$55.00
Sea side resort	25	23	70.00
Mountain resort	35	16	42.00
Motor Trip	22	14	88.50
Lake Resort	10	6	48.50
Misc.	21	14*	41.25
Totals	155	100	$57.64

*A total of 14 percent of the employees collectively had other kinds of vacations.

TABLE 8
Five-column, with rules.

New Mexico Gift Shop Inc.

SALES REPORT FOR NORTHERN REGION

City	This Year	Last Year	Increase	Percent
Santa Fe	$ 7,204	$ 6,852	$352	5.1
Albuquerque	11,368	10,476	892	8.5
Gallup	5,029	4,775	254	5.3
Tucumcari	4,279	3,740	539	14.4
Las Vegas	5,728	5,550	178	3.2
Raton	2,301	2,017	284	14.1

arrange alphabetically

How fast can you type with no more than 1 error for 30 seconds? Find out by taking two 30-second timings on lines 4–5 below. Remember to multiply the total words typed by 2 to find your 1-minute rate.

4 When you go for a ride in a car, take a look from   10

5 the window and view the sights as you move along.   20

| 1 | 2 | 3 | 4 | 5 | 6 | 7 | 8 | 9 | 10

ACCURACY

Accuracy lines should be typed as a paragraph.

Type lines 6–10 twice.

6 aaa aye aaa air aaa ail aaa aim aaa aria aaa alma

7 eee elf eee ewe eee eye eee end eee even eee earn

8 iii six iii did iii win iii fin iii city iii give

9 ooo oak ooo sod ooo own ooo ore ooo oboe ooo oleo

10 uuu sub uuu cub uuu rub uuu cup uuu sure uuu much

SPEED

Speed lines should be typed individually.

Type each line twice.

11 isle fuel flay gown keys then she for and the own

12 fish sign form wish duck they eye icy dig sow bug

13 pale idle gush slay torn roam sue hay sob man oak

14 goal bush firm chap lake city pay wit fur irk urn

15 lead coal pane risk half kept has lot yam cut fix

TAB STOPS

A formatting technique.

To make the carriage or carrier skip to a selected point, set a tab stop at that point and use the tab key.

1. Eliminate any stop that may be in the way. Press the all-clear key if your machine has one; or move the carriage or carrier to the right margin, and then hold down the tab clear key as you return the carriage or carrier.

2. Set the tab stop by moving the carriage or carrier to the point where you want it and pressing the tab set key.

3. Test the setting. Bring the carriage or carrier back to the left margin, and then press the tabulator key or bar—hold it down firmly until the carriage or carrier stops moving. It should stop where you set the tab stop.

Practice: Set a tab stop 5 spaces in from the left margin, and type *The* indented on three lines.

→ 5

The
The
The

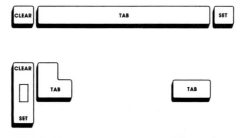

TABLE 4
Four-column, with rules.

BUDGETS FOR SCHOOL CLUBS

(Second Semester)

Name of Organization	Dues	School Contribution	Total
Athletic Club	$165	$60	$225
Business Club	85	25	110
Economics Club	60	20	80
French Club	85	25	110
Science Club	110	40	150

TABLE 5
Four-column, with rules and Totals line.

ANALYSIS OF LAST YEAR'S SALES

JULY 1 THROUGH JUNE 30

BRANCH	BUDGET	ACTUAL	PERCENT
CLEVELAND	$ 150,000	$ 150,000	115.0
DALLAS	255,000	244,000	95.7
MADISON	175,400	180,400	102.9
MINNEAPOLIS	215,400	177,500	82.4
PORTLAND	195,700	183,100	93.6
SAN FRANCISCO	300,500	278,300	92.6
TOTAL	$1,292,000	$1,213,300	93.9

TABLE 6
Five-column, with rules.

SPEAKERS' ROOM SCHEDULES

Society of Professional Editors

March 10, 19--

Speaker	Subject	Parlor A	Parlor B	Sessions
Hayen	Production	9:00	10:00	2
Mendez	Mailing	8:00	1:00	2
Orvick	Circulation		9:00	1
Rendell	Editorial	10:00		1
Swartz	Professional	1:00	8:00	2

INDENTING FOR PARAGRAPHS
A formatting technique.

When a paragraph is indented, as it is below, the indention is 5 spaces. Each indention counts as 5 strokes (1 word), the same as 5 space bar strokes would count. Use the tab to indent line 16 in the paragraph below.

2-MINUTE TIMINGS

Take two 2-minute timings on lines 16–20. Use your paper bail to proofread your copy. Circle your errors and figure your score on each timing. Format: Double spacing.

```
16        To watch the squirrel is a good lesson, some    10
17   say.  It takes some time to zip from limb to limb    20
18   and fix a place to put the food it hopes to save.    30
19   It makes the time to join a friend and bring some    40
20   happiness.                                           42
     |  1  |  2  |  3  |  4  |  5  |  6  |  7  |  8  |  9  |  10   SI 1.09
```

TYPING ALL-CAPITAL LETTERS

A formatting technique.

1. Press the shift lock. It is above one or both of the shift keys.
2. Type the words that are to be in all capitals.
3. Release the shift lock by touching the opposite shift key. (**Caution:** Release the lock before typing a stroke that, like a hyphen, cannot be typed as a capital.)

Practice: Type each line twice.

```
21   I need ONE MORE letter to FINISH the word puzzle.
22   Our team is FIRST-RATE.  We WON the CHAMPIONSHIP.
23   MARILEE and KIPP and BO were selected as LEADERS.
```

LESSON 14

GOALS
- To use the backspace key to center items horizontally.
- To center items horizontally (across) on a page.

FORMAT
- Single spacing   50-space line

KEYBOARDING SKILLS

Type each line twice.

Words
```
1   know deck file pogo jobs quey mare vote oxen hazy
```
Speed
```
2   This girl is to go to the field to work for them.
```
Accuracy
```
3   Packy quietly boxed these frozen jams with vigor.
```

SUPPLEMENTARY MATERIAL

TABLES

TABLE 1
Two-column, with
subtitle and column
headings.

Actors and Actresses
In the Order of Appearance

Roles	*Players*
The Mayor	Sandra Lewis
The Village Barber	Richard Wilson
The Oldest Daughter	Rosalie Sanchez
The Oldest Son	Benjamin Kennedy
The Visitor	Robert Benet

TABLE 2
Two-column, with
subtitle and column
headings.

EXECUTIVE OFFICERS
Capitol *Publishing* Company

Name	Position
Adriana L. Martinez	Chief Executive Officer
Nancy t. Pemberton	Vice President Executive
Harold E. Johnson	Vice President for Sales
Colleen L. Labarge	Vice President for Research
Sharon W. Woodard	V.P. for Personnel

TABLE 3
Three-column, with
subtitle and rules.

Rooms and
teacher names are
correct —
alphabetize order
of surnames in
first column.

JUNIOR ROOM ASSIGNMENTS
(First Semester)

Surname Grouping	Room	Teacher
Jackson Through Lorenz	141A	Ms. Franklin
Thomas Through Young	141B	Mr. Qually
Eastman Through Harms	142A	Ms. Yeung
Adams Through Desitaul	142B	Ms. Carlisle
Preston Through Song	143A	Mr. Kenton
Miller Through Olsen	143B	Mr. Baruch

30-SECOND TIMINGS

Take two 30-second timings on lines 4–5, or type each line twice.

4 Can you think of all the things that you would do 10

5 if you could do just as you wanted to for a week? 20

| 1 | 2 | 3 | 4 | 5 | 6 | 7 | 8 | 9 | 10 |

ACCURACY

Type lines 6–10 twice.

6 see butt happy errors flivver carriage occasional

7 off poll dizzy middle blabber possible bookkeeper

8 zoo buff radii sizzle powwows followed additional

9 inn ebbs gummy bottle accused slowness beginnings

10 Hannah took a dotted swiss dress to the Mall Inn.

SPEED

Type each line twice.

11 formal prisms blend panel busy chap cut ham is it

12 social glands visit field torn sign rid air to do

13 eighty blames audit forms half fuel apt owl of an

14 profit island slept right tidy cork fix hem am so

15 The theme for the eighth panel is When to Fix It.

FORMATTING: HORIZONTAL CENTERING

Workbook 15–16.

To center horizontally:

1. Set the carriage or carrier at the center.
2. Find the backspace key (upper left or right corner of the keyboard).
3. Say the strokes (including spaces) in pairs to yourself, depressing the backspace key once after you say each pair. If you have an odd letter left over after calling off all pairs, do *not* backspace for it.

Example: Center these
to center

4. Type the material. It should appear in the middle of the paper.

Practice: Type each of the following two drills. Use half sheets of paper. Format: Begin on line 14; double-space.

Center these
lines by using
the backspace key.

It is easy
to center
by backspacing.

JOB 14-1. CENTERING

Format the names by centering on a full sheet of paper. Double-space. Begin on line 15. Leave 5 blank lines between each group of names.

Les Boland
Bill Colburn
Stan Orlen
Jerry Longaman
Fran Mortimer

Marijane Landon
Anna Lee Lipton
Patsy Clark
Robin Salmon
Noel Wilson

Stepha Mark
Steve Fabr
Hester V. Starfire
Stella Jo Garman
Lawrence Oren

JOB 149/150-1. (Continued)
TABLE 1
MILES PER GALLON ESTIMATES

Miles per Gallon	Number of Drivers	Percentage
Less than 10	2	5.0
10 to 20	11	27.5
21 to 30	22	55.0
31 or more	5	12.5
Total	40	100.0

[1]Sheila Torrance, "Driving in the '80s," Car Report, May 1982, p. 27.

JOB 149/150-2. LETTER
Standard format (see page 92). Workbook 293–294. Body 59 words (plus 20 words for subject line).

Ms. Audrey L. Simms, Knight Insurance Company, 204 Pine Ridge Road, Boston, MA 02181 — 16 / 25
Dear Ms. Simms: Subject: Carpet Cleaning — 36

As we discussed on the telephone today, we will be able to clean the carpeting on the fourth floor of your building on Saturday, March 3. — 45 / 55 / 64

Our people will be at your office at 8 a.m. on that day to move out the furniture and vacuum the carpet before cleaning and shampooing. — 74 / 82 / 91 / 93

Thank you for doing business with us. Yours sincerely, Archie T. Maisley, Manager — 102 / 118

JOB 149/150-3. INTEROFFICE MEMO
Standard format (see page 107). Workbook 297.

[To:] Perry Davis, [From:] Helene Cotter, [Subject:] Room Reservations — 13 / 16

Please reserve Room 3004 for me on Tuesday, April 4, from 8:30 a.m. to 12 noon. We will need a slide projector and screen for our meeting. Please make arrangements to have this equipment in the room by 9 a.m. — 27 / 37 / 46 / 56 / 60

I would also like to reserve Room 3004 for April 10 from 1:30 p.m. to 3:30 p.m. I will send you my equipment requirements on the 6th. — 70 / 80 / 88 / 91

HC

JOB 149/150-4. THREE-COLUMN RULED TABLE
Standard format. Full sheet of paper.

MAJOR OIL-PRODUCING STATES*

By [Your name]

State	Capital City	Area in Sq. Miles
Texas	Austin	262,134
Louisiana	Baton Rouge	44,930
California	Sacramento	156,361
Oklahoma	Oklahoma City	68,782
Wyoming	Cheyenne	97,203

*Arranged from largest to smallest producer.

JOB 149/150-5. BUSINESS INVOICE 38644
Standard format. Workbook 299.

[To] Davidson Office Furniture / [Today's date] / 385 King Avenue / Dayton, OH 45420

Qty	Item	Unit price	Amount
10	Filing cabinets, #F780	62.50	625.00
2	Filing cabinets, #F880	72.50	145.00
6	Boxes of file folders	7.75	46.50
4	Boxes of file guides	2.50	10.00
	Total amount due		826.50

LESSON 15

GOALS
- To use the backspace key to determine a left margin.
- To block-center items on a page.

FORMAT
- Single spacing   50-space line   5-space tab and center tab

KEYBOARDING SKILLS

Type each line twice.

Words 1 both cram dyed life give junk quip owes axle size

Speed 2 Six or eight pens go to the man with the oak cot.

Accuracy 3 Quickly box five dozen afghans for W. M. Jeptham.

FORMATTING: BLOCK CENTERING

To center a group of lines (not each line separately), use the following block-centering procedure:

1. Pick the longest line in the group.
2. Backspace to center that line.
3. Set the left margin stop.
4. Begin all lines at the left margin.

Practice: Block-center each of these drills, leaving 5 lines between exercises. Begin on line 26 and double-space.

```
Centering a block
of lines is called
block centering.



LEARNING TO CENTER ITEMS
A Report by
[Your Name]
```

JOB 15-1. BLOCK CENTERING

Format the three groups of names by block centering each group. Use a full sheet of paper. Double-space. Begin on line 15. Leave 5 blank lines between each group.

Mehra Golshan	Jill Poeppelmeier	Kim Kaufenberg
Amy Tidovsky	Mike Goeke	Shakira Tadross
Steve Burton	Melody Luoma	Jenny Chojnacki
Jeff Maresca	Kevin Negilski	Ed Byrum
Jane Williamson	Lisa Serafin	Donita Steger

30-SECOND TIMINGS

Take two 30-second timings on lines 4–5, or type each line twice.

4 When you join your school pep club, you will find 10

5 all kinds of jobs that you can do to gain spirit. 20

| 1 | 2 | 3 | 4 | 5 | 6 | 7 | 8 | 9 | 10

Take two 5-minute timings on lines 3–20. Circle your errors on each.

```
 3        Many people have often wondered what might possibly be        12
 4    the greatest structure on earth.  The tallest buildings and       24
 5    the longest bridges and the mightiest dams might be closely       36
 6    examined in an attempt to identify an answer to this diffi-       48
 7    cult question.  In the minds of many people, though, one of       60
 8    the greatest structures ever built may be the Great Wall of       72
 9    China.  It's well established that its features are so very       84
10    overwhelming that astronauts could view the Wall from their       96
11    spaceship portholes.                                             100

12        The structure was built primarily by mixing just earth       112
13    and bricks.  It is wide enough at the top to permit several       124
14    people to walk abreast on it.  It winds for miles through a       136
15    large section of the country, over mountains and across the      148
16    valleys.  It was built to keep out tribes from other lands.      160
17    It is believed that building the wall required the labor of      172
18    many, many thousands of persons for many dozens of decades.      184
19    Actually, the wall was built during the reign of many vari-      196
20    ous tribal dynasties.                                            200
```

| 1 | 2 | 3 | 4 | 5 | 6 | 7 | 8 | 9 | 10 | 11 | 12 | SI 1.48 |

JOB 149/150-1. TWO-PAGE REPORT WITH TABLE AND FOOTNOTE

Double spacing. 5-space tab.

METHODS OF TRANSPORTATION

By James Rhoades

INTRODUCTION

The rising fuel costs in this country have had a profound effect on the driving habits and the means of transportation used by both young and old. The May issue of Car Report states that "student driving habits will change because of the rapidly rising fuel costs this nation is experiencing."[1] It appears that fuel costs will affect the methods by which students commute to their schools.

STATEMENT OF THE PROBLEM

The problem of this study is to reveal how students at Valley High School have changed their methods of transportation to and from school.

BACKGROUND OF THE PROBLEM

Valley High School is located between Greenville, Loan Oak, and Sulphur Springs on a 20-acre tract of land. Because of this central location, many students commute to and from school. In the past, students have commuted by driving alone in their own cars, by driving with other students, or by riding the bus.

FINDINGS

A total of 96 seniors were surveyed in the study—25 of them drove alone, 15 car-pooled with other students, and 56 rode the school bus. Of the 40 students who drove cars (either alone or in a car pool), 35 percent drove mid-size cars, 46 percent drove small cars, and 19 percent drove large cars.

An additional finding of this study revealed the miles per gallon averages for all students' cars. Table 1 below reveals that 55 percent of the cars obtained an average of 21 to 30 miles per gallon. Only one-half that number (27 percent) were able to obtain from 10 to 20 miles per gallon. Five of the students indicated that their cars were getting over 30 miles per gallon.

(Continued on next page)

ACCURACY

Type lines 6–10 twice.

6 on ear kin vat yip acre pill race upon face phony

7 we imp vex hip tag pink case limp zest lion cedar

8 in arc pin age you date jump were honk ease hilly

9 be joy tax oil fad noun tact yolk gear mink verse

10 After Kip agreed, John gave my dad a faster kiln.

SPEED

Type each line twice.

11 find this that who his and why him my be if do no

12 when wish like but out may for she me or am in to

13 them look they our the her got how by us it so up

14 what mine type now can fun put set of at on as go

15 She is to be there at a time when he can see her.

2-MINUTE TIMINGS

Take two 2-minute timings on lines 16–20. Use your paper bail to proofread your copy. Circle your errors and figure your score on each timing.

16   Watch the river move across the plain and on 10

17 to the bluff beyond. It has a tale to tell about 20

18 the ones who have gone this way. The men and the 30

19 women were not unique. They just had the zeal to 40

20 take the extra risk. 44

| 1 | 2 | 3 | 4 | 5 | 6 | 7 | 8 | 9 | 10   SI 1.16

LESSON 16

GOALS
- To count vertical lines on a page.
- To center items vertically (up and down) on a page.

FORMAT
- Single spacing   50-space line   5-space tab and center tab

KEYBOARDING SKILLS

Type each line twice.

Words   1 away vice jeep high kiln form ribs exit zero quid

Speed   2 Jan works for us but may wish to work for Pamela.

Accuracy   3 Six jet-black vans quietly zip through wet farms.

Commas (Continued)	39	I applied for the job but I have not yet been interviewed.
	40	Buy the new book at Sloan's Bookstore or order it by mail.
	41	Ann included a stamped addressed envelope with her letter.
	42	Ms. Judd wrote a short interesting letter to the engineer.
	43	We are very pleased therefore to hear about the discount.
	44	This new model will be in my opinion our most successful.
	45	For more information on this new policy call Andrea Smith.
	46	Our marketing director Rhonda Pierce developed this plan.
Semicolons	47	Order four dozen more boxes ask about a quantity discount.
	48	The television campaign begins on May 1 it ends on May 30.
	49	He may of course return the merchandise do it right now.
Question Marks	50	Gene Rand completed all the work before he left, didn't he.
	51	Arlene, where do we keep all the chronological file copies.
	52	Will the advertising copy be ready for Wednesday's meeting.
Exclamation Points	53	I cannot believe that Kyle rejected their tremendous offer.
	54	Congratulations on your promotion to director of marketing.
	55	It's true. Our firm was awarded a new government contract.
Quotation Marks	56	We must price this product under $100, said Ms. Holcroft.
	57	He replied, It is not economical to buy small quantities.
	58	Special orders should be stamped For Immediate Attention.
	59	Attach Handle With Care labels on each of the test tubes.

LESSONS 149/150

COMPETENCY CHECK

GOALS
- To type 40/5'/5e.
- To type a long report with footnotes, a letter, a memo, a ruled table, and an invoice.

FORMAT
- Single spacing   60-space line   5-space tab

PREVIEW PRACTICE

Type lines 1 and 2 twice as a preview to the 5-minute timings on page 249.

Accuracy 1 bridges wondered examined structure astronauts overwhelming

Speed 2 section several mixing answer built reign many ever was and

30-SECOND TIMINGS

Take two 30-second timings on lines 4–5, or type each line twice.

4 When you take the time to show that you are kind, 10

5 the smile on the face of a child is a joy to see. 20

| 1 | 2 | 3 | 4 | 5 | 6 | 7 | 8 | 9 | 10

ACCURACY

Type lines 6–10 twice.

6 tr tram true trek tray trip trim trap trust tribe

7 as last cast fast wasp mast ease vast tease aspen

8 re care real tore pore sore wore lore flare chore

9 op drop stop flop crop open rope hope scope slope

10 ew brew flew crew stew drew chew grew strew shrew

SPEED

Type each line twice.

11 ful grateful faithful careful fateful tactful ful

12 est greatest interest nearest biggest longest est

13 ing thinking swimming sailing sending writing ing

14 ble portable probable taxable capable visible ble

15 ure fixtures features mixture futures torture ure

2-MINUTE TIMINGS

Take two 2-minute timings on lines 16–20. Use your paper bail to proofread your copy. Circle your errors and figure your score on each timing.

16   There is no equal to the flavor of ice cream 10

17 on hot, humid days. Choices of all types are out 20

18 to engage the eye, and the snappy clerks will fix 30

19 just the mix and size to suit you best. A cup or 40

20 a cone will be fine. 44

| 1 | 2 | 3 | 4 | 5 | 6 | 7 | 8 | 9 | 10   SI 1.13

MEASURING FOR VERTICAL SPACING

Most typewriters space 6 lines to an inch. Standard typing paper is 11 inches long, so there are 11 × 6 = 66 lines on a full page or 33 lines on a half page. Some special and imported typewriters space 5¼ lines to an inch, giving 57 lines on a full page and 28 lines on a half page. A4 metric paper is slightly longer—70 lines to the page.

Practice: (1) Insert a sheet of paper, and count the single-spaced lines. (2)

Type the word *single* on six consecutive lines; then measure the lines with a ruler to see how much space they occupy.

1	single	double
2	single	------
3	single	double
4	single	------
5	single	double
6	single	------

9 Jolly Flynn was very much puzzled by Alex's quick thinking. 12

10 Why did Professor Black give you a quiz on the major texts? 24

11 Jumping quickly from the taxi, Hazel brushed a woven chair. 36

| 1 | 2 | 3 | 4 | 5 | 6 | 7 | 8 | 9 | 10 | 11 | 12

5-MINUTE TIMING

Take a 5-minute timing on lines 12–28.

12   Hiking is one of the best ways to keep in top physical 12

13 condition. Not only does it help your vital organs to keep 24

14 working well, it might also help improve your entire mental 36

15 attitude. It is important that a beginning hiker recognize 48

16 the rules that make hiking more enjoyable. First, one must 60

17 be comfortable while on the hike. All the clothing and the 72

18 shoes must fit quite well. A hiker should always wear good 84

19 shoes that are sturdy and well–fitting socks. The clothing 96

20 should be very protective for use in rugged country. Every 108

21 person should learn to keep both arms free while on a hike. 120

22 This means that each hiker must hoist all that equipment on 132

23 a backpack. Carrying a backpack requires that every person 144

24 must use good posture; otherwise, many aches might develop. 156

25 The beginning hiker should start with short distances. The 168

26 longer hike should be postponed until the person is in good 180

27 physical condition. Hiking truly provides a way to explore 192

28 the country and become physically fit. 200

| 1 | 2 | 3 | 4 | 5 | 6 | 7 | 8 | 9 | 10 | 11 | 12   SI 1.48

LANGUAGE ARTS REVIEW

As you type the following groups of sentences, you will be applying a number of language arts rules. Do your best work as you apply the rules in these sentences. Workbook 291–292.

Capitalization

29 you must cross lee, alden, main, center, and grand streets.

30 an african lion, asian tiger, and american cougar are cats.

31 they visited the red river, the caspian sea, and rice lake.

32 dr. kramer, inspector carlisle, and sergeant stabor smiled.

33 your book on regional cooking sells very well in the south.

34 turn north at the intersection; then turn west immediately.

Commas

35 As both of you already know the seminar has been canceled.

36 If you want this to get there fast send it by parcel post.

37 The conference rooms are decorated in red green and blue.

38 The returns were 6.2 7.5 and 7.9 percent on each mailing.

(Continued on next page)

FORMATTING: VERTICAL CENTERING

Workbook 17–18.

To place copy in the vertical center of a page, follow these steps:

1. Count the lines (including blanks) that the copy will occupy when typed.
2. Subtract that number from the available number of lines on your paper.
3. Divide the difference by 2 to find the number of the line on which you should begin typing (drop any fraction).

Example: To center five double-spaced lines on a half page, you need 9 lines for copy (5 typed, 4 blank); 33 − 9 = 24, and 24 ÷ 2 = 12. Begin typing on line 12.

Practice: Block-center these lines vertically on a half sheet of paper. Use double spacing.

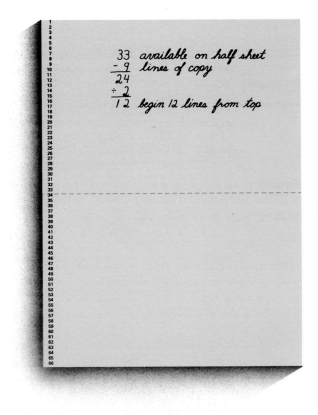

```
      To count double-spaced

      lines that you want to

      center vertically, you

  →   must count every typed

      line and all the blank

      lines in between.
```

Check: When finished typing, fold paper from top to bottom. The crease should be in the center, close to the point indicated by the arrow.

JOB 16-1. ADVERTISEMENT
Format: Center vertically and horizontally on a half sheet of paper. Double-space.

FREE GERBILS
One Month Old
→ *Both Males and Females*
See Sara Viator
Journalism Room

JOB 16-2. ADVERTISEMENT
Format: Block-center horizontally; center vertically on a half sheet of paper. Double-space.

LOST
Junior Class Ring
Sparkle-Blue Set
→ *Initials MCP*
See Marla Padraka
Room South A

Paragraph 2

Objectives: Strengthen your qualifications. Express pleasure to be a candidate.

Example: You mentioned that three people were being considered seriously for this secretarial position. I'm very glad to be one of those people. My extensive secretarial experience would prove very beneficial for your company and would provide you with the administrative expertise you requested in the newspaper advertisement.

Practice: Compose and type the second paragraph for a follow-up letter. Use any one or more of the ideas suggested on page 245.

Paragraph 3

Objectives: Express greater interest in the job. Appear optimistic about the decision.

Example: My determination to become a valuable asset to your firm is greater than ever. I look forward to a favorable decision on my employment with your company.

Practice: Compose and type the final paragraph for a follow-up letter. Use any one or more of the ideas suggested on page 245.

JOB 7. FOLLOW-UP LETTER

Compose and type a complete follow-up letter using the three paragraphs you composed as Practice exercises. Add the following parts to complete the letter: (1) return address, (2) date line, (3) inside address, (4) salutation, (5) complimentary close, and (6) signature line.

LESSON 148

LANGUAGE ARTS REVIEW

GOALS
- To type 40/5'/5e.
- To type correctly a series of sentences requiring the application of various language arts rules.

FORMAT
- Single spacing   60-space line   5-space tab

KEYBOARDING SKILLS

Type lines 1–4 once. In line 5, use your tabulator key throughout the entire line to advance from numbers to dashes. Repeat lines 1–4, or take a series of 1-minute timings.

Speed	1	It is now time to take our last final look at all our work.	12
Accuracy	2	A lazy duck quacked before jumping next to a very wise hog.	12
Numbers	3	I typed at 10 and 29 and 38 and 47 and 56 words per minute.	12
Symbols	4	It was stored @ Dock #8, and it sold for $850 (10% profit).	12
Technique	5	10 -- 29 -- 38 -- 47 -- 56 -- 10 --	

| 1 | 2 | 3 | 4 | 5 | 6 | 7 | 8 | 9 | 10 | 11 | 12

"OK" TIMINGS

Type as many "OK" (errorless) timings as possible out of three attempts on lines 6–8. Then repeat the effort on lines 9–11, page 247.

6   Jinx gave back the prize money she won for her quaint doll. 12
7   Dave quickly filled a dozen mixtures in the deep brown jug. 24
8   On the way here, this quick fox jumped back over a gazelle. 36

| 1 | 2 | 3 | 4 | 5 | 6 | 7 | 8 | 9 | 10 | 11 | 12

(Continued on next page)

LESSON 17

KEYBOARDING SKILLS

Type each line twice.

Words 1 fact bits girl with joke moon pulp quiz void exit
Speed 2 The eighty bushels of corn may be profit for Len.
Accuracy 3 Juarez vowed maximum support to buoy his legions.

30-SECOND TIMINGS

Take two 30-second timings on lines 4–5, or type each line twice.

4 Just how much more time do you think it took them 10
5 to write all these drills that fill up this book? 20
   | 1 | 2 | 3 | 4 | 5 | 6 | 7 | 8 | 9 | 10

ACCURACY

Type lines 6–10 twice.

6 er mere error infer steer power finer tower newer
7 sa said sacks sails safes sakes sandy saves sages
8 ui suit ruins fruit guide fluid juice suite squid
9 io ions lions trios adios scion idiom idiot axiom
10 we were weeps wears welds weans weeds swept weave

SPEED

Type each line twice.

11 ity activity priority charity ability quality ity
12 ial official material cordial special initial ial
13 ify simplify identify specify clarify qualify ify
14 ion deletion relation section mention lesions ion
15 age coverage mortgage average postage package age

2-MINUTE TIMINGS

Take two 2-minute timings on lines 16–20. Use your paper bail to proofread your copy. Circle your errors and figure your score on each timing. Format: Double spacing.

16   The old man who walks in the park always has 10
17 a big smile on his face. He talks to each person 20
18 who comes his way. He gives aid in his quiet way 30
19 and is excited when he makes a new friend. He is 40
20 amazed at those who join him there.   47
   | 1 | 2 | 3 | 4 | 5 | 6 | 7 | 8 | 9 | 10   SI 1.12

COMPOSING FOLLOW-UP LETTERS

The final step in the job application process is writing a follow-up letter. After you have had your interview, you should send the company a written thank you for interviewing you. Note how each numbered paragraph of the letter shown at the right achieves the goals of a follow-up letter.

① In the **opening paragraph,** you should express appreciation for the interview and reaffirm your interest in the job.

② In the **second paragraph,** you may:
   a. Add new information that might be helpful in revealing your qualifications.
   b. Express pleasure at being considered a candidate for the job.
   c. Tell how you feel about the job now that the interview has been completed.

③ In the **final paragraph,** you may do one of the following:
   a. Express even greater interest in the job.
   b. Mention that you are looking forward to a favorable decision.
   c. Make yourself available for a second interview.

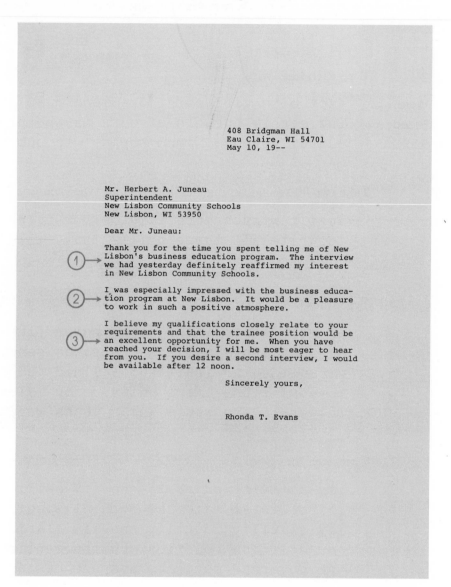

```
                    408 Bridgman Hall
                    Eau Claire, WI 54701
                    May 10, 19--


Mr. Herbert A. Juneau
Superintendent
New Lisbon Community Schools
New Lisbon, WI 53950

Dear Mr. Juneau:

     Thank you for the time you spent telling me of New
①   Lisbon's business education program.  The interview
     we had yesterday definitely reaffirmed my interest
     in New Lisbon Community Schools.

     I was especially impressed with the business educa-
②   tion program at New Lisbon.  It would be a pleasure
     to work in such a positive atmosphere.

     I believe my qualifications closely relate to your
     requirements and that the trainee position would be
③   an excellent opportunity for me.  When you have
     reached your decision, I will be most eager to hear
     from you.  If you desire a second interview, I would
     be available after 12 noon.

                    Sincerely yours,


                    Rhonda T. Evans
```

Before you compose and type your own follow-up letter, you will have the opportunity to work on each of the separate paragraphs necessary in a follow-up letter. Study the examples provided here and on the next page, and then compose your own paragraphs for a follow-up letter.

Paragraph 1

Objectives: Say thank you. Reaffirm interest.

Example: Thank you for the interesting time you spent with me this past Wednesday. My visit with you and the other members of your staff made me realize how very enjoyable it would be to work for your company.

Practice: Assume that the letter of application you wrote for Job 5 resulted in an interview. Compose and type the first paragraph of a follow-up letter to the job for which you applied.

FORMATTING: SPREAD CENTERING

To give added emphasis to a display line, spread it by leaving 1 space between letters and 3 spaces between words, like this:

T H I S   I S   S P R E A D I N G

To center a spread line, be sure to include all the spaces as you say the pairs for backspacing, like "T-space, H-space, I-space, S-space, space-space, I-space," and so on. **Practice:** Center the spread line above. Then center and spread this line: SPREAD WORDS FOR EMPHASIS.

FORMATTING ANNOUNCEMENTS

Announcements of meetings are usually displayed and are typed on either a full sheet or a half sheet of paper. To format an announcement:

1. Center the announcement vertically.

2. Center each line horizontally.

3. Use a variety of display techniques—some lines typed in capital letters and lowercase letters, some lines typed in all-capital letters, some lines spread-centered.

JOB 17-1. ANNOUNCEMENT

Standard format. Full sheet of paper. Double spacing. Spread line 5.

ANNOUNCEMENT
of the
NORTHWEST CANOE TRIP
on the
R O G U E   R I V E R
During the
First Week of July

JOB 17-2. ANNOUNCEMENT

Standard format. Full sheet of paper. Double spacing. Spread line 6.

The
Morgantown Chapter
of the
FUTURE TEACHERS CLUB
Will Meet With
DR. CAL SKIPPER
in Room S
Wednesday at Three

LESSON 18

CLINIC

GOAL
- To refine techniques for spacing, shifting, returning, tabulating, and keeping eyes on copy while typing.

FORMAT
- Single spacing   50-space line

SPACE BAR

Type each line twice.

1 ask met paw fix vib yam fog dim aye con sake even
2 jet war hot kin vet zip quo bat ace eke long oxen
3 As you know, a doe hides low before the big snow.
4 As they sat on a mat, a pup and a cat had a spat.

SHIFT LOCK

Type each line twice.

5 The SOPHOMORES were glad about having a SNOW DAY.
6 It was a DIESEL, and it was BLUE–GREEN, not GRAY.
7 She will be in the ELEVENTH grade, not the TENTH.

(Continued on next page)

Application forms vary from one company to another, but all ask for basically the same information. The illustrations at the right show two sides of an application form. This form, like most others, asks the applicant to provide information as follows (note that the numbers correspond to those included with the illustrations):

① **Date.** Include the month, day, and year.

② **Personal Data.** Be sure to provide your complete permanent address (and temporary address, if applicable)—your street address, city, state, and ZIP Code.

③ **Social Security Number.** Be prepared to fill in your social security number, because every person must have one when applying for a job.

④ **Type of Work.** A company will often inquire as to the type of position you are seeking. You may also be asked the salary you expect and the date you would be available for work. If you have special machine skills, you might be asked to identify your competencies on these machines.

⑤ **Education.** Many application forms ask for the name of your high school as well as any colleges or business schools, the dates you attended, and the courses you completed.

⑥ **Health.** Answer honestly all questions on health. The questions are essential for insurance purposes, as well as to find out who should be notified in case of medical emergency.

⑦ **Employment History.** Employers want to know about previous work experience. Past work experience may help you obtain a better entry-level position, so be as honest and as thorough as you can in completing this section.

⑧ **References.** To complete this section, use the list of references that you included in your résumé. References should be people such as past employers and former teachers, who can attest to your character, work habits, and work potential.

⑨ **Signature.** DO NOT FORGET TO SIGN THE APPLICATION FORM—and date it, too, if necessary.

JOB 6. APPLICATION FORMS

Apply for a job for which you are qualified. Workbook 287–290.

Application Form, Page 1

Application Form, Page 2

SHIFT LOCK (Continued)

8 We may choose either a TOY POODLE or a CHIHUAHUA.
9 They typed TURF instead of SURF on my manuscript.

CARRIAGE OR CARRIER RETURN

Type each line once. Return the carriage or carrier after each name.

10M Brett Caryn Robin Susie Bruce Alyn Bess Drew Beth
11M Debra Rhett Terry Carla Edwin Ezra Dale Fran Erik
12M Alexa Cyril Roxie Duane Sammy Greg Fred Evie Stan

10E Helen Julie Kathy Laura Paula Hans Olga Uris Jill
11E Nancy Henry Mella Helga Porgy Jack Lisa Joni Myra
12E Perry Yetta Jenny Price Kevin Noel Lynn Jeff Kara

TABULATOR

Set four tabs—one every 10 spaces. Type each line once; tab between words.

13 Please   tab   across   the   page.
14 It   is   so   much   faster.
15 The   spaces   go   this   way.
16 Do   you   like   typing   this?
17 Can   you   tab   better   now?

EYES ON COPY

Fill in the missing vowels as you type each line once.

18 Wh-n y-- try t- f-ll -n th- bl-nks -s y-- typ- -n
19 th- l-n-s, y-- w-ll n--d t- st-dy th- p-tt-rns -f
20 --ch -f th- w-rds. D-d y-- s-- th-t -ll -f th--r
21 v-w-ls -r- m-ss-ng? Y-- c-n f-g-r- --t --ch -ne.
22 J-st k--p y--r -y-s -n th- c-py -s y-- typ- th-m.

LESSON 19

UNIT 4 KEYBOARDING—THE NUMBERS
UNIT GOAL 25/2'/4e

GOALS
- To control 1, 2, and 3 keys.
- To format enumerations.

FORMAT
- Single spacing   50-space line   4-space tab

KEYBOARDING SKILLS

Type each line twice.

Words   1 maze elks corn idea flex give shot jobs quip whey
Speed   2 If the men do the audit work by six, they may go.
Accuracy 3 The clown from Quebec completely dazzled the man.

JOB 5. LETTER OF APPLICATION COMPOSED FROM A CLASSIFIED AD

Compose a letter of application from the information provided in one of the two classified ads below. Select the ad that most closely resembles the type of position for which you would like to apply and for which you are better qualified.

SECRETARY

The Dallas Morning News has an opening in the Data Processing Department for a secretary.

All interested applicants must type 50 wam, take shorthand at 80 wam, use transcribing equipment, and have at least two years of secretarial training and/or experience. You must be a self-motivator and work with little or no supervision.

We offer excellent working conditions and company benefits.

Send a letter of application and résumé to:

**PERSONNEL OFFICE
THE DALLAS MORNING NEWS
400 WEST ABRAMS STREET
DALLAS, TX 75214**

An Equal Opportunity Employer

FILE CLERK

Southwest Oil & Gas Company has an opening for a file clerk.

This is an entry-level position within our accounting file room. Qualifications include dependability and willingness to learn. Applicant must have had some training in basic numeric and alphabetic filing procedures.

Excellent benefits include a comprehensive medical and dental program, disability income protection, and free parking.

If interested, send a letter of application and résumé to:

**PERSONNEL DEPARTMENT
SOUTHWEST OIL & GAS COMPANY
504 STATE STREET
TEMPE, AZ 85281**

SOGCO is an Equal Opportunity Employer

FILLING OUT APPLICATION FORMS

The third step in the job application process is the completion of an application form. Most business firms have the applicant fill out an application form either before or after the interview.

Before viewing a sample application form, you might find the following suggestions helpful when you are asked to complete such a form:

1. *Be neat and accurate.* Above all else, complete the application form neatly, and be sure to check for spelling and/or grammatical errors. Make any corrections carefully.

2. *Follow instructions.* Print neatly. If you are asked to type, then be sure to align all the typewritten responses on the lines provided for that purpose. Try to complete all the blanks; but if certain items do not apply to you, print or type "Not Applicable" or "N/A" in the space provided for your answer.

3. *Do not omit continuous dates.* If you are asked to supply the dates you attended high school, be sure to enter all dates—from the beginning school year to the ending school year. If you enter your years of employment, do not omit any years that you worked.

Note: There will be many differences on application forms from different companies. Many companies are in the process of revising their application blanks to comply with existing or pending regulations regarding nondiscriminatory questions. Employers are no longer permitted to ask for the specific age of a person (age ranges are permitted because employers need to know whether an applicant is under age and needs a work permit or is eligible for social security benefits). Other questions that may not be asked are those regarding marital status, religion, and nationality.

To Practice Top Row Reaches

Type each reach slowly to feel the distance and direction of the reach.

Then type it again more smoothly.

Remember to anchor the home row fingers.

SPACE BAR

 1 KEY

Use small l for 1 if you do not have a 1 key.

Use A finger on 1 if you do have a 1 key.

Type each line twice.

4 aqa aql ala lll 1,111 11,111 1.11 11.11 and 11/11
5 ll arms, ll areas, ll adages, ll animals, or 1.11
6 My ll aides can type lll pages within ll minutes.

 2 KEY

Use S finger.

Type each line twice.

7 sws sw2 s2s 222 2,222 22,222 2.22 22.22 and 22/22
8 22 sips, 22 sites, 22 swings, 22 signals, or 2.22
9 I saw 21 ads in Column 2 of 212 papers on July 1.

3 KEY

Use D finger.

Type each line twice.

10 ded de3 d3d 333 3,333 33,333 3.33 33.33 and 33/33
11 33 dots, 33 dimes, 33 dishes, 33 daisies, or 3.33
12 She asked 231 persons 132 questions in 123 hours.

CHECKPOINT

Type lines 13–15 once. Then repeat lines 4, 7, and 10 or take two 1-minute timings on the Checkpoint.

13 At least 23 of the 32 sketches were made by 12 of   10
14 the artists for the show on March 11, 12, and 13.   20
15 We need 2 or 3 more sketches for the 3 p.m. show.   30
    | 1 | 2 | 3 | 4 | 5 | 6 | 7 | 8 | 9 | 10

2-MINUTE TIMINGS

Take two 2-minute timings on lines 16–20. Format: Double spacing, 5-space tab.

16   To see the artists paint is a joy. The zeal   10
17 with which they work to have the exact tints show   20
18 up on the pad is fun to watch. As they glide the   30
19 new brush quickly across the pad, the bright hues   40
20 take form and bring smiles to our faces.   48
    | 1 | 2 | 3 | 4 | 5 | 6 | 7 | 8 | 9 | 10 SI 1.10

2110 Ellen Court
Memphis, TN 38123
May 22, 19--

Mr. Samuel Davis
A to Z Contractors, Inc.
4701 Hanna Boulevard
Memphis, TN 38123

Dear Mr. Davis:

① One of your employees, Chris Corsi, mentioned that you have a secretarial position available at A to Z Contractors, Inc. I would like to be considered as an applicant for this position.

② My typing rate of 65 words a minute and my shorthand speed of 120 words a minute will enable me to serve your company as a competent office worker. In addition, I possess a knowledge of filing procedures and have received special training on telephone usage, as you will see in the enclosed résumé.

③ In addition to these specific office skills, I have also been an active participant at several regional competitions for parliamentary procedure. These activities have provided me with valuable human relations and oral presentation skills.

④ I am definitely interested in working for A to Z Contractors. I will telephone your office on June 4 to arrange for an interview with you at your convenience. If you wish to speak with me before that date, please telephone me at 901-555-1212.

Sincerely,

Janice L. Dale

Enclosure

LETTER OF APPLICATION

FORMATTING ENUMERATIONS

An enumeration is a series of numbered or lettered words, phrases, or sentences. Enumerations are centered vertically and block-centered horizontally. They may be double-spaced, or each lettered item may be single-spaced with a blank line between items. Titles, if used, are typed in all-capital letters and centered over the enumeration. Two blank lines separate the title from the enumeration.

Some jobs have arrows and numbers to help you space vertically. For example, ↓3 means "go down 3 lines." (Leave 2 lines blank, and type on the third line.)

JOB 19-1. ENUMERATION
Standard format. Double spacing. Full sheet of paper.

TYPING AN ENUMERATION ↓3

A. An enumeration can be a set of steps or a series of numbered or lettered words or statements.

B. It is set up so that the numbers or letters stand by themselves in the margin.

C. Each number or letter is followed by a period, and the period is followed by two spaces.

D. All lines that do not start with a number or a letter are tabbed in four spaces.

E. This job uses letters to separate the items because you have not learned all the numbers.

JOB 19-2. ENUMERATION
Retype Job 19-1. Standard format. Single spacing. Half sheet of paper.

LESSON 20

GOALS
- To control 4, 5, and 6 keys.
- To format enumerations.

FORMAT
- Single spacing   50-space line

KEYBOARDING SKILLS

Type each line twice.

Speed   1 The goal of the firm is to fix the antique autos.

Accuracy 2 Lazy Jacques picked two boxes of oranges with me.

Numbers   3 The answer is 33 when you add 12 and 21 together.

FORMATTING LETTERS OF APPLICATION

The résumé is a summary of your skills and experiences. When you send your résumé to a prospective employer, you must, of course, send a covering letter—the *letter of application*. Together, the résumé and the letter of application are your introduction to the company.

Limit your letter of application to one page—about four paragraphs, as shown in the letter on page 242. Note the exact purpose of each paragraph:

① **Introduction:** Tell the reader the purpose of the letter, which job you are applying for, and how you learned of the job.

② **Second paragraph:** Give special consideration to the qualifications you have that make you especially valuable in this position and the skills you have that can help the employer and the company. Refer to the enclosed résumé.

③ **Third paragraph:** Mention special skills that set you apart from other applicants. (Are you exceptionally well organized?)

④ **Final paragraph:** Restate your interest in the job. Ask for an interview; give the date on which you will call to set up that interview. Include your home phone number so that the employer can reach you easily.

JOB 3. LETTER OF APPLICATION

Type the letter of application shown on page 242. Standard format (see page 87 for typing a personal business letter). Use plain paper. Line 50P/60E. Center tab.

COMPOSING A LETTER OF APPLICATION

Before you compose and type your own complete letter of application, you will have the opportunity to work on each of the separate paragraphs necessary in a letter of application. Read and study the examples provided in the following paragraphs, and then compose individual paragraphs for your own letter of application.

Paragraph 1

Objectives: Specify the job applied for and mention how you found out about it.

Example: I would like to apply for the position of clerk-typist for your company. My high school English teacher, Ms. Kathleen Hutchinson, informed me of this opening.

Practice: Compose and type the first paragraph for a letter of application in which you are applying for a position as clerk-typist. Add any information that you think is necessary.

Paragraph 2

Objective: List relevant skills.

Example: The experience I gained as a typist for my father's insurance agency qualifies me for the clerk-typist position in your company, as most of my duties involved daily use of typing, filing, and communications skills. These skills would be especially beneficial to your company.

Practice: Compose and type the second paragraph for a letter of application. Include specific clerk-typist skills you possess which would be beneficial to the company.

Paragraph 3

Objective: Convince the reader that you have special skills. Sell yourself!

Example: My secretarial skills and my English skills are well above average, and I feel that I could perform any of the jobs I would be called upon to do with a minimum of error and with a high degree of competence.

Practice: Compose and type the third paragraph for a letter of application. Identify in this paragraph any special skills that you have.

Paragraph 4

Objectives: Restate your interest. Arrange an interview. Give your telephone number.

Example: It would be a pleasure to work for your company as a clerk-typist. If you wish to interview me for this position, please telephone me at (301) 555-4774 any weekday after 3 p.m.

Practice: Compose and type the fourth paragraph for a letter of application. Review the illustration on page 241 to find out what information you should include in this paragraph.

JOB 4. LETTER OF APPLICATION

Compose and type a complete letter of application using the four paragraphs you just composed. Standard format. Add the following parts to complete the letter: (1) date line, (2) return address, (3) inside address, (4) salutation, (5) complimentary close, (6) signature line, and (7) enclosure notation.

Reach Guide

Because 5 and 6 pull your hands off base, they are the hardest to control. Concentrate on them and master them, so that all the number keys will soon be easy for you.

Remember to hold those anchors.

SPACE BAR

 KEY

Use F finger.

Type each line twice.

4 frf fr4 f4f 444 4,444 44,444 4.44 44.44 and 44/44
5 44 foes, 44 films, 44 flukes, 44 folders, or 4.44
6 Show No. 4 is for May 1, 2, 3, 4, 12, 14, and 23.

 KEY

Use F finger.

Type each line twice.

7 ftf ft5 f5f 555 5,555 55,555 5.55 55.55 and 55/55
8 55 fins, 55 facts, 55 fields, 55 futures, or 5.55
9 There are 24 errors on 1,253 of the 4,135 sheets.

 KEY

Use J finger.

Type each line twice.

10 jyj jy6 j6j 666 6,666 66,666 6.66 66.66 and 66/66
11 66 jaws, 66 jokes, 66 judges, 66 jackets, or 6.66
12 Items 43, 45, and 61 are due by October 25 or 26.

CHECKPOINT

Type lines 13–15 once. Then repeat lines 4, 7, and 10 or take two 1-minute timings on the Checkpoint.

13 As you edit page 26, check line 14 to see that it   10
14 has exactly 35 spaces in it. Lines 12 and 14 are   20
15 both to be 35 spaces--space 36 is for the return.   30
    | 1 | 2 | 3 | 4 | 5 | 6 | 7 | 8 | 9 | 10

2-MINUTE TIMINGS

Take two 2-minute timings on lines 16–20. Format: Double spacing, 5-space tab.

16   When you check your typed words, you need to   10
17 examine them for thoughts as well as for how they   20
18 look. The paper bail will help you to check. It   30
19 quickly guides your eyes across the maze of lines   40
20 and helps you pick out errors with ease.   48
    | 1 | 2 | 3 | 4 | 5 | 6 | 7 | 8 | 9 | 10   SI 1.17

Ⓐ

MARTINA VALDEZ ↓2

4101 Fuller Apartments
Clio, MI 48420
313-555-2714 ↓3

Ⓑ **Educational
Background**
Clio High School; Clio, MI 48420.   Graduated
June 1982. ↓2

Major: Clerical/Secretarial ↓2

Grade Point Average: 3.66 ↓2

Business Subjects: ↓2

Ⓒ

Accounting
Typing (75 wam)
Shorthand (120 wam)
Business Machines
Business English
Business Law
Steno/Clerical Lab ↓3

**Employment
History**
Rathjen Moving and Storage
471 Vienna Road
Flushing, MI 48477
Telephone No.:   313-555-5420 ↓2

June 1982-Present
Position: General Office Clerk
Supervisor: Joyce Jones, Secretary ↓2

Duties: Composing and typing routine correspondence; filing customer records; placing and
answering telephone calls; preparing invoices
(part-time employment) ↓3

Ⓓ **References**
A complete set of references will be furnished
upon request.

RÉSUMÉ

Read the jobs on this page to review the steps for horizontal and vertical centering.

JOB 20-1. ENUMERATION

Standard format (p. 34). Type line for line. Double spacing.

VERTICAL CENTERING ↓3

1. Count the number of lines needed.
2. Subtract needed lines from the number available on the paper.
3. Divide the difference by 2 to find line on which to start.
4. If a fraction is left, drop it.
5. Check center by folding the paper from top to bottom.

JOB 20-2. ENUMERATION

Standard format. Type line for line. Double spacing.

HORIZONTAL CENTERING ↓3

1. Determine the paper center.
2. Set the carriage or carrier at the center of the paper.
3. Locate the backspace key.
4. Backspace once for every two spaces/characters in the line to be centered.
5. Type the lines.
6. Check center by folding the paper from left to right.

LESSON 21

GOALS
- To control 7, 8, and 9 keys.
- To format poems.

FORMAT
- Single spacing   50-space line

KEYBOARDING SKILLS

Type each line twice.

Speed   1 By the time the dial turns, it may be time to go.
Accuracy 2 Six bright families quickly plowed the vineyards.
Numbers   3 Lines 13, 24, and 56 were right; line 65 was not.

7 KEY

Use J finger.

Type each line twice.

4 juj ju7 j7j 777 7,777 77,777 7.77 77.77 and 77/77
5 77 jets, 77 jumps, 77 jokers, 77 joggers, or 7.77
6 We sang 34 songs for 7,657 people at 12 concerts.

FORMATTING RÉSUMÉS
(Continued)

Ⓓ **Personal Data.** By law, employers cannot ask certain questions—for example, an applicant's age. Thus many applicants choose *not* to include a personal data section. If you do choose to include a personal data section, you might wish to have such items as your height, weight, social security number, health, birth date, and marital status. If used, this section should be placed after the Education and Experience sections.

Ⓔ **Honors, Awards, and Activities.** Achievements mentioned in this section may give you an "edge" over other applicants. You should include your participation in clubs and organizations, any honors and awards you have received, and any special recognitions you have earned. You may also want to include your scholastic placement in your graduating class (such as "top 10 percent").

Ⓕ **References.** The final section of a résumé lists the names, job titles, addresses, and telephone numbers of at least three persons who can tell a prospective employer what kind of worker you are. For this reason, most people use teachers, former supervisors, and former employers as references. Before you use anyone as a reference, you *must* get permission from each individual to use his or her name. Another option for the references section is to simply include this statement: "References will be furnished upon request."

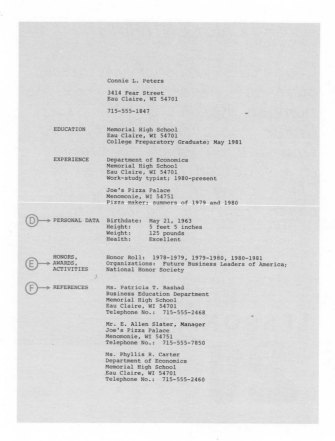

ALTERNATE FORMAT FOR RÉSUMÉS

The illustration on page 240 shows some alternate formats for the sections of a résumé. The standard format may be changed by using one or more of the alternate features.

Ⓐ The name, address, and telephone number are centered between the left and right margins.

Ⓑ Section headings are typed in initial capitals and are underscored.

Ⓒ Pertinent business courses are identified in the educational background section.

Ⓓ No references are given. Instead, a statement indicates that references will be provided upon request.

Note: No personal data section is included.

JOB 1. RÉSUMÉ

Type the résumé appearing on page 240, using the format described and illustrated on pages 238–239.

JOB 2. YOUR RÉSUMÉ

Prepare a résumé for yourself, using the guidelines introduced on pages 238 and 239. Include all sections that are pertinent and applicable to your background and experience. Do not include a section if you have no entries to place in that section. Use your typing teacher's name as one of your three references.

KEY

Use K finger.

Type each line twice.

7 kik ki8 k8k 888 8,888 88,888 8.88 88.88 and 88/88
8 88 kegs, 88 kilns, 88 knocks, 88 kickers, or 8.88
9 At 27 she has 18 titles in 36 of the 45 contests.

KEY

Use L finger.

Type each line twice.

10 lol lo9 l9l 999 9,999 99,999 9.99 99.99 and 99/99
11 99 laps, 99 loops, 99 lilies, 99 lifters, or 9.99
12 Do pages 19, 29, 39, 49, 59, 69, 79, 89, and 119.

CHECKPOINT

Type lines 13–15 once. Then repeat lines 4 (page 36), 7, and 10 or take two 1-minute timings on the Checkpoint.

13 Plant the red bulbs in beds 2, 4, 6, and 8.   Then   10
14 plant the yellow bulbs in beds 1, 3, 5, 7, and 9.   20
15 Plant the white bulbs in 3, 5, and 7 for balance.   30
    | 1 | 2 | 3 | 4 | 5 | 6 | 7 | 8 | 9 | 10

2-MINUTE TIMINGS

Take two 2-minute timings on lines 16–20. Format: Double spacing, 5-space tab.

16   The green tree in the corner of our yard has   10
17 grown just a little bit every year.   It gives the   20
18 squirrel next door a place to make a home, and it   30
19 offers shade for our big, old, lazy dog.   The big   40
20 tree has something to share with us all.   48
    | 1 | 2 | 3 | 4 | 5 | 6 | 7 | 8 | 9 | 10   SI 1.14

FORMATTING POEMS

Use the following steps when you are formatting a poem (see next page):

1. Set the left margin by centering the longest line (block-center).

2. Determine where you will type the first line (vertical centering).

3. Begin each line with a capital letter.

4. Show the scheme of the poem by indenting every other line 5 spaces.

5. Single-space stanzas; double-space between stanzas.

LESSONS 143–147

GOAL
■ To format and type papers needed when applying for a job.
FORMAT
■ Margins and tabs as needed

Now that you are near the end of your first typing course, you may soon be looking for a part-time or full-time job. In applying for a job, you will need to use your typewriting skill (1) to prepare a résumé, (2) to compose a letter of application, (3) to complete an application form, and (4) to prepare a follow-up letter. Each of these tasks is discussed below and on the following pages.

FORMATTING RÉSUMÉS

Once you have identified a job you want to apply for, your first step is to prepare a *résumé*—a summary of your training, background, and qualifications for the job.

A résumé contains different sections, depending on what information you want to include about your education, experience, personal background, and so on. The résumé illustrated on the right and on page 239 shows the basic information to include. Read directions A through F below and on page 239 for formatting résumés. Follow the margin settings, spacing directions, and tab setting shown below the illustration on the right.

Ⓐ **Heading.** For easy identification, begin the résumé with your name, address, and telephone number. Include your area code.

Ⓑ **Education.** If you have little business experience, list your education after your name, address, and telephone number. The education section should begin with the highest level of education you have completed—that is, all items should be listed in *reverse* chronological order (the most recent first). For each entry, you should include the name and address of the school, any diplomas earned and the years in which you earned them, the year you graduated, and your major area of study.

Ⓒ **Experience.** If your experience is stronger than your education, include it after your name, address, and telephone number. If not, place the experience section after the education section. For each job you include, give the name, address, and telephone number of the company, the dates of employment, your job title(s), the name and title of your supervisor, and a brief description of the duties you performed.

```
            Connie L. Peters ↓2

Ⓐ→         3414 Pear Street
            Eau Claire, WI 54701 ↓2

            715-555-1847 ↓3

Ⓑ→ EDUCATION    Memorial High School
                Eau Claire, WI 54701
                College Preparatory Graduate; May 1981 ↓3

Ⓒ→ EXPERIENCE   Department of Economics
                Memorial High School
                Eau Claire, WI 54701
                Work-study typist; 1980-present ↓2

                Joe's Pizza Palace
                Menomonie, WI 54751
                Pizza maker; summers of 1979 and 1980 ↓3

   PERSONAL DATA  Birthdate:  May 21, 1963
                  Height:     5 feet 5 inches
                  Weight:     125 pounds
                  Health:     Excellent ↓3

   HONORS,        Honor Roll:  1978-1979, 1979-1980, 1980-1981
   AWARDS,        Organizations:  Future Business Leaders of America;
   ACTIVITIES     National Honor Society ↓3

   REFERENCES     Ms. Patricia T. Rashad
                  Business Education Department
                  Memorial High School
                  Eau Claire, WI 54701
                  Telephone No.:  715-555-2468 ↓2

                  Mr. E. Allen Slater, Manager
                  Joe's Pizza Palace
                  Menomonie, WI 54751
                  Telephone No.:  715-555-7850 ↓2

                  Ms. Phyllis R. Carter
                  Department of Economics
                  Memorial High School
                  Eau Claire, WI 54701
                  Telephone No.:  715-555-2460
```

Top Margin: *On page 1, 9 lines; on continuation pages, 6 lines.*
Left/Right Margins: *10P/12E.*
Bottom Margin: *6 to 9 lines.*

Single-space within each entry; double-space and triple-space as indicated. Use 15-space tab.

JOB 21-1. POEM

Standard format. Center author's name 2 lines below the title.

RULES
↓2

By Darrell Tedrick
↓3

Rules for the classroom,
    And rules for the hall.
Rules for the lunchroom,
    And rules for the wall.

There are rules for our talking,
    And rules to make us blink.
There are rules for our listening,
    But do rules help us think?

JOB 21-2. POEM

Standard format. Type author's name starting at the center, 2 lines below the poem.

HOMEWORK
↓3

Thirteen pages in a night,
    So much homework is a fright.
Dates and math and all that stuff,
    That much homework is too rough.

I wrote and typed throughout the night,
    And do not yet have this thing right.
I have never had a job so tough,
    This time I have really had enough.
        ↓2
        By Leigh Robbins

LESSON 22

GOALS
- To control 0, ½, and ¼ keys.
- To select an appropriate format for a document.
- To arrange a document in the selected format.

FORMAT
- Single spacing 50-space line

KEYBOARDING SKILLS

Type each line twice.

Speed   1   The ducks may be the first to go to the big lake.

Accuracy   2   Twelve zebras quickly jumped high over ten foxes.

Numbers   3   Type 1 or 2 or 3 and 4 or 5 or 6 and 7 or 8 or 9.

 0 KEY

Use Sem finger.

Type each line twice.

4   ;p; ;p0 ;0; 000 2,000 30,000 4.00 50.00 and 11:00

5   600 parts, 700 planks, 800 parades, 900 particles

6   Our classes are set for 2:00 and 7:00 on Mondays.

LESSON 142

CLINIC

GOALS
- To identify which of two motions is more difficult for you and to practice them proportionately.
- To type 40/5'/5e.

FORMAT
- Single spacing   60-space line

QUOTATION MARKS WITH OTHER PUNCTUATION

Type lines 1–4 once, providing the missing exclamation points and question marks. Edit your copy as your teacher reads the answers. Then retype lines 1–4 from your edited copy.

1 Why did Tom and Flo call this design sketch "too juvenile".
2 John asked, "Where is the new copy for the advertisements."
3 Mrs. Provenzano excitedly yelled, "Call the police--hurry."
4 How Bob quibbled over those requisitions marked "Rejected".

PRETEST

Take a 1-minute timing on lines 5–7. Then take a 1-minute timing on lines 8–10. Circle and count your errors on each timing.

5 Barbara was last seen at the new dress sale late last week.   12
6 Ada stated she had traded the car off after it was wrecked.   24
7 Gerald prefers trees that have very few leaves or branches.   36
   | 1 | 2 | 3 | 4 | 5 | 6 | 7 | 8 | 9 | 10 | 11 | 12
8 It is their opinion that Jimmy will join the union at noon.   12
9 Phyllis knows her pumpkins will soon look like they should.   24
10 Phillip enjoys looking at and collecting only common coins.   36

PRACTICE

In which Pretest did you make more errors? If in lines 5–7, type lines 11–15 below six times and lines 16–20 three times. If in lines 8–10, reverse the procedure.

11 treat severe dresses cabbage afterward addressee exaggerate
12 trade tweed wears agreed career starts assets awards better
13 cares carts darts deeds fares grade grass great reads staff
14 between pleases assure tassel passes tease refer meets wash
15 sixteen referee pretty letter masses meter sewer cases fast

16 jolly imply phylon minimum million homonym opinion nonunion
17 poppy hilly onion pupil pulpy nylon milky phony plump lumpy
18 hill pink hook pool moon noon join milk mill upon look junk
19 imp import impose imposes imports impress imposing imported
20 ill chills drills fulfill willing billing goodwill waybills

POSTTEST

Repeat the Pretest to see how much your skill has improved.

5-MINUTE TIMINGS

Take two 5-minute timings on lines 7–23, page 232.

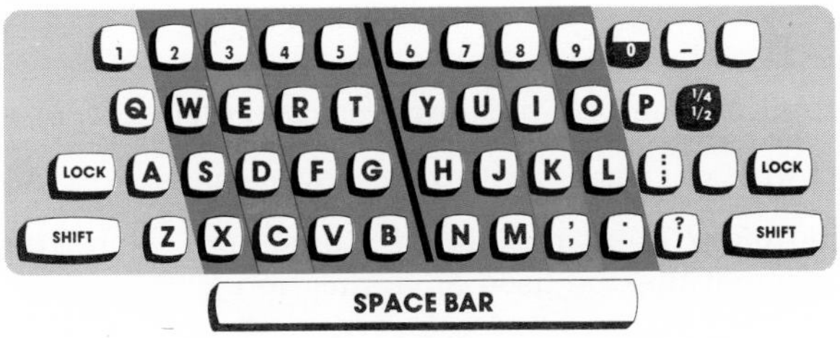

1/2 KEY

Use Sem finger.

Type each line twice.

7 ;p; ;p$\frac{1}{2}$;$\frac{1}{2}$; $\frac{1}{2}\frac{1}{2}\frac{1}{2}$ 1$\frac{1}{2}$ 2$\frac{1}{2}$ 3$\frac{1}{2}$ 4$\frac{1}{2}$ 5$\frac{1}{2}$ 6$\frac{1}{2}$ 7$\frac{1}{2}$ 8$\frac{1}{2}$ 9$\frac{1}{2}$ or 10$\frac{1}{2}$

8 Is my size 7$\frac{1}{2}$, or did he say 6$\frac{1}{2}$? Maybe it is 8$\frac{1}{2}$?

9 Mark the boxes: 10$\frac{1}{2}$ or 29$\frac{1}{2}$ or 38$\frac{1}{2}$ or 47$\frac{1}{2}$ or 56$\frac{1}{2}$.

1/4 KEY

Shift of ½.

Type each line twice.

10 ;p; ;p$\frac{1}{4}$;$\frac{1}{4}$; $\frac{1}{4}\frac{1}{4}\frac{1}{4}$ 1$\frac{1}{4}$ 2$\frac{1}{4}$ 3$\frac{1}{4}$ 4$\frac{1}{4}$ 5$\frac{1}{4}$ 6$\frac{1}{4}$ 7$\frac{1}{4}$ 8$\frac{1}{4}$ 9$\frac{1}{4}$ or 10$\frac{1}{4}$

11 I think it is 3$\frac{1}{4}$, or is it 4$\frac{1}{4}$? I think it is 5$\frac{1}{4}$.

12 Label each box: 10$\frac{1}{4}$ or 29$\frac{1}{4}$ or 38$\frac{1}{4}$ or 47$\frac{1}{4}$ or 56$\frac{1}{4}$.

CHECKPOINT

Type lines 13–15 once. Then repeat lines 4 (page 38), 7, and 10 or take two 1-minute timings on the Checkpoint.

13 If you like to work with fractions, try adding up 10

14 these: 10$\frac{1}{2}$, 29$\frac{1}{4}$, 38$\frac{1}{2}$, 47$\frac{1}{4}$, and 56$\frac{1}{2}$. If you find 20

15 the answer to be 182, you are absolutely correct. 30

| 1 | 2 | 3 | 4 | 5 | 6 | 7 | 8 | 9 | 10

2-MINUTE TIMINGS

Take two 2-minute timings on lines 16–20. Format: Double spacing, 5-space tab.

16 Getting up in the morning is quite a job for 10

17 me. I grab my yellow jacket and go for the bus-- 20

18 just in time to miss it. Five more minutes would 30

19 have done it. Next time I will not doze so long. 40

20 I can still make it. Maybe I will beat the bell. 50

| 1 | 2 | 3 | 4 | 5 | 6 | 7 | 8 | 9 | 10 SI 1.13

SELECTING AN APPROPRIATE FORMAT FOR A DOCUMENT

Selecting a format is partly a matter of learning formatting guidelines and partly a matter of using your own good judgment. You have just practiced typing a series of jobs in which you used several formatting guidelines:

1. Typing in all capitals (p. 23).
2. Indenting for paragraphs (p. 24).
3. Centering horizontally (p. 25).
4. Centering vertically (p. 29).
5. Spread centering (p. 31).
6. Typing enumerations (p. 34).
7. Spacing for titles/subtitles (pp. 34 and 38).

REVIEW OF EXCLAMATION POINT, QUESTION MARK, AND QUOTATION MARKS

1. Use an exclamation point (!) to show surprise, disbelief, or strong feeling.

   Good luck! I wish you success with your new business!

2. Use a question mark (?) at the end of a question. Note that an incomplete sentence may sometimes be used as a question.

   When will the announcement be official? Today?

3. Use quotation marks (") for someone's exact words and for words that require emphasis. Do not use quotations for short *restatements* of someone's exact words.

   He shouted, "Cancel this order!" (Exact words.)
   Is this the so-called "priceless masterpiece"? (Emphasis.)

   Note: The exclamation point in the first example goes *before* the quotation mark because the entire quotation is an exclamation. In the second example, the question mark goes *after* the quotation mark because the words in quotations do *not* make up a question.

Type lines 25–28 once. Then repeat lines 25–28 or take a series of 1-minute timings.

```
25  Congratulations!  We are glad to hear about your promotion!   12
26  Have the reports about that merger been verified?  By whom?    12
27  Jan said, "That magazine is famous for excellent features!"    12
28  Do you think that Kent will have to "work another miracle"?    12
    |  1  |  2  |  3  |  4  |  5  |  6  |  7  |  8  |  9  |  10  |  11  |  12
```

JOB 141-1. BOUND REPORT

Standard format (see pages 76, 78, and 125).

TYPING I LANGUAGE ARTS SKILLS
By [your name]

Perhaps you have asked yourself this question: "Why is it important for me to learn all these language arts rules?" The answer is that the punctuation and style rules that you are learning in this book will help you to communicate more clearly.

No, you do not have to become an "expert" in grammar and punctuation; you will have references that you can use to check rules. But you do have to master the basics -- those rules which you will use regularly as you type letters, memos, and reports. Let's review some of these rules.

PUNCTUATION RULES
We have studied the comma (and a few of its uses), the semicolon, the question mark, the exclamation point, and quotation marks. We have seen many of their most common uses.

OTHER RULES
In addition to the punctuation rules, we have studied capitalization, number usage, and spacing rules. All these have helped us write more clearly.

JOB 22-1. DISPLAY
Format: You decide (1) single-, double-, or triple-space lines; (2) spread-center a word or a line; (3) use all caps or both uppercase and lowercase letters; (4) center each line or block-center.

Bake Sale
Monday, October 24, 19--
Main lobby
11 a.m. until 1 p.m.
Sponsored by
The Language Club
Have dessert with us

JOB 22-2. DISPLAY
Format: You decide (1) single-, double-, or triple-space lines; (2) spread-center a word or a line; (3) use all caps or both uppercase and lowercase letters; (4) center each line or block-center.

You are cordially invited
to attend the annual
Winter Breakfast
for the
Student Council
Wednesday, December 13, 19--
8 to 10 a.m.
West Dining Hall
R.S.V.P. 555-7462

LESSON 23

GOALS
- To construct fractions not on keyboard.
- To type mixed numbers with constructed fractions.
- To format recipes.

FORMAT
- Single spacing   50-space line

KEYBOARDING SKILLS

Type each line twice.

Speed 1 She paid for a title to the island with the oaks.
Accuracy 2 Jack amazed Rex by pointing quickly to five haws.
Numbers 3 Type these: 10½ and 29¼ and 38½ and 47¼ and 56½.

CONSTRUCTING FRACTIONS

To construct a fraction, use the diagonal key.

Type each line twice.

4 1/3, 3/4, 4/8, 5/10, 6/12, 7/14, 9/18, and 24/48.
5 Now add 1/4, 4/8, 1/2, and 6/8. The answer is 2.
6 Other fractions are 4/10, 13/78, 9/25, and 11/60.

TYPING MIXED NUMBERS

Mixed numbers are whole numbers with fractions. Space between the number and a constructed fraction (9 3/16). Do not space between the number and a keyboard fraction (9½).

Type each line twice.

7 Type: 7 3/4, 8 9/12, 5 1/2, 34 6/9, and 85 3/10.
8 His Maltese weighs 13½ lb; my terrier weighs 15¼.
9 My room is 12 2/3 feet wide and 14 1/2 feet long.
10 This jar is 12 1/2 oz, but the other is 7 1/8 oz.
11 Melody worked 6 1/4 days in 3 of her 3 1/5 weeks.
12 There are 5¼ weeks left to my 2½-year assignment.

LESSON 141

GOALS
- To type 40/5'/5e.
- To type sentences using the question mark, exclamation point, and quotation mark rules.
- To type a one-page report applying the above language arts rules.

FORMAT
- Single spacing   60-space line   5-space and center tabs

COMMA/ SEMICOLON REVIEW

Type lines 1–6 once, providing the missing commas and semicolons. Edit your copy as your teacher reads the answers. Then retype lines 1–6 from your edited copy.

1 When Agnes is absent Bert must approve cash disbursements.
2 Joyce as you know proofread all the statistics carefully.
3 Call Kroft Plumbing and Heating for fast reliable service.
4 This lacquer is highly flammable but that one is harmless.
5 Excell Products sells fertilizer seeds and bulbs by mail.
6 The list price is $17.50 quantity discounts are available.

5-MINUTE TIMINGS

Take two 5-minute timings on lines 7–24.

```
 7       It's true for many of us that a very troublesome punc-    12
 8  tuation placement rule is where we should put the quotation    24
 9  marks when they're used with periods or commas.  If we just    36
10  follow some very basic rules, we'll soon recognize that the    48
11  exact placement of a quotation mark is really quite an easy     60
12  thing for us all to remember.                                   66
13       The first general rule we should recall is that commas    78
14  and periods always go inside the closing quotation mark.  A     90
15  good example would be to place in quotation marks the final    102
16  word in this sentence, such as "this."  Notice that even if    114
17  the last word in the sentence is placed in quotation marks,    126
18  the period is typed before that final quotation mark.  When    138
19  quotation marks appear in the middle of the typed line, the    150
20  comma at the end of that quotation would appear as follows:    162
21  The package was labeled "Pizza," so the delivery person was    174
22  very careful not to jar the package when it was moved.  All    186
23  of us should have no problems in improving the placement of    198
24  the marks.                                                     200
    |  1  |  2  |  3  |  4  |  5  |  6  |  7  |  8  |  9  |  10  |  11  |  12   SI 1.47
```

Type either lines 13–15 or 13a–15a, depending on which applies. Then repeat each line two more times or take two 1-minute timings on the Checkpoint.

Fractions on keyboard.

13 Store No. 13 will stock sizes 5¼ through 9½. The 10

14 annual sale is April 7 until April 20. A display 20

15 of 48 spring styles will be set up in 16 windows. 30

Fractions not on keyboard.

13a Store No. 3 will stock sizes 5 1/4 to 9 1/2. The 10

14a annual sale is April 7 until April 20. A display 20

15a of 48 spring styles will be set up in 16 windows. 30

| 1 | 2 | 3 | 4 | 5 | 6 | 7 | 8 | 9 | 10

2-MINUTE TIMINGS

Take two 2-minute timings on lines 16–20. Format: Double spacing, 5-space tab.

16   When you work with people every day, you get 10

17 to know what it is that they like best. You also 20

18 find out quickly what makes them frown. A little 30

19 extra effort in a dozen small ways will make your 40

20 office a pleasant place in which to do your work. 50

| 1 | 2 | 3 | 4 | 5 | 6 | 7 | 8 | 9 | 10   SI 1.20

FORMATTING RECIPES

A recipe consists of (1) a list of ingredients and (2) the directions for mixing the ingredients. To format a recipe, center the title in all-capital letters. Block-center the list of ingredients. Type the directions on a 40-space line. The recipe should be centered vertically. Leave 2 blank lines after the title and 1 blank line between the ingredients and the directions.
Note: To make numbers align at the right, set a tab for the longest number, and indent the shorter ones. If an ingredient takes more than one line, align the second line with the words on the first line.

JOB 23-1. RECIPE
Standard format. Half sheet of paper.

CHEESE WAFERS
↓3

1/2 cup butter
  1 cup grated Swiss cheese
3/4 cup flour
1/2 teaspoon salt
1/2 teaspoon dry mustard
1/8 teaspoon pepper
↓2

Blend ingredients in a bowl. Drop by teaspoonfuls, 2 inches apart, onto ungreased baking sheet. Bake at 350 degrees for 14 to 20 minutes. Cool and store in a tight container. Yield: 30.

JOB 23-2. RECIPE
Standard format. Half sheet of paper.

MERINGUE COOKIES

2 egg whites
1/8 teaspoon cream of tartar
  1 teaspoon vanilla
1/2 cup sugar
  1 cup chopped nuts or
    chocolate bits

Beat egg whites and cream of tartar until peaks form. Add remaining ingredients. Mix thoroughly, and drop by teaspoonfuls onto greased baking pan. Bake 30 minutes at 300 degrees. Cool. Yield: 40.

Type lines 5–9 once. Then repeat lines 5–9 or take a series of 1-minute timings.

```
5  Cora explained it very clearly, but Ann did not understand.   12
6  The tall, modern building on Fifth is now our headquarters.   12
7  At the end of the month-long trial, our attorneys appealed.   12
8  Jan prefers, as you know, working for a magazine publisher.   12
9  Our supervisor, Debra Kovacs, handles this account herself.   12
   |  1  |  2  |  3  |  4  |  5  |  6  |  7  |  8  |  9  |  10  |  11  |  12
```

JOB 140-1. INTEROFFICE MEMORANDUM
Single spacing. Use 50P/60E-space line. Workbook 285.

```
TO:        Nightshift Workers

FROM:      Training Director Jones

SUBJECT:   Writing Seminar
```

Last month we offered a seminar on planning meetings, and this month we will offer one to improve your writing skills. You may attend both sessions this month, but you must get approval from your shift supervisor. This new, exciting session will start on May 2, Monday. You may, if you wish, bring a recorder to the session.

SEMICOLON REVIEW

1. Two independent clauses can be joined by a comma plus *and, but, or,* or *nor.* When no conjunction is used, a semicolon is needed to join the clauses.

   Cora explained it very clearly, but Ann did not understand.
   Cora explained it very clearly; Ann did not understand.

2. If one of the clauses contains commas and a misreading is possible, use a semicolon even if a conjunction is used.

   On our way to San Francisco, we will visit our office in Chicago, Illinois; and Tucson, Arizona, may be added to our itinerary.

Type lines 10–13 once. Then repeat lines 10–13 or take a series of 1-minute timings.

```
10  Abe set the list price; Agnes Loo established the discount.   12
11  Joe wants to meet on May 12; and May 13 is Martha's choice.   12
12  Summer is the zenith of your sales season; winter is quiet.   12
13  Ask Vera for a copy of the agenda; if you prefer, call Tex.   12
    |  1  |  2  |  3  |  4  |  5  |  6  |  7  |  8  |  9  |  10  |  11  |  12
```

JOB 140-2. INTEROFFICE MEMORANDUM
Standard format. Workbook 285.

[*To*] Training Director, [*From*] Wade Reeves, [*Subject*] Writing Seminar

I would like to attend the seminar, but I have an out-of-town trip planned for that day. Could my associate, Gail Swane, attend the seminar in my place?

This seminar will be a unique, exciting one; of course, I want to be sure that one of our office employees will attend it. Ms. Swane, I am sure, will benefit much from the seminar.

LESSON 24

GOALS
- To review number-key controls.
- To build skill in typing numbers by touch.

FORMAT
- Single spacing   50-space line

PRETEST

Take two 2-minute timings on lines 1–5. Proofread your copy and circle your errors.

```
1  0101 0202 0303 0404 0505 0606 0707 0808 0909 1010   10
2  1111 1212 1313 1414 1515 1616 1717 1818 1919 2020   20
3  2121 2222 2323 2424 2525 2626 2727 2828 2929 3030   30
4  3131 3232 3333 3434 3535 3636 3737 3838 3939 4040   40
5  4141 4242 4343 4444 4545 4646 4747 4848 4949 5050   50
   |  1  |  2  |  3  |  4  |  5  |  6  |  7  |  8  |  9  |  10
```

PRACTICE

Type lines 6–10 four times. Proofread your copy and circle your errors.

```
6   1 aq1 aq1 aq1 1 11 111 11 1 11 111 11 1 11 111 11
7   0 ;p0 ;p0 ;p0 0 10 100 10 0 01 001 01 0 10 100 10
8   2 sw2 sw2 sw2 2 20 220 20 2 02 022 02 0 20 220 20
9   9 lo9 lo9 lo9 9 93 939 93 9 39 399 09 9 39 999 90
10  3 de3 de3 de3 3 33 332 38 3 38 383 03 3 38 323 30
```

Type lines 11–15 four times. Proofread your copy and circle your errors.

```
11  8 ki8 ki8 ki8 8 82 882 80 8 28 288 08 8 82 882 80
12  4 fr4 fr4 fr4 4 43 432 42 4 44 489 04 4 44 474 40
13  7 ju7 ju7 ju7 7 78 747 47 7 74 787 07 7 74 747 70
14  5 ft5 ft5 ft5 5 54 535 25 5 75 557 05 5 55 535 50
15  6 ju6 ju6 ju6 6 67 686 65 6 56 667 07 6 56 656 60
```

Type lines 16–20 four times. Proofread your copy and circle your errors.

```
16  we 23 24 25 we 23 24 25 – up 70 71 72 up 70 71 72
17  re 43 44 45 re 43 44 45 – or 94 95 96 or 94 95 96
18  ow 92 93 94 ow 92 93 94 – it 85 86 87 it 85 86 87
19  ie 83 84 85 ie 83 84 85 – ru 47 48 49 ru 47 48 49
20  qu 17 18 19 qu 17 18 19 – ye 63 64 65 ye 63 64 65
```

POSTTEST

Take two 2-minute timings on lines 1–5. Proofread your copy and circle your errors. Note your improvement.

JOB 139-1. INTEROFFICE MEMORANDUM

Standard format (see pages 59 and 107). Workbook 283.

[*To*] All Department Heads, [*From*] Lisa L. Davis, Office Manager, [*Subject*] New Office Layout

12
20
21

As you now know, we will be moving into our new building next year. When the actual move is made, office space will be assigned in accordance with current office space standards used in our company. If you think you will need more space in the new building, please let me know by the 20th.

31
40
50
59
68
77
82

A copy of the new building blueprint is enclosed so that you may study the aisle space, office layout, and square footage that has been planned.

91
100
110
115

JOB 139-2. INTEROFFICE MEMORANDUM

Standard format. Workbook 283.

TO: Lisa L. Davis, FROM: Rudy T. Barnes, SUBJECT: Office Layout

When I received the new office layout, I realized that the space allowed for my office is 50 square feet less than I now have. If our sales continue to expand as they have been expanding in the past three years, this space will not be sufficient for me. ¶ As you must realize, I cannot function with less than 175 square feet to accommodate files, furniture, and sales research area.

LESSON 140

GOALS
- To type sentences using comma and semicolon rules.
- To type two memorandums in which comma usage and semicolon rules are applied.

FORMAT
- Single spacing 60-space line 5-space tab

COMMA USAGE REVIEW

Type lines 1–4 once, providing the missing commas. Edit your copy as your teacher reads the answers. Then retype lines 1–4 from your edited copy.

1 Rodney Karen or Phil will be able to finish these orders.

2 When you land in Zurich call Jacques at our offices there.

3 We have more in the hall on the shelves and in my closet.

4 As soon as you mix all these ingredients cool this liquid.

COMMA USAGE REVIEW

3. A compound sentence is a sentence that has two independent clauses joined by the conjunction *and, but, or,* or *nor.* Place a comma before the conjunction in a compound sentence.

Pamela recommended delaying delivery, *but* Angela objected.

4. Place a comma between adjectives that modify the same noun.

Ms. Franco wrote a *clear, concise* summary.

5. Place a comma after most introductory words and phrases.

No, she has not yet approved the contract. (Word.)
Speaking distinctly, Marvin answered each question thoughtfully. (Phrase.)
For the benefit of the audience, Lisa explained her reasons. (Phrase.)

6. Use commas to set off nonessential elements and nonessential appositives.

Their offer is an excellent one, *in my opinion.*
We asked our manager, *Sarah Wells,* for approval.

LESSON 25

GOAL
- To control #, $, %, and & keys by touch.

FORMAT
- Single spacing   50-space line

KEYBOARDING SKILLS

Type each line twice.

Speed 1 This title to the island is the first to be kept.

Accuracy 2 A quick tally shows that taxi drivers whiz along.

Numbers 3 Al jumped over Nos. 10, 29, 38, 47, and 56 today.

 KEY

Shift of 3. Use D finger.

Do not space between the number and the #.

Type each line twice.

4 ded de3 d3d d3#d d#d d#d #3 #33 #333 d#d d3d #333

5 Catalog #56 weighs 38#, and Catalog #2947 is 10#.

6 My favorite ones are #10, #29, #38, #47, and #56.

 KEY

Shift of 4. Use F finger.

Do not space between the $ and the number.

Type each line twice.

7 frf fr4 f4f f4$f f$f f$f $4 $44 $444 f$f f4f $444

8 The latest rates are $10, $29, $38, $47, and $56.

9 Who bought a $56 suit at the Fashionette for $38?

CHECKPOINT

The symbol # before a number means "number"; # after a number means "pounds."

Type lines 10–13 once. Then repeat lines 4–9 or take two 1-minute timings on the Checkpoint.

10 Item #1029 lists at $38.50 but will be reduced in 10

11 June to $34.50. Item #847, which weighs 56#, can 20

12 be bought for $74. Items #1029, #3847, and #5665 30

13 will all sell for $2 in June and $3.95 in August. 40

 | 1 | 2 | 3 | 4 | 5 | 6 | 7 | 8 | 9 | 10

4 11 complaints were received about that defective motor.
5 Sarah bought 4 texts, and Jeffrey bought 5 magazines.
6 The 6 of them will meet at Twelfth Avenue and 8th Street.

5-MINUTE TIMINGS

Take two 5-minute timings on lines 7–23.

```
                      1                                2
7        Commas might be used for more than a dozen purposes in   12
              3                        4
8  our language.  We use them to separate introductory clauses    24
        5                    6                      7
9  from main clauses, we use them to separate items in series,    36
                         8                      9
10 we also use them between clauses joined by conjunctions, we    48
          10                          11                  12
11 use them to show a special emphasis, and so on, and so on.     60
                         13                      14
12      The cousin of the comma is the semicolon.  A semicolon    72
              15                        16
13 can be used between two clauses that have no conjunction to     84
      17                  18                        19
14 join them.  For example:  "Janice left for Spain yesterday;    96
                    20                  21
15 Harold will leave Sunday."  A semicolon can also be used if    108
          22                    23                      24
16 one of the two clauses joined by a conjunction contains one    120
                      25                      26
17 or more commas and could be misread.  For example:  "George    132
                  27                  28
18 plans to attend the session on Monday, Thursday, or Friday;    144
      29                  30                          31
19 and Wednesday all of us will attend."  In addition, a semi-    156
              32                  33
20 colon can be used just to show a stronger break between two    168
          34                      35                      36
21 clauses, even though a conjunction is used, as follows:  "I    180
                  37                      38
22 insist that we must change this schedule; but you must give    192
              39                      40
23 us newer costs when we meet next time."                       200
   |  1  |  2  |  3  |  4  |  5  |  6  |  7  |  8  |  9  | 10 | 11 | 12   SI 1.47
```

COMMA USAGE REVIEW

1. In a series of three or more words, numbers, phrases, or clauses, use a comma after each item in the series except the last item. In the following sentences, italics identify the items in a series:

   Our West Coast trip will take us to *Seattle, Eugene,* and *Helena.*
   She *quoted prices, checked bids,* and *prepared estimates.*

2. Use a comma after an introductory clause that begins with *if, as, when, although, since, because,* or a similar conjunction.

   Before Leroy and Carolyn arrive, let's review our agenda.
   Whenever you have time, please come to my office.

Type lines 24–27 once. Then repeat lines 24–27 or take a series of 1-minute timings.

```
24 When Mrs. Ulster arrives, we will discuss her tax problems.   12
25 Amy Zak, Paul Remy, and Bart Owens are the best applicants.   12
26 If the quality is poor, then you should retype these memos.   12
27 George drafted it, Jerry typed it, and Sharon proofread it.   12
   |  1  |  2  |  3  |  4  |  5  |  6  |  7  |  8  |  9  | 10 | 11 | 12
```

 % KEY

Shift of 5. Use F finger.

The % symbol is used only in statistical information. Do not space between the number and the %.

Type each line twice.

14 f5f f5% f%f f5f f5% f%f 5% 55% 15% 25% 25.5% 5.5%

15 The return rates are 10%, 29%, 38%, 47%, and 56%.

16 Annette scored 92%, Joe made 83%, and Ed had 74%.

 & KEY

Shift of 7. Use J finger.

Space once before and after an ampersand (&) used between words and numbers. Do not space when used between initials.

Type each line twice.

17 j7j j7& j&j j7j j7& j&j 7 & 8 & 9 & 10 & 11 & 121

18 Jean made profits of 10% & 29% & 38% & 47% & 56%.

19 Joan worked at H&S Company and then Rex & Penrod.

CHECKPOINT

Type lines 20–23 once. Then repeat lines 14–19 or take two 1-minute timings on the Checkpoint.

20 The rates given by L&S Loan Company are 18% for a   10
21 short term and 15% for a long term. P&W Loan Co.   20
22 offered 17% for short term and 14% for long term.   30
23 Dawes & Kipp have the best deal with 13% and 16%.   40

| 1 | 2 | 3 | 4 | 5 | 6 | 7 | 8 | 9 | 10

3-MINUTE TIMINGS

Using Speed Markers

The numbers in this timing are speed markers. *At the end of the timing, the number you reach will tell you your WAM speed, because the total words have already been divided by 3. For example, if you end the timing on the last letter of* which *on line 31, you typed 26 WAM.*

Take two 3-minute timings on lines 24–32. Format: Double spacing, 5-space tab.

24   I would really like to join a club at school   10
25 this year. There are so many from which to pick.   20
26 I just cannot make up my mind. There is the Swim   30
27 Club and the Ski Club; I could try out for a play   40
28 or try chess. Debate has quite a record for hard   50
29 work, and the jazz band should be an exciting new   60
30 venture too. Now which one shall I choose? Will   70
31 my friends want to help? Tell me which club will   80
32 be the best for me?   84

| 1 | 2 | 3 | 4 | 5 | 6 | 7 | 8 | 9 | 10   SI 1.09

Type lines 11–14 once. Then repeat lines 11–14 or take a series of 1-minute timings.

11   The meeting has been rescheduled for 2:45 p.m. next Monday. 12
12   Meet Ms. Quimby at the corner of 25th Avenue and 47th Road. 12
13   Jack Mazer's law office is on First Street or on 12th Road. 12
14   Rebecca allowed 30 to 45 minutes for questions and answers. 12

   | 1 | 2 | 3 | 4 | 5 | 6 | 7 | 8 | 9 | 10 | 11 | 12

JOB 138-3. LETTER

Copy is unedited and unarranged; make changes and corrections as you type it. Standard format. Workbook 281–282. Body 67 words.

Mr. Matthew G. Mitchel, Hyde Department Stoer, 4579 Third Avenue, N.E., Saint Paul, MN 55422, Dear Mr. Mitchell:

You have been our best customer since we opened our store in '72. To celebrate *our tenth anniversary this month, we are offering to all our faithful customers a special price on all forms ordered during the month of ~~July~~ June.*

If you would like to place an order for your busness forms during the Month of june, please fill out and return the form by June 1. Yours truly, Mrs. Jean Sands, Manager, Enclosure

PS: *I'll see you at approximately eight o'clock on Tuesday and will go with you to the auction at 11 a.m.*

LESSON 139

GOALS
- To practice using two comma rules.
- To type two memorandums in which two comma rules are applied.

FORMAT
- Single spacing   60-space line   5-space tab

NUMBERS REVIEW

Type lines 1–6 once applying correct number style. Edit your copy as your teacher reads the answers. Then repeat lines 1–6 from your edited copy.

1   Add precisely four grams of potassium chloride to this liquid.
2   I typed just fourteen letters, twelve memos, and eight reports yesterday.
3   They asked for exactly one thousand dollars for a deposit on any machine.

(Continued on next page)

LESSON 26

GOAL
- To control), (, ', and " keys by touch.

FORMAT
- Single spacing   50-space line

KEYBOARDING SKILLS

Type each line twice.

Speed   1   If Helen owns this land, she may wish to sell it.
Accuracy   2   Zeke was quite vexed about the joke made by Carl.
Numbers   3   Write dates as April 5, 1983 or 4/5/83 or 4-5-83.
Symbols   4   When J&R orders it at a 3.6% discount, #1 is $29.

) KEY

Shift of 0 (zero). Use Sem finger.

Space once after a closing parenthesis; do not space before it.

Type each line twice.

5   ;p; ;p) ;); ;); 10) 29) 38) 47) 56) ½) ½) ;p; ;);
6   We included 1) skis, 2) coats, 3) hats, 4) boots.
7   My rates are 1) 5%, 2) 7%, 3) 9%, 4) 16%, 5) 18%.

(KEY

Shift of 9. Use L finger.

Space once before an opening parenthesis; do not space after it.

Type each line twice.

8   lol lo(l(l l(l (10) (29) (38) (47) (56) (½) (1¼)
9   My speech (it is not too long) will cover skiing.
10   Your car (the convertible) is our favorite color.

CHECKPOINT

Type lines 11–14 once. Then repeat lines 5–10 or take two 1-minute timings on the Checkpoint.

11   When typing a symbol, follow the steps: (1) cap,   10
12   (2) strike, and (3) home. They help you feel the   20
13   motions of (1) cap, (2) strike, and (3) home in a   30
14   smooth rhythm--(1) cap, (2) strike, and (3) home.   40

   | 1 | 2 | 3 | 4 | 5 | 6 | 7 | 8 | 9 | 10

 ' KEY

Shift of 8.
Use K finger.

Or next to ; key.
Use Sem finger.

Do not space before or after an apostrophe.

Type each line twice.

15M   kik ki' k'k It's Mia's job to get Lynn's lessons.
15E   ;'; ;'; ''' It's Mia's job to get Lynn's lessons.
16   Wasn't Paul going? Isn't Jim here? Help us now.
17   We're so happy. Aren't you pleased? It's not I.

JOB 138-1. LETTER

Standard format. Workbook 277-278. Body 98 words (plus 20 words for attention line).

Locksmith City Service, 13
194 Lakeshore Drive, N.E., 18
Atlanta, GA 30324, Attention: 25
Chief Locksmith, Gentlemen: 32
Last April 15 you 36
installed the restricted 41
access locks on all the 46
doors for our new build- 51
ing. Seven keys were 55
stolen from one of our 60
employees on July 7, and 65
we would like to have 69
new locks installed on 74
the doors for which keys 79
are missing. 82
If I recall correctly, 87
you said that each lock 92
replacement would cost 97
about seventeen dollars plus 102
labor. Would the charge 107
for replacing these seven 113
locks be greater than $20 118
per lock? Please let me 123
have your estimate by 127
August 15 so that we can 132
have our locks repaired 137

as soon as possible. 141
Cordially yours, R. T. Allen, 153
Manager, cc: Ruth Richards 161

JOB 138-2. LETTER

Standard format. Workbook 279-280. Body 80 words.

Mrs. R. T. Allen, Manager, Baird Insur- 16
ance Company, 946 Pine Street, N.W., 23
Atlanta, GA 30309, Dear Mrs. Allen: 31
Thank you for your letter informing 40
me about the keys that were stolen from 48
your company. The ~~price~~ charge quoted you for 56
lock replacement was $17, and I will be 64
able to replace your locks by ~~august~~ July 15 72
or 16. 72
5 Will you need 2, 3, or 4 dupli- 81
cates of each key? On your ~~original~~ 88
order you asked for three duplicates. 96
The three duplicates for the locks that 104
will be replaced should be returned to 112
you ~~to accompany the locks.~~ when the repairs are made. Yours truly, 123
Edgar H. Hartchy, Chief locksmith, PS: 139
I will be arriving at 10 a.m. to start 147
replacing the locks. 151

NUMBERS
REVIEW

3. Spell out street names from *first* to *tenth*; use figures for street names above *tenth*. Note that ordinal numbers (*11th, 21st, 42d, 53d,* and so on) are used for street names.

They moved from *Fifth Avenue* to *19th Street*.

4. Use figures to express time with *minutes, a.m., p.m.,* and *o'clock*. (For greater formality, numbers may be spelled out with *o'clock*.) Also use figures to express years: *1981, 1983,* and so on.

The meeting should take only *15* or *20 minutes*; thus we should be able to leave by *3:45 p.m.*

CONSTRUCT AN EXCLAMATION POINT

If your machine has no exclamation point, you may construct one: (1) strike the period, (2) backspace, and (3) strike the apostrophe. Type each line once.

18 That song must have taken many months to compose!

19 My, how well she plays! She's a superb musician!

20 His accompaniment is superb! He's a new pianist!

 KEY

Shift of 2. Use S finger.

Or shift of ' key. Use Sem finger.

Type each line twice.

21M sws sw" s"s "Here," she cried.   "I am over here."

21E ;"; ;"; """ "Here," she cried.   "I am over here."

22 The signal is "blue" for up and "green" for down.

QUOTATION MARKS

Workbook 23–24.

Quotation marks are used in pairs. Often the second quotation mark is used with another punctuation mark, as shown below.

Follow these rules when using quotation marks with other punctuation:

1. Place commas and periods *before* the second quotation mark (see A and B).

2. Place colons and semicolons *after* the second quotation mark (see C and D).

3. Place question marks and exclamation marks before the second quotation mark *only if* the entire quotation is a question or an exclamation (see E). In all other cases, place the question mark or exclamation mark *after* the second quotation mark (see F and G).

Practice: Type lines 23–27 once. Use double spacing.

23   "Good morning," said Joe.   "Come in."

24   I did as he "offered": I went in.   He

25 said that I seemed "excited"; he listened.

26   "What's your news?" he asked.   "Tell me!"

27 Did he already "know"? I think he "guessed"!

CHECKPOINT

Type lines 28–31 once. Then repeat lines 16–17 (page 45) and 22 or take two 1-minute timings on the Checkpoint.

28 It's not very often that we hear the words "thank   10

29 you" or "please." Is it that we don't "care" and   20

30 "feel," or is it that we just don't "think" to be   30

31 courteous? We all "know" that we "ought" to try.   40

| 1 | 2 | 3 | 4 | 5 | 6 | 7 | 8 | 9 | 10

JOB 137-1. LETTER
Standard format (see page 169). Workbook 275–276. Body 92 words.

```
Mr. George Pera, Manager; Pera's Cam-    15
era Service, 105 Wilson Avenue, West;    23
Kingsford, MI 49801, Dear Mr. Pera:      31
      I am returning the Nobel Camera I  39
purchased from your store on Friday,     47
March 2.  As stated in your warranty,    54
there will be no charge for the fol-     61
lowing repairs:↓2                        65
```

```
  ]1. The film does not progress [    73
  ]   smoothly.  It sticks when   [    78
  ]   advancing from frame 6 to   [    83
 5]   frame 7 on the film.       5]    89
  ]2. The shutter does not work.  [    96
  ]3. The electronic F/stop does  [   103
  ]   not work properly.↓2        [   107
      Please see that these repairs are   116
made within two weeks.  My father will    124
call you at that time to pick up the      131
camera.  Cordially yours, Jeffrey S.      145
Johnson, Photographer                     152
```

LESSON 138

GOALS
- To practice using numbers rules.
- To type three letters in which these numbers rules are applied.

FORMAT
- Single spacing 60-space line 5-space tab

CAPITALIZATION REVIEW

Type lines 1–4 once, providing the missing capitals. Edit your copy as your teacher reads the answers. Then retype lines 1–4 from your edited copy.

```
1  the red river is nearby grand forks, wahpeton, and drayton.
2  i sent two letters to the president of the firm, earl jobe.
3  quinlan avenue is the site of our newest store in scranton.
4  al diaz, who imports spanish leather goods, is now in town.
```

NUMBERS REVIEW

1. Spell out numbers from 1 through 10; use figures for numbers above 10. Also spell out numbers that begin a sentence.

We will need *three* or *four* more clerks.
She estimates that the project will take *12* hours.
Eleven committee members were invited.

When numbers above 10 *and* below 10 are mixed, use figures for numbers.

Ellen surveyed *11* supervisors, *6* department heads, and *3* regional managers.

2. In technical copy, in dates, and for emphasis, use figures for all numbers.

The next meeting is scheduled for May *3* at *2:30* p.m.
The cost for *2* grams of this powder is only *$2*.

Type lines 5–10 once. Then repeat lines 5–10 or take a series of 1-minute timings.

```
5   Steve Beckley said to mix just 2 quarts of this new liquid.  12
6   We sent out 100 invitations and received just 90 responses.  12
7   Drive approximately 5.5 miles to route 122; then turn left.  12
8   Fifteen applicants were interviewed by Mrs. Mary Rodriguez.  12
9   Helen hired five clerks, two typists, and four secretaries.  12
10  Helen Greene hired 11 clerks, 2 typists, and 4 secretaries.  12
    |  1  |  2  |  3  |  4  |  5  |  6  |  7  |  8  |  9  | 10  | 11  | 12
```

GOAL
- To control __, *, ¢, and @ keys by touch.

FORMAT
- Single spacing   50-space line

KEYBOARDING SKILLS

Type each line twice.

Speed
Accuracy
Numbers
Symbols

1   It is the duty of six girls to cut down that oak.
2   Joel quickly fixed five zippers while she waited.
3   Now read this new order: 10, 29, 38, 47, and 56.
4   It's not "up" but "down."   She saw him (Joel) go.

 __ KEY

Shift of 6.
Use J finger.

Or shift of -
(hyphen).
Use Sem finger.

Workbook 25–26.

To underscore a word or a group of words: (1) type the word or words, (2) backspace to the first letter of the word or words to be underscored, (3) depress the shift lock, and (4) strike the underscore key repeatedly until all the words have been underscored. **Note:** Do *not* underscore the punctua-

tion or the space following an under-scored word or phrase. (**Exception:** If the punctuation is part of a title—as in <u>Oklahoma!</u>—then the punctua-tion *is* underscored.) *Do* underscore the punctuation or the space *within* a group of words to be underscored. See, for example, lines 6 and 7 below.

On some typewriters, the underscore key may operate continuously, like the space bar. Make sure you stop in time.

Type each line twice.

5M   ju6 ju_ j_j j_j Mary <u>did</u> say she would <u>not</u> drive.
5E   ;p_ ;p_ ;_; ;_; Mary <u>did</u> say she would <u>not</u> drive.
6   It is <u>not</u>, Linda claims, <u>very, very well written</u>.
7   Sara read her class the book <u>Alice in Wonderland</u>.

 * KEY

Shift of - (hyphen).
Use Sem finger.

Or shift of 8.
Use K finger.

Do not space between the word and the *.

Type each line twice.

8M   ;p- ;p* ;*; ;*; A style manual* is of great help.
8E   ki8 ki* k*k k*k A style manual* is of great help.
9   Rules in the reference book* help solve problems.
10   He recommends this manual* for grammar and style.

CHECKPOINT

In figuring speed, count underscored words triple.

Type lines 11–14 once.   Then repeat lines 6–7 and 9–10 or take two 1-minute timings on the Checkpoint.

11   A reference manual* is valuable for all of us who   10
12   write letters, memos, and reports.   A manual will   20
13   help to solve problems in using <u>who</u> and <u>whom</u>, for   33
14   example, and in using punctuation marks properly.   43

| 1 | 2 | 3 | 4 | 5 | 6 | 7 | 8 | 9 | 10 |

1. Capitalize proper nouns—the names of specific persons, places, or things. Capitalize common nouns when they are part of proper names.

Proper nouns:	Captain Ames	Kansas City	Chevrolet
Common nouns:	captain	city	car

   Note: Capitalize adjectives formed from proper nouns—proper adjectives such as *American, European, French*, and *Freudian*. (One common exception is *french fries*.) Also capitalize the first word of a sentence and the word *I*.

   > *She* and *I* worked for a *Greek* shipping firm.

Type lines 22–25 once. Then repeat lines 22–25 or take a series of 1-minute timings.

```
22  The Waco Paper Company is an excellent, dependable company.   12
23  Einz Plastics, a German manufacturer, supplies these pipes.   12
24  Rex Yount, a former colonel in the Marines, is our manager.   12
25  Subi, a Japanese import firm, makes high-quality materials.   12
    |  1  |  2  |  3  |  4  |  5  |  6  |  7  |  8  |  9  |  10  |  11  |  12
```

2. Capitalize *north, south, east*, and *west* when they refer to *specific* regions, are part of a proper noun, or are within an address.

   > Wesley lived in the *North* until 1982. (Specific region.)
   > He worked for the *West* End Realty Company. (Part of proper noun.)
   > His new address is 121 *South* Grand Avenue. (Part of address.)
   >
   > You must travel *east* on Route 122. (General direction.)
   > The office is on the *south* side of the city. (General location.)

   Likewise, capitalize *northern, southern, eastern*, and *western* when they refer to *specific* people or regions, not when they refer to *general* locations or directions.

   > Zambia was formerly known as *Northern* Rhodesia.
   > That warehouse will be built in the *southern* part of the state.

3. Capitalize official titles that precede names. Do not capitalize titles that follow names.

   > We asked *Mayor* Bradley to attend the reception.
   > We asked James T. Bradley, *mayor* of Scranton, to attend the reception.
   > A United States *senator* will be the main speaker.

   Note: The titles of some officials of very high rank are capitalized even when they follow or replace a name—for example, *President, Pope, Governor, Secretary General*.

Type lines 26–31 once. Then repeat lines 26–31 or take a series of 1-minute timings.

```
26  Our warehouses in the East are inadequate for our purposes.   12
27  The new metals factory is in the western part of Kalamazoo.   12
28  Vera, Jacob, and Dan handle all accounts in South Carolina.   12
29  All six distributors are north of our Bogg Street terminus.   12
30  Turn east on the Western Expressway for about 3 or 4 miles.   12
31  Eleanor lived in the Midwest before she moved to the South.   12
    |  1  |  2  |  3  |  4  |  5  |  6  |  7  |  8  |  9  |  10  |  11  |  12
```

KEY

Next to ; key.
Use Sem finger.

Or shift of 6.
Use J finger.

Do not space between the number and the symbol.

Type each line twice.

15M   ; ; ;   ;¢;   ; ; ;   ;¢;   Is it 10¢,   29¢,   38¢,   47¢,   or 56¢?

15E   jy6   jy¢   j¢j   j¢j   Is it 10¢,   29¢,   38¢,   47¢,   or 56¢?

16   Lisa has too many for 67¢ and not enough for 20¢.

17   The sales taxes total 56¢,   47¢,   38¢,   29¢,   and 1¢.

KEY

Shift of ¢ key.
Use Sem finger.

Or shift of 2.
Use S finger.

Space once before and after an @.

Type each line twice.

18M   ;¢;   ;¢@   ;@;   ;@;   She wants 21 @ 11¢, not 11 @ 21¢.

18E   sw2   sw@   s@s   s@s   She wants 21 @ 11¢, not 11 @ 21¢.

19   Pat and Ted sold them for 20 @ 14¢, not 14 @ 20¢.

20   How much are 10 apples @ 12¢ and 14 lemons @ 10¢?

CHECKPOINT

Type lines 21–24 once. Then repeat lines 16–17 and 19–20 or take two 1-minute timings on the Checkpoint.

21   The following increases were noted: cereal, 10¢;   10

22   milk, 29¢; bread, 38¢; sugar, 47¢; and beef, 56¢.   20

23   A dozen apples @ 15¢ each is also a big increase,   30

24   but buying oranges @ 20¢ is an even larger total.   40

    | 1 | 2 | 3 | 4 | 5 | 6 | 7 | 8 | 9 | 10

3-MINUTE TIMINGS

Take two 3-minute timings on lines 25–33. Use the speed markers to figure your speed. Format: Double spacing, 5-space tab.

25   When you want to mail a letter or a package,   10

26   you have a choice as to the way you want it sent.   20

27   If you want a package to be sent very fast, place   30

28   it in Express Mail. If you are not in a rush for   40

29   it to be sent, you can send it third class. Most   50

30   letters are mailed first class, but they just may   60

31   go quicker by special delivery. The size and the   70

32   weight may mean that you must change the way that   80

33   an item may be sent.   84

    | 1 | 2 | 3 | 4 | 5 | 6 | 7 | 8 | 9 | 10   SI 1.12

In Units 7 through 22, you completed 16 LABs (Language Arts Boosters) that presented modern rules of punctuation and style. In Unit 23 you will review all 16 LABs and will complete more exercises related to them. Learning activities will be introduced through (1) brief reviews of the rules, (2) examples of each rule, (3) sentence applications for each rule, and (4) production applications for each rule.

LESSON 137

UNIT 23 LANGUAGE ARTS REVIEW

UNIT GOAL
40/5'/5e

GOALS
- To use quotation marks correctly with other punctuation marks while typing sentences.
- To type a letter applying capitalization rules.

FORMAT
- Single spacing   60-space line   5-space tab

LAB 16

QUOTATION MARKS WITH OTHER PUNCTUATION

Workbook 273–274

Type lines 1–4 once, providing the missing exclamation points and question marks. Edit your copy as your teacher reads the answers. Then retype lines 1–4 from your edited copy.

1 We asked Greg, "What are the new sales quotas for January."
2 Mr. Axel ridiculed the idea that the price was a "bargain".
3 Jeffrey asked, "Did Karina Alzado approve all the designs."
4 Near the end of the commercial, two narrators yell "Hurry."

5-MINUTE TIMINGS

Take two 5-minute timings on lines 5–21.

5   There are specific language arts skills which everyone   12
6 should know. Such skills will help us improve our speaking   24
7 and writing skills, and they will permit us to express our–   36
8 selves much better. The language arts skills emphasized in   48
9 our course have by now made us more cognizant of the unique   60
10 role they play in improving our methods of expression.   71
11   In previous lessons, we learned when to capitalize and   83
12 when not to capitalize. We learned, for instance, that all   95
13 proper nouns are capitalized and that a specific place like   107
14 a city, township, county, or state is also capitalized. We   119
15 learned that numbers from 1 through 10 are spelled out, but   131
16 figures are used for numbers above 10. Several rules exist   143
17 on how and when to use the comma. For instance, a comma is   155
18 used when three or more items appear in succession. Commas   167
19 are also used at the end of an introductory clause which is   179
20 followed by a main clause. Words such as if, as, when, and   191
21 because are used to introduce these clauses.   200

| 1 | 2 | 3 | 4 | 5 | 6 | 7 | 8 | 9 | 10 | 11 | 12   SI 1.41

LESSON 28

GOALS
- To control !, +, and = keys.
- To construct special symbols.

FORMAT
- Single spacing   50-space line

KEYBOARDING SKILLS

Speed
Accuracy
Numbers
Symbols

Type each line twice.

1 The firm that they own may make a big profit now.
2 Her job was to pack a dozen equal boxes by night.
3 Mark will order 10, 29, 38, 47, and 56 varieties.
4 The book* is on sale at P&H (2 copies @ $3 each).

 KEY

Shift of 1.
Use A finger.

Or next to P.
Use Sem finger.

Or construct. (See page 46.)

Type each line twice.   Type either line A or B.

5A aql aq! a!a a!a Watch! Watch them! Watch those!
5B ;;; ;!; ;;; ;!; Watch! Watch them! Watch those!
6 Look! Look there! Look there! Look everywhere!
7 She paced: Five! Four! Three! Two! One! Go!
8 Look at the sky! You can see it from here! Wow!

 **KEYS**

+ is shift of =

Next to hyphen.
Use Sem finger.

Or next to ½.
Use Sem finger.

Type each line twice.

9 ;=; === ;=; === = A = 40, B = 35, C = 25, D = 20.
10 ;+; +++ ;+; +++ 0 + 10 + 29 + 38 + 47 + 56 = 100.
11 Yes, 3 + 3 = 6 and 9 + 9 = 18; but 3 + 18 = what?

CHECKPOINT

Space once before and after the + and the =.

Type lines 12–15 once. Then repeat lines 6–11 or take two 1-minute timings on the Checkpoint.

12 If 2 + 2 = 4 and 7 + 7 = 14, how much is 14 + 14?   10
13 Watch the ball go! It's a home run for the team!   20
14 If 4 + 6 = 10 and 6 + 4 = 10, what will 5 + 5 be?   30
15 Watch the beautiful eagle! It's building a nest!   40

| 1 | 2 | 3 | 4 | 5 | 6 | 7 | 8 | 9 | 10 |

Tables

7. Describe step by step how to type a footnote in an open (unruled) table.

8. How many lines of spaces should there be before and after a rule in a ruled table?

9. What is a source note? How is it typed?

Letters

10. How is an enumeration in a letter typed?

11. What is a *bcc* notation and what is "special" about it. Where is it typed?

12. What line length is used on baronial stationery?

Forms

13. On an invoice, where is the word *TOTAL* typed?

14. What is the difference between a purchase requisition and a purchase order?

15. Why is a "Z" rule used on printed legal forms?

JOB 136-1. LETTER IN ROUGH DRAFT ON MONARCH STATIONERY

Standard format (see page 217). Workbook 271–272. Body 89 words (plus 20 words for subject line).

Ms. Blanche Kile, 2418 Camden Avenue,   15

Flint, MI 48570, Dear Ms. Kile: Sub-   24

ject: Writing Skills Survey   30

    Enclosed is your survey on reading   38

and writing skills courses. You will note that in   48

addition to the questions we answered in   57

the survey, we have also attached 1 page   65

of "interesting" comments to the issues you raised on   74

page 3 of your survey. We think you   81

will be interested in our input on these   89

issues.   91

    We look forward to receiving a copy   99

of the results of your study. We plan   107

to share the findings of your study with   115

the entire faculty, since your topic is a   124

relevant one for us. Sincerely yours,   133

T. L. Harris, chairperson, Enclosure, cc: 148

Shirley A. Johnson, cc: Carl B. White,   155

PS: Could we have your permission to   164

duplicate the findings of your study?   171

JOB 136-2. FOUR-COLUMN RULED TABLE

Standard format (see page 159). Full sheet of paper.

Group	Boys	Girls	Totals
Freshman	237	268	505
Sophomore	295	281	576
Junior	284	277	561
Senior	301	329	630
Totals	1,117	1,155	2,272

CLASS ENROLLMENTS Fall Term

JOB 136-3. UNBOUND REPORT, PAGE 1

Standard format (see pages 117 and 118). Double-space the body.

ANIMALS AND WHERE THEY LIVE	16

March 10, 19--   27

By Paula R. West   39

Some animals spend their entire lives moving about from one home to another, but others stay in one place and have homes that last them a long time.   50 60 68 72

PERMANENT HOMES   77

Many animals, such as the ground squirrel and chipmunk, dig an underground burrow where they live "year after year after year." Bears and lions make their homes in caves or in dense thickets where they cannot be seen. Insects even make permanent homes by building hives or by digging tunnels in the ground.   87 95 104 113 122 131 140

TEMPORARY HOMES   145

Throughout the animal kingdom live animals that do not have permanent homes. They drift from place to place at certain times of the year. As an example, wild geese and other wild birds fly to warmer climates when the cold winter months arrive. Wild animals living on the African continent travel many hundreds of miles in search of water and food when the dry season approaches.   153 162 172 181 189 198 206 216 222

PHRASES   Practice lines 16–18 to build speed on familiar phrases.

16 by me, by it, by him, by her, by our, by the way,

17 or if, or so, or the, or our, or his, or her way,

18 in my, in it, in for, in our, in the, in the way,

CONSTRUCTED CHARACTERS   Every typist should know how to construct these special symbols, which are needed from time to time. Using the procedures given in Column 3, practice constructing each of the characters listed in Column 1. Then type only Column 2 centered on a full page and double-spaced.

Column 1	Column 2	Column 3
19. Cents	He charges 2¢	Small letter C, intersected by diagonal.
20. Star	✭ ✭ ✭ ✭ ✭	Capital A, typed over small letter V.
21. Caret	They try/hard (so)	Underscore and diagonal; word centered above diagonal.
22. Brackets	He /Johnston/	Diagonals, with underscores facing inside.
23. Roman numerals	Chapter XVIII	Capitals of I, V, X, L, C, D, and M.
24. Pounds sterling	£8 is English	Capital L, typed over small letter F.
25. Degrees	$32°F$ (or $0°C$)	Small letter O, raised slightly (turn cylinder by hand).
26. Military zero	Leave at Ø1ØØ	The number 0, intersected by a diagonal.
27. Times, by	What is 4 x 5	Expressed by the small letter X.
28. Divided by	120 ÷ 10 = 12	Colon, intersected by hyphen.
29. Equals	11 x 11 = 121	Two hyphens, one below the other (turn cylinder by hand).
30. Plus	87 + 18 = 105	Hyphen, intersected by diagonal or apostrophe.
31. Minus	140 – 56 = 84	Expressed by a single hyphen; space before and after.
32. Superscript	$8^2 + 6^2 = 10^2$	Type number or letter above line (turn cylinder by hand).
33. Subscript	H_2O is water.	Type number or letter below line (turn cylinder by hand).
34. Square root	$\sqrt{90000}$ is 300	Small V, off-positioned to meet diagonal, followed by underscores typed on line above.
35. Divide into	45)9045 = 201	Right parenthesis and underscores.
36. Feet and inches	Mary is 5' 2"	For feet, apostrophe; for inches, quotation mark.
37. Minutes, seconds	Time: 3' 15"	For minutes, apostrophe; for seconds, quotation mark.
38. Ellipsis	He . . . also He I	Three periods, spaced apart (but four periods if there is a sentence ending within the omitted material).
39. Section	§20. Symbols	Capital S, intersected by a raised capital S.
40. Paragraph	¶21. Symbols	Capital P, intersected by the small letter L.
41. Ratio	1:4::2:X = 8.	Use one or two colons, as appropriate.
42. Bar graph line	mmmmmmmmmmmmm	Small M, W, O, or X, typed in a solid row.

FORMATTING LEGAL FILL-IN FORMS

Workbook 216.

When typing legal documents on a form, you are required to insert the necessary information. Follow these guidelines and study the illustration to the right when typing on a preprinted legal form:

1. Align the insertions with the preprinted words.
2. Treat any blank areas on the form as follows:
   Ⓐ Fill in any blank spaces within individual lines of the form with *leaders* (a series of hyphens).
   Ⓑ Fill in any blank areas that occupy several blank lines with two horizontal underscores joined by a solid diagonal line. This is called a Z rule.
3. Leave 1 blank space between the preprinted word and the typed insertion.
4. Align margins with those of the form. **Note:** In some states erasing is not permitted on dates, addresses, amounts of money, and names.

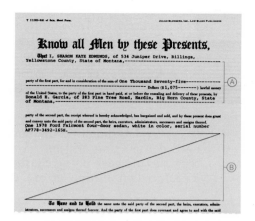

JOB 135-1. BILL OF SALE ON A FORM

Standard format. Workbook 269–270. Use the information in Job 115-2, page 194, to fill in the workbook form for a bill of sale.

LESSON 136

REVIEW

GOALS
- To answer a series of technical questions with a minimum of 80 percent competency.
- To type 40/5'/5e.
- To type a letter, a table, and a short report.

FORMAT
- Single spacing   60-space line   5-space tab and other tabs as needed

KEYBOARDING SKILLS

Type lines 1–4 once. Then do what line 5 tells you to do. Repeat lines 1–4, or take a series of 1-minute timings.

Speed   1 A whole kernel of corn was picked up by the hen last night.   12
Accuracy   2 Did Liz give Weldon your picturesque jukebox for Christmas?   12
Numbers   3 Fires raged all night at 1029 Pine, 3847 Oak, and 5610 Elm.   12
Symbols   4 We found out that 1/5 of $20 = $4 and that 10% of $40 = $4.   12
Technique 5 Use your return key after every word as you type this line.

| 1 | 2 | 3 | 4 | 5 | 6 | 7 | 8 | 9 | 10 | 11 | 12

5-MINUTE TIMING

Take a 5-minute timing on lines 5–24, page 224. Use double spacing.

TECHNICAL QUESTIONS

Compose on your typewriter answers to the following questions. Your goal is to answer 12 or more questions correctly.

Reports

1. How do the margins in a bound report differ from those in an unbound report?

2. What must be included in the heading of a magazine article?

3. What spacing is used for tables in reports?

Legal Documents

4. Where are page numbers positioned in a legal document, and what is the style for typing page numbers?

5. How wide are the margins in a legal document?

6. What is the paragraph indention for a legal document?

LESSON 29

- To review the symbol-key controls.
- To format two items that use symbols.

FORMAT
- Single spacing   50-space line

KEYBOARDING SKILLS

Type each line twice.

Speed
1 She may wish to amend the form when she signs it.

Accuracy
2 Jackey's vague quip amazed and vexed her brother.

Numbers
3 Your fingers can now find 10, 29, 38, 47, and 56.

Symbols
4 Do 10 + 29 + 38 + 47 + 56 = 180? Yes! It's 180.

REVIEW

Type each line twice.

( )
5 He listed items (10), (29), (38), (47), and (56).

+
6 Millie counted 10 + 29 + 38 + 47 + 56 to get 180.

=
7 Grades: 10 = D, 29 = C, 38 = B, 47 = A, 56 = A+.

$
8 My special rates are $10, $29, $38, $47, and $56.

¢
9 I collected 10¢, 29¢, 38¢, 47¢, and 56¢ for them.

@
10 They saw 12 pears @ $1.28 and 12 bananas @ $1.39.

CHECKPOINT

Type lines 11–12 once. Then repeat any of lines 5–10 that contain symbols you need practice in or take two 1-minute timings on the Checkpoint.

11 Anna, did you know that (9 + 9)(8 + 8) = 18 × 16?   10

12 Buy 8 @ 75¢ and 26 @ 25¢; total (plus 4%) is $13.   20

| 1 | 2 | 3 | 4 | 5 | 6 | 7 | 8 | 9 | 10 |

REVIEW

Space twice after an exclamation point at the end of a sentence.

An asterisk (*) follows a punctuation mark.

Type each line twice.

#
13 Carpet remnants were #10, #29, #38, #47, and #56.

%
14 New rates: 1% to 10%, 29% to 38%, or 47% to 56%.

!
15 Shout! Up! No! Down! There! Yes! Here! Oh!

:
16 Times listed: 10:29, 11:38, 2:47, 1:56, or 2:01.

&
17 Pair them as follows: 10 & 29, 38 & 47, 56 & 29.

*
18 Note the following: 10,* 29,* 38,* 47,* and 56.*

"
19 "Isn't it fine!" she exclaimed. "Look at it go!"

'
20 It's not that he won't speak; it's that he can't.

_
21 Please send Return of Lassie or Call of the Wild.

LESSON 135

GOALS
- To use quotation marks correctly with other punctuation marks while typing sentences.
- To type 40/5'/5e.
- To format legal fill-in forms.

FORMAT
- Single spacing   60-space line   5-space tab

LAB 16

QUOTATION MARKS WITH OTHER PUNCTUATION

Type lines 1–4 once, providing the missing punctuation marks. Edit your copy as the teacher reads the answers. Then retype lines 1–4 from your edited copy.

1 My broker said, "The quoted price is very low, so buy now."
2 Has Gary found out why the envelope is marked "Top Secret".
3 Just say to him, "Ed, when will you complete this project."
4 Ex-mayor Schwartz said, "This proposed plan is ridiculous."

1- AND 5-MINUTE TIMINGS

Take two 1-minute timings on each paragraph. Then take one 5-minute timing on the entire selection. Use single spacing for the 1-minute timings and double spacing for the 5-minute timing.

5   Stop to consider this question: "What is weather made 12
6 of?" Wind, sunshine, clouds, rain, snow, and sleet are all 24
7 brought to us by four elements: air pressure, temperature, 36
8 moisture, and wind. 40

9   Air pressure is just the weight of air pushing against 12
10 the surface of the earth. Warm air exerts less pressure on 24
11 the earth than cold air because it weighs less. Barometers 36
12 measure air pressure. 40

13   Rapid changes in temperature may create quite a severe 12
14 change in weather. If temperatures are above freezing, you 24
15 may get rain; and if they're at or below freezing, you will 36
16 have sleet or snow. 40

17   Moisture is known, of course, as precipitation. Mois- 12
18 ture reaches us from the sky as rain, snow, sleet, or hail. 24
19 However, it might possibly remain in the air as water vapor 36
20 and create clouds. 40

21   A weather pattern is drastically affected by winds. A 12
22 soft breeze may bring a very pleasant summer day, sea winds 24
23 transmit cool air over the land, and northern breezes might 36
24 provide us cool days. 40

| 1 | 2 | 3 | 4 | 5 | 6 | 7 | 8 | 9 | 10 | 11 | 12 | SI 1.41

CHECKPOINT

Type lines 22–24 once. Then repeat any of lines 13–21 (page 51) that contain symbols you need to practice or take two 1-minute timings on the Checkpoint.

22 Their #7 and #4 sizes are 30% to 40% higher here. 10
23 K&D arrived at 1:30. L&W came later on at 2:45.* 20
24 "It's Oklahoma!" Jean said. "Let's buy tickets!" 30
   | 1 | 2 | 3 | 4 | 5 | 6 | 7 | 8 | 9 | 10

3-MINUTE TIMINGS

Take two 3-minute timings on lines 25–33. Format: Double spacing, 5-space tab.

25   A jigsaw puzzle is such fun. To fit all the 10
26 shapes is a game. At first it is a game of hues, 20
27 and then it is a game of sizes, and at the last a 30
28 game of fits. Each piece looks as though it will 40
29 fit, but just one piece will do so. You can push 50
30 and squeeze all day, but only the right shape and 60
31 proper size will drop into place. Many pieces do 70
32 look equal to the holes, but only the exact match 80
33 fits in the puzzle. 84
   | 1 | 2 | 3 | 4 | 5 | 6 | 7 | 8 | 9 | 10   SI 1.13

JOB 29-1. ANNOUNCEMENT
Standard format. Double spacing. Half sheet of paper.

SWIM & SKI CLUB

Fall Roundups

from

1:30 to 4:30

Saturday, October 25, 19—

Fees: $75 each semester

JOB 29-2. ENUMERATION
Standard format. Double spacing. Full sheet of paper.

SENIOR READING LIST

1. *Ivanhoe*
2. *The Seekers*
3. *The Third Wave*
4. *A Walk Across America*
5. *Blind Ambition**
6. *Gone With the Wind*
7. *Roots*
8. *Holocaust*
9. *The Immigrants*

*Optional

LESSON 134

GOALS
- To identify how quotation marks are used with other punctuation marks while typing sentences.
- To format and type ten geographic file cards.
- To type a three-column table.

FORMAT
- Single spacing   60-space line   Tabs as needed

LAB 16

Type lines 1–4 once. Then repeat lines 1–4 or take a series of 1-minute timings.

QUOTATION MARKS WITH OTHER PUNCTUATION

1 "Tomorrow," I said, "we will discuss the budget in detail!" 12
2 Andrew asked, "Does anyone know where Anne Rodriguez went?" 12
3 Gus said, "Send requisitions to Ms. Camp for her approval!" 12
4 Did you mark them "Fragile"? Just mark each box "Caution!" 12

| 1 | 2 | 3 | 4 | 5 | 6 | 7 | 8 | 9 | 10 | 11 | 12

FORMATTING GEOGRAPHIC FILE CARDS

Whenever it is easier to file names and addresses by location rather than by last names, create *geographic file cards*.

To format geographic file cards:

1. Type the state, city, and ZIP Code on line 2 beginning 4 spaces from the left edge of the card.

2. Type the name and address a double space below the state, indented 3 spaces.

```
1234
1
2    Louisiana, Baton Rouge 70802
3
4        Mr. Glen Vance
         489 Myrtle Avenue
         Baton Rouge, LA 70802
```

JOB 134-1. GEOGRAPHIC FILE CARDS

Type a card for each contractor listed below. Standard format. Workbook 265, 267.

LOIS MEREDITH, 528 CAPITOL STREET, HOUSTON, TX 77002
LAURA HOLMES, 1678 MADRID STREET, NEW ORLEANS, LA 70122
ETHEL THOMAS, 835 CRAWFORD STREET, JACKSON, MS 39203
LEON SANCHEZ, 5019 BOLM ROAD, AUSTIN, TX 78721
RITA EVERETT, 967 GREEN STREET, BIRMINGHAM, AL 35217
SHARON LEWIS, 938 PHILLIPS STREET, HUNTSVILLE, AL 35903
JOHN ORTEGA, 167 OSCEOLA STREET, TALLAHASSEE, FL 32301
RALPH EDWARDS, 226 ACADIA STREET, ATLANTA, GA 30344

JOB 134-2. RULED TABLE

Standard format except use 8 spaces between columns. Arrange items alphabetically by name of contractor. (Use the cards you prepared in Job 134-1.)

[*Title*] Southern Insulation Contractors
[*Subtitle*] Official Members List
[*Column headings*] (1) Name (2) Street Address (3) City/State/ZIP

LESSON 30

CLINIC

GOAL
- To build keyboarding speed using 12-second timings, 30-second timings, and preview practice.
- To type 28/3'/5e.

FORMAT
- Single spacing   50-space line

PRETEST

Use the 3-minute timings from Lesson 29 (page 52) as a Pretest. Take two 3-minute timings, and determine your speed by using the faster rate.

12-SECOND TIMINGS

How fast can you type without error for 12 seconds? Find out by taking four 12-second timings on each of lines 1–3. Your speed is the number on the scale over which you stop.

1 It is time to work on my speed with fewer errors. 10
2 This is the day that you will make a better rate. 10
3 Just let your hands move over the keys with ease. 10

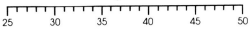

    25   30   35   40   45   50

30-SECOND TIMINGS

Take two 30-second timings on lines 4–6, or type each line twice.

4 When you can practice each day for a few minutes, 10
5 you will see how much more you can type. It is a 20
6 matter of knowing the reach for each of the keys. 30

| 1 | 2 | 3 | 4 | 5 | 6 | 7 | 8 | 9 | 10

PREVIEW PRACTICE

Preview words provide a chance to prevent errors and to increase speed. The words come from the timing and are grouped into drills. Type each line twice.

Accuracy 7 lucky exam, quite course shadow students semester

Speed 8 just were term have done hold lone all the end of

3-MINUTE TIMINGS

Take two 3-minute timings on lines 9–17. Format: Double spacing, 5-space tab.

9   The end of a semester would be just great if 10
10 it were not for the tests. It is a joy to finish 20
11 the term, to have the course done, to have a hold 30
12 on things we have mastered, etc. The lone shadow 40
13 is the course exam. But, on the other hand, some 50
14 students like tests; they see tests as the chance 60
15 to prove how much they have learned. Things that 70
16 are a puzzle to most of us are quite clear to all 80
17 those lucky persons. 84

| 1 | 2 | 3 | 4 | 5 | 6 | 7 | 8 | 9 | 10   SI 1.13

1- AND 5-MINUTE TIMINGS

Take two 1-minute timings on each paragraph. Then take one 5-minute timing on the entire selection. Use single spacing for the 1-minute timings and double spacing for the 5-minute timing.

```
                                                                        1'
 5      Each year when winter approaches, you might look up at        12

 6   the sky and view hundreds and maybe even thousands of birds      24

 7   flying toward warmer weather just to escape the severe days      36

 8   that come so soon.                                               40
                                                                       —
 9      Have you ever wondered how birds know when to commence        12

10   their flight to another area, or how they always find their     24

11   way when their extensive journey has begun, or how they en—     36

12   dure their journeys?                                             40
                                                                       —
13      In this country alone over 400 bird species travel the       12

14   flyways every year to a warm climate, and what is more sur—     24

15   prising is that they always seem to travel to the same area     36

16   as they did before.                                             40
                                                                       —
17      Why do birds migrate?  Many experts hypothesize that a       12

18   bird migrates because it can't last in the harsh winters of     24

19   the cold north; others believe that a bird migrates to find     36

20   a better food source.                                           40
                                                                       —
21      When the birds are traveling high in the sky, they use       12

22   directional signals to keep them on particular flight paths     24

23   in the flyways.  Birds have "built-in radar," a unique sys—     36

24   tem to guide them.                                               40

     |  1  |  2  |  3  |  4  |  5  |  6  |  7  |  8  |  9  | 10 | 11 | 12    SI 1.41
```

JOB 133-1. BUSINESS INVOICE 56102
Standard format (see page 113). Workbook 263.

[*To*] Safe Equipment Company / [*Today's date*] /
1457 Semple Avenue / St. Louis, MO 63112 /

3	Insulated steel safes	
	[*Unit price*] 229.99	[*Amount*] 689.97
2	Computer media safes	
	[*Unit price*] 498.99	[*Amount*] 997.98
10	Chest files	
	[*Unit price*] 75.00	[*Amount*] 750.00
7	4-Drawer file cabinets	
	[*Unit price*] 74.99	[*Amount*] 524.93
	Total amount due	2,962.88

JOB 133-2. CREDIT MEMORANDUM 8259
Standard format (see page 179). Workbook 263.

[*To*] Data Systems, Inc. / 1216 Lee Street, S.E. /
Portland, OR 97302 / [*Credits:*]

5	8″ Flexible disks (containers cracked)	
	[*Unit price*] 5.95	[*Amount*] 29.75
3	Flexible disk hanging folders (hooks bent)	
	[*Unit price*] 4.40	[*Amount*] 13.20
10	Flexible disk markers (fluid evaporated)	
	[*Unit price*] 4.05	[*Amount*] 40.50
	Total	83.45
	Delivery charges paid	3.34
	Total charges paid	86.79

LESSON 31

GOALS
- To correct errors using a variety of techniques.
- To format notes.

FORMAT
- Single spacing   60-space line

KEYBOARDING SKILLS

Type each line twice.

Speed   1 On the shelf he may find the map for the lake and the land.

Accuracy 2 Sew the azure badge on my velvet jacket before the banquet.

Numbers 3 Type 1 or 2 or 3 or 4 or 5 or 6 or 7 or 8 or 9 or 10 or 11.

Symbols 4 Pay 80% of $2.59 for #7 ledgers at Owens & Barnes Supplies.

PREVIEW PRACTICE

Type each line twice.

Accuracy 5 text dizzy covers neatly errors liquid corrects typewriter.

Speed   6 nice look will when page from take hole your have that sign

3-MINUTE TIMINGS

Take two 3-minute timings on lines 7–14. Use the speed markers to figure your speed. Format: Double spacing, 5-space tab.

7   When you correct an error that you have typed, you are   12

8   to do it as neatly as you can. A smear or a hole in a page   24

9   is a sign that you do not take pride in the text that comes   36

10 from your typewriter. If you make a page dizzy with liquid   48

11 corrections, the page will not look nice at all. That tape   60

12 which covers is fine, but you must be sure that you are not   72

13 able to see where you used it. Chalk will do on some jobs,   84

14 but it will rub off with time.   90

| 1 | 2 | 3 | 4 | 5 | 6 | 7 | 8 | 9 | 10 | 11 | 12   SI 1.11

CORRECTING ERRORS

Errors may be corrected in a number of ways: erasing, using correction tape to cover up or lift off, or using a correction fluid to cover errors.

To erase errors:

1. Turn the paper so that the error will be at the top of the cylinder.

2. Using the margin release, move the carriage or carrier as far left or right as possible (to keep eraser grit out of the operating parts of the machine).

3. Press the paper tightly against cylinder with fingertips.

4. With a typewriting eraser, erase each letter to be deleted; use light up-and-down strokes.

5. Turn the paper back to writing line.

6. Insert the correction.

Practice

Type this: There are four rules to remember. Try to learn then today.

Correct it to: There are five rules to remember. Try to learn them today.

Purchase Order 384

Computer Supplies, 5078 Lakeshore Drive, New Orleans, LA 70146. 3 Tape storage cabinets, Model TSC-8816 @ $171.65 = $514.95; 4 Tape storage cabinets, Model TSC-9816 @ $211.50 = $846; 1 Sliding door cabinet, Model TSC-7800 @ $141 = $141; 20 Tape canisters, Model TC-10 @ $14.50 = $290; 20 Tape canisters, Model TC-7 @ $9.70 = $194. Total = $1,985.95.

Purchase Order 385

Harrison Business Furniture, 1698 Manitou Road, Rochester, NY 14626. 1 Office desk, Model 2-DT-7703 @ $299.00 = $299; 1 Swivel desk chair, Model 2-DC-7702 @ $129.99 = $129.99; 1 Corner table, Model F2-AX-67 @ $134.50 = $134.50; 1 Side chair, Model DE-7750-N @ $135.00 = $135; 1 File cabinet, Model EFC-1613 @ $71.35 = $71.35. Total = $769.84.

JOBS 131/2-5 AND 131/2-6. PURCHASE REQUISITION 1031 AND PURCHASE ORDER 386

Prepare a purchase requisition and purchase order for May Clark in the Sales Department. Order from Harrison Business Furniture. Requisition: Single-space. Purchase order: Standard format. Workbook 261.

5 Standard staplers, Model OS-5647 @ $12.95 = $64.75; 2 3-hole Punches, Model OS-7413-38 @ $19.00 = $38; 5 Fluorescent swivel lamps, Model OS-8203-38 @ $72.99 = $364.95; 10 cans Spirit duplicator fluid, Catalog No. OS-9578 @ $7.99 = $79.90; 3 12″ Electric clocks, Model OS-6285-38 @ $15.99 = $47.97. Total = $595.57.

LESSON 133

GOALS
- To recognize how quotation marks are used with other punctuation marks while typing sentences.
- To practice typing invoices and credit memorandums.

FORMAT
- Single spacing   60-space line   5-space tab and other tabs as needed

LAB 16

QUOTATION MARKS WITH OTHER PUNCTUATION

Type lines 1–4 once. Then repeat lines 1–4 or take a series of 1-minute timings.

```
1  Is the report titled "Study of Broadcast Media in Arizona"?   12
2  "No," said Ms. Quimby, "these statistics are not accurate!"   12
3  Hurry!  I must mark all the cartons "Biological Specimens"!   12
4  "Can we have five or six days to complete this?" she asked.   12
   |  1  |  2  |  3  |  4  |  5  |  6  |  7  |  8  |  9  |  10  |  11  |  12
```

Place a question mark *before* the second quotation mark when the words quoted form a question. In all other cases, place the question mark *after* the second quotation mark.

"What is the date of the next stockholders' meeting?" asked Carole. (Because the quoted words form a question, the question mark is placed *before* the second quotation mark.)

Does anyone know why these folders are stamped "Confidential"? (The word in quotations does *not* form a question.)

Likewise, place an exclamation point *before* the second quotation mark when the words quoted form an exclamation. In all other cases, place the exclamation point *after* the second quotation mark.

Alicia said, "I can't believe that my design won first prize!" (The words in quotations are an exclamation.)

I think it's ridiculous to say that this product is "overpriced"! (The word in quotations does *not* form an exclamation.)

FORMATTING NOTES

Informal notes are short and therefore are usually typed on a half sheet of paper. To format informal notes:

1. Use a 60-space line.
2. Begin date at the center on line 7.
3. Leave 4 blank lines between date and salutation.
4. Type salutation at the left margin.
5. Leave 1 blank line between salutation and body (the message).
6. Indent paragraphs 5 spaces from the left margin.
7. Single-space each paragraph, but double-space between paragraphs.
8. Type the closing a double space below the body, beginning at the center.

JOBS 31-1 AND 31-2. INFORMAL NOTE

Type the note below and check it for format. Correct all errors. Then retype the note; address it to someone in your class. Standard format.

Date   November 18, 19--
                                                      ↓5

Salutation   Dear Club Member:
                                      ↓2

Body   We have planned a special program on diving techniques for
our next Swimming Club meeting. Lisa Cammero, last year's city
diving champion, will demonstrate proper diving for all of us.
                                                                    ↓2

          The meeting will be held at the Civic Center in the pool
area at 7 p.m., Wednesday, November 29. You won't need a pass
to enter. We have made special arrangements for everyone to
swim free for this meeting.
                          ↓2

Closing   Bring your suit and join us.

Signature   *Gloria*

LESSON 32

GOALS
- To correct errors by squeezing and spreading characters and spaces.
- To type notes.

FORMAT
- Single spacing   60-space line

KEYBOARDING SKILLS

Type lines 1–4 on page 54 twice each.

CORRECTING ERRORS   Workbook 29–30.

Problem: In making a correction, how can you squeeze in an extra letter?
Answer: Move the word a half space to the *left* so that only a half space precedes and follows it.

To do this, you must keep the carriage or carrier from spacing normally. You can use one of three ways to control the carriage or carrier movement: (1) press your fingertips against the end of the platen or carrier, (2)

Type lines 5 and 6 twice as a preview to the 5-minute timings below.

Accuracy 5 search typing ability personal employer carefully emotional
Speed   6 always public mature touch adept loyal might work such when

**5-MINUTE
TIMINGS**

Take two 5-minute timings on lines 7–23.

7   When employers search for a new office worker, they do   12
8 so by looking at many things. Such a worker must have good   24
9 skills that might be quite hard to find. For instance, the   36
10 adept office worker must work quickly and carefully. Also,   48
11 the valued office worker must be at ease while working with   60
12 other personnel as well as with the general public. If you   72
13 wish to work in an office, you should touch up your skills.   84
14   The skills to work on are the professional skills such   96
15 as typing, shorthand, and math; the personal skills such as   108
16 need for initiative, being on time, and working with others   120
17 in the office; and, of course, the emotional skills such as   132
18 ability to work under stress, to be loyal to your employer,   144
19 and "to keep the business of an office in an office." When   156
20 a mature person works in an office, these skills are always   168
21 easy to observe. Just by being aware of the nature of work   180
22 in an office, you will be able to do the work with zeal and   192
23 become a winner; and that's important.   200

| 1 | 2 | 3 | 4 | 5 | 6 | 7 | 8 | 9 | 10 | 11 | 12 | SI 1.39

JOBS 131/2-1 AND 131/2-2. PURCHASE REQUISITIONS

Type the information in Jobs 131/2-1 and 131/2-2 on two purchase requisition forms. Single-space. Workbook 257.

Purchase Requisition 1029

To expand the computer storage facilities, Virginia Hanes, Director / Computer Center, needs the following items: 3 Open tape-storage cabinets; 4 Double-door tape-storage cabinets; 1 Sliding door cabinet; 20 10½" tape canisters; 20 7" Tape canisters. Obtain the supplies from Computer Supplies, 5078 Lakeshore Drive, New Orleans, LA 70146.

Purchase Requisition 1030

A new sales position has been added to Saratoga Enterprises, 413 Main Street East, Rochester, NY 14604. Charles Fuhrman, Facilities Manager, is ordering the following furniture from Harrison Business Furniture, 1698 Manitou Road, Rochester, NY 14626: 1 24" × 54" Desk; 1 Swivel desk chair; 1 Corner table; 1 Side chair with arms; 1 4-drawer 52" File cabinet.

JOBS 131/2-3 AND 131/2-4. PURCHASE ORDERS

Type the information in Jobs 131/2-3 and 131/2-4 (page 221) on two purchase order forms. Standard format. Workbook 259.

depress the halfspace key if your machine has one, or (3) partly depress the backspace key.

Practice: Type lines *a* and *b* *exactly* as shown; then insert *said* in each of the two blank areas in line *b*.

By squeezing

a   You say that you will help us.   You say that you will work.
b   You   that you will help us.   You   that you will work.

Problem: How do you spread a word so that it will occupy an extra space?
Answer: Move the word a half space to the *right* so that 1½ spaces precede and follow it. This requires

your controlling the carriage or carrier just as you did in the preceding exercise.
Practice: Type lines *c* and *d* *exactly* as shown; then insert *say* in each of the two blank areas in line *d*.

By spreading

c   You said that you will help.   You said that you will do it.
d   You   that you will help.   You   that you will do it.

PREVIEW PRACTICE

Type each line twice.

Accuracy
Speed

5   for amazed friend special whether hobbies thoughts choosing
6   also joke gift your will when what that how you may has the

3-MINUTE TIMINGS

Take two 3-minute timings on lines 7–14. Format: Double spacing, 5-space tab.

```
                 1              2              3              4
7        When you select a gift for a friend, how do you decide    12
              5              6              7              8
8    what it will be?  You will be amazed at the hours which you    24
                   9             10             11            12
9    spend choosing the exact gift.  You may choose a gift to be    36
            13             14             15            16
10   worn, or you may choose a gift to be read.  The gift may be    48
           17             18             19            20
11   a joke which brings a smile.  You could also note whether a    60
             21             22             23            24
12   friend is active or quiet, and you could check hobbies that    72
            25             26             27            28
13   your friend has.  The gift will convey the special thoughts    84
            29             30
14   that you have for your friend.                                 90
     |  1  |  2  |  3  |  4  |  5  |  6  |  7  |  8  |  9  |  10  |  11  |  12    SI 1.13
```

JOBS 32-1 AND 32-2. INFORMAL NOTE

Type the note below and check the format. Correct all errors. Then retype the note; address it to someone in your class. Standard format.

December 5, 19--

Dear Fred

Several of us are planning a trip for spring break. We want to come to the beach. Our break falls the last week in March this year. Is this the same week that you will have off? We hope that we can get together with you if it is.

Would you recommend some motels where you think that we might stay for the week? We need to make our plane reservations before Christmas, and we would like to make our motel plans at the same time.

See you soon

Rick

Take a 5-minute timing on lines 11–28. Type six times each word on which you made an error, hesitated, or stopped during the 5-minute timing. Then take a 5-minute timing to see how much your skill has improved.

```
                          1                              2
11      Do you realize that a more attractive office will most    12
              3                              4
12      Do you realize that a more attractive office will most    24
        5                         6                    7
13      Do you realize that a more attractive office will most    36
                    8                         9
14   likely cause an office worker to produce at a higher level?   48
             10                     11              12
15   likely cause an office worker to produce at a higher level?   60
                     13                        14
16   likely cause an office worker to produce at a higher level?   72
                15                           16
17   More attractive color selections will be seen in offices of   84
        17                     18                 19
18   More attractive color selections will be seen in offices of   96
                      20                        21
19   More attractive color selections will be seen in offices of  108
              22                    23                  24
20   the next decade.  Quite a few of the colors we select for a  120
                            25                26
21   the next decade.  Quite a few of the colors we select for a  132
                    27                    28
22   the next decade.  Quite a few of the colors we select for a  144
        29                   30                      31
23   new office will be those judged to best reflect light.  The  156
                      32                    33
24   new office will be those judged to best reflect light.  The  168
              34                    35                    36
25   new office will be those judged to best reflect light.  The  180
                    37
26   colors can help to diffuse light.                            187
                      38
27   colors can help to diffuse light.                            193
              39                        40
28   colors can help to diffuse light.                            200
     |  1  |  2  |  3  |  4  |  5  |  6  |  7  |  8  |  9  |  10  |  11  |  12    SI 1.38
```

**LESSONS
131/
132**

UNIT 22 FORMATTING BUSINESS FORMS

UNIT GOAL
40/5'/5e

GOALS
- To use quotation marks correctly while typing sentences.
- To type three purchase requisitions and three purchase orders (from unarranged and incomplete copy).

FORMAT
- Single spacing   60-space line   5-space tab and other tabs as needed

LAB 15

QUOTATION MARKS

Type lines 1–4 once, providing the missing quotation marks. Edit your copy as your teacher reads the answers. Then retype lines 1–4 from your edited copy.

```
1   Now, Duane said, we will have accurate costs available.
2   Her so-called crazy idea, we think, is really quite sane.
3   I strongly recommend Dr. Joan Peterson, replied Jeremiah.
4   Send Kevin the exact schedule of each meeting, said Kent.
```

LESSON 33

GOAL
- To use the bell to make line-ending decisions.

FORMAT
- Single spacing   60-space line

KEYBOARDING SKILLS

Type each line twice.

Speed   1 Dick may wish to type the forms with the aid of some codes.
Accuracy 2 My lazy, gray dog curled up very quietly and went to sleep.
Numbers   3 Kay had to try 546 samples before she found any of No. 329.
Symbols   4 He read "How to Type" in Max's August issue of Office News.

PREVIEW PRACTICE

Type each line twice.

Accuracy 5 new jazz music sounds country classical different depending
Speed   6 like tune have fast slow beat show rock mind much tale rich

3-MINUTE TIMINGS

Take two 3-minute timings on lines 7–14. Format: Double spacing, 5-space tab.

```
                1              2              3              4
 7        Which kind of music do you like best?  A jazz tune can      12
              5              6              7              8
 8  have a fast or a slow beat, depending on the mood the tunes       24
          9              10             11             12
 9  are meant to show.  Rock music has a different beat and can       36
          13             14             15             16
10  bring a new set of moods to mind.  Much of folk music has a       48
          17             18             19             20
11  tale of joy or grief as its text.  Country tunes are like a       60
          21             22             23             24
12  folk tune, but they are a blend of other types.  Music that       72
          25             26             27             28
13  is classical has rich tones of quiet or blaring sound.  The       84
          29             30
14  choice is as wide as you wish.                                    90
    |  1  |  2  |  3  |  4  |  5  |  6  |  7  |  8  |  9  | 10  | 11  | 12    SI 1.14
```

RIGHT MARGIN BELL   Workbook 31.

To help make the right margin even, a bell rings when the carriage or carrier approaches the margin. Depending on the machine, the bell may ring as few as 8 or as many as 15 spaces before the margin. (Check *your* machine. How many spaces before the margin does it ring?)

Assume that your machine will ring 8 spaces before the right margin. Assume, too, that you have set your right margin at 85 (80 plus 5 spaces). The bell will ring when you reach 77. When the bell rings, you must decide how best to end the line closest to 80— preferably without dividing words. Here are some typical line-ending decisions:

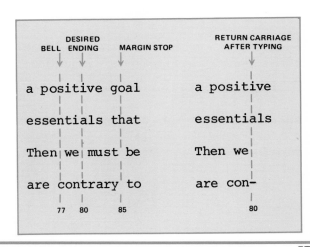

JOB 129-1. LETTER ON BARONIAL STATIONERY
Standard format. Workbook 255–256. Body 66 words.

Ms. Roberta Kile, Office Administration De- 16
partment, Mayville State College, Mayville, 25
ND 58257, Dear Ms. Kile: 31

We are pleased to be able to take part in 41
your survey on reading and writing skills. I 50
have completed your survey and am returning 59
it as you requested in your letter. 66

My colleagues and I had some comments on 75
the issues you raised in your survey, and our 85
reactions appear on the enclosed sheet. 93

We look forward to receiving a copy of the 102
survey results. Yours truly, Frank S. James, 117
Chairperson 120

JOB 129-2. LETTER ON BARONIAL STATIONERY
Standard format. Workbook 255–256. Body 65 words.

Mr. James P. Hill, Manager, Lomax Sales 16
Associates, 20627 Hawthorne Boulevard, 24
South, Torrance, CA 90503, Dear Mr. Hill: 33

Thank you for the catalog showing your line 43
of office supplies. We were indeed interested 52
in looking at the volume of metric supplies 61
your store carries. 65

Next week Ms. Lang from our Long Beach 74
store will be in Torrance to view your line of 84
metric supplies. 87

You will be receiving our fall order by the 97
end of the week. Thank you again for the 105
catalog. Very truly yours, Karen T. Booker, 120
Office Manager 126

LESSON 130

CLINIC

GOALS
- To use quotation marks correctly while typing sentences.
- To type 40/5'/5e.
- To improve your typing speed on 12-second timings and 5-minute timings.

FORMAT
- Single spacing   60-space line   5-space tab and every fifth space thereafter

LAB 15

QUOTATION MARKS

Type lines 1–4 once, providing the missing quotation marks. Edit your copy as your teacher reads the answers. Then retype lines 1–4 from your edited copy.

1 David said, We will obviously need a quiet place to work.
2 The photo is fuzzy because of the poor lens, said Robert.
3 Joe and Vera know the combination of the safe, Will said.
4 Ask Xaveria for help on these projects, Marisa suggested.

12-SECOND TIMINGS

Type lines 5–7 four times, or take four 12-second timings on each line. For each timing, type with no more than one error. Repeat the procedure on lines 8–10.

5 A small tug pushed the liner into the quay and to the pier. 12
6 We would prefer to take a lot of quizzes, not one big exam. 12
7 If you put the sodas in the fridge, they will soon be cold. 12
8 All they want to do is to sit in the shade of the big oaks. 12
9 We had a kit of tools that we could use to fix the engines. 12
10 The two of them sat in the soft sand and soaked up the sun. 12

25   30   35   40   45   50   55   60

MAKING LINE-ENDING DECISIONS BY USING RIGHT MARGIN BELL

¶ means start a new paragraph.

JOB 33-1. INFORMAL NOTE

Note: Do not divide a word at the end of any line. Standard format.

[*Current date*] / Dear [*Use a friend's name*], / How do you like the way this note looks? I'm typing it in my typing class. We are practicing listening for the bell at the end of a line. We must type the note without dividing words. ¶Our teacher says that we will learn how to type reports soon. Then I can type all my papers for my English class. / Until next time, / [*Sign your name*]

JOB 33-2. INFORMAL NOTE

Retype Job 33-1 using a 50-space line. Do not divide words.

JOB 33-3. INFORMAL NOTE

Retype Job 33-1 using a 40-space line. Do not divide words.

LESSON 34

GOALS
- To align typed words on a page.
- To align words on a printed postal card.

FORMAT
- Single spacing   60-space line

KEYBOARDING SKILLS

Type lines 1–4 on page 57 twice each.

PREVIEW PRACTICE

Type each line twice.

Accuracy 5 quite other means nicely change around expanding attractive
Speed 6 page make from just such that they some type both line them

3-MINUTE TIMINGS

Take two 3-minute timings on lines 7–14. Format: Double spacing, 5-space tab.

```
                  1              2            3              4
 7        To format words on a page means to make them look just    12
              5            6            7            8
 8  as attractive as you can.  It also means that you plan them     24
             9            10           11           12
 9  in such a way that they are easily read.  One way to change     36
              13           14           15           16
10  a format of a page is to type some parts in all caps and to     48
              17           18           19           20
11  type other parts in both caps and lowercase.  Expanding the     60
              21           22           23           24
12  letters in a line or two makes them stand out from the maze     72
             25           26           27           28
13  of words quite nicely.  The use of a box around word groups     84
              29           30
14  makes it simple to read a page.                                 90
    |  1  |  2  |  3  |  4  |  5  |  6  |  7  |  8  |  9  |  10  |  11  |  12    SI 1.16
```

FORMATTING POSTAL CARD MESSAGES

Workbook 32.

Postal cards are often used to send very short impersonal messages. To format a postal card:

1. Set margins for a 45-space line.
2. Type the date on line 3, beginning at the center.
3. Type the salutation on line 5.
4. Begin the message on line 7.
5. Single-space paragraphs; double-space between paragraphs.
6. Type the sender's name a double space below the message, at the center.
7. Begin all lines except date and sender's name at the left margin.

1- AND 5-MINUTE TIMINGS

Take two 1-minute timings on each paragraph. Then take one 5-minute timing on the entire selection. Use single spacing for the 1-minute timings and double spacing for the 5-minute timing.

```
 5       Animals are capable of defending themselves in various   12
 6    ways.  Defense to some means to run or fly away, to some it   24
 7    means to hide, to some it means to play dead, and to others   36
 8    it means to fight.                                             40

 9       The rabbits are very quick and can often run away from    12
10    their enemies.  They are also quite good at making a zigzag   24
11    jump as they bound off.  Birds, of course, will escape most   36
12    enemies by flight.                                             40

13       Some animals are very good at hiding as a means of de-    12
14    fense.  Some are hidden by their colors; others can use the   24
15    shape of their body to hide.  For example, a tiger can hide   36
16    well in the shadows.                                           40

17       An "expert" at playing dead, of course, is an opossum.    12
18    When it is threatened, the opossum closes its eyes and lets   24
19    its body go limp.  Even when it's bitten, it will remain in   36
20    this quiet position.                                           40

21       Many animals choose to fight as a defense.  Members of    12
22    the deer family might bite, kick, or use their antlers when   24
23    defending themselves.  Large members of the cat family will   36
24    use their sharp claws.                                         40
      |  1  |  2  |  3  |  4  |  5  |  6  |  7  |  8  |  9  | 10 | 11 | 12   SI 1.37
```

FORMATTING LETTERS ON BARONIAL AND MONARCH STATIONERY

Workbook 253–254.

Some firms have their short letters typed on either baronial stationery (5½″ by 8½″—metric A5: 148 by 210 mm) or monarch stationery (7¼″ by 10½″—about 181 by 263 mm). The more commonly used is baronial.

1. To format letters on baronial stationery:
   a. Date: line 12.
   b. Inside address: line 16 (↓4).
   c. Line length: 40P/50E.
2. To format letters on monarch stationery:
   a. Date: line 14.
   b. Inside address: line 19 (↓5).
   c. Line length: 40P/50E or 50P/60E.

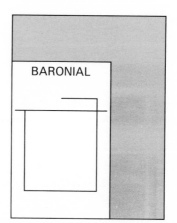
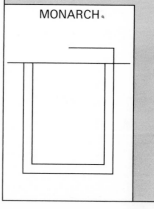

Form Messages. Sometimes postal cards are used to send out standardized "form" messages. A reminder for a dental appointment (like the one shown below) is an example. When you type a form message, (1) do not fill in the date, (2) type only the word *Dear,* and (3) leave space for any information to be filled in later.

JOB 34-1. POSTAL CARD FORM MESSAGES

Prepare four form messages on postal cards. Do not type the words shown in color. Use Workbook 33. Save your work for use in Job 34-2.

```
                                                                1
                                                                2
                          (Current Date)                        3
Line 3                                                          4
                                                                5
Line 5    Dear (Put in name of client)                          6
                                                                7
Line 7    Our records show that your last dental checkup        8
          was (Fill in date of last checkup).                   9
                                                               10
          It is now time to schedule another checkup.          11
          Call us at 555-2936 to make an appointment.          12
                                                               13
                    Ann Tschanz, D.D.S.                        14
                                                               15
                                                               16
                                                               17
                                                               18
                                                               19
                                                               20
                                                               21
```

ALIGNING

1. Locate exactly the printing point between the aligning scales.

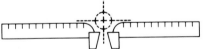

2. Insert paper. Shift it until the end of the printing is exactly in the printing point.

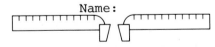

3. Strike the space bar three times. Type the insertion.

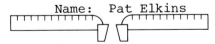

Practice 1. At four different places on a sheet of paper, type the printed guide words illustrated here. Use double spacing. Remove the paper, insert it, then fill in the requested data—yours, not the data used in the illustration.

Practice 2. Repeat Practice 1 on the other side of the paper.

```
 Date: October 3, 19--
 Name: Pat Elkins
Grade: 10
  Age: 16
 City: Topeka
State: Kansas
```

JOB 34-2. FILL-IN POSTAL CARD MESSAGES

Send cards to the people listed at the right using the cards you prepared in Job 34-1. Be sure to align the fill-ins. Addresses do not have to be typed because printed labels will be used.

Kathleen Davis—last checkup June 13
Oliver Treadway—last checkup June 15
Margaret Tolley—last checkup May 3
Jose Martino—last checkup May 15

JOB 127/8-4. LETTER WITH POSTSCRIPT AND *BCC* NOTATION

Standard format. Make corrections in spelling, grammar, and punctuation, and provide other editing revisions as you type. Workbook 251–252. Body 106 words (plus 20 words for subject line).

Mr. Ted Moore, Shield Products Inc., 582 College (Ave)., Des Moines, IA 5934(l), Subject: Dear Mr. Moore: Slides for Equipment Training

This year at Central ^state^ College we are expanding our information procesing program.

No ¶ Although we do not have the funds to purchase a large volume of word procesing equipment, we have been able to secure enough funds to provide our students with two <u>crt</u>'s for the com/ing year.

To acquaint our students with machines from other manufacturers, we would like to develop a slide/tape program for there use. May we have permi/sion to tour your word processing department for the pur-pose of developeing a portion of this /slide/ /tape /program?

I would like to call you at 10 A.M. on Friday to discus our visit. Yours truly, Jean R. Hall, Business Teacher, Ps: I will bring some sample slides with me so that you can see how we are going to use theese materials.

LESSON 129

GOALS
- To identify when quotation marks are used while typing sentences.
- To type at least 40/5'/5e.
- To format letters on baronial and monarch stationery.

FORMAT
- Single spacing   60-space line   5-space tab

LAB 15

Type lines 1–4 once. Then repeat lines 1–4 or take a series of 1-minute timings.

QUOTATION MARKS

1 June Mendez said, "Request more information on these forms." 12
2 Label this item "Caution" so that it gets extraspecial care. 12
3 "The issue," answered Vonda, "is whether you should cancel." 12
4 Verna insisted, "The best glue on the market is Stick-Glue." 12

| 1 | 2 | 3 | 4 | 5 | 6 | 7 | 8 | 9 | 10 | 11 | 12

LESSON 35

GOALS
- To type words on ruled lines.
- To type words on a lined, fill-in postal card.

FORMAT
- Single spacing   60-space line   5-space tab

KEYBOARDING SKILLS

Type each line twice.

Speed
Accuracy
Numbers
Symbols

1 Alene's neighbor owns six or eight antique autos right now.
2 Five lizards very quickly jumped into the box on the table.
3 we 23 up 70 to 59 or 94 it 85 yi 68 et 35 op 90 ur 74 re 43
4 File cards (unlined) will be purchased 100 @ 59¢ at school.

PREVIEW PRACTICE

Type each line twice.

Accuracy
Speed

5 who senior others flowers citizen service students projects
6 their time work with some done take read like and the to by

3-MINUTE TIMINGS

Take two 3-minute timings on lines 7–14. Format: Double spacing, 5-space tab.

```
                  1              2              3              4
7       Many students give hours of their time to work for the      12
              5              6              7              8
8   service projects in their towns.  Some jobs are done with a      24
                 9             10             11             12
9   group, while some are not.  Students work with kids at some      36
                13             14             15             16
10  parks, and they work with kids who are ill.  They take food      48
                17             18             19             20
11  to senior citizens and read to those who are blind.  Bright     60
              21             22             23             24
12  flowers and green trees are planted, and trash is picked up      72
              25             26             27             28
13  by some students.  These nice young people like helping out     84
              29             30
14  others in many different ways.                                   90
    |  1  |  2  |  3  |  4  |  5  |  6  |  7  |  8  |  9  | 10  | 11  | 12    SI 1.20
```

TYPING ON RULED LINES

1. Preliminary step: On a blank sheet, type your name and underscore it. Note (a) exactly where the underscore touches or almost touches the aligning scale and (b) exactly how much room is between the letters and line.

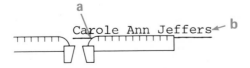

2. Now insert the paper with the ruled lines, and adjust it so that one of the ruled lines is in the position of an underscore.
The ruled line should look like this:

3. Type what is to be on the line.

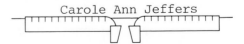

Practice: At various places and angles on a page, type underscore lines 30 spaces long. Remove the paper. Reinsert it. Type your name on each line.

Manufacturer	Model	Storage
W. P. Systems	J43	Disk
Word Data Inc.	VIP	Diskette
Speed Terminal	PAC-II	Tape
First Typing	215	Card

Please call me if you would like to use one of the above machines while your Model 200 is being repaired. Very truly yours, Allen H. Jacobs, Manager

PS: If your Model 200 is not repaired by the 6th, you may keep the machine you loaned until the Model 200 has been returned.

JOB 127/8-3. LETTER WITH *BCC* NOTATION

Block format. Workbook 249–250. Body 119 words (plus 20 words for subject line).

Dr. R. L. Stern, Chairperson, Business Education, **Department** Bronx   21

City College, 738 White Plains Road, Bronx, NY 10473, Dear Dr.   36

Stern: Subject: Keyboard Training   43

We would like you to share the enclosed brochures with your   56

students who might be interested in a business career. Our ~~key~~   68

~~board~~ training program is open to those who have a ~~special~~ desire   80

to work in the area of word processing.   88

We will provide key board training on four of the **most** popular text-   103

editing machines. When the training has been completed, the   115

graduates will **be assigned to an office where they will** work as interns for at least eight weeks.   135

This Training Employment Program has proven to be a very   147

popular one, as we have ~~already~~ placed over 250 trainees in firms   159

throughout the state in the past ③ years. We hope your students   173

will be added to ~~this~~ **our** list too. Sincerely, Claire V. Speel,   189

Training Director, bcc: Jayne Ross   198

FORMATTING FILL-INS ON RULED LINES

Because postal card messages are often used as reply cards, they may have ruled lines to show where information should be filled in. Short fill-ins are usually centered:

1. Insert and adjust the card so that the ruled line is in the position of the underscore.
2. Position the printing point at the beginning of the ruled line.
3. Space across the line, counting the spaces.
4. Then count the spaces of the copy to be typed on the line.

5. Subtract the spaces to be typed (Step 4) from the spaces available (Step 3).
6. Divide the difference by 2; drop any fraction. Indent that number of spaces to reach the starting point (for the fill-in).

Long fill-ins may follow a colon or be typed from margin to margin:

1. Begin two spaces after a colon. **or:**
2. Set your left margin at the beginning of the rule and your right margin at the end of the rule. Type from margin to margin; do not type beyond the edges of the ruled line.

JOB 35-1. RULED FILL-INS ON REPLY CARDS

Use the information below to complete the reply cards. Standard format. Workbook 35.

1. *Coach,* John Lantz, *Sport,* football, *Players,* Bill Jones, Ed Lukins, Joe Eads, Paul Johns, Ted Ley.
2. *Coach,* Mary Allen, *Sport,* volleyball, *Players,* Anne Reed, Kathy Nickel, Pam Rizzo, Lori Robins, Tammy Colton.
3. *Coach,* Chris Spangs, *Sport,* tennis, *Players,* Don Tia, Patty Kipp, Fred Vines, Willie Parks, Julie Scheper.
4. *Coach,* Fred Caton, *Sport,* baseball, *Players,* Gloria Gimbrone, Kelly Maxton, Pam Avery, Jeff Meyer, David Paxton.

```
Reservations for the January 15 Annual Sports
Banquet are now being taken.  If you plan to
attend, please list the names of the members
of your group and return the card with $5.50
for each person.  Deadline:  December 1, 19--

Name of coach_____Joe Witzman_____

Sport_____Cross country_____

Members of group:  Rick Sizemore, Jason

Underleider, Jayne Bishop, Sally Jones,

Bernie Beyler
```

LESSON 36

REVIEW

GOALS
- To type 30/3'/5e.
- To review formatting and operating techniques used for typewriting.
- To demonstrate knowledge of basic terminology and rules for using the typewriter.

FORMAT
- Single spacing 60-space line 5-space tab

PREVIEW PRACTICE

Type each line twice as a preview to the 3-minute timing on page 62.

Accuracy 1 quite errors adjust through learned symbols numbers letters

Speed 2 each have type with page your make soon will that well book

JOB 127/8-1. LETTER WITH SUBJECT LINE, POSTSCRIPT, AND *BCC* NOTATION

Block format (see page 173). Workbook 245–246. Body 125 words (plus 20 words for subject line).

Ms. Rose T. Sands, Safety Life Insurance Company, 227 Chama Road, Clovis, NM 88101, Dear Ms. Sands:, Subject: New Product Line for CRT

 As a user of our word processing equipment for the past ten years, we know you will be quite interested in the enclosed brochures on our new line of products.

 Note on the brochure marked "Sample" that you will now be able to input data 20 percent faster on our new text-editing machines be-cause we increased our line length, and we changed our format design for letters. Also note on page 5 of the same brochure that the visual display has been enhanced by providing an improved, softer contrast between print and background image.

 Mr. James Lessard, our sales rep in Sante Fe, will be calling you by the end of next week to set up an appointment for demonstrating the new Editor 500. Sincerely yours, John W. Grace, Branch Manager, PS: Because of the immaculate condition of your 400-S, we will give you a fabulous deal on trade-in. bcc: T. R. Jordan

17	106
25	115
36	124
37	133
47	143
56	146
65	156
70	165
80	174
89	187
97	199
	207
	218
	220

FORMATTING TABLES WITHIN LETTERS

When a table or display is typed in a letter or memo, follow these guidelines:

1. Precede and follow the table with at least 1 blank line.
2. Center the table within the margins and indent at least 5 spaces on each side. If the table is too wide, select intercolumnar spaces that will limit the table width to preserve the indention.
3. Single-space the body of the table.

Note: Add 20 words to the body count for the display.

JOB 127/8-2. LETTER WITH A TABLE

Block format. Workbook 247–248. Body 77 words.

Mrs. June R. Tijerina / Claims Department / Golden Insurance Company / 18416 Market Street / San Francisco, CA 94102 / Dear Mrs. Tijerina: /

 Thank you for your call on Friday, June 25, requesting the loan of a Model 250 while your machine is in our shop for repairs. We do not have a Model 250 available at this time, but you may want to consider using one of the machines described in the table below. We currently have these machines in the shop, and you can use one of them at no charge while your Model 200 is being repaired.

(Continued on next page)

3-MINUTE TIMINGS

Take two 3-minute timings on lines 3–10. Format: Double spacing.

```
                  1              2              3            4
 3       You have almost completed the first level of the book.      12
        5              6              7          8
 4   You have learned how to type letters, numbers, and symbols.      24
        9              10             11         12
 5   With these, you have learned to format words on a page, and      36
        13             14             15         16
 6   you have learned how to adjust your machine and correct any      48
        17             18             19         20
 7   errors that you make.  The skill with which you type is now      60
        21             22             23         24
 8   growing with each day.  Soon you will learn to compose your      72
        25             26             27         28
 9   own words as you type.  You will zip through a page and fix      84
        29             30
10   errors quite well in seconds.                                    90
     |  1  |  2  |  3  |  4  |  5  |  6  |  7  |  8  |  9  |  10 |  11 |  12    SI 1.20
```

TECHNICAL QUESTIONS

Type one- or two-word answers to the following 15 questions.

1. If you type 60 words in 2 minutes, what is your speed for 1 minute?

2. If you type 15 words in ½ minute, what is your speed for 1 minute?

3. How many times do you strike the hyphen key to make a dash?

4. How many spaces follow a period at the end of a sentence?

5. How many spaces follow a period in the initials of a person's name?

6. How many blank lines separate single-spaced paragraphs?

7. What does the term *keyboarding* mean?

8. How many times do you backspace to center a line with 15 strokes?

9. How many spaces are there between letters when a title is spread centered?

10. To center a 15-line, single-spaced display on a half page, on what line would you begin?

11. An all-cap title is separated from the body of an item by how many blank lines?

12. If a subtitle follows an all-cap title, the two are separated by how many blank lines?

13. How many spaces follow a period in an enumeration?

14. What does the term *formatting* mean?

15. Most typewriters have how many vertical lines to an inch?

JOB 36-1. ENUMERATION
Standard format.

Participating 4-H Clubs
For the Year 19--
1. Bell Brook
2. Camden
3. Clearcreek Local
4. Edgarsville
5. Farmington
6. Mohawk Valley
7. Seven Mile
8. Spring Valley

JOB 36-2. INFORMAL NOTE
Standard format.

(Date)
Dear Sally and Joe
Our 4-H Club judging will take place the last Friday in July at the Allen County Fairgrounds.
We would like to have you come to see our projects. Ann has an especially well-fed steer, and I am going to compete in the advanced bake-off.
See you at the fair!
Ed

LESSONS 127/128

GOALS
- To recognize when quotation marks are used while typing sentences.
- To type business letters with three special parts: *bcc* notation, subject line, and postscript.
- To format a table within a letter.

FORMAT
- Single spacing   60-space line   5-space tab and as needed

LAB 15

QUOTATION MARKS

Type lines 1–4 once. Then repeat lines 1–4 or take a series of 1-minute timings.

```
 1  Gus said, "Send requisitions to Ms. Camp for her approval."   12
 2  Mark these packages "Fragile," Jo; "they're very delicate."   12
 3  "About two dozen boxes were damaged in the fire yesterday."    12
 4  "Please ask Laura for a copy of the June inventory report."    12
    |  1  |  2  |  3  |  4  |  5  |  6  |  7  |  8  |  9  |  10  |  11  |  12
```

Use quotation marks around the *exact* words of a speaker or writer. Do not use quotations for *restatements* of someone's exact words. Also use quotation marks around words that need special emphasis, such as words following *so-called* and *marked*. **Note:** Always place commas and periods before the second quotation mark when they are used.

"The contract," said Mrs. Berry, "will help us to hold down costs for the next few years." (Exact words.)

This so-called "inexpensive" product could cost us a fortune! (Special emphasis.)

5-MINUTE TIMINGS

Take a 5-minute timing on lines 5–19. Type six times each word on which you made an error, hesitated, or stopped during the 5-minute timing. Then take a 5-minute timing to see how much your skill has improved.

```
 5    Autumn in the "northlands" is very exciting.  You jump up in the    14
 6  early morning; walk out under a clear, azure blue sky; and notice a   28
 7  strong chill in the air.  The leaves have lost their brilliant green.  It   42
 8  appears that they have been tinted by a so-called "passerby."  However,   57
 9  during the late night hours a frost has painted the green to hues of   71
10  brown, yellow, red, and orange.  It is really a breathtaking panorama   85
11  in technicolor.  The leaves barely move in the quietly persistent   98
12  breeze.  Then, suddenly, a brisk puff lifts them from the limbs and   112
13  carries them gently like feathers to the ground below.  You watch as   126
14  legions of leaves jump free and float to the earth, covering it like a   140
15  quilted blanket that looks much like moss.   148
16    As you glance down at the grass, you can no longer see any large   162
17  droplets of dew like those that had clung to each blade, bright in the   176
18  early morning summer sun.  Those drops of dew have been "crystal-   189
19  lized."  Now their appearance possibly may deceive you.   200
    |  1  |  2  |  3  |  4  |  5  |  6  |  7  |  8  |  9  |  10  |  11  |  12  |  13  |  14   SI 1.34
```

JOB 36-3. DISPLAY
Format: You decide. Use a full sheet of paper.

Program for Judging
4-H Club Projects
Hereford steers at 9:00
Angus steers at 9:30
Shorthorn steers at 10:00
Open class at 10:30
Showmanship at 11:00
Lunch break
Beginner's bake-off at 1:00
Advanced bake-off at 2:00
Beginning sewing projects at 3:00
Complete outfit projects at 3:30
Booth displays at 4:00

JOB 36-4. POSTAL CARD MESSAGE WITH LINED FILL-INS
Type the card shown below. Type a second card for Ann Kelly, who is participating in the Angus steer competition. She has been in 4-H for 6 years and is 17 years old. She belongs to the same club as Ed does, and she has the same advisers. Standard format. Workbook 37.

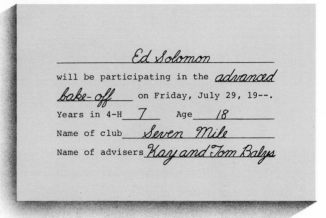

        Ed Solomon
will be participating in the advanced
bake-off   on Friday, July 29, 19--.
Years in 4-H 7   Age   18
Name of club   Seven Mile
Name of advisers Kay and Tom Balys

LESSON 37

COMPETENCY CHECK

GOALS
- To type 30/3'/5e.
- To demonstrate competency in basic operating techniques of the typewriter.
- To demonstrate competency in basic formatting procedures on the typewriter.

FORMAT
- Single spacing   60-space line   5-space tab

PREVIEW PRACTICE

Accuracy
Speed

Type each line twice as a preview to the 3-minute timing below.

1 to school active realize express campaign question politics
2 part they read will know what hand type more want join that

3-MINUTE TIMINGS

Take two 3-minute timings on lines 3–10. Format: Double spacing, 5-space tab.

```
                    1              2              3              4
3       High school students can be an active part of politics   12
4   if they choose.  They can keep up with the news for the day   24
5   and know what issues are at hand.  They can type letters to   36
6   be put in papers to question and express points of view for   48
7   the public to read.  If they choose to be more active, then   60
8   they may want to join a campaign team and work for a person   72
9   who seeks an office.  All students realize that their votes   84
10  will also be the way to speak.                               90
    |  1  |  2  |  3  |  4  |  5  |  6  |  7  |  8  |  9  |  10  |  11  |  12    SI 1.20
```

JOB 125/6-4. LETTER

Retype Job 125/6-3, replacing the second paragraph with the material below. Standard format with indented paragraphs. Workbook 239–240. Body 99 words.

We think you will be *quite* interested in our ~~complete~~ *all new* line of office templates and office layout grids. *In for your use.* We have all the latest supplies needed by the office managers who wish to re/design their offices by using the ~~modern~~ open ~~office~~ plans.

JOB 125/6-5. UNEDITED, UNARRANGED LETTER

Standard format. Make corrections in spelling, grammar, and punctuation as you type. Workbook 241–242. Body 126 words (plus 20 for attention line).

Metro Towers, 401 Beach Street, Fort Worth, TX 76111, Atention: Manager, Ladies and Gentlemen:

Fleet Window Cleaning are one of the newest high rise window cleaning company's in the Fort Worth area and we would like to tell you about our grand opening special. Just give us a few moments of your time to help you become aware of our fine service.

We will wash any and every window in your bilding, to include storm and screan windows. We have rates for weekly monthly or yearly contracts and will make bids on jobs you wish did on short notice. We are fully insured and give free estimites on any job requested this month.

Clean windows reflect your concern for good public relations. Wo'nt you let Fleet help you improve your image. Call us today and make arangements for our free estimate. Sincerly yours, Anne W. Shane, Managre, cc: Ken Wells and Chris Armstrong

JOB 125/6-6. UNEDITED, UNARRANGED LETTER

Standard format with indented paragraphs. Make corrections in spelling and punctuation, and provide other editing revisions as you type. Workbook 243–244. Body 147 words (plus 20 words for attention line).

Key Products Inc., 124 Second Street, Cleveland, OH 44131, Atention Purchasing Manager, *Ladies and* Gentleman:

In your may ten letter you asked that we arrange a time that we both could get together to discus the purchase of new dry copy machines and supplies for your firm. As I will be in Cleveland, ~~Ohio~~, next week Tusday miht be the best *time* for our meeting. Do you think it ~~might~~ *would* be a good idea to start ~~right~~ at 8 A.M. so that we coud discuss not only the purchase of new machines but also the other options of machine aquisition that you might like to consider. You might like to trade *in* your ~~old~~ machines or rent some ᶠof our new machines on a trial basis—with an option to buy the machines of course!

I will call you tomorow afternoon at 4:00 P.M. to finalize our plans for the meeting. I look forward to working with you and to showing you all our new dry copy machines. yours very truly, Edward *a.* Vincent, Sales Representative [*Send copies to Sally Bolton, Mark Kaiser, and Theresa Santos.*]

You have just taken a job as a faculty assistant during your study hall. You are working for Jane Bowman, who is head of the Speech Department at Clover Hill High School. She is getting ready for a regional speech tournament to be held at Clover Hill. Your job is to help her with all of the paperwork for the tournament.

JOB 37-1. ENUMERATION

Prepare a list of the participating schools that will be involved in the tournament. Put them in alphabetic order. Standard format.

Participating Schools
Speech Tournament
December 23, 19--
1. *Wayne Township High School*
2. *Martinsburg High School*
3. *Clover Hill High School*
4. *Yorktown Career Center*
5. *Crockett High School*
6. *Addams High School*
7. *St. Joseph's High School*
8. *Lee Joint Vocational School*

JOB 37-2. DISPLAY

Format: You decide (see page 39).

PROGRAM
Fifth Annual
Regional Speech Tournament
Clover Hill High School
Saturday, December 23, 19--
Extemp I, 9:00, Room 102
Extemp II, 9:00, Room 104
Prepared Speech I, 10:30, Room 106
Prepared Speech II, 10:30, Room 108
Lunch, 12:00, West Commons
Debate I, 1:00, Room 102
Debate II, 1:00, Room 104
Closing Assembly, 2:30, Auditorium

JOB 37-3. INFORMAL NOTE

Standard format.

(Date)
Dear Mr. Salvato:
Thank you for approving the schedule for the regional speech tournament at Clover Hill High School. It is an honor for us to host the tournament, and your support of it will make it the best tournament ever. Lisa Comerchero will contact you next week to explain the closing assembly. We appreciate your volunteering to make the opening introductions.

[Leave room for Ms. Bowman to sign her name.]

JOB 37-4. POSTAL CARD MESSAGE WITH RULED FILL-INS

Complete one postal card as shown below. Then complete one card for each of the other seven schools listed in Job 37-1; for these cards, fill in only the school name, not the sponsor name or the number of participants. Standard format. Workbook 39, 41.

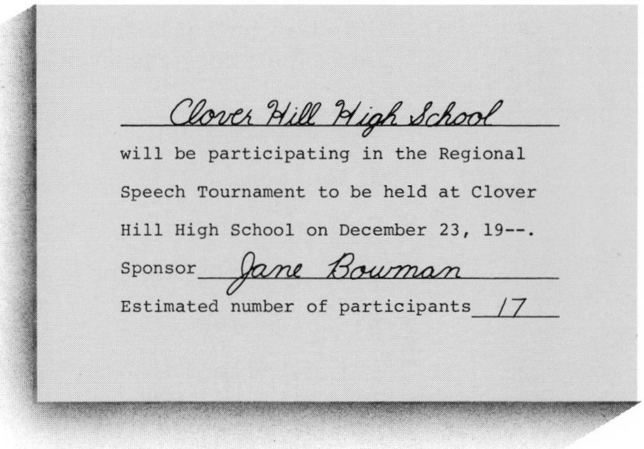

Clover Hill High School
will be participating in the Regional
Speech Tournament to be held at Clover
Hill High School on December 23, 19--.
Sponsor *Jane Bowman*
Estimated number of participants *17*

JOB 125/6-2. LETTER

Standard format with indented paragraphs. Workbook 235–236. Body 84 words (plus 20 words for attention line).

```
Dahl Dairy Products, 1145 Rock Street        16
Rockford, IL 61101, Attention:  Man-         24
ager, Ladies and Gentlemen:                  30

        This morning we received your        38
letter awarding us the bid for design-       46
ing an office layout for your new            53
branch store in DeKalb. We are indeed        60
pleased that we were chosen to               67
work on this important project.              73
We have enclosed three designs               81
```

```
that incorporate an open office              88
concept such as the one we                   93
looked at in your office last week.  I      101
will call next week to confirm the          108
desired layout.                             111

        We look forward to working with     120
you in designing the offices                126
of the DeKalb branch. Yours                 134
very truly, Dwight R. Straight,             146
President cc: Ms. Fontaine and Mr. Parks    158
```

FORMATTING ENUMERATIONS IN LETTERS

When typing enumerations in a letter, use the following guidelines: (1) To display the enumeration, indent it 5 spaces from both margins. (2) Precede and follow each enumerated item with 1 blank line. (3) Single-space each turnover line. (4) Indent each turnover line 4 spaces. Add 20 words to the body count for the display.

JOB 125/6-3. LETTER

Standard format with indented paragraphs. Workbook 237–238. Body 102 words (plus 20 words for attention line).

```
L&S Office Supplies, 13980 Peach Grove, Van Nuys, CA 91423,            20
Attention:  Office Manager, Ladies and Gentlemen:                     32
                very
¶ We are  pleased to send you a copy of the new catalog that shows our  48
                          #            complete
line of office supplies.  In it you will find our line of products.    62
                                                    metric
¶ We think you will be interested in our following line of supplies:   78
    1.    A4 File Folders  These folders will hold both standard-size   89
                                    to
                -size
          and legal paper.                                             94
    2.    A3 to A8 Metric Paper for small poster boards and name tags. 109
    3.    C6/7 and DL envelopes (small and large envelopes).           121
  ¶ We look forward to receiving your order from our catalog  We in-    132
vite you to visit our Lane Street Store and view our complete line    145
                                        P.
of office supplies.  Yours truly, James Mason, Manager                162
```

LEVEL 2

FORMATTING FOR PERSONAL USE

Take a 5-minute timing on lines 5–22. Type six times each word on which you made an error, hesitated, or stopped during the 5-minute timing. Then take a 5-minute timing to see how much your skill has improved.

```
                      1                              2
 5      The office of the future is going to see quite a large   12
                 3                         4
 6      The office of the future is going to see quite a large   24
          5                  6                      7
 7      The office of the future is going to see quite a large   36
                          8                    9
 8   change from today's office.   One of the amazing things that   48
              10                      11                12
 9   change from today's office.   One of the amazing things that   60
                          13                   14
10   change from today's office.   One of the amazing things that   72
                  15                    16
11   will happen is that we may no longer see offices with fixed   84
        17                    18                      19
12   will happen is that we may no longer see offices with fixed   96
                     20                    21
13   will happen is that we may no longer see offices with fixed   108
               22                  23                      24
14   walls.   Instead, movable walls might be used so that a firm   120
                        25                    26
15   walls.   Instead, movable walls might be used so that a firm   132
                   27                    28
16   walls.   Instead, movable walls might be used so that a firm   144
          29                    30                      31
17   will be able to change the office layout when a new project   156
                        32                    33
18   will be able to change the office layout when a new project   168
               34                    35                      36
19   will be able to change the office layout when a new project   180
                        37
20   team requires more room to work.                            186
                   38
21   team requires more room to work.                            193
               39                  40
22   team requires more room to work.                            200
      |  1  |  2  |  3  |  4  |  5  |  6  |  7  |  8  |  9  |  10 |  11 |  12   SI 1.32
```

In this unit, you will have to read the letters to see if you should add an enclosure notation. You will also have to remember to use the current date and your initials—no reminders are provided.

JOB 125/6-1. LETTER

Standard format (see page 169). Workbook 233–234. Body 98 words (plus 20 words for attention line).

Elementary Education Department, Mayville State College, Mayville, ND 58257, Attention Chairperson, Ladies and Gentlemen:

The enclosed survey is being sent to all schools in the state to find out how you teach reading and writing skills in the lower level courses.

In addition to your answers to each of the questions on page 1 and page 2 of our survey, we would welcome your comments to the issues we have listed on page 3. If necessary, please feel free to use additional sheets for your comments. We look forward to receiving your answers to our survey. A copy of the results of our survey will be mailed to you in a few weeks. Yours truly, Blanche Kile, Researcher, cc: Chris Van Vleit

School reports, letters, tables, various forms—these are some of the many messages that you will need to type for personal use. To prepare such messages effectively, you must improve your ability to keyboard by touch with speed and accuracy on the alphabet, number, and symbol keys, and you must learn the basics of formatting such messages.

In Level 2, "Formatting for Personal Use," you will:

1. Demonstrate keyboarding accuracy and speed on straight copy with a goal of 35 words a minute or more for 3 minutes with no more than 5 errors.

2. Demonstrate improved skill in the control of the nonprinting parts of the typewriter.

3. Detect, mark with proofreaders' marks, and correct errors in typewritten copy.

4. Use a typewriter to format reports, letters, tables, and forms for personal use.

5. Apply rules for correct use of word division, capitalization, numbers, and punctuation in communications.

LESSON 38

UNIT 7 PREPARING FOR PRODUCTION TYPING   UNIT GOAL 32/3'/5e

GOAL
- To apply some rules of word division.

FORMAT
- Single spacing   60-space line   5-space tab

KEYBOARDING SKILLS

Type lines 1–4 once. Then do what line 5 tells you to do as you type it. Repeat lines 1–4, or take a series of 1-minute timings.

Speed	1	If they handle the work right, the eight may make a profit.	12
Accuracy	2	Our packing the dozen boxes for fresh jam was quite lively.	12
Numbers	3	We counted 38, 47, and 56; they counted 10, 29, 38, and 47.	12
Symbols	4	Mark 38¢, 49¢, and 50¢ after each item shown with a # sign.	12
Technique	5	Return the carriage or carrier after each word as you type.	

| 1 | 2 | 3 | 4 | 5 | 6 | 7 | 8 | 9 | 10 | 11 | 12

1- AND 3-MINUTE TIMINGS

Take two 1-minute timings on each paragraph. Then take one 3-minute timing on the entire selection. Use single spacing for the 1-minute timings and double spacing for the 3-minute timing.

6   Have you ever gone to a flea market? At flea markets,   12
7 people try to sell their crafts, junk items, or things they   24
8 no longer can keep or store in an attic.   32

9   Often it happens that one person can use any old thing   12
10 that someone else seems most anxious to get rid of. Such a   24
11 sale makes both buyers and sellers glad.   32

12   Sometimes it amazes people to find that what they hate   12
13 so much, others like. A vase you do not like in your house   24
14 may be quite right in a neighbor's home.   32

| 1 | 2 | 3 | 4 | 5 | 6 | 7 | 8 | 9 | 10 | 11 | 12   SI 1.23

PRACTICE

Type lines 11–36 twice each. Then retype any lines featuring letters you made errors on in the Pretest. Use single spacing.

A	11	acreage	adverse	aboard	acquit	alias	arena	ajar	auto	art	ask
B	12	boulder	bouquet	beware	broken	baker	bumpy	busy	bias	ban	bet
C	13	chamber	caption	candid	cavern	cynic	comet	calm	coat	cat	cry
D	14	deposit	diagram	domain	during	drive	drift	dust	doze	dim	dry
E	15	elegant	eternal	emerge	emblem	elect	enter	even	easy	elk	eye
F	16	feather	forgive	fiscal	fabric	fling	field	fuse	form	fix	for
G	17	glisten	gainful	gasket	govern	gravy	going	goat	gulf	gun	gym
H	18	housing	harvest	health	height	heart	haste	hint	hand	ham	hem
I	19	iceberg	impulse	impede	insect	infer	inept	idle	into	ire	imp
J	20	journal	justice	joyful	jungle	judge	juice	join	joke	jet	jam
K	21	kitchen	keynote	kidney	kindle	knife	knack	kind	kite	kin	kit
L	22	license	lecture	legion	locker	logic	lemon	late	lawn	lax	lye
M	23	monthly	morning	method	mishap	might	match	mock	mink	mid	mow
N	24	neither	neglect	napkin	nation	noted	noisy	nail	next	nag	now
O	25	outlast	outgrow	origin	oxygen	ocean	onion	oath	once	oat	oak
P	26	playful	prairie	pencil	prefer	pride	poise	paid	past	par	pet
Q	27	quintet	quarrel	quarry	quiver	quote	quilt	quip	quid	quo	qt.
R	28	reflect	reptile	result	remark	range	ridge	rack	rail	rye	rig
S	29	soldier	someone	sample	shower	spoke	split	sway	salt	sew	sap
T	30	thirsty	tactful	trance	threat	tease	think	tray	town	tax	tar
U	31	unknown	upright	useful	urgent	urban	upset	ugly	undo	urn	use
V	32	voucher	vicious	volume	versus	vault	vague	vice	vest	vow	via
W	33	whoever	wrinkle	within	winter	wrist	wound	went	wild	wed	web
X	34	exploit	relaxed	expect	expand	excel	exile	next	axle	six	lax
Y	35	yardage	yawning	yearly	yellow	yucca	yummy	year	yawn	yam	yet
Z	36	zippers	zealous	zigzag	zither	zippy	zebra	zing	zest	zoo	zap

POSTTEST

Repeat the Pretest on page 208 to see how much your skill has improved.

LESSONS 125/126

UNIT 21 FORMATTING LETTERS

UNIT GOAL
40/5'/5e

GOALS
- To use question marks correctly while typing sentences.
- To type business letters with two special parts: a *cc* notation and an attention line.
- To format enumerations in letters.

FORMAT
- Single spacing   60-space line   5-space tab

LAB 14

QUESTION MARKS

Workbook 231–232.

Type lines 1–4 once, providing the missing question marks. Edit your copy as your teacher reads the answers. Then retype lines 1–4 from your edited copy.

1 When will Dr. Zukov and Mr. Kim arrive at the airport, Jim.
2 Does Sean have an exact transcript of the press conference.
3 Will you be able to carry all those boxes with you, George.
4 How many questions were asked at the end of Bill's meeting.

RULES OF WORD DIVISION

When your typewriter bell rings, you must often decide whether you have space to complete a word or whether you should divide it. To divide words, follow the rules given below; other rules will be given in Lesson 39.

1. Divide only between syllables. If you are not sure where a syllable ends, use a dictionary. Never guess—some words are tricky.

   Examples: syl-la-ble   prod-uct   chil-dren   pro-ject (v.)   proj-ect (n.)

2. Do not divide:

   a. A word pronounced as one syllable: *shipped, strength, tire.*
   b. A word of 5 or fewer letters: *about, into.*
   c. Any contraction: *couldn't, can't, o'clock.*
   d. Any abbreviation: *dept., UNICEF, a.m.*

3. Leave a syllable of at least 2 letters on the upper line.

   Line 1: to-   ab-   around   **not** a-
   Line 2: gether   solute   round

4. Carry to the next line a syllable of at least 3 letters (or 2 letters and a punctuation mark that follows the word):

   Line 1: full-   cov-   teacher   **not** teach-
   Line 2: est   er,   er

JOB 38-1. DIVIDING WORDS BY SYLLABLES

Type lines 15–17. Then study each word and draw a vertical line on your paper between syllables if the word may be divided. Check your answers. Then retype lines 15–17 from your edited copy, inserting hyphens at the correct division points.

15   knowledge doesn't children worthwhile tricky; settle profit

16   stop leading steamed mfg. p.m. UNESCO planned signed worthy

17   around, court; mixer, sixty, shouldn't, service area; into.

JOB 38-2. LISTENING FOR THE BELL

Type the paragraph below. Some words will have to be divided at the end of the line, so listen for the bell. If you make the correct line-ending decisions, all lines except for the last will end evenly. Format: Double spacing, 50-space line, 5-space tab.

Do not divide words at end of more than 2 consecutive lines.

18   All of us need to watch our diets to maintain good health. If

19   you do not know much about nutrition, then you should start to

20   learn--now. Eating habits can destroy good health or can help

21   you attain good health, so be sure to eat wholesome food at ev-

22   ery meal. If you would like to read some information on nutri-

23   tion, visit your library or your local bookstore. Also, be sure to

24   learn how vitamin supplements ensure that we receive the mini-

25   mum daily requirements of vitamins and minerals.

JOB 123-1. DISPLAY WITH LEADERS

Standard format. Full sheet of paper and a 50-space line. Single-space the body.

[Handwritten copy:]

single-
space {

SENIOR CLASS PLAY
"The Disappearance of T. J. Walker"
May 4, 19--
Central High School Auditorium

Player   Role
Kenny Loftsgard . . . . . . T. J. Walker
Maria Sanchez . . . . . . Mrs. Walker
Jane Zejdlik . . . . . . Carol Walker
Frank Stantzel . . . . . Detective Ryan
Bernice Larson . . . . . Detective Unness
Bill Rodgers . . . . . . Tom Wright
Paul Johnston . . . . . Sgt. LeRoy Foster
Annette Vango . . . . . Ms. Peterson
Pete Weingard . . . . . Mr. Benson
Beth Talwani . . . . Ticket Agent
Emily Rice . . . . . . Dr. Swanson

LESSON 124

CLINIC

LAB 14

Type lines 1–4 once, providing the missing question marks. Edit your copy as your teacher reads the answers. Then retype lines 1–4 from your edited copy.

QUESTION MARKS

1 Has James Maxon submitted his estimates for this contract.
2 Does Jean agree that the azure cover is the brightest one.
3 Has Karen Boll rescheduled her meeting yet.   For what date.
4 Has Pattie or Henry arrived yet.   When should they be here.

PRETEST

Take a 5-minute Pretest on lines 5–10, repeating the paragraph until time is called. Circle each incorrect letter, and use the practice lines on page 209 to improve your skill. Use double spacing.

```
5        A typist might think that only his or her machine will    77 142
6   be found on a job, but typists frequently exchange machines    89 154
7   or elements to use what is most effective for the job.  The   101 166
8   typist is free to zero in on what is best:  one print style   113 178
9   or another, pica or elite, a correction key or other method   125 190
10  of correction, and so on.                                     130 195
    |  1  |  2  |  3  |  4  |  5  |  6  |  7  |  8  |  9  |  10  |  11  |  12  |  SI 1.39
```

LESSON 39

GOAL
- To apply additional rules of word division.

FORMAT
- Single spacing   60-space line   5-space tab

KEYBOARDING SKILLS

Type lines 1–4 once. Then do what line 5 tells you to do. Repeat lines 1–4, or take a series of 1-minute timings.

Speed
Accuracy
Numbers
Symbols
Technique

1 Helen paid the city firm for the land she owns by the lake. 12
2 Quickly fix the seven wires that jeopardized the big camps. 12
3 Please vote, when you can, for Laws 10, 29, 38, 47, and 56. 12
4 Use these percentages when you write a chart: 38% and 56%. 12
5 Center your name; then center your teacher's name below yours.

| 1 | 2 | 3 | 4 | 5 | 6 | 7 | 8 | 9 | 10 | 11 | 12

1- AND 3-MINUTE TIMINGS

Take two 1-minute timings on each paragraph. Then take one 3-minute timing on the entire selection. Use single spacing for the 1-minute timings and double spacing for the 3-minute timing.

6   Do you want to get better grades in school? Then here 12
7 are a few tips you should follow for doing good work in all 24
8 courses, no matter which ones they are. 32
9   You should prepare for each class, so that you will be 12
10 able to respond when there is any chance to discuss a major 24
11 issue or a point made by another student. 32
12   Discover what all your teachers expect of each student 12
13 in and out of class. Listen. Be exact in all answers that 24
14 you give on a quiz. Know all the facts. 32

| 1 | 2 | 3 | 4 | 5 | 6 | 7 | 8 | 9 | 10 | 11 | 12   SI 1.25

MORE RULES OF WORD DIVISION

Workbook 43–44.

Rule	Preferred	Avoid
1. Divide a compound word between the whole words that it contains. Similarly, divide a hyphenated compound word after the hyphen.	business–men under–stand father–in–law clerk–typist	busi–nessmen un–derstand fa–ther–in–law clerk–typ–ist
2. Divide after a one-letter syllable unless it is part of a suffix. Divide between two consecutive, separately pronounced vowels.	sepa–rate simi–lar radi–ation valu–able	sep–arate sim–ilar rad–iation valua–ble
3. When dates, personal names, street names, and long numbers must be broken, do not separate parts that must be read as units. Follow preferred examples.	June 10, / 1982 132 Eastern / Road Ms. Elsie / Berndt 1,583,– / 000,000	May / 21 132 / Eastern Road Mr. / Swenson 2,– / 567

(Continued on next page)

30-SECOND TIMINGS

Take two 30-second timings on lines 5–7, or type the paragraph twice.

5 You do not save very much time when you indent with the tab 12
6 key, but if the tab stop is set correctly, you do know that 24
7 each tab is quite uniform and each indention is just right. 36

| 1 | 2 | 3 | 4 | 5 | 6 | 7 | 8 | 9 | 10 | 11 | 12

PRETEST

Take a 5-minute Pretest on lines 8–24. Then circle and count your errors. Use the chart below to determine which lines to type for practice.

8 Have you ever felt [1]run down, tired, and [2]fatigued? The 12
9 symptoms [3]listed above are common to [4]many of us today. They 24
10 affect [5]our job performance, [6]they limit the fun we have [7]with 36
11 our family and [8]friends, and they might even [9]affect our good 48
12 health. [10]Here are just a few ways [11]that we can quickly mini-[12] 60
13 mize the problems and [13]become more active persons [14]in all the 72
14 things we do [15]daily. 76
15 It is essential[16] that we get plenty of [17]sleep so that we 88
16 are rested[18] when we get up each morning.[19] We must eat a good[20] 100
17 breakfast so that we can[21] build up energies for [22]the day that 112
18 follows. Physi[23]cal exercise is a necess[24]ity, and it might be 124
19 the [25]one most important ingred[26]ient in building up our [27]energy 136
20 reserves. We must [28]take part in exercises [29]that make us per- 148
21 spire, [30]make our hearts beat faster,[31] and cause our breathing[32] 160
22 rate to increase apprec[33]iably. All these things [34]can help us 172
23 increase our [35]energies and make us heal[36]thier people. Can we 184
24 not [37]enjoy life more if we [38]concentrate on these items?[39] 195

| 1 | 2 | 3 | 4 | 5 | 6 | 7 | 8 | 9 | 10 | 11 | 12 SI 1.39

PRACTICE

In the chart below, find the number of errors you made on the Pretest. Then type each of the designated drill lines four times.

Pretest errors	0–1	2–3	4–5	6+
Drill lines	28–32	27–31	26–30	25–29

Accuracy

25 ever tired perspire problems fatigued breakfast performance
26 many above energies physical symptoms essential appreciably
27 might limit quickly exercise minimize important concentrate
28 heart sleep morning building healthier breathing ingredient

Speed

29 listed common family energy people today have ever felt you
30 friend health become hearts affect enjoy even many they our
31 active person things faster builds these have with beat and
32 plenty rested follow things causes items each that when all

POSTTEST

Repeat the Pretest to see how much your skill has improved.

4. Divide after a prefix or before a suffix.

| super-sonic | su-personic |
| legal-ize | le-galize |

5. Avoid dividing the last word on a page.

JOB 39-1. WORD DIVISION PRACTICE

Clear your tabulator; then set tab stops 20 spaces and 40 spaces from the left margin. Type lines 15–19, which show all syllable breaks for the words given. Then retype lines 15–19, showing only the *best* division point for each word.

15	sep-a-rate	in-tro-duce	re-ad-just
16	crit-i-cal	grad-u-a-tion	ret-ro-ac-tive
17	time-ta-ble	le-gal-ize	care-less-ness
18	eye-wit-ness	pre-ma-ture	val-u-a-ble
19	reg-u-late	su-per-star	cen-ter-piece

JOB 39-2. WORD DIVISION PRACTICE

Using the same margins and tabs as in Job 39-1, type lines 20–23. Then decide on the *best* division point for each word given. **Hint:** Some words or phrases cannot be divided.

20	Dr. Hamill	radiation	international
21	1,265,610,000	May 31, 1984	cross-reference
22	masterpiece	$265.22	facilitate
23	September 21	Ms. E. Swenson	23 Mulberry Avenue

LESSON 40

GOALS
- To recognize how words are capitalized while typing sentences.
- To type from rough draft.

FORMAT
- Single spacing   60-space line   5-space tab

LAB 1

CAPITALIZATION

Type lines 1–4 once. Then repeat lines 1–4 or take a series of 1-minute timings.

1	Jane's instructor, Ms. Patterson, teaches in New York City.	12
2	Gerald hopes to travel to Mozambique and Germany next year.	12
3	Dr. Frey, the new museum director, bought a rug in Bangkok.	12
4	Today, Global Airlines travels to most countries in Europe.	12

| 1 | 2 | 3 | 4 | 5 | 6 | 7 | 8 | 9 | 10 | 11 | 12 |

Capitalize a proper noun (the name of a specific person, place, or thing): *Ms. Patterson, Germany, New York, Kleenex, Spanish.*

Note: Common nouns such as *museum, high school,* and *city* are also capitalized when they are part of proper names: *Carnegie Museum, Patterson High School, New York City.*

Capitalize the first word of a sentence.

Corporations in the city contribute to public museums.

FORMATTING SOURCE NOTES IN TABLES

A *source note*, which tells the source of information in a table, can be typed as a subtitle or as a footnote. If typed as a footnote:

1. Do not use an asterisk (*).
2. Type the word *Source* in all-capital letters, and use a colon after it.
3. Type the source note before footnotes (if any).

JOB 121/2-4. TABLE WITH LEADERS

Standard format. Full sheet of paper and a 50-space line. Double-space the body.

CLIMATIC Extremes

Measurement	Extreme
Highest Temperature	136 degrees
Lowest Temperature	-127 degrees
Greatest rainfall	74 inches*
Longest hotspell	162 days**
Greatest snowfall	76 inches*

Source: Information Please Almanac

* In 24 hours
** 100 degrees Fahrenheit or above

JOB 121/2-5. UNARRANGED TABLE WITH LEADERS

Standard format. Full sheet of paper and a 50-space line. Arrange in ascending order by page number; correct spelling errors.

THE COMPLETE DESK REFERENCE

Table of Contents*

Usage	210
Grammer	171
Numbers	87
Speling	132
Abreviations	105
Word Division	166
Compound Words	152
Capitolization	70
Plurels and Possesives	119
Punctuation: Other Marks	40
Punctuation: Majer Marks	1

*Part 1.

LESSON 123

GOALS
- To identify when question marks are used while typing sentences.
- To type at least 39/5'/5e.
- To type leadered displays.

FORMAT
- Single spacing   60-space line   5-space tab and tab at center

LAB 14

Type lines 1–4 once. Then repeat lines 1–4 or take a series of 1-minute timings.

QUESTION MARKS

1 Can you collate all these copies of the manuscript by noon? 12
2 Who requested a dozen extra copies of the January printout? 12
3 When did Marge and Karen schedule the meeting with Michael? 12
4 Have all invitations been printed? When will we mail them? 12

| 1 | 2 | 3 | 4 | 5 | 6 | 7 | 8 | 9 | 10 | 11 | 12

12-SECOND TIMINGS

Type each line four times, or take four 12-second timings on each line. For each timing, type with no more than one error.

5 If the order is a big one, we will make a profit this year. 12
6 We will do all we can to help them win the big prize today. 12
7 He cannot go there if he is to come here first for an hour. 12

25   30   35   40   45   50   55   60

PROOFREADERS' MARKS

Workbook 45–46

When corrections must be made in copy, professional writers, editors, proofreaders, and typists use proofreaders' marks. These symbols are quick and easy to use, and they make typing from a rough draft faster or easier for the typist. Study the proofreaders' marks shown below.

Proofreaders' Mark	Draft	Final Copy	Proofreaders' Mark	Draft	Final Copy
SS Single-space	SS first line / second line	first line / second line	/or— Delete and change	pa_r_ragraph / and so _if_ it	paragraph / and so it
ds Double Space	ds first line / second line	first line / second line	••• Don't delete	can _we_ go	can we go
◡ Omit space	to gether	together	/ Lowercase letter (make letter small)	/Business	business
# Insert space	It#may be	It may not be	≡ Capitalize	mrs. Wade	Mrs. Wade
Move as shown	it is (not)	it is	⌐ Move to right	it is so]	it is so
∽ Transpose	(is/it) so	it is so	5 Indent 5 spaces	5 Let it be	Let it be
◯ Spell out	the only (1)	the only one	⌐ Move to left	⌐let us	let us
¶ Paragraph	¶ If he is	If he is	∧ Insert punctuation mark	style∧and	style, and
∧ Insert word	and so∧it	and so it	⊙ Make it a period	other way⊙	other way.
Delete	it may be	it may			

JOB 40-1. PARAGRAPH COPY WITH PROOFREADERS' MARKS

Type a corrected copy of the paragraph below, making all changes indicated by proofreaders' marks. Format: Double spacing, 60-space line, 5-space tab. Half sheet of paper. Center title on line 7.

Cooking Chinese Style

¶ The chinese cook foods so that neither the color nor vitamins are lost

in the pan. So, if you want to cook chinese style, make sure that you

cook your vegetables in a Wok (with a touch of oil) rather than a skillet,

and do not over cook. With a Wok, the cook can toss food about so that the heat

is evenly spread. ¶ The chinese like their vegetables to be crisp

and very fresh. Have you ever tasted foods cooked in a Wok?

JOBS 40-2 AND 40-3. ENUMERATION WITH PROOFREADERS' MARKS

Format: Block-center on a half sheet of paper a corrected copy of the rough draft shown on page 71. Center the copy vertically on the page. Then retype on a full sheet of paper, using double spacing.

70 / LESSON 40   70

PRACTICE

In the chart below, find the number of errors you made on the Pretest. Then type each of the designated drill lines four times.

Pretest errors	0–1	2–3	4–5	6+
Drill lines	25–29	24–28	23–27	22–26

Accuracy
22 below sports begins replace covering concealed temperatures
23 those change states outdoors freezing equipment participate
24 quite frigid suited popular northern activities inexpensive
25 which winter tennis fishing swimming absolutely underground

Speed
26 certain almost anyone safety these lying when snow fall are
27 support before unless strong enjoy areas fans gone golf all
28 minimum inches spring enough don't winds well days most who
29 someone select direct enjoys water going that must your ice

POSTTEST

Repeat the Pretest on page 204 to see how much your skill has improved.

JOB 121/2-1. DISPLAY WITH LEADERS

Standard format. Full sheet of paper and a 50-space line. Double-space the body.

N O T I C E

The following committee assignments are made for the Junior Class Prom:

Lisa Bender .... Refreshments

Yaki Husharu .... Invitations*

Fernando Lopez .... Theme

Mark Mitchell .... Cleanup

Bonnita Valdez .... Entertainment

*Also responsible for decorations.

JOB 121/2-3. TABLE WITH LEADERS

Standard format. Full sheet of paper and a 50-space line. Single-space the body.

JOB 121/2-2. TABLE WITH LEADERS

Standard format. Half sheet of paper, 40-space line.

AVERAGE MILES PER GALLON
(TOTAL DISTANCE TRAVELED: 9,000 MILES)

MONTH	MILES PER GALLON
JANUARY	25.6
FEBRUARY	27.3
MARCH	25.8
APRIL	26.9
MAY	24.7
JUNE	23.1

NORTH DAKOTA ZIP CODES
Cities in Walsh County

Cities	ZIP Code
Adams	58201
Fairdale	58229
Fordville	58231
Edinburg	58227
Grafton	58243
Hoople	58237
Minto	58261
Parkriver	58270

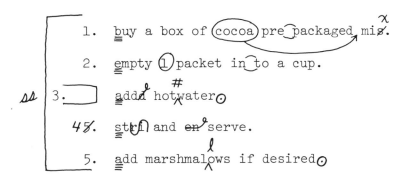

how to make hot cocoa

1. buy a box of cocoa pre-packaged mix.

2. empty 1 packet in to a cup.

3. add hot water.

4. stir and serve.

5. add marshmallows if desired.

LESSON 41

GOALS
- To identify how words are capitalized while typing sentences.
- To use proofreaders' marks in editing copy and to type from rough draft.

FORMAT
- Single spacing   60-space line   5-space tab

LAB 1

CAPITALIZATION

Type lines 1–4 once. Then repeat lines 1–4 or take a series of 1-minute timings.

1 Our supervisor, Mrs. Jezarian, is flying to Iraq next year.   12
2 El Duo Corporation, a Spanish company, does this work best.   12
3 Lincoln Center will feature a hula dance group from Hawaii.   12
4 My French teacher will visit the Grand Canyon during March.   12

| 1 | 2 | 3 | 4 | 5 | 6 | 7 | 8 | 9 | 10 | 11 | 12

1- AND 3-MINUTE TIMINGS

Take two 1-minute timings on each paragraph. Then take one 3-minute timing on the entire selection. Use single spacing for the 1-minute timings and double spacing for the 3-minute timing.

5   Jazz and blues music have the same roots from the past   12
6 in black gospel singing; slaves had just religion and music   24
7 to escape the hardships of their lives.   32

8   When days were bad, captives wrote and sang the blues.   12
9 When life was freer, jazz was sung to express joy. Both of   24
10 these are popular with all races today.   32

11   Whether played and sung by a lone guitarist or done by   12
12 a quintet, the music and the mood are sensed best by people   24
13 if they grasp the meaning of the words.   32

| 1 | 2 | 3 | 4 | 5 | 6 | 7 | 8 | 9 | 10 | 11 | 12   SI 1.26

LESSONS 121 / 122

GOALS
- To recognize when question marks are used while typing sentences.
- To type leadered tables.
- To format "source" notes in tables.

FORMAT
- Single spacing   60-space line   5-space tab and other tabs as needed

LAB 14

QUESTION MARKS

Type lines 1–4 once. Then repeat lines 1–4 or take a series of 1-minute timings.

```
1   What is my expense budget for the last quarter of the year?   12
2   When did Maria decide to transfer to our office in Seattle?   12
3   Did John know why sixty or more members voted against this?   12
4   In your opinion, should we approve Mr. Adzick's loan?  Why?   12
    |  1  |  2  |  3  |  4  |  5  |  6  |  7  |  8  |  9  |  10 |  11 |  12
```

Use a question mark (?) at the end of a question. Note that the question sometimes may not be a complete sentence:

Has the new contract been approved? When?
Who was named to head the committee? Shirley Anderson?

PRETEST

Take a 5-minute Pretest on lines 5–21. Then circle and count your errors. Use the chart on page 205 to determine which lines to type for practice.

```
5        When the snow begins to fall and the temperatures drop     12
6    to below freezing, sports fans in all those northern states    24
7    change their sports activities.  Gone are the tennis, golf,    36
8    and swimming.  To replace these sports are those quite well    48
9    suited to the cold, frigid days of winter.  One of the most    60
10   popular winter sports for many who enjoy fishing is that of    72
11   ice fishing.  It is a sport in which almost anyone can par-    84
12   ticipate, but did you know that it is inexpensive to enjoy?    96
13       Before going ice fishing, you must be certain that the    108
14   ice is strong enough to support you and all your equipment.    120
15   To be absolutely safe, don't go out on the ice unless there    132
16   is a minimum of six inches of ice covering the water.  Also    144
17   watch for thin ice that could be lying over a concealed un-    156
18   derground spring.  You should select an area that is not in    168
19   the direct path of the cold winds if you are going to stand    180
20   outdoors as you fish.  For safety, try to take someone else    192
21   along with you.                                                195
     |  1  |  2  |  3  |  4  |  5  |  6  |  7  |  8  |  9  |  10 |  11 |  12   SI 1.37
```

JOB 41-1. TYPING FROM A HANDWRITTEN DRAFT

Format: Double spacing, 60-space line, 5-space tab. Half sheet of paper. Begin on line 7.

Smoking and Sleeping

¶ Smoking has been linked to many health problems, including lung cancer and heart disease. Now it also appears to cause sleeping problems.

¶ A recent 2-year study in Washington of 100 smokers and non-smokers found that non-smokers fall asleep after an average of 30 minutes, while it takes smokers about 50 to 70 minutes. That's because the nicotine in cigarettes is a stimulant.

JOB 41-2. ROUGH-DRAFT ENUMERATION

Standard format. Half sheet of paper.

ds

do you read bumper stickers?

1. Some ask questions: "Have you Hugged your Child today?"

2. Some give answers: "Don't follow me. I'm lost too."

3. Some are serious: "60 is Thirfty."

4. Some are for small cars: "I'm Pedaling As Fast as I can."

JOB 41-3. ROUGH-DRAFT ENUMERATION

Standard format. Half sheet of paper.

HINTS FOR HELPING THE NEW DRIVER

1. keep in mind that the new driver needs more time to deal with traffic.

2. inform a new driver well in advance of the need to make a turn at a certain corner.

3. give practice driving in the rain.

4. give give practice parking the car.

FORMATTING TABLES WITH FOOTNOTES

Workbook 229–230.

When a footnote appears in a table, it is typed much the same as a footnote in a report. To format footnotes in unruled and ruled tables:

Tables Without Rulings. (1) Separate the footnote from the body of the table with a 10P/12E underscore. (2) Single-space before typing the underscore; double-space after it. (3) Indent the footnote 5 spaces and type it the length of the table, with single spacing; double-space between footnotes.

(4) Type an asterisk or another symbol at the beginning of a footnote to indicate its use in the table.

Tables With Rulings. (1) Type the footnote a double space below the final rule. (2) Follow steps 3 and 4 under "Tables Without Rulings."

Note: The footnote reference in the body of a table should be counted as part of the key line if it follows the longest entry in the column.

JOB 120-1. THREE-COLUMN TABLE
Standard format. Full sheet of paper.

SEVEN WONDERS OF THE WORLD
By Sheila Thomas

Structure	Location	Date of Construction*
Colossus	Rhodes (Greece)	280 B.C.
Hanging Gardens	Babylon (Iraq)	600 B.C.
Mausoleum	Halicarnassus (Turkey)	350 B.C.
Pharos	Alexandria (Egypt)	270 B.C.
Pyramids	Giza (Egypt)	2800 B.C.
Statue of Zeus	Olympia (Greece)	500 B.C.
Temple of Artemis	Ephesus (Turkey)	350 B.C.

* Dates listed are approximate.

FORMATTING DECIMALS IN TABLES

Numbers usually align at the right; however, in decimal numbers, the decimals must be aligned when typed. The key line may be a combination of two lines, as illustrated in Job 120–2.

JOB 120-2. FIVE-COLUMN TABLE
Standard format. Full sheet of paper.

CHEMICAL ELEMENTS
(Noble Gases)

Name	Chemical Symbol	Atomic Number	Atomic Weight	Date of Discovery
Argon	Ar	18	39.948	1894
Helium	He	2	4.0026	1895
Krypton	Kr	36	83.80	1898
Neon	Ne	10	20.183	1898
Radon	Rn	86	122.00	1900
Xenon	Xe	54	131.30	1898

JOB 120-3. RULED TABLE, UNARRANGED COPY
Standard format. Half sheet of paper.

[*Title*] States Bordering Arkansas
[*Subtitle*] (Listed Alphabetically)
[*Column headings*] State, Position of Border, Length of Border*
[*Body*] Louisiana, South, 170 miles; Mississippi, East, 150 miles; Missouri, North, 325 miles; Oklahoma, West, 200 miles.
[*Footnote*] *In miles.

LESSON 42

GOALS
- To capitalize words correctly while typing sentences.
- To type 32/3'/5e.
- To align roman numerals in an outline and to format an outline.

FORMAT
- Single spacing   60-space line   5-space tab

LAB 1

Type lines 1–4 once, providing the missing capitals. Edit your copy as your teacher reads the answers. Then retype lines 1–4 from your edited copy.

CAPITALIZATION 10'

1 Their teacher, ms. quartz, hopes to visit sicily this year.

2 The buhl planetarium in pittsburgh is a great place to see.

3 The president of our company also serves the jacox company.

4 He bought a swiss clock at the st. louis auction last week.

1- AND 3-MINUTE TIMINGS 15'

Take two 1-minute timings on each paragraph. Then take one 3-minute timing on the entire selection. Use single spacing for the 1-minute timings and double spacing for the 3-minute timing.

5   You simply do not go rafting down the quick river that   12

6 flows through the Grand Canyon without skills and plenty of   24

7 help. The many hazards are truly great.   32

8   It's one of the longest waterways in the world, and it   12

9 has rapids that are fearsome to hear. see, and run; but the   24

10 first trip can be filled with excitement.   32

11   The lovely canyon is rocky, thorny, and hot in summer.   12

12 Sometimes it is so windy that the spray and sand hit you in   24

13 the face with a brisk and stinging jolt.   32

| 1 | 2 | 3 | 4 | 5 | 6 | 7 | 8 | 9 | 10 | 11 | 12 | SI 1.26

FORMATTING AN OUTLINE 25'

To format an outline of, for example, a term paper, follow these rules:

1. Set your margins so that the outline will be approximately centered horizontally. Or if you wish, use the same margins as those used in your term paper.

2. Center the outline vertically, or type the title on line 13 if you are using a full sheet of paper.

3. Align the periods after the roman numerals, like this:

   I.
  II.
 III.

Use the margin release key and backspace from the left margin for roman numerals that take more than one space.

4. Use single spacing, but leave 2 blank lines before and 1 blank line after a line that begins with a Roman numeral.

5. Indent each subdivision 4 more spaces.

  I.##
    A.##
      1.##
        a.##
          (1)## (etc.)

Numbers are usually aligned on the right. However, when numbers appear with other alphabetic data (such as with 4 reams in the column to the right) in a table column, it is permissible to align the numbers at the left.

JOB 119-1. THREE-COLUMN RULED TABLE

Standard format. Full sheet of paper.

SUPPLIES INVENTORY
Typewriting I, Room 142

Item	Number	Reorder
Paper	4 reams	No
Ribbons	5 boxes	Yes
Textbooks	38	No
Copyholders	35	Yes
Machine covers	30	Yes

JOB 119-2. THREE-COLUMN RULED TABLE

Standard format. Half sheet of paper.

TYPEWRITING SPEEDS
Beginning Typewriting

Student	Speed	Increase
Helen	45	8
Juan	41	5
Randy	35	4
Shelby	34	2
Stacy	45	4

JOB 119-3. THREE-COLUMN RULED TABLE

Standard format. Full sheet of paper.

AREA CODES/TIME ZONES
Selected Nebraska Cities

City	Time Zone	Area Code
Alliance	Mountain	308
Lincoln	Central (Mountain)	402
McCook	Central	308
North Platte	Central	308
Scottsbluff	Mountain	308
Wayne	Central	402

(handwritten notes: "place this column last"; "#" over Area Code)

LESSON 120

GOALS
- To format footnotes and decimal numbers in tables.
- To produce ruled tables.

FORMAT
- Single spacing   60-space line   Center tab and other tabs as needed

KEYBOARDING SKILLS

Type lines 1–4 once. In line 5, backspace and underscore each word containing double letters immediately after typing it. Repeat lines 1–4, or take a series of 1-minute timings.

Speed	1	The key to the problem with both their maps is their shape.	12
Accuracy	2	Jack bought five exquisite bronze bowls at Pam's yard sale.	12
Numbers	3	We set our tabs at 10, 29, 38, 47, and 56 for the problems.	12
Symbols	4	Only 9% of #47 and 8% of #56 were sold on the 1st (Monday).	12
Technique	5	They, too, shall give three good yells when the bell tolls.	

| 1 | 2 | 3 | 4 | 5 | 6 | 7 | 8 | 9 | 10 | 11 | 12

JOB 42-1. OUTLINE

Format the outline shown below. Use a half sheet of paper and single spacing. 50-space line. Set tab stops 4, 8, and 12 spaces from your left margin.

FORMING A BICYCLE TOURING CLUB

Align periods after roman numerals.

    I.   PLAN A SHORT TRIP.

        A. Take a one-day city tour.
        B. Take a weekend trip.
           1. Go to a state park.
             a. Eat at a country inn.
             b. Camp overnight.
           2. Go to Lake Erie.

Leave 2 blank lines before and 1 blank line after lines that begin with roman numerals.

   II.   PLAN A LONG TRIP.

        A. Write to other clubs in our country.
        B. Write to clubs in foreign countries.

  III.   TAKE CLASSES IN BIKE SAFETY.

JOB 42-2. OUTLINE

Standard format. 30-space line. Half sheet of paper.

MAKING FRIENDS
I. Join a Club
A. School Clubs
1. The Business Club
2. Junior Achievement
3. Y-Teens
B. Out-of-School Clubs
II. Get a Pen Pal
III. Take Up a Sport
A. Join a Team
B. Learn a New Sport
1. Tennis
2. Golf
3. Skiing

You may replace tennis, golf, or skiing with your favorite sports.

Take a 5-minute Pretest on lines 5–21. Then circle and count your errors. Use the chart below to determine which lines to type for practice.

```
                                 1                                2
 5        Have you ever been through an actual haunted house?  I      12
              3                             4
 6   would really enjoy going into one, but I have never had the      24
       5                    6                            7
 7   opportunity of doing so.  Actually, I am somewhat afraid of      36
                      8                          9
 8   what may be in store for me if such a wish would come true!      48
              10                         11                    12
 9   I visualize seeing ghosts or monsters and having them chase      60
                          13                       14
10   me rapidly down the stairs and out a window or door!  Worse      72
                 15                          16
11   yet, I also view being trapped in a dark room with them and      84
         17                    18
12   not being able to locate the exit!                              91
                         19                          20
13        Exactly what causes those fears to overcome us?  Where     103
            21                         22                         23
14   do we first begin to be afraid?  When thinking about it, we     115
                             24                       25
15   really have to laugh at ourselves; then we quickly see just     127
                 26                       27
16   how foolish we were to be scared.  Ghosts and monsters come     139
         28                       29                       30
17   from fantasy.  In fact, many of these fears probably arose,     151
                     31                       32
18   for the first time, when our older brothers or sisters were     163
             33                       34                       35
19   trying everything they could to keep us out of their rooms.     175
                             36                       37
20   When we can look at it in that light, there is no longer an     187
                 38                    39
21   unreasonable fear.  We laugh about it!                          195
     |  1  |  2  |  3  |  4  |  5  |  6  |  7  |  8  |  9  |  10  |  11  |  12   SI 1.37
```

In the chart below, find the number of errors you made on the Pretest. Then type each of the designated drill lines four times.

Pretest errors	0–1	2–3	4–5	6+
Drill lines	25–29	24–28	23–27	22–26

Accuracy

```
22   been ever have actual foolish brothers somewhat opportunity
23   some what into fantasy quickly probably ourselves visualize
24   true come wish sisters trapped overcome actually everything
25   door down them really exactly rapidly monsters unreasonable
```

Speed

```
26   afraid trying house would enjoy going think about fear that
27   seeing scared never doing store chase laugh these look when
28   ghosts really stair worse being cause fears arose were just
29   stairs causes fears where first begin older could fact view
```

Repeat the Pretest to see how much your skill has improved.

LESSON 43

GOALS
- To build typing speed.
- To type 32/3'/5e.

FORMAT
- Single spacing   60-space line   5-space tab

KEYBOARDING SKILLS

Type lines 1–4 once. Then do what line 5 tells you to do. Repeat lines 1–4, or take a series of 1-minute timings.

Speed
Accuracy
Numbers
Symbols
Technique

1 The eight may make a profit if they handle the forms right.   12
2 Quietly pick up the box with five dozen gum and candy jars.   12
3 On May 29 and June 10, I will use 38, 47, and 56 if we can.   12
4 Jarris & Sons buys from Wilson & Harris and M&E in Houston.   12
5 Type line 2; remove your paper; reinsert; align and retype over the original.

| 1 | 2 | 3 | 4 | 5 | 6 | 7 | 8 | 9 | 10 | 11 | 12

PREVIEW PRACTICE

Type lines 6 and 7 twice as a preview to the Pretest.

Accuracy
Speed

6 rapids without waterways longest hazards rafting excitement
7 windy help trip sand it's jolt with hear down that many hit

PRETEST

Take a 3-minute timing on lines 5–13, page 73.

PRACTICE

Type each line three times, and take a series of 1-minute timings on each line, working to increase your speed.

8   tool well soon keep look fill need less been eggs ebbs burr   12
9   ball miss mill pass good pool feel sees toss seem will book   12
10 wall door hood food ooze buff mitt cuff putt miff mutt full   12

11 Both the men may go to town if he pays them for their fuel.   12
12 She may make the girls do the theme for their eighth panel.   12
13 They paid for the pen and the box, so I paid for the forks.   12

| 1 | 2 | 3 | 4 | 5 | 6 | 7 | 8 | 9 | 10 | 11 | 12

12-SECOND TIMINGS

Type each line four times, or take four 12-second timings on each line. For each timing, type with no more than one error.

14 Now is the hour to come to the aid of those of us who work.   12
15 She works with them and with the boss in this small office.   12
16 They put a box down the chute and into a van waiting there.   12

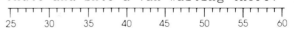

25   30   35   40   45   50   55   60

30-SECOND TIMINGS

Take two 30-second timings on lines 17–19, or type the paragraph twice.

17 There is no quick way to learn to spell. But if you are an   12
18 expert typist, there is one very good method for you. Just   24
19 teach your fingers to spell as you zip through the lessons.   36

| 1 | 2 | 3 | 4 | 5 | 6 | 7 | 8 | 9 | 10 | 11 | 12

POSTTEST

Repeat the Pretest twice to see how much your speed has improved.

1- AND 5-MINUTE TIMINGS

Take two 1-minute timings on each paragraph. Then take one 5-minute timing on the entire selection. Use single spacing for the 1-minute timings and double spacing for the 5-minute timing.

20   When you decide to redecorate a room, or move to a new   12

21 apartment, or help a friend getting settled in a new place,   24

22 you must make many decisions. How could this place be made   36

23 more pleasant?   39

24   After all the furniture is in place, you should decide   12

25 where to put wall hangings. Would a picture look better on   24

26 one wall, or would it look better on another? It must look   36

27 exactly right!   39

28   Once these kinds of decisions have been made, you will   12

29 begin the hanging process. First, you might want to locate   24

30 the horizontal center of the wall on which you have decided   36

31 to hang an item.   39

32   Then ask somebody to hold the picture steady while you   12

33 step back a little way and determine how high this painting   24

34 should be placed. Many paintings and other items look best   36

35 at eye level.   39

36   Once you have completed this procedure, you can use it   12

37 again and again to help you in placing pictures on the wall   24

38 quickly and easily. All you have to do is just get started   36

39 and keep going!   39

| 1 | 2 | 3 | 4 | 5 | 6 | 7 | 8 | 9 | 10 | 11 | 12   SI 1.36

LESSON 119

UNIT 20 FORMATTING TABLES

UNIT GOAL
39/5'/5e

GOALS
- To use exclamation points correctly while typing sentences.
- To type three ruled tables.

FORMAT
- Single spacing   60-space line   5-space tab and other tabs as needed

LAB 13

Type lines 1–4 twice, providing the missing exclamation points. Edit your copy as your teacher reads the answers. Then retype lines 1–4 from your edited copy.

EXCLAMATION POINTS

1 Stop. We already have several dozen copies of these forms.

2 Congratulations. I'm happy that you've been promoted, Kay.

3 Wow. Our water taxes for last quarter have almost doubled.

4 Yes. Joan Kim has been awarded first prize for her design.

LESSON 44

GOALS
- To capitalize words correctly while typing sentences.
- To format a one-page report.

FORMAT
- Single spacing   60-space line   5-space tab

LAB 1

Type lines 1–4 once, providing the missing capitals. Edit your copy as your teacher reads the answers. Then retype lines 1–4 from your edited copy.

CAPITALIZATION

1   I hope that ms. sajovic and ms. quinn fly to great britain.

2   We met mr. and mrs. dextor when they visited san francisco.

3   We wrote to the peking art museum about the chinese sketch.

4   A big american flag was flying atop new zenith high school.

12-SECOND TIMINGS

Type each line four times, or take four 12-second timings on each line. For each timing, type with no more than one error.

5   The new moon went over the hills and out of sight too soon.   12

6   We know that he had the spools when he left here about six.   12

7   If the wind hits the leaves, they will come down very soon.   12

     25   30   35   40   45   50   55   60

30-SECOND TIMINGS

Take two 30-second timings on lines 8–10, or type the paragraph twice.

8   On a clear day the view from the top of a tall building can   12

9   be lovely. The azure sky looks so inviting that you expect   24

10   a quiet cloud to be a magic jet plane to fly you to Utopia.   36

| 1 | 2 | 3 | 4 | 5 | 6 | 7 | 8 | 9 | 10 | 11 | 12

FORMATTING A ONE-PAGE REPORT

Many reports are short enough to fit on one page. To format a one-page report:

1. Set margins for a 60-space line on a pica typewriter (60P) and for a 70-space line on an elite typewriter (70E).

2. Center the title on line 13. Type the title in all-capital letters.

3. Center the subtitle a double space below the title. Use initial caps. The subtitle may further explain the title or may be a *by-line*—the name of the author of the report. Triple-space after typing the subtitle or by-line.

4. Double-space the body of the report.

5. Indent paragraphs 5 spaces.

JOB 44-1. ONE-PAGE REPORT

Type the one-page report shown on page 77. Standard format. Workbook 49.

LESSON 118

CLINIC

GOALS
- To practice using the number keys on which more drill is needed.
- To build skill in typing numbers.
- To type 39/5'/5e.

FORMAT
- Single spacing   60-space line   5-space tab

KEYBOARDING SKILLS

Type lines 1–4 once. Then do what line 5 tells you to do. Repeat lines 1–4, or take a series of 1-minute timings.

Speed | 1 She paid Laurie to fix the ivory box that the visitor made. | 12
Accuracy | 2 A frozen bird squawked vigorously as Joseph coaxed him out. | 12
Numbers | 3 Players 29, 38, 47, and 56 all scored 10 points last night. | 12
Symbols | 4 On 1/31 we received a 9% raise, from $1,200/week to $1,308. | 12
Technique | 5 Strike your return key after typing each word in this line.

| 1 | 2 | 3 | 4 | 5 | 6 | 7 | 8 | 9 | 10 | 11 | 12

PRETEST

Take a 2-minute timing on lines 6–9, or type them twice to find out which number keys are the most difficult for you to type. Keep your eyes on your copy as you type. Circle each digit where an error was made.

6 4703 6051 8954 5607 1283 7826 5316 0914 9065 7283 9413 8972 | 12
7 3145 2364 5603 8917 4823 0543 7951 2541 7068 6079 7286 9012 | 24
8 8942 5613 7084 9508 5263 7420 8162 7395 9481 5369 4327 6110 | 36
9 4378 6250 9064 1357 7072 1431 5923 7045 8968 2648 9019 8123 | 48

| 1 | 2 | 3 | 4 | 5 | 6 | 7 | 8 | 9 | 10 | 11 | 12

PRACTICE

Type lines 10–19 once. Then repeat any of the lines that stress the errors you circled in the Pretest.

1 | 10 I have 1 tulip, 1 rose, 11 zinnias, 11 violets, and 1 iris.
2 | 11 We donated 2 quarters, 2 dimes, 22 nickels, and 22 pennies.
3 | 12 When multiplying 3 times 13, we get 39; 3 times 3 equals 9.
4 | 13 Study page 44 in Chapter 4 and read page 444 in Chapter 14.
5 | 14 The mileage between cities was 5, 45, 85, 95, 125, and 165.
6 | 15 On 6/6/76 and 6/16/76 we sold 66 units of Item 66 for $666.
7 | 16 Series 7 was used in 77 high schools in the area in 7/7/82.
8 | 17 On the 18th we bowled scores of 88, 118, 181, 188, and 208.
9 | 18 Their winning numbers are 9919, 9929, 9939, 9949, and 9959.
0 | 19 The metric system is founded on tens: 10, 20, 30, 40, etc.

POSTTEST

Repeat the Pretest to see how much your skill has improved.

CARE OF YOUR RECORDS ↓13
↓2
By Jane Baxter
↓3

The most important part of taking care of your records is protecting them from dust. What harm will dust do to your records? Dust settles into the record grooves, and when the stylus hits the dust, your records can be hurt in two ways.

First, the stylus will grind dust into the soft vinyl grooves, creating pock marks that will be heard as "clicks and pops" the next time you play the record.

Second, the stylus will pick up the dust as it goes along, which will keep the stylus from tracking clearly or cause it to skid to the end of the record.

The best way of keeping dust off your records is to put a cover on your machine, even when a record is playing. The only time the cover should be off is when you are changing a record.

Never store your records in the plastic wrap that they come sealed in. This material will shrink when it is exposed to heat, which can cause your records to warp during hot weather if they are stored in the wrap.

A legal contract is an agreement between two or more parties. It is usually in typed format, and it is enforceable by law.

JOB 117-1. LEGAL CONTRACT
Standard format. Workbook 225, 227.

```
            EMPLOYMENT   C O N T R A C T                           12

        THIS CONTRACT, made and signed on this 10th day of June,   26
                    the firm of
by and between Crane and Garth, of 701 Rome Street, Flushing, New  42

York, Party of the first part, and Ms. Erma Ostlund, 628 High Bluff  55
                                           second
Road, Portland, Maine, party of the first part.                    65

   10   Article 1.  The party of the second party covenants and    77

agrees to and with the party of the first party, to represent the  90
       of the first part
party as agent of the firm in the State of Maine for the period of 105

1 year, or twelve (12) months, beginning on June 20 and ending 1   119

year hence on June 19; and the said party of the second part does  132

agree to perform all the duties subject to this employment, to in- 145

clude, among others, attending District Sales Meetings heretofore  158

scheduled for the months of July, August, March, and May.         170

        ARTICLE 2.  The said party of the first part covenants and 183
                   said party of the
agrees to pay the second part for the performance of those duties  200

the sum of fifteen thousand three hundred dollars ($15,300), in    212
      monthly
equal installments of One Thousand Two Hundred Seventy-Five Dollars 228
                               first
($1,275), to be paid upon the fifth day of each calendar month, starting 242
         August
with July 1; plus a commission of nine percent (9%) of the annual  255

sales in that state over the average of the 3 three preceding years. 269
                                              ceding
        In Witness Thereof, the parties have, in the presence      284
                            to this contract
of each other, hereunto set their hands and seals, the day and     297

year first written above.                                          302

Party of the First Part:                Party of the second part:  314


_____               _____  329

D. L. Wilde, Vice President             Erma Ostlund               339


_____               _____  354

Witness to Signature                    Witness to Signature       365
```

JOB 44-2. ONE-PAGE REPORT

Type the report shown below. Standard format (see page 76).

WHAT MESSAGE ARE YOU SENDING?

By [*Your name*]

Without your saying a word, your posture and your walk might tell people what is on your mind. Although your walking style may not tell the whole story, it can send a message about your moods. Check the way you walk.

When you walk at a slow pace, with your head down and hands in your pockets, you tell others that you want to be alone. If your shoulders are drooped, your head is downcast, and your gait is a kind of shuffle, you are telling others that you feel sad. But when you walk at a brisk pace, hold your head up, look relaxed, swing your arms, and use your entire body, you express a sense of openness to everyone.

LESSON 45

GOALS
- To format a one-page report with side headings.

FORMAT
- Single spacing 60-space line 5-space tab

KEYBOARDING SKILLS

Type lines 1–4 once. Then do what line 5 tells you to do. Repeat lines 1–4, or take a series of 1-minute timings.

Speed	1	Then the boys moved with their friends to the right corner.	12
Accuracy	2	Jack Dorp and Vera Lopez quietly bought six new farm tools.	12
Numbers	3	The May 3 group included 38 men, 47 women, and 56 children.	12
Symbols	4	Contracts were sent to L&R and to T&W but not to Rod & Loo.	12
Technique	5	As you retype line 4, underscore all proper nouns in it.	

| 1 | 2 | 3 | 4 | 5 | 6 | 7 | 8 | 9 | 10 | 11 | 12

3-MINUTE TIMINGS

Take a 3-minute timing on lines 6–13. Type six times each word on which you made an error, hesitated, or stopped during the 3-minute timing. Then take a 3-minute timing to see how much your skill has improved.

6 Strong legs, quick reflexes, and great team spirit are 12
7 what it takes to play the really fast game of soccer. Both 24
8 men and women can play, since skill--not size--is required. 36
9 Long the most widely played sport in Europe, soccer in this 48
10 country is all the rage. It is beloved in other countries, 60
11 too, such as Brazil and Japan. Many high schools that have 72
12 had football as a major team sport have dropped the game in 84
13 favor of soccer, since players are less likely to get hurt. 96

| 1 | 2 | 3 | 4 | 5 | 6 | 7 | 8 | 9 | 10 | 11 | 12 SI 1.26

FORMATTING SIDE HEADINGS IN REPORTS

Side headings divide reports into sections. To format side headings:
1. Type the side headings in all-capital letters.
2. Triple-space (leaving 2 lines blank) before a side heading.
3. Double-space (leaving 1 line blank) after a side heading.

JOB 45-1. REPORT WITH SIDE HEADINGS

Type the report shown on page 79. Standard format.

LESSON 117

GOALS
- To use exclamation points correctly while typing sentences.
- To type at least 39/5'/5e.
- To format a legal contract.

FORMAT
- Single spacing   60-space line   5-space tab and other tabs as needed

LAB 13

EXCLAMATION POINTS

Type lines 1–4 once, providing the missing exclamation points. Edit your copy as your teacher reads the answers. Then retype lines 1–4 from your edited copy.

1 Be careful. It is difficult to see very well in this haze.
2 Work quietly. Do not make noise. You will disturb others.
3 No. Daren cannot fix all these machines in just four days.
4 Great. Paul completed the project weeks ahead of schedule.

1- AND 5-MINUTE TIMINGS

Take two 1-minute timings on each paragraph. Then take one 5-minute timing on the entire selection. Use single spacing for the 1-minute timings and double spacing for the 5-minute timing.

1'

5   Today, a quick way to get from one place to another is   12
6   by plane. There are many airlines from which to select for   24
7   your flight. Airlines throughout the country provide daily   36
8   service to all.   39

9   If you are going to fly by airplane for the very first   12
10 time, you should contemplate arriving at the terminal about   24
11 an hour before your plane will depart so you can check your   36
12 extra baggage.   39

13   When flying on a large aircraft, you may choose to sit   12
14 in a smoking seat or nonsmoking seat. You can ask a ticket   24
15 agent for your preference when you are checking in for your   36
16 airline flight.   39

17   Would slight changes in air pressure affect your ears?   12
18 If increased pressure causes your ears to plug, chew gum or   24
19 some other substance so that your ears stay open during the   36
20 entire flight.   39

21   If you are flying across country or on some other long   12
22 trip, bring along something to read such as a magazine or a   24
23 new book. Or you might read some of the magazines that the   36
24 airline offers.   39

| 1 | 2 | 3 | 4 | 5 | 6 | 7 | 8 | 9 | 10 | 11 | 12   SI 1.33

HANDLING AND STORING YOUR RECORDS

By Gordon MacIntosh

Taking good care of your records is very important to good sound. Here are some basic things you should do to make sure that your records keep their clear tone.

CARE IN HANDLING

Hold your records at the edges with two hands or balanced with your thumb at the outer edge and the tips of your fingers on the center label. Don't touch the playing surface of the record. Your fingers leave skin oils and moisture that act as glue for the dust that settles there.

CARE IN STORING

After each time you play one of your records, put it back in its inner sleeve and then in its jacket. Store your records upright, away from heat and the direct rays of the sun.

Before playing a record, sweep the dust away with a velour pad that comes in the form of a wooden block with a handle. Use the pad with a wiping and lifting motion. However, the best record-care product will not do much good for your records if you use it only twice a year.

JOB 116-1 (Continued)

may possess at the time of my death, together with all my insurance 227

policies thereon. All the rest of my estate, of whatever kind, I 240

bequeath and give to my beloved Husband, Charles Duane Johnson. 253

        FOURTH: I direct that my Husband, Charles Duane 264
Johnson, shall not be required to furnish any security, unless 279
contrary to any law; nor shall he be liable for loss, damage, or 292
destruction of said property. 298

        IN WITNESS WHEREOF, I have hereunto set my hand and 309
seal this fifteenth day of March, in the year one thousand nine 322
hundred and eighty-one. 327

_____ 337

        THE ABOVE INSTRUMENT, consisting of two pages, was 352
subscribed by Carolyn Ann Johnson in our presence and was acnowl- 365
edged by her to each of us; and she at the same time declared the 378
above to be her Last Will and Testament; and we, at her request, 391
in her presence and in the presence of each other, have hereunto 404
signed our names as hereto witnesses. 412

_____ residing at _____ 427

_____ residing at _____ 442

_____ residing at _____ 457

Page 2 of 2   *(Typist: Don't forget to add page number to first page.)*

JOB 116-2. RESOLUTION

Standard format. Use plain paper. Copy is unedited and unarranged; make changes and corrections as you type.

R E S O L U T I O N

WHEREAS Ralph Marshall Thompson is retiring from her position as Chairman of the Business Department at Moore High School after having served this comunity for a total of twenty years; and

WHEREAS he devoted all his efforts to provide the students of Moor High High School with a highly credable and worthwhile start on careerrs of there onw, and all the while he has acted in a selfless and generos manner in his actions; and

Whereas he has given generously of himself in the encouragment and assistance of all those who were fortuntae enough too work with her personnally, to the end that all the teachers and all his peers have learned and gained much from this wise and gentel person; and

WHEREas he has proved himself a wise and discerning leader, and a men endowed as much with openess of heart and hand as with wisdom, so that his name is a legend in this school and that he is loved for what he is more then for what he has done; therefore be it

RESOLVED, that the faculty of the Business Department, the entire administrative staff at Moore High School, and the members of the School Board do, for his devotion to education and to this school system in which he has worked for the passed twenty years, commend

RALPH MARSHALL THOMAS

JOB 45-2. REPORT WITH SIDE HEADINGS

Retype Job 44-2, page 78, inserting side headings as follows: Before the first paragraph, YOUR WALKING STYLE; before the second paragraph, WHAT OTHERS SEE. Standard format.

LESSON 46

GOALS
- To recognize how words are capitalized while typing sentences.
- To produce a one-page report with side and paragraph headings.

FORMAT
- Single spacing 60-space line 5-space tab

LAB 2

CAPITALIZATION

Type lines 1–4 once. Then repeat lines 1–4 or take a series of 1-minute timings.

1 North Dakota and South Dakota are states north of Nebraska. 12
2 Just five bankers went to the West to tour Northern Realty. 12
3 Jo Proxmire is moving from West Virginia to the West Coast. 12
4 Go quickly to 1700 East Graham, on the south side of Azusa. 12
   | 1 | 2 | 3 | 4 | 5 | 6 | 7 | 8 | 9 | 10 | 11 | 12

Capitalize *north, south, east,* and *west* when they refer to definite regions, are part of a proper noun, or are within an address.

  in the West   West Company   610 West Carson Street

Do not capitalize *north, south, east,* and *west* when they merely indicate direction or general location.

  Drive *west* on Hatteras Street.
  We live in the *south* part of Italy.

12-SECOND TIMINGS

Type each line four times, or take four 12-second timings on each line. For each timing, type with no more than one error.

5 Once the boy began to laugh, all of us began to laugh also. 12
6 Where in the world can we find an island on which to relax? 12
7 Now is the time for all of us to rush and join a good team. 12
   25   30   35   40   45   50   55   60

30-SECOND TIMINGS

Take two 30-second timings on lines 8–10, or type the paragraph twice.

8   All of us need to relax our minds each day. You may not be   12
9   able to use a technique such as yoga, but you can realize a   24
10 true inner peace by thinking about happy days in your life.   36
    | 1 | 2 | 3 | 4 | 5 | 6 | 7 | 8 | 9 | 10 | 11 | 12

FORMATTING PARAGRAPH HEADINGS IN REPORTS

Paragraph headings further subdivide a report. To format paragraph headings:

1. Type paragraph headings at the beginning of a paragraph in *initial* *caps*; that is, capitalize the first letter of each important word.

2. Underscore paragraph headings.

3. Follow paragraph headings by a period and 2 spaces.

LESSON 116

GOALS
- To identify when exclamation points are used while typing sentences.
- To format a last will and testament and a resolution.

FORMAT
- Single spacing 60-space line 10-space tab and center tab

LAB 13

EXCLAMATION POINTS

Type lines 1–4 once. Then repeat lines 1–4 or take a series of 1-minute timings.

1 Hurry! To mail a dozen orders today, we must work quickly. 12
2 No! Jo will not change her decision regarding this matter. 12
3 That was the most exciting basketball game Flo ever played! 12
4 Quick! Look at that pretty rainbow across the eastern sky! 12

| 1 | 2 | 3 | 4 | 5 | 6 | 7 | 8 | 9 | 10 | 11 | 12

LAST WILL AND TESTAMENT

A last will and testament is a document that enables people to ensure that their belongings are distributed as they wish after they die.

JOB 116-1. WILL
Standard format (see page 194). Workbook 221, 223.

LAST WILL AND TESTAMENT   14
OF   17
Carolyn A. Johnson   ↓3   30

I, Carolyn Ann Johnson, residing in the City of Dayton,   45
County of Hennepin, State of Minnesota, do hereby make and declare 58
this to be my Will and Testament, hereby rescinding all former Wills 73
and Codicils by me at any time made.   80

FIRST: I hereby direct that all of my just debts and   92
funeral expenses be paid out of my estate, as soon as practicable after 106
my death. I further direct that my executor, hereinafter named, 119
defend any claim against my estate.   126

SECOND: I hereby appoint my Husband, Charles Duane   138
Johnson, as sole executor of my estate; and I direct that no bond 150
be required of him in performing these duties.   161

THIRD: I hereby give and bequeath to my beloved Husband,   173
Charles Duane Johnson, all automobiles, books, china, clothing,   186
fixtures, furniture, glass, household goods and supplies, jewelry, linen, 201
ornaments, plaques, silverware, tapestries, and appliances that I 214

(Continued on next page)

JOBS 46-1 AND 46-2. REPORT WITH SIDE AND PARAGRAPH HEADINGS

Type the one-page report with side and paragraph headings as shown below. Standard format. Then retype the report using single spacing.

About Apples

PICKING APPLES

If you live near apple-growing farms, you can get the very freshest fruit, along with some fresh air and exercise, by going to a pick-your-own orchard. These fruit farms often post signs on roads or run ads in local papers. Call in advance to see if you need to bring baskets and to check on the kinds of apples they grow.

RATING APPLES

Big apples may look solid, but often they are mealy and mushy inside. Small- or medium-sized fruit may taste better. Here are some names of apples and their features to help you get the right kind of apple for your needs.

Northern Spy. This kind of apple is somewhat tart and is best for baking because it holds its shape well when cooked.

Cortland. This apple is somewhat tart, too, but it has a nice crunch. It is best for salads because it won't discolor as fast as some others.

Red and Golden Delicious. Both kinds are good to eat; both kinds are sweet and juicy.

Remember that paragraph headings are typed in capital and lowercase letters at the beginning of a paragraph, underscored, and followed by a period and 2 spaces.

LESSON 47

GOALS
- To identify how words are capitalized while typing sentences.
- To produce from rough-draft copy a one-page report with run-in references.

FORMAT
- Single spacing   60-space line   5-space tab

LAB 2

CAPITALIZATION

Type lines 1–4 once. Then repeat lines 1–4 or take a series of 1-minute timings.

1 On Saturday, he will zip to South Carolina for an election.   12

2 Back East in my home town of Quincy, Maine, we like to ski.   12

3 When we visit Mississippi, we enjoy our long journey South.   12

4 I live at 16 East Sixth Avenue, but I will soon move North.   12

| 1 | 2 | 3 | 4 | 5 | 6 | 7 | 8 | 9 | 10 | 11 | 12

FORMATTING LEGAL PAPERS

Workbook 215–216.

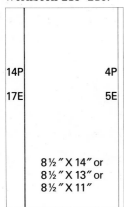

14P
17E

4P
5E

8½″ X 14″ or
8½″ X 13″ or
8½″ X 11″

Legal paper has a double vertical line ruled 14P/17E spaces from the left edge and a single vertical line 4P/5E spaces from the right edge. To format copy on legal paper:

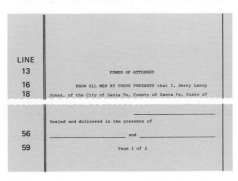

LINE
13   POWER OF ATTORNEY
16   KNOW ALL MEN BY THESE PRESENTS that I, Jerry Leroy
18   Jones, of the City of Santa Fe, County of Santa Fe, State of

Sealed and delivered in the presence of
56   and
59   Page 1 of 2

1. Set margin stops 2 spaces inside the vertical ruled lines.
2. Center the title of the document between the margins.
3. Indent paragraphs 10 spaces.
4. Double-space unless directed to do otherwise.
5. Maintain a top margin of 12 blank lines on the first page, 9 blank lines on others.
6. Center page numbers between the margins about 6 lines from the bottom of the page. The phrase to use is "Page 1 of 3," "Page 2 of 3," and so on. Omit the page number from a one-page document.

POWER OF ATTORNEY

A power of attorney gives one person the power to act as an agent, or proxy, for another.

JOB 115-1. POWER OF ATTORNEY
Standard format. Workbook 217.

POWER OF ATTORNEY↓₃   10
KNOW ALL MEN BY THESE PRESENTS   20
that the undersigned does hereby constitute   28
and appoint Jan R. Heinz, James R. Espinoza,   37
and Kyle R. Moen, and each of them, the true   46
and lawful attorneys and proxies of the un-   55
dersigned, with full power of substitution, and   64
revocation for and in the name, place, and   73
stead of the undersigned, to vote upon and act   82
with respect to all the shares of Common Stock   92
without par value of HENDERSON PROD-   99
UCTS, INC., standing in the name of the   107
undersigned on the books of the Company as   115
at the time of the meeting, at the Scheduled   125
Meeting of the Stockholders of the Company   134
to be held at the LeBaron Hotel in Dallas,   142
Texas, on Thursday, March 21, 19--, at 10:00   151
a.m. and at any and all adjournments thereof,   160
with all the powers the undersigned would   168
possess if personally present, hereby ratifying   178
and confirming all that said attorneys and   186
proxies or any of them shall do or cause to be   196
done by virtue hereof.   201
WITNESS the hand and seal of the under-   210
signed this   day of   , 19 ↓₃   219
_____   227

BILL OF SALE

A bill of sale is an agreement by which one person agrees to sell a piece of personal property to another.

JOB 115-2. BILL OF SALE
Standard format. Workbook 219.

BILL OF SALE↓₃   7
KNOW ALL MEN BY THESE PRESENTS   16
That I, Grace Ann Roth, of 548 Blue Jay   24
Drive, Flint, Genesee County, State of Mich-   33
igan, party of the first part, for the sum of Six   43
Thousand Dollars ($6,000), to me in hand   51
paid, at or before the ensealing and delivery   61
of these presents by James Earl Grant, of 247   70
Cedar Street, Ingham County, State of Mich-   78
igan, party of the second part, do sell and grant   89
and convey unto the said party of the second   99
part my 1982 Buick Regal, serial number   106
KT1038-56-47-29S.   110
TO HAVE AND TO HOLD the same unto   118
the said party of the second part forever. And   128
I do covenant and agree to defend the sale of   137
the said automobile against all and every   145
person.   147
IN WITNESS WHEREOF, I have hereunto   155
set my hand and my seal on the sixth day of   164
June in the year of one thousand nine hundred   173
and   175
   ↓₃
_____   183
   ↓₂ 188
Sealed and Delivered
in the Presence of ↓₃   191
_____   197

Type each line four times, or take four 12-second timings on each line. For each timing, type with no more than one error.

```
 5  When you turn the pages in the book, do not make any sound.   12
 6  The sail of the boat caught the wind, and we scooted north.   12
 7  The skies were gray; then the rain became a heavy downpour.   12
            |    |    |    |    |    |    |    |
           25   30   35   40   45   50   55   60
```

Take two 30-second timings on lines 8–10, or type the paragraph twice.

```
 8  As a cause of hearing loss, nothing exceeds the damage that   12

 9  is done by loud noises.  If you work quite near a very loud   24

10  machine, you may become dizzy or possibly injure your ears.   36
      |  1  |  2  |  3  |  4  |  5  |  6  |  7  |  8  |  9  | 10  | 11  | 12
```

When you are writing a report in which you refer to or quote an idea, fact, or statement of someone else, you should give your readers the source of this information. In this way, you give credit to the original author. You also aid your readers, who may want to find additional information on the subject about which you are writing.

In this lesson you will practice using run-in references in a report. Format a book reference as follows: Author, book title, publisher, place of publication, year of publication, page number (if reference is being made to a specific page).

(Note the underscored book title.)

(John Speer, Airplanes, McGraw-Hill Book Company, New York, 1981, p. 10.)

Format a reference to a magazine article as follows: Author [*if known*], "article title," name of magazine, date, page number. (Note the quotation marks for the article title and the underscored magazine title.)

(Beth Zeiman, "The Friendly Skies," Time, September 4, 1981, p. 88.)

JOB 47-1. REPORT WITH RUN-IN REFERENCES

Type the following one-page report with run-in references. Standard format.

A HISTORY OF PARACHUTING
by Grace ackerman #

There are clues that many years ago the chinese tried to invent a sort of "roof tent" for jumping. But, the parachute as we know it was not made until the 1700s. (Ted Terrance, A History of Flying, Glenmore Press, New York, 1980, p. 104.) Balloonists worked to build a *type of* parachute because they *needed* wanted a safe way to land if the balloon burst.

(Continued on next page)

JOB 113/4-1 (Continued)

charge or if you will have to 578
provide your own training. The 584
equipment you buy must be 590
easy to operate by both 594
the dictators and the transcribers. 602

And lastly, be sure that the 609
equipment you buy is flexible 615
and will be able to meet 620
the changes that will take 625
place in your business in the 631
years to come. 634

CENTER SURROUNDINGS 640

Once you know what kind 646
of equipment you are going 651
to buy, you must also decide 657
just where that equipment 662
is going to be placed. What- 668

ever space you choose, you 674
must control the air in the 679
office both for the protection 685
of the equipment and for the 691
comfort of the operator. Is 697
the air too cold or too warm? 703
Is it clean? And does it have 709
the right humidity level? 715

Because of all the typing, 721
reading, handwriting, and edit- 727
ing that are done in a word 733
processing center, it is impor- 739
tant to have the right lighting. 746

Sound must also be controlled 752
so that excessive noise does 757
not affect people's health and 763
performance on the job. 769

LESSON 115

GOALS
- To recognize when exclamation points are used while typing sentences.
- To format and type legal papers.

FORMAT
- Single spacing   60-space line   5-space tab and other tabs as needed

LAB 13

EXCLAMATION POINTS

Type lines 1–4 once. Then repeat lines 1–4 or take a series of 1-minute timings.

1 Wow!   Frank Klinger said that my raise will be retroactive!   12
2 It's just amazing!   None of us has ever heard such a story!   12
3 I can't believe it!   I scored six points more than Quentin!   12
4 Yes!   My manager said, "I will close at 2 p.m. on Fridays!"   12
   | 1 | 2 | 3 | 4 | 5 | 6 | 7 | 8 | 9 | 10 | 11 | 12

To indicate surprise, disbelief, or strong feeling, place an exclamation point at the end of a statement or sentence.

Congratulations! I wish you success in your new job.
Oh, no! I sent the check to the wrong address!
Hurry! We must be at the airport by 3 p.m.!

invention #

    In france a man by the name of garnerin made the first drop in
a cone-shaped parachute. (Scot Webber, "Sky Diving," <u>Sports Today</u>,
May, 1981, p. 154.) He made many jumps but got air sick because of
the wobbly ride down. Then a friend told him to cut a hole in the
top of the chute, allowing air to flow through. This cone shape with
a hole in the top is still used today.

<u>modern uses</u>

    With the use of air planes in world war I, we were able to drop
supplies by para chute to our forces deep in hosstile lands. the parachute
pack has saved the lives of ~~lots of~~ many pilots. Today there are ~~lots~~ all kinds of
people who enjoy the sport of sky diving.

The modern style for month/year dates does not use a comma.

JOB 47-2. REPORT WITH RUN-IN REFERENCES

Retype Job 47-1. Insert a run-in reference after the first sentence in the third
paragraph, as follows:

(Sarah Rosenblatt, <u>Heroes of World War I</u>, Victor Ludwig and
Company, Boston, 1978, p. 271.)

LESSON 48

GOALS
- To capitalize words correctly while typing sentences.
- To type 32/3'/5e.
- To produce a one-page report with an enumeration and run-in references.

FORMAT
- Single spacing   60-space line   5-space tab

LAB 2

CAPITALIZATION

Type lines 1–4 once, providing the missing capitals. Edit your copy as your
teacher reads the answers. Then retype lines 1–4 from your edited copy.

1 Jean Azar moved from the northeast in april or may of 1980.

2 During the Civil War, the north attacked southern shipping.

3 Our south side high school is two miles south of knoxville.

4 The northern and southern railroad travels north to quebec.

Thus, like its predecessors, word processing systems have had great influence on the amount of work produced in the office of today. The completion of more work is made possible through the use of such equipment as the automatic typewriter and the cathode ray tube. Magnetic tape and magnetic card typewriters are able to capture on tape or card all that is placed into the machine and change or delete those words or sections that must be revised before the final copy is typed. The cathode ray tube shows on a screen above the keyboard what is being placed into the storage unit of the typewriter. The keyboard of this machine allows for changes to be made very easily in the text, and these changes are displayed on the screen.

DICTATION EQUIPMENT

Many different kinds of input dictation equipment for word processing are available. You can buy portable units that can be carried away from your desk, and these units are small enough to fit into your coat pocket. A desk-top unit can be purchased from many different suppliers. Many of these units operate with cartridges or cassette tapes; you can dictate, transcribe, or perform both functions on these machines.

Some offices have centralized systems that use private wire connections to all dictators. Sometimes, a telephone system can be used for a word processing dictation system. The number of people capable of using this system at one time is limited only by the number of telephone extensions in use in the office.

SELECTING EQUIPMENT

When choosing input equipment for your word processing center, you should weigh several factors. The cost factor, of course, is very important. Prices will vary greatly, depending on the options and special features you wish to have and the number of units you want. You must decide whether you want a service contract. You must be sure that service can be obtained on short notice and that the people who service your equipment are well trained.

You must set up a training session for all the people who are going to operate the equipment. Find out if the manufacturer will train operators free of

(Continued on next page)

Take a 3-minute Pretest on lines 5–12. Then circle and count your errors. Use the chart below to determine which lines to type for practice.

```
                    1              2              3              4
 5      Outer space is an exciting new place about which we do    12
           5              6              7              8
 6  not know very much.  Science has tried to guess some of the    24
             9             10             11             12
 7  answers to the questions, but we need more facts.  We have,    36
        13             14             15             16
 8  of course, done amazing feats in space, such as land on the    48
        17             18             19             20
 9  moon and shake hands during a walk in space among the stars    60
          21             22             23             24
10  and planets; but there are vast areas still to be explored.    73
        25             26             27             28
11  Do you think that you would like to take a fun journey into    84
           29             30             31             32
12  outer space?  Would you be afraid to encounter the unknown?    96
    | 1 | 2 | 3 | 4 | 5 | 6 | 7 | 8 | 9 | 10 | 11 | 12    SI 1.26
```

PRACTICE

In the chart below, find the number of errors you made on the Pretest. Then type each of the following designated drill lines four times.

Pretest errors	0–1	2–3	4–5	6+
Drill lines	16–20	15–19	14–18	13–17

Accuracy

```
13  walk feats areas space tried place amazing unknown exciting
14  land shake among outer hands facts answers science explored
15  not stars guess about would course afraid journey encounter
16  be you has there hands which think during planets questions
```

Speed

```
17  know very much into new the but and you fun not is an we do
18  some need more like have done such that moon vast take area
19  space tried facts feats areas land know much into are be to
20  hands outer place would shake walk more some like has if so
```

POSTTEST

Repeat the Pretest to see how much your skill has improved.

FORMATTING REFERENCES

Two References in a Row. When a reference notation in a report refers to a book or magazine article that is the same as the one immediately preceding, you may shorten it by using the abbreviation *Ibid.* (meaning "in the same place"). Add a page number if the page is different.

    Ibid., p. 63.

Two References in the Same Work. When a reference notation in a report refers to a book or magazine article fully identified in an earlier reference—but not the one immediately preceding—it may be shortened as follows: Author's surname, page number.

    Speer, p. 11.

Formatting Enumerations in a Report. When an enumeration appears in a report, indent the enumerated items 5 spaces on both sides. If the items take more than 1 line, single-space each item and double-space between items.

JOB 48-1. REPORT WITH ENUMERATION AND RUN-IN REFERENCES

Type the report shown on page 85, providing the needed capitalization. Edit your copy as your teacher reads the correct capitalization. Standard format.

Take two 1-minute timings on each paragraph. Then take one 5-minute timing on the entire selection. Use single spacing for the 1-minute timings and double spacing for the 5-minute timing.

```
13      Locating a good job is one of the most critical things   12
14   you'll do in life.  There very well might be dozens of jobs  24
15   that will be appealing to you and for which you have suffi-  36
16   cient training.                                              39
17      A large number of people find good jobs through ads in   12
18   their local newspapers.  The ads may often quote the skills  24
19   and background you need for the positions for which you may  36
20   like to apply.                                               39
21      Friends might also prove to be a good source for hear-   12
22   ing about job openings that exist; they might learn about a  24
23   job that is going to be opening in the future for which you  36
24   could soon apply.                                            39
25      A fourth source for finding out about a new job may be   12
26   the firms that know just which jobs are vacant.  Employment  24
27   firms are excellent at finding out about positions that are  36
28   now in demand.                                               39
29      These are but a few of the various sources that you'll   12
30   use as you look for a job.  It's important to know that you  24
31   must use a number of options to be assured of the very best  36
32   job possible.                                                39
```
```
| 1 | 2 | 3 | 4 | 5 | 6 | 7 | 8 | 9 | 10 | 11 | 12 |   SI 1.30
```

JOB 113/4-1. BUSINESS REPORT

Standard format. Workbook 213–214.

THE ADVENT OF WORD PROCESSING

By Don Martin

HISTORY

The concept of word processing has been with us for
quite a few years, back to
the late 1800s when C.L.
Sholes from Wisconsin in-
vented the first typewriter
for commercial production
(1873). The touch system
(1889) used on the typewriter
was responsible for changing
the outlook of the modern
office in terms of the amount
of work that could be done
by a typist who used all the
fingers working at the task
instead of just two or four
fingers. Dictating machines were
also responsible for causing
rapid changes in the office.

(Continued on next page)

PASTA

By joyce pavavatti

How well can you apply the rules of capitalization?

WHO FIRST MADE PASTA?

You may think that pasta came from italy, but it has for many, many years been part of the diet of the people of china. (Alfonse Conti, Great Foods, Howe House, new york, 1979, p. 144.) Some sources say that the chinese first made pasta and that marco polo found it in china and brought it back to rome. Other sources say this is not so because pasta was referred to in old roman writings. (Ibid., p. 145.)

IS PASTA GOOD FOOD?

Pasta is easy to digest and low in fat. Although it is also low in protein, the meat or cheese served with noodles and other types of pasta raises the protein content and food value of the dish. (Ruth Roth, "Cut Your Food Bill," Foods Today, june 1981, p. 14.)

When you buy your pasta at the store, be sure the product is made from semolina, which holds its shape well during cooking.

For best results, keep in mind these pointers:

Indent enumerations 5 spaces on each side. Single-space turnovers.

1. don't rinse cooked pasta unless it will be used in a salad.

2. Don't overcook pasta; test it often to be sure it is tender but firm.

3. Serve it at once. (conti, p. 267.)

**ONE-PAGE REPORT WITH ENUMERATION AND RUN-IN REFERENCES
(ELITE TYPE)**

Level 4 of *Gregg Typing, Series Seven*, continues to focus on the formatting of business documents. In Level 4 you will:

1. Demonstrate keyboarding accuracy and speed on straight copy with a goal of 40 words a minute or more for 5 minutes with no more than 5 errors.

2. Correctly proofread copy for errors and edit copy for revision.

3. Apply production skills in keyboarding and formatting copy for four categories of business documents from six input modes.

4. Complete and compose documents required for a job application sequence.

5. Apply rules for correct use of punctuation, capitalization, and numbers in communications.

LESSONS 113 / 114

UNIT 19 FORMATTING REPORTS

UNIT GOAL
39/5'/5e

GOALS
- To use semicolons correctly in compound sentences while typing.
- To type a business report from handwritten copy.

FORMAT
- Single spacing   60-space line   5-space tab

LAB 12

SEMICOLONS IN COMPOUND SENTENCES

Workbook 211–212.

Type lines 1–4 once, providing the missing semicolon in each of the compound sentences. Edit your copy as your teacher reads the answers. Then retype lines 1–4 from your edited copy.

1 Jim Mazer is the new manager ask him for more information.
2 This quarter was very rewarding we made a million dollars.
3 Carole gave explicit instructions see her October 12 memo.
4 You and I will discuss this with Bart let's meet at 2 p.m.

"OK" TIMINGS

Type as many "OK" (errorless) timings as possible out of three attempts on lines 5–7. Then repeat the effort on lines 8–10.

5 Those folks who won big money prizes have vexed Jacqueline.   12
6 The four women in the jury box quickly spotted Dave dozing.   24
7 The judge may require the work to be typed with extra care.   36

8 Judy weaves quickly at large beaches for extra prize money.   12
9 Jack swung my ax quite rapidly, chopping five logs by size. 24
10 The next job was quietly sized up by that very good farmer.   36
   | 1 | 2 | 3 | 4 | 5 | 6 | 7 | 8 | 9 | 10 | 11 | 12

PREVIEW PRACTICE

Type lines 11 and 12 twice as a preview to the 5-minute timing on page 191.

Accuracy   11 job good apply future various critical appealing employment
Speed   12 most that have find like also they firm just know must very

LESSON 49

GOALS
- To build typing accuracy.
- To type 32/3'/5e.

FORMAT
- Single spacing   60-space line   5-space tab

KEYBOARDING SKILLS

Type lines 1–4 once. Then do what line 5 tells you to do. Repeat lines 1–4, or take a series of 1-minute timings.

Speed   1   She is busy with the work but is to go to town for the pay.   12
Accuracy   2   Wes vexed Jack by quietly helping to farm a dozen zucchini.   12
Numbers   3   Do not take 10, 29, and 38 in place of 47 and 56 right now.   12
Symbols   4   Order #29 is for 38 pounds of #10 nails by the end of June.   12
Technique 5   Type line 3 in all caps; release the shift lock as you type the numbers.

       | 1 | 2 | 3 | 4 | 5 | 6 | 7 | 8 | 9 | 10 | 11 | 12

PRETEST

Take a 3-minute timing on lines 5–12, page 84.

PRACTICE

Type lines 6–9 three times. Then type lines 10–13 three times.

6   sws swim swam swell swaps swish sweeps swanky sweats sweets
7   kik skim skid kindly skinny skimpy killer skips skins skimp
8   lol long love loosen clouds sloppy floods loyal along loses
9   ded deer deck dealer seeded headed leaded ceded deeds deuce

10 waw wade wage awake waist waxen awards warden waxers wander
11 lil like lilt milky light slips lilies flight limber slices
12 drd draw drab draft drama drawn drills droopy drives dreads
13 nkn inks pink skunk ankle chunk linked banker tanker dunker

"OK" TIMINGS

This version of a 30-second timing is used to build your accuracy on alphabetic copy. Try to type as many 30-second "OK" (errorless) timings as possible out of three attempts on lines 14–16. Then repeat the effort on lines 17–19.

14   Things seem to happen just right for some people. When the   12
15   good chance comes along to be seized, they are quick to get   24
16   the exact vision of how the lucky moment can work for them.   36

17   Quite by chance you may have seen a person of the other sex   12
18   do a crazy thing. You want to explode in laughter, but you   24
19   just smile. The other person smiles back. You feel great.   36

       | 1 | 2 | 3 | 4 | 5 | 6 | 7 | 8 | 9 | 10 | 11 | 12

POSTTEST

Repeat the 3-minute timing on page 84 to see how much your skill has improved.

LEVEL 4

BUSINESS FORMATTING

LESSON 50

GOALS
- To capitalize words correctly while typing sentences.
- To format a personal-business letter.

FORMAT
- Single spacing   60-space line   5-space tab

LAB 2

Type lines 1–4 once, providing the missing capitals. Edit your copy as your teacher reads the answers. Then retype lines 1–4 from your edited copy.

CAPITALIZATION

Workbook 53–54.

1 I moved to james plaza, which is south of butternut square.
2 The hotel is on north valley drive, just north of oak road.
3 On my birthday we may fly north to vermont for some skiing.
4 We will drive to the west coast next week for a short rest.

12-SECOND TIMINGS

Type each line four times, or take four 12-second timings on each line. For each timing, type with no more than one error.

5 The man and the woman got a day off and got their pay also. 12
6 Did you see that our new red car is in the lot, out of gas? 12
7 It is not at all clear to us why he is to get a part of it. 12

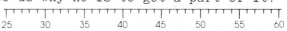

25   30   35   40   45   50   55   60

FORMATTING PERSONAL-BUSINESS LETTERS

A letter from an individual to a department store concerning a personal bill or to a company asking for a job interview is called a *personal-business letter*. A personal-business letter has these standard parts:

Heading. The heading consists of a return address (the writer's address) and the date.

Opening. The opening is the inside address (the address of the person or firm to whom the letter is being sent) and the salutation or greeting.

Body. The message of the letter.

Closing. A complimentary closing, such as *Yours truly* or *Sincerely yours*, and the name of the writer.

To format a personal-business letter:

1. Use standard-size paper (8½ by 11 inches or 216 by 279 mm) or A4 paper (210 by 297 mm, or 8¼ by 11¾ inches).

2. Set margins for a 50-space line (pica) or a 60-space line (elite).

3. Begin the return address on line 13, at the center.

4. Type the date on the line below the return address, aligned with it.

5. Type the inside address 5 lines below the date, at the left margin.

6. Type the salutation, followed by a colon, a double space below the inside address.

7. Begin the message a double space below the salutation. Single-space paragraphs, but double-space between paragraphs. Block paragraphs at the left margin.

8. Type the complimentary closing, followed by a comma, a double space below the body, beginning at the center.

9. Type the writer's name 4 lines below the complimentary closing, beginning at the center. This space is for the writer's signature.

The format described here is the most commonly used letter style and is considered to be the standard format. This style is known as *modified-block style.*

JOBS 50-1 AND 50-2. PERSONAL-BUSINESS LETTER

Type the letter shown on page 88. Standard format. Then retype the letter, using your own address in the return address position, the current date, and your own name as the writer.

Take two 5-minute timings on the paragraphs below.

```
 3      Can you remember how easy it was when you were younger   12
 4  and didn't have to worry about money?  In those years, your   24
 5  parents paid for what you needed or what you couldn't quite   36
 6  do without; you didn't even have to give a thought to where   48
 7  the money had originated.  Now, however, you have dozens of   60
 8  places where your limited amount of earnings must be spent.   72
 9  Most of us know exactly how much money we can spend, and we   84
10  must make wise decisions and set realistic priorities about   96
11  spending.                                                     98
12      Because you must make these wise, realistic judgments,   110
13  it is best to plan a budget.  You, the wage earner, must be  122
14  careful enough to plan ahead.  Items such as food, housing,  134
15  transportation, and any other necessities must be taken out  146
16  first.  Only after all of these have been taken care of can  158
17  you afford to turn your attention to such items as clothing  170
18  and entertainment.  Then you should also think about saving  182
19  some of that money you worked to earn.                       190
   |  1  |  2  |  3  |  4  |  5  |  6  |  7  |  8  |  9  |  10  |  11  |  12   SI 1.44
```

JOB 112-1. LETTER

Standard format. Body 79 words (plus 20 words for subject line). Workbook 209–210.

[*Today's date*] / Mr. Roger Braum / 2476 Flora 13
Avenue / San Jose, CA 95130 / Dear Mr. 21
Braum: / Subject: July 14 Luncheon 29

It was a real pleasure to learn that you will 38
be our speaker for the July 14 luncheon meet- 49
ing. Your presentation, "The Office of the 57
80s," will be well received by all our members. 67

The enclosed luncheon tickets are for you 77
and your wife. The program will begin at 85
1 p.m., and you will have about 50 minutes in 94
which to give your talk. 99

Thank you again, Mr. Braum, for agreeing 108
to take part in our annual meeting. / Yours 118
very truly, / Ms. Jane R. Windom / President 131
/ [*Your initials*] / Enclosure / cc: Scott Webb / 138
cc: Brenda McDaniel / PS: The overhead pro- 148
jector and screen will be in the room for your 157
presentation. 160

JOB 112-2. THREE-COLUMN TABLE

Standard format. Double-space on a full sheet of paper. 10 spaces between columns.

MAJOR LAKES IN CANADA

Name of Lake	Square Miles	Location
Great Bear	12,275 ...	N.W. Territories
Winnipeg	9,465 ...	Manitoba
Athabasca	3,120 ...	Saskatchewan
Nipigon	1,870 ...	Ontario
Melville	1,133 ...	Newfoundland

JOB 112-3. PURCHASE ORDER

Standard format. Workbook 207 bottom.

Purchase Order 350 / J. R. Company / 1201 Hite Street / Akron, OH 44307 / 4 Three-drawer filing cabinets, Model F330 @ $68.75 = $275.00; 2 boxes File folders, #31862 @ $8.25 = $16.50; 2 boxes Filing labels, #15562 @ $1.65 = $3.30; Total $294.80.

Heading
Writer's address
Date

672 Western Parkway ↓13
Park City, UT 84060
April 10, 19-- ↓5

Opening
Name
Inside address
Salutation

Mrs. Violet Logan
LaVista High School
2400 Highland Avenue
Park City, UT 84060 ↓2

Dear Mrs. Logan: ↓2

Body

Last fall I was a student in an advanced course in typing that you taught at the high school on Monday evenings, starting September 4. I received an "A" grade in the course. ↓2

Perhaps you will remember that you helped me get a typing job at the Mesa Clinic in Salt Lake City. I have been working for two months now for Dr. Joel Weiss, and I enjoy my work a great deal. But I find that I need more practice in typing medical terms and filling out forms for patients. ↓2

Do you know where I can take a course in typing for medical office workers? I would be grateful if you would send any brochures about such a course to my home. The address is at the top of this letter. ↓2

Sincerely yours, ↓4

Closing
Complimentary
  closing
Writer's name

Nadine Hooper

JOB 111-2. LETTER

Standard format. Body 63 words (plus 20 words for subject line). Workbook 205–206.

[*Today's date*] / Ms. Sarah Clem / 1183 Cecil   ₁₃
Avenue / San Jose, CA 95128 / Dear Ms.   ₂₃
Clem: / Subject: Banquet Speaker   ₂₉

    Thank you for agreeing to be our banquet   ₃₈
speaker for the March 14 annual luncheon.   ₄₇
We look forward to hearing your presentation,   ₅₆
"Future Trends in the Office."   ₆₂

    Our luncheon will begin at 12 noon, and the   ₇₂
program is now scheduled to begin at 1:30   ₈₀
p.m. Luncheon tickets are enclosed for your   ₈₉
use.   ₉₀

    Once again, thank you for agreeing to speak   ₁₀₀
to our group. / Yours truly, / Carl A. Spears /   ₁₁₅
President / [*Your initials*] / Enclosure / cc: ₁₂₃
Andrew Thomas and Joyce Greene / PS: Please   ₁₃₂
let me know if you have any special equipment   ₁₄₁
needs for your talk.   ₁₄₅

JOB 111-3. CREDIT MEMORANDUM

Standard format. Workbook 207 top.

[*To*] Custom Sporting Goods / [*Today's date*] / 290
Cheyenne Avenue, S. / Tulsa, OK 74103 /
[*Shipped*] Trailways Express

6	Ladies' bowling trophies, 18″		
	[*Unit price*] 12.50	[*Amount*]	75.00
2	League championship trophies, 24″		
	[*Unit price*] 18.00	[*Amount*]	36.00
	Amount credited		111.00
	Delivery charge refund		5.37
	Total amount credited		116.37

JOB 111-4. THREE-COLUMN TABLE

Standard format. Double-space on a full sheet of paper.

MAJOR RIVERS IN THE UNITED STATES

Name of River	Miles in Length	Source
Mississippi	2,350	Minnesota
Missouri	2,320	Montana
Yukon	1,770	Canada
Arkansas	1,460	Colorado
Red	1,270	Oklahoma
Columbia	1,240	Canada

LESSON 112

COMPETENCY CHECK

GOALS
- To type at least 38/5'/5e.
- To demonstrate competency in typing a letter, a ruled table, and a purchase order.

FORMAT
- Double spacing 60-space line 5-space tab

PREVIEW PRACTICE

Type each line twice as a preview to the timings on page 188.

Accuracy   1 priorities realistic decisions clothing saving dozens quite
Speed   2 you wage best about budget earner limited without judgments

LESSON 51

GOALS
- To type a personal-business letter in correct format.
- To address small envelopes and fold letters to fit small envelopes.

FORMAT
- Single spacing   60-space line   5-space tab

KEYBOARDING SKILLS

Type lines 1–4 once. Then do what line 5 tells you to do. Repeat lines 1–4, or take a series of 1-minute timings.

Speed
Accuracy
Numbers
Symbols
Technique

1 It is his fault if he does not help us find the six orders. 12
2 Jumping quickly from the taxi, Hazel brushed a woven chair. 12
3 Please get some price tags for 10¢, 29¢, 38¢, 47¢, and 56¢. 12
4 "Why must I leave?" she asked. "Well," we said, "why not?" 12
5 Depress the shift lock and type line 4 in all-capital letters.

| 1 | 2 | 3 | 4 | 5 | 6 | 7 | 8 | 9 | 10 | 11 | 12

1- AND 3-MINUTE TIMINGS

Take two 1-minute timings on each paragraph. Then take one 3-minute timing on the entire selection. Use single spacing for the 1-minute timings and double spacing for the 3-minute timing.

6   The Inca Indians lived hundreds of years ago near what 12
7 is now Peru; they were a great nation well known for unique 24
8 buildings, which can still be seen in jungle ruins. 34
9   The temples that stand can be searched for clues about 12
10 these people and their way of life. Some knowledge exists, 24
11 for we know that they were a people of many skills. 34
12   The Incas still have lots of secrets which are lost in 12
13 the haze of their culture. The best kept secret is why the 24
14 Incas vanished. In time, we may learn the secret. 34

| 1 | 2 | 3 | 4 | 5 | 6 | 7 | 8 | 9 | 10 | 11 | 12   SI 1.24

JOB 51-1. PERSONAL-BUSINESS LETTER

Standard format. Use your own return address and the current date; use your own name as the writer. Body 127 words.

B&B Agency / 4 Rockefeller Plaza / New York, NY 10020 / Ladies and Gentlemen: / In our class in office practice, our teacher showed your new film, You CAN Succeed. All of us enjoyed it very much. I thought the film was really good for young people who are trying to decide whether they want a career in business. ¶ Our Business Club will hold its state meeting next year. As I am a member of the group that will plan the program, I should like to suggest this film for one of our sessions at the state meeting. ¶ Will you please let me know as soon as possible how much it would cost our organization to rent the film You CAN Succeed for viewing next March. / Yours truly,

LESSON 111

GOALS
- To answer a series of technical questions with a minimum of 80 percent competency.
- To type a credit memo, a report, a letter, and a table.
- To type 38/5'/5e.

FORMAT
- Single spacing   60-space line   5-space tab

TECHNICAL QUESTIONS

Compose and type answers to the following questions. Your goal is to answer 16 or more questions correctly.

Reports

1. Are minutes of a meeting single- or double-spaced?

2. How do you type the page 2 heading of a magazine article?

3. What is the minimum acceptable bottom margin for all pages of a report?

4. What are the minimum acceptable side margins you may use on an unbound report?

5. How do you display a table in a report?

Tables

6. What vertical spacing is used before and after a ruled line in a table?

7. In tables containing figures, do you align the numbers on the left or on the right?

8. How many times do you space vertically between the last line of a table and the final horizontal ruling?

9. What are leaders?

Letters

10. How many pica or elite spaces are used in the line length of a standard business letter?

11. Does a *cc* notation precede or follow an enclosure notation when both are used in a letter?

12. What salutation do you use when using an attention line?

13. What does *bcc* mean?

14. Is a *cc* notation typed on the original copy of a letter so the addressee will see it?

15. In what order would you type the following notations at the bottom of a letter: postscript, reference initials, carbon copy notation, enclosure?

16. How do you type an attention line in letters? on envelopes?

Forms

17. How many spaces are left between the printed guide words and the ones typed on a memo?

18. What is a credit memorandum?

19. What is an invoice?

20. What is a statement of account?

JOB 111-1. REPORT

Standard format. Double-space on plain paper.

LEGAL TYPING   7

Some Basic Differences in Format   29

The typing of legal papers can present some   41
problems for the typist who has never before   50
had to prepare such documents. However, a   58
quick review of legal typing should clarify   67
most of the questions.   72

LINE LENGTH   76

If legal paper is used, the line length is   86
established by the rules on both sides of the   96
paper. A typist should type within these lines,   105
which are placed at 14P/17E spaces from the   114

left edge and 4P/5E spaces from the right   122
edge.[1]   125

PARAGRAPHS AND MARGINS   132

Paragraph Indentions. A 10-space para-   149
graph indention is used on legal papers.   157

Top and Bottom Margins. On the first page   176
of the paper, the typist should use a top margin   186
of 12 lines. On other pages a 9-line top margin   196
is used. The bottom margin is always about   205
6 lines.[2]   209
                                                            215

[1]Alan C. Lloyd et al., Typing 1, General   234
Course, Gregg Division, McGraw-Hill Book   245
Company, New York, 1982, p. 194.   251
   [2]Ibid.   257

FORMATTING SMALL ENVELOPES (No. 6¾)

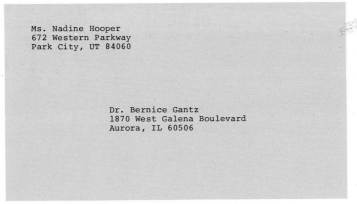

```
Ms. Nadine Hooper
672 Western Parkway
Park City, UT 84060




          Dr. Bernice Gantz
          1870 West Galena Boulevard
          Aurora, IL 60506
```

No. 6¾ (6½ by 3⅝ inches, or 165 by 92 mm)
Metric: No. C7/6 (162 by 81 mm, or 6⅜ by 3⅛ inches)

Envelopes contain two addresses—the mailing address, to which the letter is sent, and the writer's return address.

1. To format a return address, begin on line 3, in 5 spaces from the left edge. Single-space the address.
2. To format the mailing address, begin the addressee's name and address on line 12, at 20 spaces from the left edge of the envelope. Single-space the address.

In all addresses, type the city, state, and ZIP Code on one line. Remember to leave 1 space between the state and the ZIP Code number.

FOLDING LETTERS FOR SMALL ENVELOPES

To fold a letter for a small envelope, bring the bottom edge up to ⅜ inch (10 mm) from the top edge, fold the right-hand third toward the left, fold the left-hand third toward the right. Then insert the last crease into the envelope.

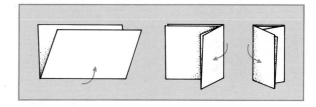

JOB 51-2. ADDRESSING SMALL ENVELOPES

Address three envelopes as follows: (1) as shown in the illustration of the small envelope above, (2) for the letter in Job 51-1, page 89, and (3) for the letter in Job 50-2, pages 87–88. Workbook 55.

LESSON 52

GOALS
- To recognize how numbers are expressed while typing sentences.
- To produce two personal-business letters, with addressed envelopes.

FORMAT
- Single spacing   60-space line   5-space tab

LAB 3

NUMBER STYLE

Type lines 1–4 once. Then repeat lines 1–4 or take a series of 1-minute timings.

```
1  Jack ordered five boxes of pads and eight boxes of pencils.   12
2  This aircraft will hold 152 passengers and 12 crew members.   12
3  Fourteen members of the panel voted in favor of my quizzes.   12
4  The room is precisely 8.5 meters long and 4.57 meters wide.   12
   |  1  |  2  |  3  |  4  |  5  |  6  |  7  |  8  |  9  |  10  |  11  |  12
```

Spell out numbers from *1* through *10*; use figures for numbers above *10*. (**Exception:** Spell out any number that begins a sentence.)

Only *three* offices have been painted.
Send *12* brochures and *75* order forms to Ms. Ames.
Fifteen applicants were interviewed today.

In technical copy and for emphasis, use figures for numbers: *4 p.m., 3 liters, 2.5 miles, 7 spaces, 12 lines, page 9, $8.*

```
13      Looking for a place to live can be frustrating as well    12
14   as exciting; many different points must be examined before,   24
15   during, and after this search.  In order to make what seems   36
16   to be a hazy issue clear, you should make a listing of pros   48
17   and cons for all apartments that you see.  Needless to say,   60
18   you should consider important points when making this list;   72
19   you must put each point in proper perspective as well.        83
20         In making your list of pros and cons, quiz yourself on  95
21   the following aspects.  How long will you have to travel to  107
22   get to work?  If you don't own an auto, how near are public  119
23   transportation lines?  Is your apartment furnished, or must  131
24   you provide the furniture?  Will you have to pay all of the  143
25   utilities?  What kinds of recreational facilities might you  155
26   have access to?  Must you sign a lease, or can you just pay  167
27   rent every month?  How large a security deposit is required  179
28   prior to your occupancy?  How much rent will you pay?         190
     |  1  |  2  |  3  |  4  |  5  |  6  |  7  |  8  |  9  |  10  |  11  |  12    SI 1.39
```

What Increases Your Accuracy?

Sitting right and not moving.

Typing with fingers ONLY.

Keeping arms and wrists quiet.

Typing steadily, not speedily.

Thinking each letter to yourself.

Keeping your wits about you.

Keeping calm about your errors.

FORMATTING POSTAL CARD ADDRESSES

To format addresses on postal cards, follow the format for small envelopes:

1. Type a return address (if necessary) on line 3, 5 spaces from the left edge.

2. Begin the mailing address on line 12, 20 spaces from the left edge.

Remember to single-space all addresses. Type the city, state, and ZIP Code on one line; leave 1 space between the state name or abbreviation and the ZIP Code.

```
GAMMA EPSILON CHAPTER
2122 Bradford Place
Fort Worth, TX 76112



          Ms. Anita Griffin
          3501 Hanover Avenue
          Dallas, TX 75225
```

JOB 110-1. POSTAL CARDS

Using the alphabetic file cards you prepared in Job 109-1, send a postal card to each of the new initiates regarding the next meeting. The meeting will take place on February 21, 19--. The return address is Gamma Epsilon Chapter, 2122 Bradford Place, Fort Worth, TX 76112. Standard format. Workbook 201–204.

Take two 30-second timings on lines 5–7, or type the paragraph twice.

```
5  If there is a blaze in a home near us, we can be so excited     12
6  that we want to dash to see it.  So many observers may come     24
7  that they quite often jeopardize the work of fire fighters.     36
   |  1  |  2  |  3  |  4  |  5  |  6  |  7  |  8  |  9  |  10  |  11  |  12
```

JOB 52-1. PERSONAL-BUSINESS LETTER

Standard format. Address an envelope. Envelope: Workbook 57. Body 132 words.

Notice that the number 5 has been circled—the proofreaders' mark for spelling out a numeral.

62 Hadley Avenue/Dayton, OH 45419/October 19, 19–/ LaViva Foods, Inc./1200 East Brady Street/Erie, PA 16505/ Ladies and Gentlemen:/Yesterday I bought ⑤ LaViva frozen pizzas for a party I had last night. Although I baked the pizzas as directed, the crust was tough, and the sauce was so bitter that we could not eat them. I had to throw them out. ¶ Today I took my receipt to the Fair Price market where I bought the pizzas. The manager gave me a refund; then he asked me to write to you because he thought that you should know about this problem. ¶ I hope that you will check this matter so that your food products will always be up to your usual high standards. The code number on the boxes was CX-463./Yours truly,/ Peggy Hamner

JOB 52-2. PERSONAL-BUSINESS LETTER

Standard format. Use your own return address and the current date; use your name as the writer. Address an envelope. Envelope: Workbook 57. Body 122 words.

Mr. Edward L. Brown, Manager / The Skyline Motel / Mercer, PA 16137 / Dear Mr. Brown: / Last week my two friends and I stayed at your motel for a weekend of skiing in the area. As members of the Skyline Ski Club and guests at your motel, we were to be given free ski-tow passes. ¶ When I got home, however, I checked the bill dated _____ [*fill in last Sunday's date*] and discovered that we were charged $36 for the use of the ski tow. Since we are all members of the Skyline Ski Club, we should not have been charged for the use of these facilities. ¶ I would appreciate your taking the time to correct our bill and send me a check for the sum of $36, the amount of the overcharge. My address is at the top of this letter. / Sincerely,

FORMATTING BUSINESS MAILING LABELS

When using sheets of labels, type the left-hand labels first; then move the margin stop and type the right-hand labels. Start each name and address 10P/12E from the left edge, and estimate the vertical center for each entry.

```
Ms. Anita Griffin
3501 Hanover Avenue
Dallas, TX 75225
```

JOB 109-3. BUSINESS MAILING LABELS

Type a mailing label for each person in Job 109-2; follow the illustration to the right. Standard format. Workbook 199.

LESSON 110

GOALS
- To use semicolons correctly in compound sentences while typing.
- To type at least 38/5'/5e.
- To format postal card addresses.

FORMAT
- Single spacing   60-space line   5-space tab

LAB 12

Type lines 1–4 once, providing the missing comma *or* semicolon in each of the compound sentences. Edit your copy as your teacher reads the answers. Then retype lines 1–4 from your edited copy.

SEMICOLONS IN COMPOUND SENTENCES

1 Alex made copies for everyone he mailed them the next day.
2 Katie went to Brazil and she plans to stay there one week.
3 Call Ann quickly or write her a letter explaining my idea.
4 Just file these five or six copies discard all the others.

PRETEST

Take a 5-minute Pretest on lines 13–28 on page 185. Circle and total your errors. Use the chart below to find the number of errors you made on the Pretest. Then type each of the designated drill lines four times.

PRACTICE

Pretest errors	0–1	2–3	4–5	6+
Drill lines	8–12	7–11	6–10	5–9

Accuracy

5 can for security consider exciting different transportation
6 you many examined important needless apartments frustrating
7 well live looking furniture furnished occupancy perspective
8 see all listing following utilities facilities recreational

Speed

9 aspects search should public lease every large live pay you
10 deposit points making access lines kinds might rent how can
11 required proper travel place clear point; list sign pay all
12 points before during after order seems issue must line owns

POSTTEST

Repeat the Pretest (lines 13–28), page 185.

LESSON 53

GOALS
- To identify how numbers are expressed while typing sentences.
- To format two business letters.

FORMAT
- Single spacing   60-space line   5-space tab

LAB 3

NUMBER STYLE

Type lines 1–4 once. Then repeat lines 1–4 or take a series of 1-minute timings.

1 Eighty-eight students will tour Europe for five long weeks. 12
2 Just mix 12.5 grams of powder in 10.5 liters of the liquid. 12
3 I will purchase 13 pairs of socks, 15 blazers, and 22 ties. 12
4 Yes, 14 students from my college are among the 77 scholars. 12
   | 1 | 2 | 3 | 4 | 5 | 6 | 7 | 8 | 9 | 10 | 11 | 12

12-SECOND TIMINGS

Type each line four times, or take four 12-second timings on each line. For each timing, type with no more than one error.

5 Most of the good guys in the movie were wearing white hats. 12
6 Her jolly friends have been glad that she has done so well. 12
7 He has found that a bit of music is a help when he studies. 12

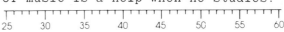

25   30   35   40   45   50   55   60

FORMATTING BUSINESS LETTERS

Workbook 59–60.

A business letter represents a company, not an individual, and is therefore typed on printed letterhead—official company stationery on which are printed the company's name, address, and telephone number.

The parts of the business letter—heading, opening, body, closing—are similar to the parts of the personal-business letter. However, there are some differences.

1. Most of the heading information is already included in the letterhead; only the date must be added.

2. In a business letter the closing includes not only the writer's name but also his or her title. (Together the name and title lines are called the *writer's identification*.)

3. The closing in a business letter includes the typist's initials (see page 93).

To format a business letter: (1) Type the date on line 15, beginning at the center. (2) Type the writer's title on the line below the writer's name, aligned with it. (3) Type the initials of the typist at the left margin, a double space below the writer's title. Type the initials without periods in either lowercase letters or in all-capital letters.

This format is most commonly used in business and is considered to be the standard format. It is known as *modified-block style*.

JOB 53-1. BUSINESS LETTER
Type the letter on page 93. Standard format. Workbook 61, 63–64. Body 178 words.

JOB 53-2. BUSINESS LETTER
Standard format. Workbook 65–66. Body 111 words.

Remember

Titles of books and magazines are underscored with an unbroken line.

[*Today's date*] / Ms. Jane Petit / 462 West Omaha Avenue / Akron, OH 44301 / Dear Ms. Petit: / Thank you for your letter telling us how much you enjoyed the story that appeared in the June issue of Young Views about new careers in the health field. ¶ We are sending you the booklet you asked for, Your Future as a Health Worker. There is, of course, no charge for the booklet. ¶ We hope that you will continue to follow your plans to train for a job in the health professions. If we can be of any further service to you, please write to us or call our toll-free number: (800) 555-6000. / Very truly yours, / Henry J. Templer / Editor in Chief [*Your initials*]

LESSON

GOALS
- To identify how semicolons are used in compound sentences while typing.
- To format and to type alphabetic file cards.
- To format and to type business mailing labels.

FORMAT
- Single spacing   60-space line   Tabs as needed

LAB 12

Type lines 1–4 once. Then repeat lines 1–4 or take a series of 1-minute timings.

SEMICOLONS IN COMPOUND SENTENCES

```
1  I may be able to help you with this; Vera may also be free.   12
2  Yes, Joan types quickly; she is also an expert in spelling.   12
3  Max Dubron prefers the new procedures; Ella Zeldon doesn't.   12
4  Ken works in our Dallas office; he may be transferred soon.   12
   |  1  |  2  |  3  |  4  |  5  |  6  |  7  |  8  |  9  |  10  |  11  |  12
```

FORMATTING ALPHABETIC FILE CARDS

Workbook 188.

Names and addresses that are frequently referred to are often kept on 5 by 3 cards for quick reference. If the cards are arranged in alphabetic order by last name, they are called *alphabetic file cards*.
   To format alphabetic file cards:

1. Start typing the person's name on line 2, 4 spaces from the left edge of the card.

2. Type the person's last name first, followed by the first name and middle initial or middle name (if any).

3. Type titles such as *Miss, Ms., Mr., Mrs., Dr.,* and *Prof.* in parentheses after the name.

4. Type the address a double space below the name, indented 3 spaces.

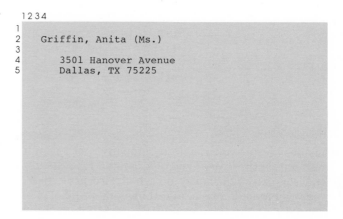

```
  1234
1
2    Griffin, Anita (Ms.)
3
4       3501 Hanover Avenue
5       Dallas, TX 75225
```

JOB 109-1. ALPHABETIC FILE CARDS
Type a card for each name in the table below. Standard format. Workbook 195, 197.

INITIATES OF GAMMA EPSILON CHAPTER

November 14, 19--

Dr. Scott Harbison	7730 Idlewood Lane	Dallas, TX 75230
Miss Diane Goertzen	3433 Kaywood Drive	Dallas, TX 75209
Mr. Domingo Andrada	225 Shady Lane	Fort Worth, TX 76116
Ms. Louise Baum	2532 Eastridge Drive	Fort Worth, TX 76117
Dr. Margaret Dodson	7050 Arapaho Road	Garland, TX 75042
Mr. Joseph Yamata	5842 Live Oak Drive	Irving, TX 75061
Mr. Alvin Watson	2407 Greenhill Drive	Mesquite, TX 75150
Mrs. Gloria Tucker	1715 Langdon Road	Mesquite, TX 75149

JOB 109-2. THREE-COLUMN TABLE
Arrange the file cards you typed in Job 109-1 in alphabetic order (by last name). Then type the table above, arranging the names alphabetically. Standard format. Full sheet of paper.

Letterhead

LaVIVA FOODS, Inc.

1200 East Brady Street
Erie, Pennsylvania 16505
814-555-7000

↓ 15

Date
Line 15

July 14, 19--

↓ 5

Ms. Peggy Hamner
62 Hadley Avenue
Dayton, OH 45419

↓ 2

Dear Ms. Hamner:

↓ 2

We are very sorry to learn that you could not eat the five LaViva frozen pizzas you bought at your local store last week. Thank you for writing to us about this matter. We want all our customers to be pleased with our products.

↓ 2

When our pizzas leave our plant, they are fresh, with all the flavor frozen in; but sometimes the shipper or the grocer does not put the pizzas in the freezer right away. The food begins to defrost, and when at last the pizzas are put in the freezer case, they have lost their true flavor. There is nothing we can do about this.

↓ 2

We want to give you a gift for trying to help us. If you will take this letter to your Fair Price store, your grocer will give you free $10 worth of LaViva frozen foods of your choice. We hope that you will enjoy these great foods and that you will continue to buy our pizzas.

↓ 2

Closing

Sincerely yours,

↓ 4

Writer's name
and job title

Dominic Sparanta
Vice President

↓ 2

Typist's initials

km

BUSINESS LETTER, STANDARD FORMAT

Take two 1-minute timings on each paragraph. Then take one 5-minute timing on the entire selection. Use single spacing for the 1-minute timings and double spacing for the 5-minute timing.

8 Have you ever been on a fairly long trip by car simply to find   14
9 yourself bored because you did not have much to do? You, the   26
10 passenger, have many options available to minimize boredom.   38

11 One answer to the boredom is to read some books in the car. You   14
12 will find a paperback at the local bookstore; and as you read, you can   28
13 obtain many hours of entertainment and enjoyment.   38

14 But you, a passenger, can do much more than just read. There are   14
15 dozens of activities and games that can be played while you travel;   28
16 magnetic checkers and chessboards can be great fun.   38

17 There are also games where passengers count particular types of   14
18 signs or landmarks, or you might choose to partake in guessing games   27
19 with other passengers. And extra players add fun.   38

20 Therefore, if you are a person who does not quite like riding along   15
21 on an extended trip, plan ahead. Think of all the nice activities you   29
22 and others can participate in while traveling.   38

| 1 | 2 | 3 | 4 | 5 | 6 | 7 | 8 | 9 | 10 | 11 | 12 | 13 | 14   SI 1.42

FORMATTING STATEMENTS OF ACCOUNT

A statement of account summarizes a customer's transactions during a specific period (usually a month).

To format a statement of account:

1. Align fill-ins in the heading with guide words.
2. Begin typing the body a double space below the horizontal rule; single-space the body.
3. Visually center the date in the first column. Abbreviate long months. To align numbers on the right, space twice before typing one-digit numbers.
4. Begin items in the Reference column 2 spaces after the vertical rule.
5. Visually center amounts of money in the Charges, Credits, and Balance columns.

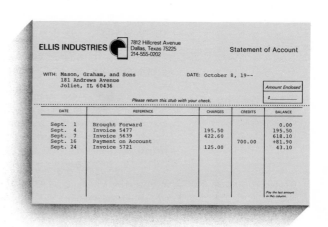

JOB 108-1. STATEMENT OF ACCOUNT
Workbook 193.

[To] Red's Sport Shop / West Acres Shopping Center / Fargo, ND 58102

May 1 Brought forward [Balance]72.00
    10 Payment [Credit]72.00
       [Balance]00.00
    15 Invoice 3559 [Charges]234.00
       [Balance]234.00

JOB 108-2. STATEMENT OF ACCOUNT
Set tabs as needed. Workbook 193.

[To] Clarks' Sports Center / South Washington Shopping Center / Grand Forks, ND 58201

July 1 Brought forward [Balance]135.50
    15 Invoice 3575 [Charges]89.25
       [Balance]224.75
    18 Payment [Credits]100.00
       [Balance]124.75

LESSON 54

GOALS
- To express numbers correctly while typing sentences.
- To type 34/3'/5e.
- To format business letters with enclosures.
- To address large envelopes and fold letters to fit in large envelopes.

FORMAT
- Single spacing 60-space line 5-space tab

LAB 3

NUMBER STYLE

Type lines 1–4 once, correcting any errors in number-style rules. Edit your copy as your teacher reads the answers. Then retype lines 1–4 from your edited copy.

1 Joann listed 100 items to be discussed in the next meeting.

2 The engineer said that the precise diameter is 1.75 meters.

3 We need 10 samples, but they shipped us only 4 or 5.

4 426 women attended the huge convention.

1- AND 3-MINUTE TIMINGS

Take two 1-minute timings on each paragraph. Then take one 3-minute timing on the entire selection. Use single spacing for the 1-minute timings and double spacing for the 3-minute timing.

```
                  1            2            3           4    1'
 5     Health foods may seem ridiculous to some of us; but if  12
              5            6            7           8
 6  you enjoy pure and natural foods, you know what a change it  24
              9           10           11
 7  makes in your life when you eat all-natural foods.          34
            12           13           14           15
 8     It is a fact that most people who eat health foods all   12
            16           17           18           19
 9  the time require less medical care.  If you play a sport or 24
            20           21           22
10  exercise and get plenty of rest, you are sensible.          34
            23           24           25           26
11     Explore health foods like fruits, fresh produce, nuts,  12
            27           28           29           30
12  grains, and dairy foods; they make up a basic diet that all 24
            31           32           33           34
13  need to preserve their strength for zestful lives.          34
    |  1  |  2  |  3  |  4  |  5  |  6  |  7  |  8  |  9  |  10  |  11  |  12    SI 1.26
```

FORMATTING ENCLOSURE NOTATIONS

Whenever an item is sent within a letter, the word *Enclosure* is typed on the line below the reference initials. The enclosure notation reminds the sender to include the item, tells the receiver to look for the item, and serves as a record on the file copy. For more than one item, type *2 Enclosures, 3 Enclosures,* and so on.

```
                              John Harman Jones
                              President

TCW
3 Enclosures
```

FORMATTING PURCHASE ORDERS

When a purchase requisition has been approved, the purchasing department completes a purchase order.

To format a purchase order:

1. Use the standard format for invoices.
2. Visually center the catalog number in the column marked "Catalog No."
3. Type the word *Total* aligned with the *D* in *Description*.

JOB 107-2. PURCHASE ORDER

Type and arrange the information below on a purchase order, using the illustration above as your guide. Workbook 191.

Purchase Order 345. Hanson Supplies Inc., 1248 Meridian Avenue, San Jose, CA 95125. 1 Carpet, Style 8962, 14' × 30' @ $6/sq ft = $2,520.00; 13 Office chairs, Model 498E @ $45 = $585.00; 1 Executive chair, Model 499EX @ $125 = $125.00; 1 Conference table, Model 50CT @ $454.00 = $454.00. Total = $3,684.00.

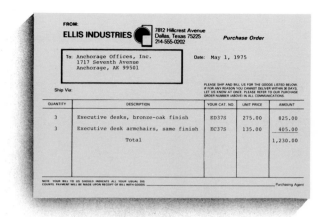

LESSON 108

GOALS
- To recognize how semicolons are used in compound sentences while typing.
- To format and to type a statement of account.

FORMAT
- Single spacing   60-space line   5-space tab and as needed

LAB 12

SEMICOLONS IN COMPOUND SENTENCES

Type lines 1–4 once. Then repeat lines 1–4 or take a series of 1-minute timings.

```
1  Ms. Wall is our personnel director; she is now on vacation.   12
2  Jeff must go to Zurich quickly; May is on her way to Zaire.    12
3  Alex's report is due next week; he has nearly completed it.    12
4  Bertha is in charge of this project; give her all my bills.    12
   |  1  |  2  |  3  |  4  |  5  |  6  |  7  |  8  |  9  |  10  |  11  |  12
```

In LAB 7 (page 132), you learned to use a comma before *and, but, or,* and *nor* in compound sentences. When no conjunction is used, place a semicolon between the two independent clauses.

Larry took a bus; Mary went by plane. (No conjunction joins the two independent clauses. A semicolon is needed.)

We have an office in New York; we will have one in Boston soon.

12-SECOND TIMINGS

Type each line four times, or take four 12-second timings on each line. For each timing, type with no more than one error.

```
5  Where in the world can we find an island on which to relax?   12
6  Once the rain began to pour, it just went on and on and on.   12
7  Now is the right time for you to sell the old black trucks.   12
   25      30      35      40      45      50      55      60
```

JOB 54-1. BUSINESS LETTER

Standard format. Prepare the small addressed envelope that is to be enclosed. Workbook 67–68. Body 94 words.

(Today's date) Mr. Rudolph Martino/412 Ash Street/Terre Haute, IN 47804/Dear Mr. Martino:

We are pleased that you plan to enter our pizza bake-off contest and test your skills in making pizza. ¶ The first round of the bake-off will be on Sunday, May 10, at 1 p.m. at the Erie Home Show. You must be 18 years old or under to enter, and we ask that you bring all your own supplies. Twenty-six persons have already entered. ¶ If you will need a hotel room in Erie, please use the enclosed envelope to send me your reservation request. Good luck next Sunday./Sincerely yours,/Alfred J. Leary/Director of Public Relations/(Your initials)/Enclosure

Workbook 69–70.

FORMATTING LARGE ENVELOPES (NO. 10)

To format a large envelope:

1. (a) Type a return address. Begin on line 3, 5 spaces from the left edge. Single-space the address. **Or:** (b) If the envelope already has a printed return address, type the sender's name on the line above the address. Block the name if the address is blocked; center the name if the address is centered.

2. Begin the mailing address on line 14, 40 spaces from the left edge. Single-space the address, and remember to leave only 1 space between the state and the ZIP Code.

FORMATTING SPECIAL ENVELOPE DIRECTIONS

To format special directions:

1. Type an on-arrival direction (such as *Personal* or *Confidential*) on line 9, aligned at left with the return address. Use capital and small letters, and underscore the direction.

2. Type a mailing direction (such as *Special Delivery* or *Registered*) on line 9, ending about 5 spaces from the right edge of the envelope. Use all-capital letters. Do not underscore.

Nathan Parks

THOMPSON & EVANS
LAWYERS BUILDING
PITTSBURGH, PA 15219

Confidential   SPECIAL DELIVERY

Ms. Linda T. Humphries
5650 Southeast Fremont Street
Atlanta, GA 30315

No. 10 (9½ by 4⅛ inches, or 241 by 105 mm)
Metric: No. DL (220 by 110 mm, or 8⅝ by 4⅜ inches)

GOALS
- To format and to type purchase requisitions and purchase orders.

FORMAT
- Single spacing   60-space line   Tabs as needed

KEYBOARDING SKILLS 8'

Type lines 1–4 once. In line 5, backspace and underscore each underscored word immediately after typing it. Repeat lines 1–4, or take a series of 1-minute timings.

Speed   1 It is easy for them to type this short, brief line of type. 12
Accuracy 2 If we find the precise quiz, just give Bob an exam quickly. 12
Numbers   3 On 10/29/56 we drove 38 miles to Waco and 47 miles to Hico. 12
Symbols   4 Is #47 selling @ $.38 or $.56? It sold for 45¢ (20% less). 12
Technique 5 They _may_ soon _know_ how _good_ they are as _they_ type _the_ work. 12

| 1 | 2 | 3 | 4 | 5 | 6 | 7 | 8 | 9 | 10 | 11 | 12

12-SECOND TIMINGS 6'

Type each line four times, or take four 12-second timings on each line. For each timing, type with no more than one error.

6 It is their wish to go to the city by auto when they do go. 12
7 Their goal is to do the work by the sixth or eighth of May. 12
8 Their firm is paid to paint half the signs for those towns. 12

25   30   35   40   45   50   55   60

36'

FORMATTING PURCHASE REQUISITIONS

Purchasing goods or services is a two-step procedure in most companies: First a *purchase requisition* is completed and sent to the purchasing department. Then the purchasing department completes an *official purchase order* and sends it to the supplier.

To format a purchase requisition:

1. Align the fill-ins in the heading with the guide words.

2. Begin typing the body a double space below the ruled line.

3. Visually center the quantity in the *Quantity* column.

4. Begin the description 2 spaces after the vertical rule. Single-space items that take more than one line. Double-space between items. Indent turnover lines 3 spaces.

5. Insert the suggested supplier's name and address as an address block, 2 spaces after the vertical rule.

6. Do not fill in the bottom portion of the form. This will be completed by the purchasing department.

Purchase Requisition No.
TO: Purchasing Agent--ALEUTIAN ALLSAVE--2713 Third Avenue--Anchorage, AK 99501

Department: Medical   Date of Request: August 9, 19--
Location: Ground Floor   Date Wanted: September 15, 19--
Person: Dr. Steubens

Reason: To implement expanded services

Approvals: _____   _____
          Signature of Department Head   Other Signature Required

QUANTITY	DESCRIPTION	SUGGESTED PURCHASE SOURCE
1	Gladstone 76 Instrument Sterilizer Catalog No. 4498-IS12	Alaskan Medical Supplies 213 Willoughby Avenue Juneau, AK 99801

PURCHASING DEPARTMENT INFORMATION
Ordered From: _____   Purchase Order Number: _____
                                 Date Ordered: _____
                                 Date Received: _____

JOB 107-1. PURCHASE REQUISITION

Type and arrange the information below on a purchase requisition, using the illustration above as your guide. Workbook 191.

Purchase Requisition 1116. Mark Grove, Sales Manager, Room 710, needs the following items to renovate the conference room on May 12: 1 Green shag carpet, 14' × 30'; 13 Baylor office chairs; 1 Parman executive chair; 1 Walnut conference table, 3' × 20'. Order from Smythe Supplies, 250 Pine, Akron, OH 44302.

JOB 54-2. ADDRESSING LARGE ENVELOPES

Address three envelopes, using the copy given in (1) the illustration at the bottom of page 95, (2) the letter in Job 54-1 on the top of page 95, and (3) the letter in Job 53-1 on pages 92–93. Workbook 71, 73.

FOLDING A BUSINESS LETTER

To fold a letter for a large envelope, (1) fold up the bottom third of the paper, (2) fold the top third over the bottom third, and (3) insert the letter into the envelope, with the last crease going first.

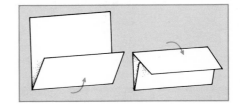

LESSON 55

CLINIC

GOALS
- To build typing speed.
- To type 34/3'/5e.

FORMAT
- Single spacing   60-space line   5-space tab

KEYBOARDING SKILLS

Type lines 1–4 once. Then do what line 5 tells you to do. Repeat lines 1–4, or take a series of 1-minute timings.

Speed | 1 | Kay got the forms for the firm and may also work with them. | 12
Accuracy | 2 | Six jumbo elephants quickly moved the wagon from the blaze. | 12
Numbers | 3 | You can take the 1:38 bus, the 4:56 bus, or the 8:47 train. | 12
Symbols | 4 | Grant & Harris developed the Kenyan, Smith & Blake project. | 12
Technique | 5 | Retype line 3. Underscore only the figures—not the words.

| 1 | 2 | 3 | 4 | 5 | 6 | 7 | 8 | 9 | 10 | 11 | 12

PRETEST

Take a 3-minute timing on lines 6–14.

6   A batik is a dyed cloth that has hot wax painted on it   12
7   to form a design. The artist melts wax, tints it different   24
8   colors, paints a design, and then dyes each cloth.   34
9   But some artists paint the cloth with clear wax. Then   12
10   the batik is dyed again and again, using many colors. Just   24
11   the part not coated with that wax is then colored.   34
12   The second method requires more work on the part of an   12
13   artist, but the colors in the finished batik will have more   24
14   zest and look brighter to those who see the cloth.   34

| 1 | 2 | 3 | 4 | 5 | 6 | 7 | 8 | 9 | 10 | 11 | 12   SI 1.26

In the chart below, find the number of errors you made on the Pretest. Then type each of the designated drill lines four times.

Pretest errors	0–1	2–3	4–5	6+
Drill lines	25–29	24–28	23–27	22–26

Accuracy

22 clean vision quantity friends everyone finished suggestions
23 search school waiting repairs majority essential automobile
24 drive almost drizzle certain entertain ourselves windshield
25 time nation reduced pressure condition inspected obstructed

Speed

26 chance family could hours such tank care view help come not
27 owning course there tears when must here rain long trip gas
28 should wipers tires belts they have auto also many they six
29 visit check often quick items level alone ripe them has our

POSTTEST

Repeat the Pretest on page 178 to see how much your skill has improved.

FORMATTING CREDIT MEMORANDUMS

Workbook 187.

A credit memorandum is a form used to let a customer know that a credit (deduction) has been made to his or her account.

To format a credit memorandum:

1. Use the standard format for business invoices.
2. Type the words *Total amount credited* (instead of *Total amount due*) aligned with the *D* in *Description*.
3. Format any adjustments as follows:

Amount credited	75.15
5% Sales tax refund	3.76
Transportation refund	3.45
Total amount credited	82.36

ELLIS INDUSTRIES
7812 Hillcrest Avenue
Dallas, Texas 75225
214-555-0202

Credit Memorandum
No.

TO: Williams and Finch, Inc.   DATE: October 8, 19--
181 Danvers Street
Normal, IL 61761

Your account has been credited as follows:

QUANTITY	DESCRIPTION	UNIT PRICE	AMOUNT
6	Regulation Type F Basketballs, damaged in transit	11.90	71.40
1	Basketball Inflation Pump and Needle, not ordered	3.75	3.75
	Amount credited		75.15
	5% Sales tax refund		3.76
	Transportation refund		3.45
	Total amount credited		82.36

JOB 106-1. CREDIT MEMORANDUM 756

Workbook 189.

[*To*] Alamosa Sports Equipment / 204 Main Street / Alamosa, CO 81101 / [*Credits:*]

10   Racquetball rackets, Model 75H
(handle wrapping defective)
[*Unit price*] 19.50   [*Amount*] 195.00
5   Racquetball gloves, right hand
(elastic torn)
[*Unit price*] 4.75   [*Amount*] 23.75

Amount credited	218.75
Transportation refund	17.50
Total amount credited	236.25

JOB 106-2. CREDIT MEMORANDUM 757

Workbook 189.

[*To*] C & R Sports Inc. / 378 Delaware Avenue, N.E. / St. Petersburg, FL 33703 / [*Credits:*]

3   Fastdart dart boards, 36"
(boards not ordered)
[*Unit price*] 15.65   [*Amount*] 46.95
12   Bullseye darts, #4560
(dart tips damaged)
[*Unit price*] 12.50   [*Amount*] 150.00

Amount credited	196.95
Transportation refund	8.76
Total amount credited	205.71

PRACTICE	Practice the words in the Pretest on which you made errors or slowed down. Type each word at least three times.
30-SECOND TIMINGS	Take three 30-second timings on each paragraph on page 96. Try to increase your speed each time.
1-MINUTE TIMINGS	Take two 1-minute timings on each paragraph on page 96. Try to maintain your 30-second speed.
POSTTEST	Repeat the Pretest on page 96 twice to see how much your skill has improved.

UNIT 10 FORMATTING TABLES

UNIT GOAL
34/3'/5e

GOALS
- To express numbers correctly while typing sentences.
- To format 2-column tables and 3-column tables.

FORMAT
- Single spacing 60-space line Tabs as needed

LAB 3

Type lines 1–4 once, correcting any errors in number-style rules. Edit your copy as your teacher reads the answers. Then retype lines 1–4 from your edited copy.

NUMBER STYLE

1 Over 250 people attended the party for Jacqueline and Gary.

2 90 pens were left on the desk for their art instructor.

3 About 5 or 6 members of the club attended the meeting.

4 6 students helped the 120 senior citizens plan that tour.

30-SECOND TIMINGS

Take two 30-second timings on lines 5–7, or type the paragraph twice.

5 All of us must make decisions every day. Some of these are   12

6 quite routine, but others can be of major importance. Good   24

7 citizens work at always making logical and exact decisions.   36

| 1 | 2 | 3 | 4 | 5 | 6 | 7 | 8 | 9 | 10 | 11 | 12

FORMATTING TABLES

A table lists data in columns and rows. For quick understanding and easy reference, most tables are worded concisely.

A table can be included as part of a letter, memo, or report, or it can be displayed on a separate sheet of paper.

When a table is typed on a separate sheet of paper, it is centered horizontally and vertically. Standard formatting instructions apply. Use double spacing unless directed to do otherwise.

To format the body of a table horizontally, follow these steps:

1. Clear the margins and tabs on the machine.

2. Identify a "key line." Find the longest entry in each column and add 6 spaces between the columns, as shown below and on page 98:

```
To Kill a Mockingbird        Shakespeare
                    123456
```

(**Note:** Six spaces are standard, but you may use any number of spaces that will make the table attractive and easy to read.)

(*Continued on next page*)

LESSON 106

GOALS
- To use commas to set off appositives while typing sentences.
- To type credit memorandums.

FORMAT
- Single spacing   60-space line   5-space tab and as needed

LAB 11

Type lines 1–4 once, providing the missing commas for each line. Edit your copy as your teacher reads the answers. Then retype lines 1–4 from your edited copy.

COMMAS WITH APPOSITIVES

Workbook 185–186.

1 We thank you Ms. Gamble for all your help on our project.
2 Our employer the Quincey Corporation is moving to Boston.
3 Gregg Hanley's office the huge corner office was painted.
4 Ask our manager John Appezzatto to send five dozen boxes.

PRETEST

Take a 5-minute Pretest on lines 5–21. Then circle and count your errors. Use the chart on page 179 to determine which lines to type for practice.

```
                    1                              2
5         The laws in this country permit us to drive an automo-    12
              3                         4
6    bile; many of us do so prior to finishing high school.  The    24
        5                  6                           7
7    majority of us today believe that we must own an automobile    36
                           8                      9
8    to search for a new job, entertain ourselves, or visit good    48
            10                        11                      12
9    friends.  When we own an auto, we must be sure to check for    60
                           13                     14
10   repairs frequently.  Here are six quick suggestions that we    72
              15
11   could certainly follow.                                        77
              16                        17
12        We must be certain to check for such things as the oil    89
        18                  19                      20
13   level, the quantity of gas in the car, and the air pressure    101
                      21                        22
14   in the tires.  Obviously, we must clean the windshield with    113
            23                        24                    25
15   care so that our view is not obstructed.  We should observe    125
                           26                        27
16   the condition of the windshield wipers so that if it should    137
              28                        29
17   drizzle or rain, our vision will not be reduced.  The drive    149
        30                        31                      32
18   belts should also be inspected for rips or tears.  We could    161
                 33                        34
19   possibly find ourselves waiting many hours for another per-    173
              35                        36                      37
20   son to assist us if a belt tears, leaving us stranded while    185
                           38
21   we're on an extended trip.                                     190
     |  1  |  2  |  3  |  4  |  5  |  6  |  7  |  8  |  9  |  10  |  11  |  12    SI 1.39
```

3. From the center of the page, back-space-center the key line and set the left margin stop at the point to which you backspaced.

4. Space across the paper to the start of the next column (the width of column 1 plus 6 spaces) and set a tab stop. No matter how many columns there are in the table, use the margin stop for the first column and a tab stop for each additional column.

5. When you type a table, use your tabulator to move from column to column as you type each line.

JOB 56-1. TWO-COLUMN TABLE

Format a copy of the table shown below. Standard format. Half sheet of paper.

Title

CLASSICS FOR TEENAGERS

Body with two columns

Animal Farm	Orwell
Frankenstein	Shelley
Lord of the Flies	Golding
Moby Dick	Melville
Romeo and Juliet	Shakespeare
To Kill a Mockingbird	Lee

Column width is determined by longest item in a column.

Key line

To Kill a Mockingbird   Shakespeare
123456

JOB 56-2. TWO-COLUMN TABLE

Standard format. Half sheet of paper.

GIRLS' LACROSSE RECORDS

Goals in a game	Chris Chester
Goals in a season	Charlene Hvorecky
Goals by a freshman	Lynn Armstrong
Goals by a sophomore	Barb McCoy
Goals by a junior	Karen Schultz
Goals by a senior	Lee Van Ban
Assists in a game	Chris Chester
Assists in a season	Gwen Chan

JOB 56-3. THREE-COLUMN TABLE

Standard format. Half sheet of paper.

HOME TEAMS IN VARIOUS STATES

Georgia	Atlanta	Falcons
Maryland	Baltimore	Colts
Illinois	Chicago	Bears
Missouri	Kansas City	Chiefs
Missouri	St. Louis	Cardinals
Washington	Seattle	Seahawks

6	abide	bevel	crude	ditch	eaves
7	groan	hinge	igloo	judge	knock
8	meter	mourn	ounce	prowl	quart
9		slack	toast	until	venue
10		fixed	youth	zebra	adorn
11		clock	doubt	every	fable
12			heart	imply	joist
13			learn	music	north
14			phase	query	react
15				tempt	union
16				worry	exams
17				zings	again

PRETEST

Take a 2-minute Pretest on lines 18–26; then take a 2-minute Pretest on lines 27–34. Circle and count your errors on each Pretest. Double spacing; 5-space tab.

Speed

18   Typing has for many years been a useful skill to those   12
19 who wish to work in the field of business. People who wish   24
20 to study other careers also realize it is useful. In fact,   36
21 there are not many who can claim that this skill is not one   48
22 of the best to possess.   54
23   In the past few years, though, a similar skill has ap-   66
24 peared in schools all across this land. Keyboarding is the   78
25 name of the skill; and it, too, will soon enjoy a degree of   90
26 fame because of its many uses.   95

Accuracy

27   Keyboarding is very useful to those who aspire to work   12
28 in the field of business but who do not wish to acquire the   24
29 expert skill that is often associated with those who pursue   36
30 careers in business education or in the secretarial area.   48
31   This course is primarily for all those people who want   59
32 to learn as soon as they can how to operate the keyboard by   71
33 touch so that they can program their own personal computers   83
34 or communicate with a computer housed in their own company.   95

| 1 | 2 | 3 | 4 | 5 | 6 | 7 | 8 | 9 | 10 | 11 | 12   SI 1.39

PRACTICE

In which Pretest did you make more errors? If in the speed lines (18–26), type the speed lines below six times and the accuracy lines three times. If in the accuracy lines (27–34), reverse the procedure.

Speed

35 keyboarding degree years skill those claim been has for the
36 business similar useful though field enjoy wish can not one
37 appeared possess typing people across work also fact, land.
38 because careers realize schools there many soon its and too

Accuracy

39 can touch their course pursue personal business secretarial
40 they that those housed expert program computers communicate
41 this with learn often acquire company primarily keyboarding
42 very soon field aspire operate careers education associated

POSTTEST

Repeat the Pretests.

LESSON 57

GOALS
- To format subtitles and to align numbers and decimals in tables.

FORMAT
- Single spacing   60-space line   Tabs as needed

KEYBOARDING SKILLS

Type lines 1–4 once. Then do what line 5 tells you to do. Repeat lines 1–4, or take a series of 1-minute timings.

Speed   1   If they give him a good price, he might take a lot of them.   12
Accuracy   2   Jeff quickly amazed the audience by giving six new reports.   12
Numbers   3   The years to remember are 1910, 1929, 1938, 1947, and 1956.   12
Symbols   4   Please find #2938, #4756, #1029, #1038, and #1947 for them.   12
Technique   5   Retype line 3. Underscore each of the years.

| 1 | 2 | 3 | 4 | 5 | 6 | 7 | 8 | 9 | 10 | 11 | 12

PRETEST

Take a 3-minute Pretest on lines 6–14. Then circle and count your errors. Use the chart below to determine which lines to type for practice.

6   High tech is the name given to a basic and useful type   12
7   of design that is changing the concept of modern living and   24
8   things we use daily. It has long enjoyed a quiet appeal in   36
9   places like stores and restaurants, but now it is coming to   48
10   be used in homes. High tech designs are not expensive, and   60
11   they are built to last. They come in a wide range of zany,   72
12   bright colors; things such as water pipes, tire rubber, and   34
13   window glass are often used with style in high tech designs   96
14   and are fun to own and use.   102

| 1 | 2 | 3 | 4 | 5 | 6 | 7 | 8 | 9 | 10 | 11 | 12   SI 1.26

PRACTICE

In the chart below, find the number of errors you made on the Pretest. Then type each of the designated drill lines four times.

Pretest errors	0–1	2–3	4–5	6+
Drill lines	18–22	17–21	16–20	15–19

Accuracy   15   own basic quiet stores design concept expensive restaurants
16   built style pipes range bright rubber window appeal designs
17   use and are they tech living modern useful designs changing
18   now but used come water things colors coming places enjoyed

Speed   19   glass daily wide zany such tire come like home with has not
20   homes given high tech name type long used they last now are
21   appeal living useful given basic things daily long type use
22   colors bright stores water pipes style glass range zany are

POSTTEST

Repeat the Pretest to see how much your skill has improved.

JOB 104-1. LETTER

Block format (see page 172). Workbook 183–184. Body 66 words (plus 20 words for subject line).

(Today's date)/Shield Home Inspection_{^Inc.}/1800 South Elm Street/Grand   19

Forks, ND 58201/Dear Mr. Shields̶/:/Subject: Home Repairs Check   34

              home *Mrs. Anne Shiek,*

    A ^*home* buyer has asked that I contact you to arrange for an in-   51

           of the ^*foundation*   *i*   *year*

spection ^on a home that we repa̶red last M̶arch. ⟨Please send all   101

charges for this inspection to my office.⟩   110

    At the buyer's request, *I will would like you to inspect the basic*   78

                                  repairing

workmanship and materials used ⟩in ~~renovating~~ the foundation for the   91

house at 1210 South Elm (St.)/Sincerely yours,/Gordon H. ~~Hampton~~ *Hall*/   120

Building Contractor/(Your initials)/cc: Mr. & Mrs. Ralph M. Ernst   132

bcc: Kay West *P. S. Please let me know the exact day you plan to*   146

make the inspection.   150

LESSON 105

CLINIC

GOALS
- To review tabulator key and margin-release-key operations.
- To type 38/2'/2e.

FORMAT
- Single spacing   60-space line   Tabs every 8 spaces

KEYBOARDING SKILLS

Type lines 1–4 once. In line 5, use your tabulator key to advance from one word to the next through the entire line. Repeat lines 1–4, or take a series of 1-minute timings.

Speed   1   If an auditor signs the key amendment, I may work for them.   12

Accuracy   2   Have five more wax jugs been glazed quickly for two people?   12

Numbers   3   With 56 precincts tallied, Gray had 3,847; Green had 2,910.   12

Symbols   4   Interest on the $247 loan was 9 3/4%, which came to $24.08.   12

Technique   5   and   nor   the   too   den   mop   see   for

    | 1 | 2 | 3 | 4 | 5 | 6 | 7 | 8 | 9 | 10 | 11 | 12

TAB AND MARGIN RELEASE REVIEW

Set your left margin at 20 and your right margin at 62. Set a tab every 10 spaces. Type lines 6–17 on page 177. Use the tabulator key to move from column to column. Use the margin release key to complete the typing of the last word in each line.

FORMATTING SUBTITLES IN TABLES

Workbook 77.

NUMBERS IN COLUMNS

Subtitles in tables are formatted the same way as subtitles in other documents: (1) Center the subtitles. (2) Double-space before and triple-space after them. (3) Use initial caps.

Align numbers. Numbers are aligned at the right. If a column of numbers contains items with decimals or amounts of money with decimals, as shown at the right, the decimals should be aligned.

Key line. Use the longest item in the column—just as you would if the column contained words. If the column contains a dollar sign, be sure to include it in the key line.

Margin and Tabs. Since spacing forward and backward will be needed to align the number items at the right, set the margin or tab stops for the digit that requires the least forward and backward spacing (note where the margin and the tabs were set for the illustration at the right).

```
        HEMP'S DEPARTMENT STORE
                                    ↓2
        Fall Clearance Sale
                                    ↓3
 564        Silk Ties          $10.62
  19        Belts                 1.43
   5        Wool Sweaters        19.95
1500        Pairs Socks            .75
 M            T                  T
```

JOB 57-1. THREE-COLUMN TABLE WITH SUBTITLE AND NUMBERS

Type the copy in the column to the right. Standard format (see pages 97 and 98). Double spacing. Half sheet of paper.

ASTRO CONSTRUCTION
Number of Employees on June 30

Warehouse	Lima, OH	116
Plant	Denver, CO	1,235
Office	New York, NY	954
Branch	Seattle, WA	28
Branch	Chicago, IL	39
Branch	Atlanta, GA	9
Branch	Dallas, TX	11

JOB 57-2. THREE-COLUMN TABLE WITH SUBTITLE AND NUMBERS

Standard format. Double spacing. Half sheet of paper.

The Great Race
Kilometers Completed by City Business Club Members

G. Craig	Beaver High	12.6
W. Kahn	Denby High	10.5
L. Mervis	Lincoln High	8.0
R. Bennett	Oliver High	7.2
S. Bellini	Gladstone High	6.1
A. Dever	Kenton High	5.7

Take a 5-minute Pretest on lines 5–20. Circle and count your errors.

When You Type:

Sit all the way back in the chair.

Sit erect, leaning forward slightly.

Set your feet squarely on the floor.

Place your ankles 6 to 8 inches apart.

```
 5        If you attend college upon graduation from high school  12
 6   next year, choose the school you feel will be acceptable to  24
 7   you.  Certain issues must be looked at; and you, the gradu-  36
 8   ating senior, should assess all of them very carefully.  In  48
 9   making a choice, it's essential that you discuss the issues  60
10   with all of your good friends who are attending the schools  72
11   in which you might choose to enroll.  You should also go to  84
12   the college campuses that are of great interest to you.      95
13        While you are in high school is the time to plan for a  107
14   program of study you wish to pursue in college.  Inquire at  119
15   several schools to ascertain whether the college you'd like  131
16   to attend has the precise program of your choice.  You must  143
17   also identify just where you'd like to go to school.  Would  155
18   you prefer staying quite close to home, or would you prefer  167
19   attending college in another state far away from home?  You  179
20   ought to consider your total cost and the school size.       190
     |  1  |  2  |  3  |  4  |  5  |  6  |  7  |  8  |  9  |  10  |  11  |  12    SI 1.38
```

PRACTICE

Type the accuracy lines (21–24) below as a group four times. Type the speed lines (25–28) four times each.

Accuracy

```
21   cliff allow attend allied channel baggage attorney accuracy
22   hills flood enroll collar fulfill drilled colleges carriage
23   proof kitty occupy hidden outdoor illness marriage loudness
24   stuff small tariff rotten warrant spelled withheld socially
```

Speed

```
25   armchair burdened auditor chicken apathy burden burst dough
26   delegate eloquent educate friends fairly height flick lapse
27   latitude neighbor husband network layout sickly mayor rough
28   identify urgently statute without taught waited sorry visit
```

POSTTEST

Repeat the Pretest.

FORMATTING A POSTSCRIPT (*PS:*)

A postscript (*PS:*) is an additional message typed in paragraph form at the end of a letter. To format a postscript:

1. Double-space after the last item in the letter.
2. Type the postscript at the left margin if paragraphs were blocked; indent it if paragraphs were indented.
3. Type *PS:*, leave 2 spaces, and type the message.

```
                              Sincerely your

                              Matthew R. Hal
                              Purchasing Dep
     jbo

     PS:  Please let us know within a week if you
     items in stock.
```

LESSON 58

GOALS
- To recognize how numbers are expressed while typing sentences.
- To format tables with blocked column headings.

FORMAT
- Single spacing   60-space line   Tabs as needed

LAB 4

Type lines 1–4 once. Then repeat lines 1–4 or take a series of 1-minute timings.

NUMBER STYLE

1 They have fine new offices at 171 Seventh Avenue in Queens. 12
2 The Orin Building is located at 56th Street and West Fifth. 12
3 They built a new zoo at 462 Sixth Avenue--or is it Seventh? 12
4 Our jet departs at 11:45 a.m. and arrives 30 minutes later. 12

| 1 | 2 | 3 | 4 | 5 | 6 | 7 | 8 | 9 | 10 | 11 | 12

Spell out street names from *first* through *tenth*; use figures for street names above *tenth*. Also use figures for all house numbers except *one*: *One Third Avenue, 12 West 22 Street, 7 Fifth Avenue.*

Use figures to express most periods of time: *45 minutes, 10:15 a.m., 7 o'clock, 30 days.* Use figures for dates: *May 9, 1989.*

12-SECOND TIMINGS

Type each line four times, or take four 12-second timings on each line. For each timing, type with no more than one error.

5 See if this paper will fit in the slot near the right wall. 12
6 We hope to get a big order from one of the firms near here. 12
7 Sue did her best to get a pup that we can keep in the yard. 12

25   30   35   40   45   50   55   60

FORMATTING BLOCKED COLUMN HEADINGS

Column headings in tables clarify the data in each column and eliminate unnecessary words. In draft copies and in informal correspondence, column headings may be blocked.

To format blocked column headings:
1. Begin the column heading at the left edge of the column (at the margin or tab stop).
2. Type the column heading in initial caps and underscore it.
3. Triple-space before and double-space after a column heading.

MEMBERSHIP NOMINEES ↓2

Report of the
Membership Committee ↓3

Juniors   Seniors ↓2

Sally Hollins   Richard Belemy
Max Schroeder   Alice Bickmore

JOB 58-1. TWO-COLUMN TABLE WITH BLOCKED COLUMN HEADINGS

Type the copy in the column to the right. Standard format. Half sheet of paper.

JOB 58-2. THREE-COLUMN TABLE WITH BLOCKED COLUMN HEADINGS

Retype Job 58-1 adding the name of the country as column 1. Use the column heading *Country*. Standard format. Half sheet of paper.

International TRAVELERS' FORECAST #
Today's Projected Weather Conditions
ea 2 - #

# City	# Forecast
Amsterdam	Cloudy
Frank furt	rain
Peking	Fair *it*
London	Heavy Fog
Mexico City	hazy
Tel Aviv	Clear

FORMATTING A BLIND CARBON COPY (*BCC*) NOTATION

When you do not want the addressee to know that a carbon copy is being sent to someone else, use a blind carbon copy (*bcc*) notation on all copies *but not on the original letter*.

To format a *bcc*:

1. Type the *bcc* notation on line 7 at the left margin of the carbon copies.

2. Use the same style for the *bcc* as you would use for a *cc* notation.

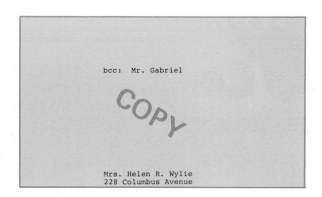

JOB 103-2. LETTER

Block format (see page 172). Workbook 179–180. Body 65 words.

[*Today's date*] / Mr. Gardner F. West / Ling- 13
Champion Company / 105 Royal Lane / Com- 20
merce, TX 75428 / Dear Mr. West: 28

We will be pleased to welcome your group 37
and take you on a visit of our plant on the 46
date you suggest. 49

If you can, please arrange your arrival for 59
about 9:30 in the morning. We will have our 68
guides waiting for you. 73

The tour takes an hour and a half. It 83
involves walking about two miles—tell your 92
members to wear their walking shoes! / Cor- 101
dially yours, / Elizabeth Hawkins / Guest 112
Receptionist / [*Your initials*] 116

JOB 103-3. LETTER

Standard format with indented paragraphs (see page 171). Workbook 181–182. Body 37 words.

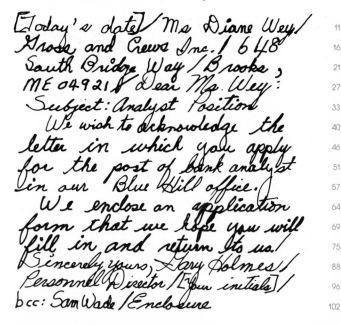

GOALS
- To use commas to set off appositives while typing sentences.
- To format a postscript notation.
- To type 35/5'/5e.

FORMAT
- Single spacing   60-space line   5-space tab

LAB 11

Type lines 1–4 once, providing the missing commas for each line. Edit your copy as your teacher reads the answers. Then retype lines 1–4 from your edited copy.

COMMAS WITH APPOSITIVES

1 The best runner is Phil Jones a new student at Maxim High.
2 If you have questions, call our service manager Ann Smith.
3 Get in touch with the dean Dr. Leonard for an assignment.
4 Will Liz be available on Tuesday August 21 for a meeting?

Paper turned lengthwise has the following dimensions: Width, 110 pica spaces or 132 elite spaces. Depth, 51 lines.

JOB 58-3. FOUR-COLUMN TABLE WITH BLOCKED COLUMN HEADINGS

Standard format. Full sheet of paper turned lengthwise.

PORTLAND TOWN HALL
Winter Program of Events

Date	Topic	Speaker	Location
January 15	Books	L. T. Borman	Downtown YMCA
January 29	Music	Sandra Cotts	East End Library
February 12	Real Estate	Fred T. Hamma	South High School
February 26	Theater	Betty Jean Bay	College Club
March 10	Business	Stuart Green	Civic Hall

LESSON 59

GOALS
- To identify how numbers are expressed while typing sentences.
- To format tables with short centered column headings.

FORMAT
- Single spacing   60-space line   Tabs as needed

LAB 4

NUMBER STYLE

Type lines 1–4 once. Then repeat lines 1–4 or take a series of 1-minute timings.

```
1  My jet should depart at 10:47 a.m. and arrive at 12:34 p.m.    12
2  Eighty-six people will attend the workshops in New Zealand.    12
3  Meet Bart at 12 o'clock on 142d Street near Seventh Avenue.    12
4  Amy lives quietly on Third Avenue, but she prefers Seventh.    12
   |  1  |  2  |  3  |  4  |  5  |  6  |  7  |  8  |  9  |  10  |  11  |  12
```

30-SECOND TIMINGS

Take two 30-second timings on lines 5–7, or type the paragraph twice.

```
5  Success is very much needed by all in the learning process.    12
6  The exercises that the students type must nct cause them to    24
7  just quit working; students need their work recognized too.    36
   |  1  |  2  |  3  |  4  |  5  |  6  |  7  |  8  |  9  |  10  |  11  |  12
```

FORMATTING SHORT CENTERED COLUMN HEADINGS

When a column heading is shorter than the longest line in a column, the heading should be centered over the column. Follow these formatting directions:

1. Subtract the number of spaces in the column head from the number of spaces in the longest line in the column.

2. Divide the answer by 2 (drop any fraction) and indent the column head that many spaces.

```
            Date

      September 12
      September 30
      October 10
```

In the column above, the heading is 4 spaces long; the longest line is 12. Thus 12 − 4 = 8 and 8 ÷ 2 = 4. Indent the head 4 spaces from the start of the column.

FORMATTING A CARBON COPY NOTATION

1. One line below your reference initials (or below the enclosure notation, if there is one), type *cc:*, leave 2 blank spaces, and type the name of the person receiving the copy.

2. Type each additional name on a separate line, aligned with the name on the first line. Do not repeat *cc:* before each name.

```
                          Sincerely yours,


                          Karen Bouchard
                          Director

BPT
Enclosure
cc:  Mr. Crawsen
     Ms. Daniels
```

ASSEMBLING A CARBON PACK

Carbon packs consist of ① the sheet of paper or letterhead on which your original correspondence is to be typed, ② the carbon paper containing the carbon ink that transfers to all sheets but the original, and ③ the onionskin or other thin sheets of paper on which you wish to make carbon copies.

When assembling a carbon pack, make sure the carbon (shiny) side faces the copy paper—not the original.

To insert a carbon pack into your typewriter, you must first straighten the sides and top of the carbon pack so that all edges are even.

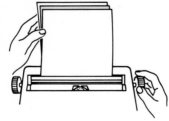

After you have straightened the carbon pack, hold it with your left hand with the carbon side (and the copy paper) facing you. Now turn the cylinder smoothly with your right hand. Continue turning the cylinder until you have advanced to the vertical position where you want to start typing.

JOB 103-1. LETTER
Standard format with indented paragraphs (see page 171). Workbook 177–178. Body 76 words.

[Today's date] / Mr. Rick Menlo / Time- 12
keeper watches Co. / 225 Eighth Ave. / 19
New York, NY 10027 / Dear Mr. Menlo: 28

Enclosed is the defective Time- 36
keeper watch to which I refered in my 44
recent letter of May 10. We have had 50
this watch in our repair shop on 4 dif- 59
ferent occasions but have been unable 66
to resolve find the problem. 71

Would you, Mr. menlo, please ask 79
your repair shop to isolate the cause 86
of the problem--a stem date that does 94
not release. If we cannot correct the 102
defect, we will shall have to give the owner 110
a new watch. / Yours Truly, / Leslie E. 123
Lauson / Manager, Dallas Region / [Your 132
initials] / Enclosure / cc: Mr Conrad 136
White 137

JOB 59-1. TABLE WITH SHORT CENTERED COLUMN HEADINGS
Standard format. Half sheet of paper.

OAKDALE HIGH SCHOOL
Varsity Field Hockey Schedule

Date	Opponent	Site
September 12	Ellis	Home
September 21	St. Agnes	Away
September 30	Quaker Valley	Home
October 10	Keystone	Home
October 18	Winchester	Away

JOB 59-2. TABLE WITH SHORT CENTERED COLUMN HEADINGS
Standard format. Half sheet of paper.

WINTER TOURNAMENT
Varsity Basketball

Player	Position
B. Ligurski	R. Forward
D. Swenson	L. Forward
C. Brewster	R. Guard
C. Kanter	L. Guard
D. Sirinek	Center

JOB 59-3. TABLE WITH SHORT CENTERED COLUMN HEADINGS
Standard format. Half sheet of paper.

GEMS OF THE WORLD _#
Origin of the most Precious Stones
2—#

Gem	Country
Emerald	Colombia
amethyst	Brazil
Opal	Australia
diamond	South africa ᵃ
Ruby	Burma

JOB 59-4. TABLE WITH SHORT CENTERED COLUMN HEADINGS
Standard format with 8 spaces between columns. Full sheet of paper.

EXPEDITIONS TO THE NORTH POLE
By ice, air, and sea #
2—#

Name	Vehicle	Year
Byrd	airplane	1926
Norge	Dirigible	1927 6
Nautilus	Submarine	1958
Plaisted	Snow mobile	1968
Herbert	Dog sled	1969
Arktika	Icebreaker	1077 9

LESSON 60

GOALS
- To express numbers correctly while typing sentences.
- To type 34/3'/5e.
- To format tables with long and short centered column headings.

FORMAT
- Single spacing   60-space line   Tabs as needed

LAB 4

Type lines 1–4 once, correcting any errors in number-style rules. Edit your copy as your teacher reads the answers. Then retype lines 1–4 from your edited copy.

NUMBER STYLE

1 His jet from Mexico to Quebec leaves at eight-fifteen p.m. today.

2 You are invited to attend our sorority meeting at two-thirty p.m.

3 7 days ago she bought 2 new skirts and 3 blazers.

4 I walked down 6th Avenue last evening looking for a sale.

FORMATTING LETTERS IN BLOCK STYLE

Another style that is used to format letters is known as the *block style*, where *all* letter parts begin at the left margin. Margins and vertical spacing remain the same.

JOB 102-2. LETTER

Block format. Workbook 173–174. Body 68 words (plus 20 words for subject line).

[*Today's date*] / Mr. Paul Abernathy / Night-   13
light Hotel Inc. / 2670 Blue Bird Drive / Great   22
Neck, NY 11023 / Dear Mr. Abernathy: /   30
Subject: Sales Meeting   36

Last year we had the pleasure of holding our   46
sales meeting at your hotel. Our meeting was   55
a big success; and a large part of our good   64
fortune was due, of course, to the excellent   73
services we received from your hotel.   81

We would like to return   86
to your hotel for our next meet-   93
ing. Would you, therefore, please   100
let me know what your group   105
rates are for this year. /Sincerely/   114
J. J. Reynolds / Program Chairperson /   122
[Your initials]   123

JOB 102-3. LETTER

Block format. Workbook 175–176. Body 78 words.

[*Today's date*] / Mr. Adam T. Weight / 141 Rice   14
Street / LaGrange, TX 38046 / Dear Mr.   22
Weight: / Subject: Luncheon Speaker   30

How delighted I am that you have agreed to   39
speak at our closing luncheon for the Adver-   48
tising Club's annual meeting in Nashville on   57
March 14.   59

As one of the country's foremost authorities   69
on consumerism, you will certainly be able to   78
provide us with important, relevant informa-   88
tion. All of us look forward to hearing you.   96

Your plane tickets and hotel confirmation   105
will be sent to you shortly. The honorarium   114
of $250 will be sent by the end of March.   123
Yours truly, / Joan T. Parks / [*your initials*]   132

LESSON 103

GOALS
- To identify how commas are used to set off appositives while typing sentences.
- To learn how to use carbon packs.
- To format *cc* and *bcc* notations.

FORMAT
- Single spacing 60-space line 5-space and center tabs

LAB 11

COMMAS WITH APPOSITIVES

Type lines 1–4 once. Then repeat lines 1–4 or take a series of 1-minute timings.

1 The book I want, <u>Principles of Management</u>, is out of stock.   22
2 My brother, John Quinn, is a fullback on the football team.   12
3 Your next workshop will be on Valentine's Day, February 14.   12
4 Sue Krzyskowski, our personnel manager, recruits employees.   12

| 1 | 2 | 3 | 4 | 5 | 6 | 7 | 8 | 9 | 10 | 11 | 12

PRETEST 4′

Take a 3-minute Pretest on lines 5–13. Then circle and count your errors. Use the chart below to determine which lines to type for practice.

```
                      1              2              3              4
 5        Antiques are old items that have become valued objects    12
              5              6              7              8
 6   with the passing of time.  Rugs, lamps, chairs, silverware,    24
              9              10             11             12
 7   and objects of art are bought and sold at auctions and by a    36
              13             14             15             16
 8   number of great experts around the world.  Antiques are big    48
              17             18             19             20
 9   business, and each year some items become the rage with all    60
              21             22             23             24
10   those who like to collect.  Prices zip up and down with the    72
              25             26             27             28
11   demand, but antiques can be a good way to invest some money    84
              29             30             31             32
12   that you plan to save.  Just be sure not to toss out an old    96
              33             34
13   piece that may be worth money.                               102
     |  1  |  2  |  3  |  4  |  5  |  6  |  7  |  8  |  9  |  10 |  11 |  12    SI  1.28
```

PRACTICE 7′

In the chart below, find the number of errors you made on the Pretest. Then type each of the designated drill lines four times.

Pretest errors	0–1	2–3	4–5	6+
Drill lines	17–21	16–20	15–19	14–18

Accuracy

```
14   become objects private antiques passing business silverware
15   demand valued chairs bought number around experts business,
16   rage just rugs that have money those world collect auctions
17   with sold lamps items invest prices become objects antiques
```

Speed

```
18   prices some down with good save zip who all big are art old
19   collect money items that like each year out not may you way
20   become items those plan toss save time some sure and are up
21   valued invest shops just each sure sold that with can of be
```

POSTTEST 4′

Repeat the Pretest to see how much your skill has improved.

25′

FORMATTING LONG CENTERED COLUMN HEADINGS

Workbook 78.

When a column heading is longer than any item in the column, the column is centered under the heading. To format the column under the heading:

1. Subtract the number of spaces in the longest line in the column from the number of spaces in the heading.

2. Divide that answer by 2 (drop any fraction), and indent the column that number of spaces. In the example, 23 − 13 = 10 and 10 ÷ 2 = 5. Indent the column 5 spaces.

3. Reset the left margin or tab stop to the point of the indention.

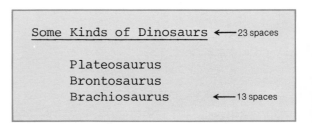

Note: When the column heading is longer than the column, regard the heading as part of the key line.

LESSON 102

GOALS
- To recognize how commas are used to set off appositives while typing sentences.
- To format letters in two styles: blocked with indented paragraphs and full-blocked.

FORMAT
- Single spacing   60-space line   5-space and center tabs

LAB 11

COMMAS WITH APPOSITIVES

Type lines 1–4 once. Then repeat lines 1–4, or take a series of 1-minute timings.

```
1 Our educational consultant, Jan Newby, is highly qualified.  12
2 Mr. Williams, our resident expert, was amazed at this idea.  12
3 We have planned to hold the next meeting on Monday, May 27.  12
4 It is best for you, our client, to know everything we know.  12
  |  1  |  2  |  3  |  4  |  5  |  6  |  7  |  8  |  9  |  10 |  11 |  12
```

An appositive is a word or a phrase that further describes or identifies a person or a thing. Use two commas to separate an appositive within a sentence. Use one comma if the appositive begins or ends the sentence.

Mrs. Baker, *the national sales manager,* approved the raises.
(The words *the national sales manager* further identify *Mrs. Baker.*)

This account was handled by a local firm, *Adams & Fells.*

The seminar has been rescheduled for next Monday, *August 12.*

FORMATTING LETTERS WITH INDENTED PARAGRAPHS

The letters that you have typed in this course have all been formatted in *modified-block style,* with the date, complimentary closing, writer's name or name and title indented to the center. A variation of this style is to also indent the first line of each paragraph 5 spaces.

JOB 102-1. LETTER

Standard format with indented paragraphs. Workbook 171–172. Body 90 words.

[*Today's date*] / Dr. Sheng Y. Hwang / 2205   13
Auburn Street / Portland, ME 04105 / Dear   21
Dr. Hwang: 24

Thank you for your recent request for a copy   35
of a letter written by Dr. E. L. Stewart to   44
Congresswoman Kate Crews.   49

As chairperson for the committee that used   60
that letter as evidence in the case Bear vs.   69
King, I must inform you that I am not per-   77
mitted to reveal the contents of the letter to   86
you until the case has been closed.   94

Mr. Lee Hurst, who was also involved in   102
this case, may be able to assist you. He was   111
in close contact with Dr. Stewart on this   119
matter. / Yours truly, / W. L. Safranski /   135
Member of Congress / [*Your initials*]   142

JOB 60-1. TABLE WITH LONG CENTERED COLUMN HEADINGS
Standard format. Half sheet of paper.

DINOSAURS

A Parade Through Time

Some Kinds of Dinosaurs	Millions of Years Ago
Plateosaurus	225
Brontosaurus	185
Brachiosaurus	170
Tyrannosaurus Rex	136

JOB 60-2. TABLE WITH LONG CENTERED COLUMN HEADINGS
Standard format. Half sheet of paper.

YEARBOOK ADVERTISERS

Signed Contracts for This Year

Business or Company Name	Local Mailing Address
American Plumbing	120 Second Avenue
Haroldson Printing	15 Third Avenue
Modern Furniture	Fifth and Main
Shaeffer Real Estate	23 Tenth Street
Wagner Equipment	500 Fourth Avenue

JOB 60-3. TABLE WITH CENTERED COLUMN HEADINGS
Standard format. Half sheet of paper.

PARIS

Places of Interest	Location
Eiffel Tower	Avenue de la Bourdonnais
Palais du Louvre	Quai du Louvre
Notre Dame	Ile de la Cité
Arc de Triomphe	Avenue des Champs Elysées

2. After an attention line, use the salutation *Gentlemen:*, *Ladies:*, or *Ladies and Gentlemen:*.

3. On the envelope, type and underscore the attention line in capital and small letters on line 9, 5 spaces from the left edge.

Note: Because the attention line will add two lines (one typed, one blank), add 20 words to the body count to determine placement.

JOB 101-1. LETTER

Type a speed draft of the following letter. Copy at your fastest rate without correcting your errors. Use today's date. Use address and attention line in illustration on page 169. Standard format. Workbook 165–166. Body 82 words (plus 20 words for attention line).

Enclosed are the Southeast Region	8
reports for funds raised in the city of	16
Juneau. *I am happy to report*	22
that this year we improved on	28
our fund-raising program and	34
as a result were able to	39
meet our quota.	42
Our next report is not due	49
until the middle of next month.	55
By that time we should be able to pre-	63
dict how close we will come to our	70
yearly goal. We believe we will be	77
able to exceed our goal by at	83
least $5,000./ Yours truly,/	91
Ann B. Clifton / Juneau	100
Manager /[Your initials]/Enclosures	105

JOB 101-2. LETTER

Use proofreaders' marks to indicate any needed corrections in the draft of Job 101-1. Then retype a corrected copy of the letter. Standard format. Workbook 167–168.

FORMATTING A SUBJECT LINE

A subject line briefly identifies the main topic of a letter. To format a subject line:

1. Type the subject line in initial caps at the left margin between the salutation and the body of the letter, preceded and followed by 1 blank line.

2. Follow the word *Subject* with a colon and 2 spaces.

Note: The subject line, like the attention line, occupies two lines—add 20 words to the body count to determine placement.

> Dear Ms. King:
>
> Subject: Battlefield Charity Dance
>
> I am pleased that you thought of our firm in
> tion with your charity dance. We have found

JOB 101-3. LETTER

Standard format. Workbook 169–170. Body 53 words (plus 20 words for subject line).

[Today's date] / Ms. Anne B. clifton /	12
Juneau Manager / United Charities	18
Campaign / Juneau, AK 99801 / Dear Mrs. *Ms.*	26
Clifton: / Subject: Juneau Campaign	34
Thank you for your report on the	42
Alaska *Juneau* fund-raising campaing. We are *always*	51
happy to hear that the campaign is	58
going well so in your region.	64
The other regions in Anchorage and	69
Fairbanks are also doing quite well;	74
consequently, and, this may be a banner year for our	85
campaign. We all look forward to re-	91
ceiving your *final* report. / Yours truly, /	102
Ralph B. Jones / Alaska Manager / [Your	114
initials]	

LESSON 61

GOALS
- To type 34/3'/5e.
- To review the number keys.

FORMAT
- Single spacing   60-space line   5-space tab

KEYBOARDING SKILLS

Type lines 1–4 once. Then do what line 5 tells you to do. Repeat lines 1–4, or take a series of 1-minute timings.

Speed	1	The man is to go to town and then make six panels for them.	12
Accuracy	2	My fine black ax just zipped through the wood quite evenly.	12
Numbers	3	The 29 boys and 38 girls ate 47 pies and 56 pancakes today.	12
Symbols	4	These forms cost 10¢, 29¢, and 38¢ each, depending on size.	12
Technique	5	Type line 3; then underscore the words and not the numbers.	

| 1 | 2 | 3 | 4 | 5 | 6 | 7 | 8 | 9 | 10 | 11 | 12 |

3-MINUTE TIMINGS

Repeat the Pretest/Practice/Posttest routine on page 104.

NUMBERS

Type lines 23–32 four times.

23   woe 293 yer 634 tot 595 pet 035 tip 580 owe 923 pow 092 092

24   tip 580 yip 680 row 492 tow 592 you 697 tie 583 tee 533 533

25   wet 235 pie 083 rip 480 pit 085 rut 475 pop 090 too 599 599

26   were 2343 your 6974 tire 5843 pour 0974 weep 2330 pity 0856

27   wire 2843 pout 9075 toot 5995 peep 0330 type 5603 pyre 0643

28   wore 2943 yore 6943 tour 5974 pore 0943 writ 2485 peer 0334

29   wipe 3802 poor 0994 tout 5975 poet 0935 riot 4895 putt 0755

30   root 4995 trey 5436 yoyo 6969 ewer 3234 yipe 6803 rout 4975

31   troop 54990 trout 54975 tutor 57594 puppy 07006 putty 07556

32   write 24853 witty 28556 wiper 28034 rotor 49594 route 40753

LESSON 62

GOALS
- To express numbers correctly while typing sentences.
- To format memorandums on plain paper and on forms.

FORMAT
- Single spacing   60-space line   5-space tab

LAB 4

NUMBER STYLE

Workbook 81–82.

Type lines 1–4 once, correcting any errors in number-style rules. Edit your copy as your teacher reads the answers. Retype lines 1–4 from your edited copy.

1   Should Jack go to 6th Street or to 8th Avenue for fun?

2   They live near 16th Street; she lives closer to twenty-third Street.

3   Their plane stopped for forty-five minutes in Iraq around 6:30 a.m.

4   18 zealots have studied four years for the bar exams.

LETTER-PLACEMENT GUIDE

Workbook 159–160.

Some employers prefer using a variable placement plan for very short or very long letters. The variables are shown in the chart below.

Words in Body	Line Length	Date Typed on	From Date to Inside Address	Space for Signature
Under 75	40P/50E	Line 15	5–8 lines	3–6 lines
75–225	50P/60E	Line 15	5 lines	3 lines
Over 225	60P/70E	Lines 12–15	4–5 lines	2–3 lines

JOB 100-1. LETTER

Standard format (see page 92). Workbook 161–162. Body 65 words.

[*Today's date*] / Ms. Elvera Carver / 708 Garland Road / Garland, TX 17
75041 / Dear Ms. Carver: 23

    As you requested in our recent conversation, we are sending you 36
more information about opportunities to own and operate your own 49
Campus Bookstore. ¶ The enclosed materials describe some of the 63
many benefits of our franchises. Of course, there are many more. For 77
more information, make an appointment with one of our representa- 90
tives by completing the enclosed card and returning it to us at your 104
convenience. Sincerely yours, / Kenneth J. Mills / Marketing Director 124
/ [*Your initials*] / Enclosures 128

LESSON 101

GOALS
- To format an attention line in a letter.
- To format a subject line in a letter.

FORMAT
- Single spacing   60-space line   Tab at center

KEYBOARDING SKILLS

Type lines 1–4 once. In line 5, backspace and underscore each underlined word immediately after typing it. Repeat lines 1–4, or take a series of 1-minute timings.

Speed	1	The world's fuel problem may also signal a big proxy fight. 12
Accuracy	2	Calm Rex quit many jobs while driving a bus for a park zoo. 12
Numbers	3	They hoped for 3,856. Only 2,947 paid; 10 did not show up. 12
Symbols	4	An asterisk (*) showed the loss to be $7,946.50 as of 12/8. 12
Technique	5	It is not up to us to pay the bill by the time we get home.

| 1 | 2 | 3 | 4 | 5 | 6 | 7 | 8 | 9 | 10 | 11 | 12 |

FORMATTING AN ATTENTION LINE

Workbook 163–164.

When a letter is addressed directly to a company, an attention line may be used to route it to a particular person or department.

1. Type the attention line in initial caps at the left margin, a double space below the inside address and a double space above the salutation. Use a colon after the word *Attention*.

```
United Charities Campaign
258 North Star Drive
Anchorage, AK 99503

Attention:  Campaign Manager

Ladies and Gentlemen:
```

Take two 1-minute timings on each paragraph. Then take one 3-minute timing on the entire selection. Use single spacing for the 1-minute timings and double spacing for the 3-minute timing.

```
5       Quilts, or padded covers used on top of beds as lovely        12
6   spreads or just bedding, have a long history.  Quilting has       24
7   been done worldwide and has been considered as an art.            35

8       A large part of the social life of our rural folks was       12
9   built around a group party, like a quilting bee.  The women      24
10  in a village often met and made many new, warm quilts.           35

11      Quilts that were made of strips of cloth of all colors       12
12  and of crooked shapes were called crazy quilts.  These were      24
13  a part of the exciting days of our early Western life.           35
    |  1  |  2  |  3  |  4  |  5  |  6  |  7  |  8  |  9  |  10  |  11  |  12      SI 1.27
```

FORMATTING MEMOS

Workbook 83.

Memorandums, or memos, are messages written among people in the same organization or business. Less formal than letters, memos have no salutations and no complimentary closings; and they may be typed on half sheets or full sheets, depending on the length. Memos are used so often that most companies use standard memo forms on which the guide words *To, From, Subject,* and *Date* are printed. (The company name and other information may also be printed on the form.) However, memos can also be typed on plain paper. Look at the illustrations on page 108 as you read the formatting directions below.

To format a memo on plain paper:

1. Set margins for 50P/60E.
2. Type the word *Memorandum* in all-capital letters, centered on line 7.
3. Triple-space after *Memorandum.* Type the guide words (*Date:, To:, From:, Subject:*) double-spaced at the left margin in all-capital letters.

4. Type the words that follow the guide words 10 spaces from the margin (2 spaces after *Subject:*).
5. Triple-space after the heading to the body of the memo. Single-space the body; double-space between paragraphs.
6. Type the writer's initials a double space below the body, beginning at the center.
7. Type any notation as in letters (a double space below the writer's initials, typed at the left margin).

To format a memo on a printed form:

1. Set the left margin stop 2 spaces after the longest guide word, and fill in the heading information.
2. Set the right margin stop so that the right margin is approximately the same number of spaces as the left margin.
3. Align the writer's initials with the date.

GOALS
- To use commas to set off nonessential elements.
- To format a short letter.

FORMAT
- Single-spacing   60-space line   5-space tab

LAB 10

COMMAS FOR NONESSENTIAL ELEMENTS

Workbook 157–158.

Type lines 1–4 once, providing the missing commas for each line. Edit your copy as your teacher reads the answers. Then retype lines 1–4 from your edited copy.

1 When will you and Janice arrive in Kalamazoo Mrs. Santori?
2 This is as you know your next chance to take this course.
3 We look forward to hearing you speak to our group Dr. Lon.
4 The vice president must consequently be in command today.

PRETEST

Take a 2-minute Pretest on lines 5–13; then take a 2-minute Pretest on lines 14–22. Circle and count your errors on each Pretest.

Speed

5   Do you at times feel like relaxing with an interesting   12
6 book to read? You, too, will soon find much enjoyment from   24
7 the right book; and here are some good hints to be followed   36
8 when choosing the book that is right for you.   45
9   Choose the author you feel will be appealing. Look to   57
10 see what the author has already written. This will usually   69
11 tell you if an author's style and manner of expression seem   81
12 right for you. Did you realize authors have unique writing   93
13 styles?   95

Accuracy

14   You could also decide whether you want to read fiction   12
15 or nonfiction. If you prefer to gain knowledge, nonfiction   24
16 might be the wiser choice. But if you would prefer to gain   36
17 entertainment from most of the books, fiction may be a wise   48
18 pick.   49
19   The length of the book may also be judged. Some read–   61
20 ers like a shorter book so that they may have a wide choice   73
21 of reading materials; others like to settle down for a long   85
22 period of time with a lengthy, interesting novel.   95

| 1 | 2 | 3 | 4 | 5 | 6 | 7 | 8 | 9 | 10 | 11 | 12 | SI 1.37

PRACTICE

In which Pretest did you make more errors? If in the speed lines (5–13), type the speed lines below six times and the accuracy lines three times. If in the accuracy lines (14–22), reverse the procedure.

Speed

23 approach attacked applied deepest accord borrow apply bless
24 billiard channels grammar legally dollar follow ditto issue
25 formally helpless payroll settled looked pegged lobby shall
26 neatness suddenly stalled witness settle thrill skill teeth

Accuracy

27 desks candy candid angora charged antique category although
28 labor flush forgot costly fatigue drought happiest entitled
29 quail parks orient length leaflet history packages marketed
30 waist spent system senses tenants quality vitality surgical

POSTTEST

Repeat the Pretest.

JOB 62-1. MEMORANDUM
Standard format. Full sheet of plain paper.

TITLE
all caps, centered
on line 7.

GUIDE WORDS
in all caps; tab 10
for copy that
follows.

BODY
50P/60E, single
spacing.

**WRITER'S
INITIALS**
Align at center.

MEMORANDUM ↓ 7
↓ 3

DATE: January 4, 19--

TO: Sue Booth, President, South Side High Business Club

FROM: Tom Dunn, President, Green High Business Club

SUBJECT: Joint Meeting ↓ 3

I have enclosed a copy of the rough draft of the program for
the next joint meeting of our clubs, which we discussed on the
telephone last week. Notice, Sue, that I have moved the date
from February 10 to March 6 because of a conflict with a
basketball game at our school. ↓ 2

Please talk over the events planned with your officers and
make any changes you like. Then call me at the school before
the end of the week so that I can get my members working on
the details. ↓ 2

TD ↓ 2

Enclosure

JOB 62-2. MEMORANDUM ON A PRINTED FORM
Workbook 85.

**PRINTED
GUIDE
WORDS**
Aligned
at the
bottom,
2 spaces
after the
colons.

**WRITER'S
INITIALS**
Aligned
with
date.

**TYPIST'S
INITIALS**

MEMORANDUM

TO: Pat Smith   DATE: May 1, 19--

FROM: George Zonn, Vice President

SUBJECT: Tour of the Building

Lehigh Valley High School will be sending us 15
students for a tour of the building on Thursday,
May 10. This program is one of many that we do
each year for the young people at the high school.
Ms. Hansen, head of the office program at Lehigh
Valley, always looks forward to our helping her
give her students a look at the real office.

The students will be with us from 9 a.m. to 12 noon.
Would you come to my office at 9 a.m. on Thursday,
May 10, to assist me in forming small groups and
conducting the building tour?

GZ

DM

LESSON 99

CLINIC

GOALS
- To improve your typing skills on the Selective Practice routine.
- To type 37/2'/2e.

FORMAT
- Single spacing   60-space line   5-space tab

KEYBOARDING SKILLS

Type lines 1–4 once. Do what line 5 tells you to do. Repeat lines 1–4, or take a series of 1-minute timings.

Speed 1 Ms. Lela Dow owns a pair of authentic ivory and clay bowls. 12
Accuracy 2 Next month Phil may just quit work and buy five cozy games. 12
Numbers 3 Marathon Runners #10, 29, and 56 were all tied at 38:56:00. 12
Symbols 4 In Cruz's new book, A NEW MATH, does 2 + 2 = 4? Of course! 12
Technique 5 As you type this line, use your return key after each word.

| 1 | 2 | 3 | 4 | 5 | 6 | 7 | 8 | 9 | 10 | 11 | 12

PRETEST

Take a 2-minute Pretest on lines 6–12; then take a 2-minute Pretest on lines 13–19. Circle and count your errors on each Pretest.

Speed 6   It is again that time of the year when skiers hurry to 12
7 get out their boots, jackets, skis, goggles, plus all other 24
8 equipment and charge to those slopes at the first sign of a 36
9 heavy snowfall. When that first ideal snow appears on that 48
10 high slope, it's usually an exciting moment for most skiers 60
11 in this country. Do you think you would like to enjoy this 72
12 same sport? 74

Accuracy 13   Our lungs will not get in shape if we delay starting a 12
14 specific exercise program. The young and old all need lots 24
15 of good exercise. Many who were just lazy now receive lots 36
16 of exercise by running. Like many people, you can run at a 48
17 slow jog along any route, or you can run at a swift pace if 60
18 you want. Much is gained by pursuing a planned program for 72
19 exercising. 74

| 1 | 2 | 3 | 4 | 5 | 6 | 7 | 8 | 9 | 10 | 11 | 12   SI 1.34

PRACTICE

In which Pretest did you make more errors? If in the speed lines (6–12), type the speed lines below six times and the accuracy lines three times. If in the accuracy lines (13–19), reverse the procedure.

Speed 20 altitude calendar amateur clarity badges client awoke delay
21 diligent enlarged drought helpful edited gentle flies heavy
22 jubilant slightly loyalty planted highly likely lucky pearl
23 obsolete thorough statute warmest roamed stolen sedan story
24 delegate surprise student garment farmed joyful style plays

Accuracy 25 check bound burned anyway diploma belongs colorful audience
26 front doubt growth dental foundry century friendly economic
27 loyal hunch lovely inside kitchen healthy mechanic identify
28 twice round walnut shaped specify musical tendency punching
29 slump fifty hyphen cement brought license comedian multiply

POSTTEST

Repeat the Pretest.

LESSON 63

KEYBOARDING SKILLS

Type lines 1–4 once. Then do what line 5 tells you to do. Repeat lines 1–4, or take a series of 1-minute timings.

Speed 1 All of us are glad that the six of you came over to see us. 12
Accuracy 2 Paul reviewed the subject before giving Max and Kay a quiz. 12
Numbers 3 Sean sold several thousands of #380, #477, #566, and #2910. 12
Symbols 4 Try to locate reports #10, #29, #38, #47, and #56 for them. 12
Technique 5 Retype line 1, capitalizing the first letter of every word.

| 1 | 2 | 3 | 4 | 5 | 6 | 7 | 8 | 9 | 10 | 11 | 12

12-SECOND TIMINGS

Type each line four times, or take four 12-second timings on each line. For each timing, type with no more than one error.

6 When will that bookstore have more copies of the blue book? 12
7 They will move home from the city when they need more cash. 12
8 How soon can you help them get some cash to move back here? 12

25   30   35   40   45   50   55   60

JOBS 63-1 AND 63-2. MEMORANDUMS FROM SCRIPT

Standard format. Type two copies: one on plain paper, the other on a printed form. Workbook 87 top.

Memorandum/Date: (Today's)/To: Jo Anne Jones, Group Leader/FROM: Ruth Lee, Chairperson/SUBJECT: Fund Drive for Children's Home ¶ Thank you for your excellent report, Jo Anne. You, Sybil, and Dick did a great job! ¶ It is good to know that all the classes supported the drive and that we went over our goal of $300. ¶ Don't forget to take the money to the Children's Home before Saturday. Last year we missed the deadline, so our school did not get any credit for our hard work. ¶ If I can be of assistance to you in any way, please let me know. /RL

We must not let that happen this year.

JOBS 63-3 AND 63-4. MEMORANDUM

Standard format. Type two copies of the memo on page 110: one copy on plain paper; the other, on a printed form. Workbook 87 bottom.

```
 5        Yesterday, my puppy took me along on a walk.  First, I    12
 6        Yesterday, my puppy took me along on a walk.  First, I    24
 7        Yesterday, my puppy took me along on a walk.  First, I    36
 8   started walking slowly, but she quickly seized command.  We   48
 9   started walking slowly, but she quickly seized command.  We   60
10   started walking slowly, but she quickly seized command.  We   72
11   began the walk, of course, in normal fashion; but just as I   84
12   began the walk, of course, in normal fashion; but just as I   96
13   began the walk, of course, in normal fashion; but just as I  108
14   approached the end of the sidewalk, she tugged, tore loose,  120
15   approached the end of the sidewalk, she tugged, tore loose,  132
16   approached the end of the sidewalk, she tugged, tore loose,  144
17   and zipped across the driveway excitedly.  Then, I followed  156
18   and zipped across the driveway excitedly.  Then, I followed  168
19   and zipped across the driveway excitedly.  Then, I followed  180
20   behind.                                                      182
21   behind.                                                      184
22   behind.                                                      185
     |  1  |  2  |  3  |  4  |  5  |  6  |  7  |  8  |  9  |  10  |  11  |  12   SI 1.40
```

JOB 98-1. RULED TABLE WITH LEADERS

Standard format. Double-space on a full sheet of paper. 10 spaces between columns, with leaders.

CONVERSION CHART

From Standard to Metric Measurements

To change	To	Multiply by
Feet	Meters	.3048
Gallons	Liters	3.7853
Inches	Centimeters	2.5400
Miles	Kilometers	1.6093

JOB 98-2. FIVE-COLUMN UNARRANGED TABLE

Double-space on a full sheet of paper. Add horizontal rules. Type numbers in Area column in numeric order, with *Area 1* first. Compute averages that are missing. Standard format.

[*Title*] QUARTERLY REPORT OF SALES
[*Subtitle*] April Through June
[*Column headings*] Area, April, May, June, Average
[*Body of table*]

Area	April	May	June	Average
3	$10	$47	$57	$38
4	38	23	41	
2	74	65	83	
1	33	82	65	
5	40	44	63	49

```
DATE:      (Today's)
TO:        Ray Falk, Order Clerk
FROM:      kay Bright, Sales
SUBJECT:   Order No. 264-1002
```
¶ a few weeks ago we placed an order for a slide projector for use in
are classes, which we hold here in the building the year. during the order
was approved, but we have not recieved the goods. ¶ We are really
anxious about this order because a speaker who will be here in ② weeks
wants to use a slide projector. Will you please check on this order for
me and let me no know when the equipment will be sent to us? ¶ If delivery
can not be made by next monday, we will need to rent a projector. So
I would appreciate your prompt attention to this matter. / kb

LESSON 64

GOALS
■ To recognize how commas are used in a series while typing
  sentences.
■ To format ruled forms.

FORMAT
■ Single spacing   60-space line   5-space tab

LAB 5

COMMAS IN SERIES

Type lines 1–4 twice. Then take a series of 1-minute timings on each line.

1 The tools, parts, and tires were in the drive near the car.   12
2 I bought a new sweater, a winter jacket, and quilted boots.   12
3 The fruit rolls, pies, cakes, and donuts are most tempting.   12
4 Fritz and Helen joined John, Sally, and Maline in the park.   12
   | 1 | 2 | 3 | 4 | 5 | 6 | 7 | 8 | 9 | 10 | 11 | 12

In a series of three or more numbers, phrases, or clauses, use a comma after each
item in the series except the last.

Numbers: This model costs $12, $15, or $18.
Words: Abco manufactures nuts, bolts, and locks.
Phrases: We went into the plane, onto the runway, and into the air.
Clauses: Mel cooked the food, Janice made the salad, and Bob made the dessert.

30-SECOND TIMINGS

Take two 30-second timings on lines 5–7, or type the paragraph twice.

5 To be an expert in typing, you need to spend quite a lot of   12
6 time on drill work, which at times can be a big job, unless   24
7 the teacher recognizes the need for variety in each lesson.   36
   | 1 | 2 | 3 | 4 | 5 | 6 | 7 | 8 | 9 | 10 | 11 | 12

JOB 97-2. FINANCIAL STATEMENTS: THE INCOME STATEMENT
Standard format. 60-space line.

```
                     Baker and Brown Inc. ↓2
                  SUMMARY INCOME STATEMENT ↓2
                For the Month Ended June 30, 19-- ↓3

SALES ......................................... ↓2      $38,564.39
COST OF GOODS SOLD
     Beginning Inventory ...............$26,378.00
     Inventory Purchases ...............  9,587.60
     Total Available ...................$35,965.60
     Ending Inventory ..................  23,724.60
          Cost of Goods Sold ........... ↓2            12,241.00
GROSS PROFIT ON SALES ................. ↓2             $26,323.39
EXPENSES
     Selling Expense ...................$ 6,536.96
     Rent Expense ......................  3,699.50
     Heat and Light ....................    731.54
     Depreciation of Equipment .........  2,250.50
          Total Expenses ...............               13,218.50
NET INCOME BEFORE TAXES ............... ↓2             $13,104.89
```

LESSON 98

GOALS
- To use commas to set off nonessential elements while typing sentences.
- To type at least 37/5'/5e.
- To type tables with leaders and rules.

FORMAT
- Single spacing 60-space line 5-space tab and as needed

LAB 10

COMMAS FOR NONESSENTIAL ELEMENTS

Type lines 1–4 once, providing the missing commas. Edit your copy as your teacher reads the answers. Then retype lines 1–4 from your edited copy.

1 Aquivane Industries in my opinion should handle this job.

2 All of us must of course submit our responses by June 30.

3 If those projects are late though Gus must pay a penalty.

4 When you arrive in Oxnard Mrs. Luzinski we will meet you.

5-MINUTE TIMINGS

Take a 5-minute timing on lines 5–22 on page 166. Type six times each word on which you made an error, hesitated, or stopped during the 5-minute timing. Then take a 5-minute timing to see how much your skill has improved.

FORMATTING FORMS

Well-designed forms are set up so that data can be typed using standard vertical spacing and common tabs for horizontal spacing. However, when there is not enough space on a line, you will have to squeeze in the information in the space available.

To format ruled forms:

1. Look at the form before typing it to see where common tabs can be set.
2. Check the information to be placed on each line to see if you have enough space or if you will have to type the information on two lines.
3. Make sure the ruled line is in the position of the underscore and is straight.

```
MEMBERSHIP APPLICATION
The Business Club

Name  Mary Wong                          Grade 10
Address 308 Parker Drive, Pittsburgh, PA 15216    Phone 555-5327
Homeroom teacher  Mr. Henderson          Unit  South
Business subjects taken  Typewriting, general business

Other school activities  Gymnastics Club, Drama Club

Why do you want to be a member of The Business Club? I hope to become a secretary, and I
want to belong to an organization related to my future career.
When is the best time to contact you for an interview?  My study hall is during the second
period, or I can be available after school any day except Monday or Friday.
```

```
REQUEST FOR TRANSPORTATION

Requesting school  Washburn High School    Date of event  November 24, 19--
                   First National State Bank of Connecticut
Destination     6072 North Broadway, Bridgeport, CT
Purpose of trip  Observe banking jobs    School group  Office procedures class
Number of students  28                   Leaving time   1:15 p.m.
Pickup location       High school parking lot  Returning time  3:30 p.m.


Signature of Teacher                      Signature of Principal

November 1, 19--
Date of Request                           Approval of Transportation Officer

Bus assigned                              Driver assigned
```

JOB 64-1. MEMBERSHIP APPLICATION
Workbook 89 top.

Jerry Killian is a junior who lives at 12 Oak Drive, Pittsburgh, PA 15214. His phone number is 555-8937. His homeroom teacher is Ms. Taylor, and the homeroom is in the East Unit. He has taken Accounting and Business Law and is a member of the band and golf team. He wants to be in The Business Club to learn more about accounting and computer sciences. His study hall is fourth period, and he can be interviewed at that time.

JOB 64-2. MEMBERSHIP APPLICATION
Workbook 89 bottom.

Marianne Weatherby is a sophomore who lives at 3492 Southwind Drive, Nashville, TN 37217. Her phone number is 555-7739. Her homeroom teacher is Mr. Johnson, and her homeroom is in the West Unit. She has taken Shorthand, Typewriting, and Word Processing and is a member of the girls' basketball team and the symphonic choir. She also works part-time as a gas station attendant. She wants to join The Business Club because she is interested in meeting other students who are going to major in business in college. She doesn't have any study halls but can stay after school on Tuesdays for an interview.

JOB 64-3. REQUEST FOR TRANSPORTATION
Workbook 91 top.

The Mitchell High School Business Club is requesting a bus for 25 students to attend a word processing installation located in the Americana Insurance Company at 12 East First Street in Mitchell. The trip is scheduled for November 9. The bus should pick up the students at the main entrance to the high school at 8:30 a.m. and will return to school at 1 p.m. The purpose of the trip is to see how a word processing center operates. The date of the request is October 20. (Signatures should not be typed.)

JOB 64-4. REQUEST FOR TRANSPORTATION
Workbook 91 bottom.

The Winchester Career Center Business Club is requesting a bus for 32 students to attend regional skills contests located at Montgomery County Joint Vocational School on Hathaway Road. The contests are scheduled for December 5. The bus should pick up the students at the south entrance at 9:30 a.m. and will return to school at 5:30 p.m. The purpose of the trip is to allow students to participate in regional skills competition. The date of the request is November 10.

FORMATTING FINANCIAL STATEMENTS

Workbook 156.

Periodic financial statements help businesses to analyze cash flow, profit and loss, and other important financial information. Among the monthly, quarterly, or yearly statements that are commonly used in business are the balance sheet and the income statement.

Because it is important to compare current financial statements with past statements, they should be formatted consistently.

To format financial statements:

1. Vertically center the statement. Use single spacing (but if the statement is to be displayed on a separate page, use double spacing).

2. Set margins to an assigned line length (usually 60, 65, or 70 spaces).

3. Position money columns only 2 spaces apart (not 6) for easiest reading. Set tabs for the money columns by backspacing from the desired line-ending point.

4. Type major entries in all-capital letters. Double-space before major entries.

5. Capitalize the first letter of each major word in subentries.

6. Use leaders to carry the eye from the first column to the second column.

7. Indent subentries 5 spaces from the left margin.

8. Indent Total lines 5 spaces from the beginning of the line above.

9. Type a single rule to separate groups of numbers that must be added or subtracted.

10. Type a double rule to indicate totals. Use the platen release lever as you turn up the paper for the second line. (The platen release lever allows you to temporarily change the line of writing.)

JOB 97-1. FINANCIAL STATEMENTS: THE BALANCE SHEET

Standard format. 65-space line.

```
                    The Foundation Club

                       BALANCE SHEET

              For the Year Ending June 30, 19--
                                            ↓3

ASSETS
     Supplies on Hand ........................ $231.60
     Cash in Bank ............................  478.59
     Accounts Receivable .....................  166.42
          Total Assets .......................          $876.61
                                                            ↓2
LIABILITIES
     Accounts Payable ........................ $265.98
     Refunds on Memberships ..................   75.00
          Total Liabilities ..................          $340.98
                                                            ↓2
EQUITY
     Capital ................................. $415.75
     Profit from Club Activities ............  119.88
          Total Equity .......................           535.63
               Total Liabilities and Equity ..          $876.61
```

Major entry—all caps.

Subentry—initial caps; indent 5 spaces.

Total line—initial caps; indent 10 spaces.

Grand total—indent 15 spaces.

LESSON 65

GOALS
- To identify how commas are used in series while typing sentences.
- To format display forms.

FORMAT
- Single spacing   60-space line   5-space tab

LAB 5
COMMAS IN SERIES

Type lines 1–4 twice. Then repeat lines 1–4 or take a series of 1-minute timings.

```
1  We packed our clothes, food, and a tent in the large trunk.   12
2  Joyce wrote about cities, tall buildings, and busy offices.   12
3  I very much like to play tennis, racquetball, and baseball.   12
4  We lost 38 balls, 29 bats, and 10 helmets with our luggage.   12
   |  1  |  2  |  3  |  4  |  5  |  6  |  7  |  8  |  9  |  10  |  11  |  12
```

12-SECOND TIMINGS

Type each line four times, or take four 12-second timings on each line. For each timing, type with no more than one error.

```
5  The one problem is that he might not wish to take the work.   12
6  We know that they can do this work as well as we can do it.   12
7  Why did Joe and the dog not see you at the end of the path?   12
```
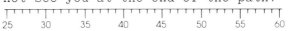
```
                    25    30    35    40    45    50    55    60
```

30-SECOND TIMINGS

Take two 30-second timings on lines 8–10, or type the paragraph twice.

```
8   A big study which explores the question of trust shows that   12

9   people who trust others are very happy folks; they can zero   24

10  in on thoughts that keep them well adjusted and well liked.   36
    |  1  |  2  |  3  |  4  |  5  |  6  |  7  |  8  |  9  |  10  |  11  |  12
```

FORMATTING DISPLAY FORMS

Forms such as certificates and membership cards look best when the names are centered on the lines provided. Either all capitals or capital and lowercase letters can be used. Spread centering can be used also. Signatures are not typed.

JOB 65-1. CERTIFICATES
Type four certificates for students who participated in Region III contests for The Ohio Business Education Association. All certificates should be dated December 10, 19—. Format: Center items on the lines. Workbook 93, 95.

Geoffrey Collins placed first in Region III in Advanced Data Processing; Colleen Kennedy placed second in Region III in Advanced Information Communications; Jim Hustad placed first in Region III in Beginning Accounting; and Allison Akers placed third in beginning Stenography.

JOB 65-2. MEMBERSHIP CARDS
Prepare cards for the applicants in Jobs 64-1 and 64-2. When typing the school year, use the current year for September to June. Format: Center items on the lines. Workbook 97 top.

JOB 96-1. TWO-COLUMN TABLE WITH LEADERS

Standard format. Double-space on a half sheet of paper. 45-space line.

SCHOOL LUNCH ENTREES

Greenville High School

Monday	Turkey with dressing
Tuesday	*Hot beef sandwich*
Wednesday	Tacos and beans
Thursday	*Barbeque with chips*
Friday	*Tuna casserole*

JOB 96-2. TWO-COLUMN TABLE WITH LEADERS AND RULES

Standard format. Single-space on a half sheet of paper. 35-space line.

E X O D U S

Table of Contents

Chapter	Page
Jordan Beyond	1
This Land Is Mine	197
A Eye for a Eye	321
Awake in glory	714
With Wings as Eagles	579

LESSON 97

GOALS
- To identify how commas set off nonessential elements while typing sentences.
- To improve accuracy on "OK" timings.
- To format and to type financial statements.

FORMAT
- Single spacing   60-space line   Tab at center

LAB 10

COMMAS FOR NONESSENTIAL ELEMENTS

Type lines 1–4 once. Then repeat lines 1–4, or take a series of 1-minute timings.

```
1  Please let us know, Dr. Lu, if there is anything we can do.   12
2  That would be an excellent time, therefore, for the picnic.   12
3  You should be aware of all of the qualifications, Ms. Lund.   12
4  Dr. James V. Zak will, as usual, act as committee chairman.   12
   |  1  |  2  |  3  |  4  |  5  |  6  |  7  |  8  |  9  |  10  |  11  |  12
```

"OK" TIMINGS

Type as many 30-second "OK" (errorless) timings as possible out of three attempts on lines 5–7. Then repeat the attempt on lines 8–10.

```
5  Jack quietly gave some dog owners most of his prize boxers.   12
6  Roxie picked off the amazing yellow jonquils by the cavern.   24
7  Kay bought five or six cans to award as equal major prizes.   36

8  Vicky placed a dozen jugs from Iraq on the waxed tabletops.   12
9  Paul reviewed the subject before giving Max and Kay a quiz.   24
10 With all kinds of gripes, Buz rejected every required exam.   36
   |  1  |  2  |  3  |  4  |  5  |  6  |  7  |  8  |  9  |  10  |  11  |  12
```

GOALS
- To use commas in series correctly while typing sentences.
- To type 35/3'/5e.
- To format and produce three invoices.

FORMAT
- Single spacing   60-space line   5-space tab

LAB 5

COMMAS IN SERIES

Type lines 1–4 once, providing the missing commas. Edit your copy as your teacher reads the answers. Then retype lines 1–4 from your edited copy.

1   The children played with the blocks trucks and tricycles.

2   Mr. Velez typed his quizzes tests and exams on Wednesday.

3   Jo fixed the brakes checked the oil and added antifreeze.

4   Can they make some fudge taffy popcorn and candy apples?

1- AND 3-MINUTE TIMINGS

Take two 1-minute timings on each paragraph. Then take one 3-minute timing on the entire selection. Use single spacing for the 1-minute timings and double-spacing for the 3-minute timing.

```
                    1                2                3             4    1'
5       The energy from coal can do lots of jobs for us.  Coal    12
                5              6             7                8
6   gives power for machines and heat for our homes.  Coal also   24
            9            10            11
7   helps scientists to make things that better our lives.       35
        12           13            14              15
8       Today plastics, many drugs, and types of food dyes are   12
        16           17            18            19
9   made from coal.  With a possible fuel shortage now, a large  24
        20         21              22            23
10  effort will be made to make coal fill this urgent need.      35
            24           25              26            27
11      We realize that our search for fuels will make a drain   12
            28           29            30            31
12  on our natural resources.  So we must be on guard and watch  24
            32           33            34            35
13  that we do not let greedy folks exploit our quantities.      35
    |  1  |  2  |  3  |  4  |  5  |  6  |  7  |  8  |  9  |  10  |  11  |  12   SI 1.29
```

FORMATTING INVOICES   Workbook 84.

Invoices vary in size, length, and complexity, but all have the same general format, as shown on page 114. A printed invoice form includes the company name and its return address, the guide words *To:* and *Date:*, and the word *Invoice.* For ease in typing invoices, the column areas are ruled.

To format invoices:

Heading. Begin typing the name and the date 2 spaces after the guide words. Align the typed words with the bottom of the guide words.

Quantity, Unit Price, and Amount Columns. The entries in these columns should be centered visually within each ruled area. Type an underscore under the last entry in the Amount column. The underscore should be as long as the longest entry. **Remember**: Columns of numbers align at the right. Set margin or tab stops for the length of the entry most frequently used, and backspace or space in for other entries.

Description Column. Set a tab 2 spaces to the right of the vertical rule. Double-space between entries. Single-space turnovers when an entry is more than one line. Indent turnovers 3 spaces.

Total Amount Due Line. Type the words *Total amount due* in the Description column, approximately aligned with the *D* in the word *Description.* Type the numbers in the Amount column.

(Continued on next page)

5   My gardening talents, as they have guessed, are almost 12

6   My gardening talents, as they have guessed, are almost 24

7   My gardening talents, as they have guessed, are almost 36

8   infamous. There seems to exist a basic mystique around how 48

9   infamous. There seems to exist a basic mystique around how 60

10 infamous. There seems to exist a basic mystique around how 72

11 to keep gardens growing, and I have never, or almost never, 84

12 to keep gardens growing, and I have never, or almost never, 96

13 to keep gardens growing, and I have never, or almost never, 108

14 been able to do it well. Zillions of persons, both men and 120

15 been able to do it well. Zillions of persons, both men and 132

16 been able to do it well. Zillions of persons, both men and 144

17 women, do gardens. They have a skill I just am not able to 156

18 women, do gardens. They have a skill I just am not able to 168

19 women, do gardens. They have a skill I just am not able to 180

20 master. 182

21 master. 184

22 master. 185

| 1 | 2 | 3 | 4 | 5 | 6 | 7 | 8 | 9 | 10 | 11 | 12 | SI 1.39

FORMATTING TABLES WITH LEADERS
Workbook 155.

Leaders are rows of periods that lead the reader from one column to the next. Leaders are especially helpful in financial statements, tables of contents, programs, and menus.

To format leadered tables:

1. Set the left margin and tab stops for the table.
2. Find the point on the scale where the final period on each line of leaders will be typed. The final period should be 1 blank space before the item in the second column.
3. Type the first item in the first line, space once, and type the line of periods. Remember to stop 1 space before the item in the second column.
4. Repeat step 3 for each item.

Practice: Type the table below, following the instructions for formatting tables with leaders. Use single spacing and a 40-space line to center the table on a half sheet of paper.

TABLE OF CONTENTS

How to Type With Carbons 139

How to Make Erasures 140

How to Crowd Letters 140

How to Center Horizontally 141

How to Type a Proxy 158

How to Type Minutes 185

Spacing. Begin the body of the invoice a double space below the horizontal rule. Single-space each entry; double-space between entries, including the Total amount due line.

Note: Dollar signs are not needed in the Unit Price or Amount columns because only dollar amounts are listed there.

JOB 66-1. INVOICE

Type a copy of the invoice shown below. Standard format. Workbook 97 bottom.

SWISSVALE HIGH BUSINESS CLUB
1036 HIGHLAND AVENUE
SWISSVALE, PA 13821

TO: Ms. Marion Mertz
Music Department

DATE: June 11, 19--

INVOICE

QUANTITY	DESCRIPTION	UNIT PRICE	AMOUNT
300	2-page concert programs	.06	18.00
2	Offset masters	1.10	2.20
800	1-page handouts	.03	24.00
1	Stencil	.75	.75
40	Invitations	.08	3.20
	Total amount due		48.15

FORMATTING QUANTITY COLUMNS WITH WORDS

Sometimes the Quantity column contains words as well as numbers. (See examples at the right.) The numbers must align at the right just as they would in a plain number column. The entire entry (both number and word) should be visually centered in the Quantity column. Use the longest number and the longest word.

QUANTITY	DESCRIPTION
3 boxes	Paper clips
1 pkg.	Carbon paper
125	Envelopes

JOB 66-2. INVOICE

Standard format. Workbook 99 top.

[Today's date]
TO: Dr. James Fetter, Principal
Swissvale High School
1036 Highland Avenue
Swissvale, PA 13821

500	Parents' Night programs @ .05	25.00
500	Course information sheets @ .03	15.00
3	Offset masters @ 1.10	3.30
2	jars Colored ink @ 4.75	9.50
5	boxes Gold stars (for programs) @ 1.04	5.20
	Total amount due	58.00

JOB 95-3. THREE-COLUMN UNARRANGED TABLE

Standard format. Double-space on a full sheet of paper. Add horizontal rules.

[*Title*] DEGREE ABBREVIATIONS

[*Subtitle*] Selected From <u>American Universities and Colleges</u>

[*Column headings*] Abbreviation, Title, Classification

[*Line 1*] D.D., Doctor of Divinity, Honorary

[*Line 2*] D.P.A., Doctor of Public Administration, Earned and Honorary

[*Line 3*] D.Sc., Doctor of Science, Earned and Honorary

[*Line 4*] LL.D., Doctor of Laws, Usually Honorary

[*Line 5*] Pharm. D., Doctor of Pharmacy, Earned and Honorary

LESSON 96

GOALS
- To recognize how commas set off nonessential elements while typing sentences.
- To format and to type tables with leaders.

FORMAT
- Single spacing   60-space line   5-space tab

LAB 10

COMMAS FOR NONESSENTIAL ELEMENTS

Type lines 1–4 once. Then repeat lines 1–4 or take a series of 1-minute timings.

1 It is, however, going to be quite late when we finish here. 12

2 You will, nonetheless, be required to stay until we fix it. 12

3 Joan, too, will represent our school in the skills contest. 12

4 Zach will, in the meantime, be our candidate for secretary. 12

| 1 | 2 | 3 | 4 | 5 | 6 | 7 | 8 | 9 | 10 | 11 | 12

Words, phrases, or clauses that are not essential to the meaning of a sentence are set off by commas. Names in direct address are also considered nonessential. Use two commas to set off nonessential elements within a sentence. Use one comma if a nonessential element appears at the end or at the beginning of a sentence.

We are planning, *as you know*, to reject their offer.
A quantity discount is available, *of course*.
Lisa requested, *moreover*, that the catalog be reprinted.
You will receive a copy, *Mr. James*, with your next invoice. (Direct address.)

5-MINUTE TIMINGS

Take a 5-minute timing on lines 5–22 on page 162, typing each new line three times (omit the blank lines—they are there to help you keep your eyes on the copy). Type six times each word on which you made an error, hesitated, or stopped during the 5-minute timing. Then take a 5-minute timing to see how much your skill has improved.

FORMATTING ADJUSTMENTS TO INVOICES

Adjustments such as delivery charges, sales taxes, and discounts are typed before *Total amount due* and aligned with it, as shown at the right. First type *Amount due* (a subtotal) a double space below the last entry. Then type the adjustment line (or lines) single-spaced below *Amount due*, with a rule under the last adjustment line.

Double-space and then type *Total amount due*.

```
Amount due                   343.35
Sales tax 6%                  20.60
Delivery charges              15.00

Total amount due             378.95
```

JOB 66-3. INVOICE
Standard format. Use today's date. Workbook 99 bottom.

To: Scott Klein, Treasurer, The Business Club
Swissvale High School
1036 Highland Avenue
Swissvale, PA 13821

45 cans	Coke, ginger ale, and orange soda @ .30	13.50
6 dozen	Cookies @ .99	5.94
3 dozen	Cupcakes @ 1.89	5.67
5 bags	Potato chips @ .98	4.90
61	Ice cream bars @ .40	24.40
	Amount due	54.41
	Sales tax 6%	3.26
	Total amount due	57.67

LESSON 67

GOALS
- To type 35/3'/5e.
- To practice typing symbols.

FORMAT
- Single spacing   60-space line   5-space tab

KEYBOARDING SKILLS

Type lines 1–4 once. Then practice smooth shift-key control by capitalizing the proper nouns in line 5. Repeat lines 1–4, or take a series of 1-minute timings.

Speed	1	He may wish to pay them if and when they go to town for us.	12
Accuracy	2	Bernard won five major prizes equal to your six big checks.	12
Numbers	3	Please order 10 cakes, 29 pies, and 38 quarts of ice cream.	12
Symbols	4	Jo may write to Dop & Co., Smith & Sons, and Howe & Blaker.	12
Technique	5	Lyle Jinx Lisa Dora Lulu Mina Jack Boyd Nate Hank Jane Saul	12

| 1 | 2 | 3 | 4 | 5 | 6 | 7 | 8 | 9 | 10 | 11 | 12

GOAL
- To format and type two-line column headings in tables.

FORMAT
- Single spacing   60-space line   Tabs at center and as needed

KEYBOARDING SKILLS

Type lines 1–4 once. In line 5, use the shift lock for each word in all-capital letters. Repeat lines 1–4, or take a series of 1-minute timings.

Speed 1 Rush him eight bushels of corn, but make him sign for them. 12
Accuracy 2 Park my gray, bronze jet and quickly wax it for five hours. 12
Numbers 3 Our bills for the week came to $10, $29, $38, $47, and $56. 12
Symbols 4 Listen! I did <u>not</u> say 12 was 1/4 of 60. Did <u>you</u> say that? 14
Technique 5 Go to ADAMS, not to WHITMAN or LANKIN or EDMORE or LANGDON.

| 1 | 2 | 3 | 4 | 5 | 6 | 7 | 8 | 9 | 10 | 11 | 12

FORMATTING TWO-LINE COLUMN HEADINGS

When a column heading is much longer than any item in the column, the column heading is typed on two lines. To format two-line column headings:

1. Align one-line column headings with the second line of two-line column headings.

2. Center each line. Subtract (a) the number of characters in the shorter line from (b) the number of characters in the longer line.

3. Divide that answer by 2 (drop any fraction), and indent the shorter line by that number of spaces. In the example, 9 − 5 = 4, and 4 ÷ 2 = 2. Indent the shorter line 2 spaces, as in this example:

Suggested ←9
Price ←5

4. Underscore the words in each line in open tables; do not underscore in ruled tables.

Practice: Center each of the following two-line column headings:

Number of	Daily	Unit
Units	Expenses	Price

JOB 95-1. THREE-COLUMN TABLE
Standard format. Double-space on a full sheet of paper.

BASKETBALL SCORES
December Games

Home Team's Score	Visitor's Score	Difference
68	66	+ 2
72	81	− 9
59	52	+ 7
65	66	− 1
77	58	+19

JOB 95-2. THREE-COLUMN TABLE
Standard format. Double-space on a full sheet of paper.

Schedule of Summer Seminars

Topic	Date	Expected Attendance
Time Management	July 6-9	15
Interview Techniques	July 20-23	19
Decision Making	August 2-5	16
Financial Planning	August 9-11	15
Accounting Principles	August 16-18	12

SYMBOL PRACTICE

Type each line twice, or take a series of 1-minute timings on lines 6–12.

6   John claims Order #38 is for 38#, but Order #38 is for 29#.   12
7   Yes, Jo, it is better to buy 20 @ 15¢ than to buy 10 @ 21¢.   12
8   The box is (1) big, (2) wrapped, and (3) too heavy to lift.   12
9   He said, "Pay the $56 or I'll call the state police today."   12
10 Give Lake & Dun 10%, B&G 12%, Mann & Scot 11%, and T&L 13%.   12
11 Type an asterisk (*) next to the most important references.   12
12 As an example, please write 29 + 38 = 67 on the chalkboard.   12
13 If you <u>must</u> drive to Ohio, then be <u>sure</u> to use a seat belt.

| 1 | 2 | 3 | 4 | 5 | 6 | 7 | 8 | 9 | 10 | 11 | 12

12-SECOND TIMINGS

Type each line four times, or take four 12-second timings on each line. For each timing, type with no more than one error.

14 We would prefer to take a lot of quizzes, not one big exam.   12
15 A small tug pushed the liner into the quay and to the pier.   12
16 If you put the sodas in the fridge, they will soon be cold.   12

          25   30   35   40   45   50   55   60

PREVIEW PRACTICE

Type lines 17 and 18 twice as a preview to the 1- and 3-minute timings below.

Accuracy

17 bolts wrought machines products nonsteel tranquil civilized

Speed

18 could about write least build books paper long iron ore new

1- AND 3-MINUTE TIMINGS

Take two 1-minute timings on each paragraph. Then take two 3-minute timings on the entire selection. Use single spacing for the 1-minute timings and double spacing for the 3-minute timings.   1'

                1   2   3   4
19   Iron and steel are the most useful and least expensive   12
          5   6   7   8
20 metals we have. Iron ore is needed to make steel, which in   24
          9   10   11
21 turn is used to make things from bolts to battleships.   35
          12   13   14   15
22   Iron is not new to a civilized world; wrought iron was   12
          16   17   18   19
23 used by people long before they could read and write. Some   24
          20   21   22   23
24 nations have failed because they lacked iron and steel.   35
              24   25   26   27
25   Steel is used to build the machines which produce just   12
          28   29   30   31
26 about all the nonsteel products needed for a tranquil life,   24
          32   33   34   35
27 such as plastic, paper, fibers, books, cans, and jars.   35

| 1 | 2 | 3 | 4 | 5 | 6 | 7 | 8 | 9 | 10 | 11 | 12   SI 1.29

FORMATTING RULED TABLES

Workbook 153–154.

Summary words like Total *or* Average *are blocked at the left on the column. The words may be typed in all-capital letters or in initial caps.*

To format ruled tables, such as the one illustrated at the right, follow these guidelines:

1. Center the table horizontally and vertically.

2. Using your key line, set your left margin. Then space across for the key line as you set your tabs. This will help you determine how wide to type the ruled lines in the table.

3. Type the ruled lines (the underscores) the exact length of the key line. Single-space before each ruled line, and double-space after each ruled line.

4. End the table with a single ruled line, typed the length of the key line.

Practice: Type the table below on a full sheet of paper. Use double spacing. The table should occupy 16 lines.

```
          TEST MILES
                       ↓2
        Western Region
                         ↓1
   _____
                                  ↓2
        Month        Miles
                             ↓1
   _____
                                  ↓2
   July             197
   August           386
   September        205
   October          417
                         ↓1
   _____
                                  ↓2
   AVERAGE          301
                         ↓1
   _____
```

FORMATTING COLUMNS WITH WORDS AND NUMBERS

You have previously learned that words align on the left and numbers align on the right. Sometimes columns contain a mixture of both words *and* numbers.

To format a column of words and numbers, align all entries at the left, as if they were all words.

JOB 94-1. THREE-COLUMN RULED TABLE

Standard format. Double-space on a full sheet of paper.

SPORTS CAR EXHIBITS
(Final Entries)

Car	Model	Country
Corvette	Convertible	United States
Datsun	280ZX	Japan
Ferrari	410	Italy
Jaguar	E-Type	Great Britain
Porsche	911	West Germany

GOALS
- To use commas in series correctly while typing sentences.
- To format long reports.

FORMAT
- Single spacing   60-space line   5-space tab

LAB 5

Type lines 1–4, providing the missing commas. Edit your copy as your teacher reads the answers. Then retype lines 1–4 from your edited copy.

COMMAS IN SERIES

Workbook 103–104.

1 I hope to go through Germany Holland and Italy next year.

2 Their figures for January are $125.50 $162.19 and $14.24.

3 Look up these numbers: 263-12 410-79 244-83 and 766-42.

4 Harold Betty Alice and Sam have worked on these quizzes.

SKILL DEVELOPMENT DRILL

Type each line twice.

Speed

5 Did she pay the neighbor to fix the oaken box for the coal?

6 I am to go to work for the audit firm by the eighth of May.

Accuracy

7 Jeff amazed the audience by quickly giving six new reports.

8 Five bright boys could work extra now to pass a major quiz.

Numbers

9 She sold 1,234 in June, 3,456 in July, and 7,890 in August.

10 The winning bulletins were numbered 56, 47, 38, 29, and 10.

Symbols

The symbol " also means "inches."

11 The five maple boards measured 10", 29", 38", 47", and 56".

12 I bought 10 shares @ 29, 38 shares @ 47, and 56 shares @ 1.

FORMATTING LONG REPORTS

A *long report* is one that takes more than one page. Long reports usually contain side headings and/or paragraph headings.

The first page of a long report is formatted in the same manner as a one-page report: (1) the title is typed on line 13; (2) margins are set for a 60-space pica or a 70-space elite line; and (3) the body of the report is double-spaced. The bottom margin for any full page should contain a minimum of 6 blank lines or a maximum of 9 blank lines.

To format continuation pages in a long report:

1. Type the page number (the word *page* is unnecessary) on line 7 at the right margin. (Do not type a page number on the first page.)

2. Begin the text of the report on line 10, a triple space below the page number.

↓ 7
2

↓ 3

BOTTOM MARGINS

The bottom margin on each page should be a minimum of 6

or a maximum of 9 lines deep. On standard paper with 66 lines,

```
X   29   Mix wax jinx apex fixed extra reflex expend excited x-rayed
Y   30   Yes you yard your yeast yield yonder yearly yardage younger
Z   31   Zip zig zone zinc zesty zebra zenith zodiac zoology zealous
```

POSTTEST   Repeat the Pretest on page 152 to see how much your skill has improved.

GOALS
- To use commas after introductory words and phrases while typing sentences.
- To type ruled tables.

FORMAT
- Single-spacing   60-space line   5-space tab and as needed

LAB 9

Type lines 1–4 once, providing the missing commas. Edit your copy as your teacher reads the answers. Then retype lines 1–4 from your edited copy.

COMMAS AFTER INTRODUCTORY WORDS AND PHRASES

Workbook 151–152.

```
1   Speaking rapidly Kent explained the reasons for the delay.
2   In any event Ms. Smithe should finish before the deadline.
3   During the question-and-answer period Jan was outstanding.
4   In the first place Ms. Maizley is not a computer operator.
```

1- AND 5-MINUTE TIMINGS

Take two 1-minute timings on each paragraph. Then take one 5-minute timing on the entire selection. Use single spacing for the 1-minute timings and double spacing for the 5-minute timing.

```
                  1                         2                   1'
5      Old furniture can look as good as new again.  A marred   12
           3                       4
6   chair or table can become a thing of beauty and a source of  24
       5                  6                      7
7   pride to you with a little bit of concentrated effort.       35
                          8                     9
8      To begin, you must carefully and thoroughly remove the    12
           10                   11
9   old finish.  To do this, just apply a thick coat of a paint  24
       12                    13                  14
10  or varnish remover.  Then scrub it away with steel wool.     35
                        15                      16
11     Next, it's important to sand the furniture, being sure    12
         17                      18
12  to eliminate any rough spots.  At the same time, you should  24
       19                  20                      21
13  repair any cuts or scratches that have damaged the wood.     35
                            22                  23
14     Once you have completed these steps, you can restain a    12
         24                        25
15  piece of furniture.  The stain should dry quickly, and then  24
       26                      27                    28
16  you can apply the first coat of varnish to the article.      35
                        29                      30
17     Finally, you should smooth the article with new pieces    12
           31                    32
18  of steel wool to remove any rough areas that have appeared,  24
       33                      34                  35
19  apply a second coat of varnish, and gaze at your work.       35
      |  1  |  2  |  3  |  4  |  5  |  6  |  7  |  8  |  9  | 10  | 11  | 12   SI 1.35
```

Standard format.

LONG REPORTS

A Report for Typing 1

by (Your name)

¶ A long report is one that takes more than ① page. To prepare long reports that are consistent and attractively arranged, follow the guidelines given in this paper.

GENERAL RULES

A long report is typed on a line of 60 pica or 70 elite spaces, with the body double-spaced. The Main headings—title, subtitle (optional), and author's name—is centered. Side headings are typed at the left margin in all caps, preceded by 2 blank lines.

HEADINGS AND TOP MARGINS

First Page. The main heading of two or three double-spaced lines as shown above begins on Line 13, leaving a top margin of 12 blank lines. The main heading is followed by 2 blank lines. This page is counted, but no page number is typed on page 1.

Other Pages. The heading of each other pages consists of the page number. (The word Page is not necessary.) The page number is backspaced from the right margin on line 7. Leaving 6 lines in the top margin. The page number is followed by 2 blank lines, so that the body of the report will always resume on line 10 on each continuation page.

Start page 2 here. → BOTTOM MARGINS

The bottom margin on each page should be a minimum of 6 or a maximum of 9 lines. On standard paper with 66 lines, the last line of typing should appear on line 57, 58, 59, or 60. if it is necessary to break a paragraph, at least 2 lines should be typed on the first page and 2 lines on the following page.

CLINIC

GOALS
- To strengthen accuracy by practicing alphabetic drills.
- To type 37/5'/5e.

FORMAT
- Single spacing   60-space line   Tabs every 5 spaces

KEYBOARDING SKILLS

Type lines 1–4 once. In line 5, use your tabulator key to advance from one word to the next through the entire line. Repeat lines 1–4, or take a series of 1-minute timings.

Speed	1	When I visit the island, I may go down to the lake to fish.	12
Accuracy	2	Quietly, six zebras jumped back over the eight brown rafts.	12
Numbers	3	Diane should not take 10, 29, and 38 in place of 47 and 56.	12
Symbols	4	On 10/29 he (Bart) paid $87, which is 36% less than I paid.	12
Technique	5	as at if be or an up to in ad is it	

     | 1 | 2 | 3 | 4 | 5 | 6 | 7 | 8 | 9 | 10 | 11 | 12

PRETEST

Take a 5-minute Pretest on lines 5–20 on page 152. Circle your errors, and use the Practice lines below and on page 158 to improve your skill. Use double spacing.

PRACTICE

Type lines 6–31 below and on page 158. Then repeat any of the lines that stress the letter errors you circled in the Pretest. Use single spacing.

A	6	Apt ale arch ache arena alibi acquit abound achieve absolve
B	7	Bag bid busy baby bacon basis behave basket bandage brought
C	8	Cup can cost core candy cargo cement center caption cabinet
D	9	Dig did dawn dive drive doubt design digest dentist default
E	10	End eye each edge eight earth enrage extend enforce engrave
F	11	Fly fin fret form fixed float forest formal fragile fortune
G	12	Get gem gift gaze giant going gadget govern garbage gesture
H	13	Hay hen howl huge house horse handle hanger honesty horizon
I	14	Ill ice itch inch index input insure intact impulse iceberg
J	15	Job jar just jinx joker jumpy jigsaw jingle journey jewelry
K	16	Kid key knit knot knock knife kitten kidney kingdom kitchen
L	17	Let lye land lane latch lance ladies length lantern lasting
M	18	Map mud mail make mouth mound marvel magnet martial machine
N	19	New nap name nail niece night nickel nephew neglect neither
O	20	Out old ouch oath onion other object oblige ostrich oatmeal
P	21	Pay par plot plug prowl print pantry pastel poultry prairie
Q	22	Qt. quo quiz quit quest quick quaver queasy qualify quarter
R	23	Rot rub raid raft ridge right raging random reverse romance
S	24	Say sea self sold smack snake scarce scheme shingle shorten
T	25	Tub tip tent team trash tempt tendon temper trouble textile
U	26	Use urn used urge usher until uproar unkind upright unlatch
V	27	Vat van view vote vocal virus victim virtue varsity vehicle
W	28	Won why wish went while where wrench weight without whistle

(Continued on next page)

To avoid typing in the bottom margin, use ~~any~~ one of these: ~~procedures:~~

Indent and SS

1. Count the lines; stop on line 57, 58, 59, or 60.
2. Before inserting the paper, draw a *very* light pencil line at the right edge about 2 inches from the bottom as a caution signal; erase it when you finish and remove the page.
3. On a separate sheet, draw heavy lines to show where the margins should be. Put this "visual guide" under the ~~page~~ *paper* on which you type; the lines will show through to help you maintain correct margins on every page of the report.

5

LESSONS 69/70

GOALS
- To recognize how commas are used after introductory clauses while typing sentences.
- To format text references and footnotes.

FORMAT
- Single spacing   60-space line   5-space tab

LAB 6

INTRODUCTORY IF, AS, AND WHEN CLAUSES

Type lines 1–4 once. Then repeat lines 1–4 or take a series of 1-minute timings.

1 If Barte Gomez calls while we are out, just take a message.   12
2 As David quickly noticed, your extra hours are paid double.   12
3 When Yvette explained zero budgeting, she did so very well.   12
4 Although Jack left quickly, he missed the bus to Kalamazoo.   12

Use a comma after an introductory clause that begins with *if, as, when, although, since, because,* or a similar conjunction. Note the examples in lines 1–7.

12-SECOND TIMINGS

Type each line four times, or take four 12-second timings on each line. For each timing, type with no more than one error.

▶ 5 As we started to dance, the lights were quickly turned off.   12
▶ 6 When the moon came up, the lake was a huge sheet of silver.   12
▶ 7 When it began to rain, they had to call a halt to the game.   12

25   30   35   40   45   50   55   60

FORMATTING AN ITINERARY

An itinerary is an outline of the details of a planned trip. It includes departure and arrival times, meeting times, flight plans, and other essential information. To format an itinerary on plain paper:

1. Set your margins for a 60P/70E line.
2. Set 5-space and 30-space tabs.
3. Type the itinerary heading as follows:
   a. Type *ITINERARY* centered on line 13.
   b. Double-space, and then type the name of the person for whom the itinerary is prepared at the left margin.
   c. On the same line as the person's name, type the date on which the trip will begin. Backspace this date from the right margin.
   d. Double-space, and then center the names of the city(ies) to be visited; begin with the departure city. Use a dash (two hyphens) to separate the city names.
4. Double-space after the heading information, and begin typing the day-to-day schedule. Beginning at the left margin, type the day, month, and date of departure.
5. Double-space. Indent all time and reminder notes 5 spaces from the left margin. Whenever time zones are changed, specify the time zone after each time.
6. Indent 30 spaces to type the description information for each notation in the left column. Indent any turnover lines 2 spaces from the 30-space tab.
7. Underscore departure and arrival cities and the word *Accommodations*.
8. For itineraries longer than 1 page, leave a bottom margin of 6 to 9 lines. Type page numbers on all pages except the first, beginning on line 7 at the right margin.

JOB 92-1. ITINERARY
Standard format.

```
                              ITINERARY

   M. J. Donaldson                           December 10, 19--
                                         c
                        (Memphis--San Francisp)

   Sunday, December 10
        9:35 a.m., CST        Depart Memphis, Memphis Municipal Airport,
                                 United Air Lines Coach (Y) one stop
                                 Flight 433, Boeing 727, lunch served.

        1:02 p.m., PST        Arrive San Francisco, San Francisco
                                 International Airport.

                              Accommodations:  Mark Hopkins hotel,
                                ① Nob Hill.

        5:30 p.m.             Depart hotel for Chinatown visit.
   Monday, December 11
          All day
          Reminder            Convention at Mark Hopkins Hotel.
                              Call Pat Wolton to confirm dinner arrange-
                                 ments for tomorrow.
   Tuesday, December 12                Mark
        9 a.m.-5 p.m.         Convention at Hopkins Hotel.
        7 p.m.                Dinner with Pat Wolton.
   Wednesday, December 13
        10:30 a.m.            Depart hotel for airport.
          noon                                    San Francisco
        12 p.m., PST          Depart San Francisco International Airport,
                                 United Air Lines Coach (Y) two stops
                                 Flight 700, Boeing 727, lunch served.

        7:15 p.m., CST        Arrive Memphis, Memphis Municipal Airport.
```

Take a 3-minute Pretest on lines 8–16. Then circle and count your errors. Use the chart below to determine which lines to type for practice.

```
8      Every day the sun sends out to Earth quiet jet streams    12
9   of sunlight, which are a new and vital source of energy.  A   24
10  nation like ours could adequately fill its needs for energy   36
11  sources if the rays of the sun could be kept and stored, as   48
12  in a tank.  Solar energy could be used to heat homes and to   60
13  run engines, but more research must be done to find ways to   72
14  store the excess heat from the sun.  We all must constantly   84
15  work to save fuel; if we rely on the sun rather than oil or   96
16  coal, the possibility of a shortage is zero.                 105
    |  1  |  2  |  3  |  4  |  5  |  6  |  7  |  8  |  9  |  10  |  11  |  12    SI  1.30
```

PRACTICE

In the chart below, find the number of errors you made on the Pretest. Then type each of the designated drill lines four times.

Pretest errors	0–1	2–3	4–5	6–7
Drill lines	20–24	19–23	18–22	17–21

Accuracy

```
17  quiet could stored energy source research sunlight shortage
18  be zero earth rather nation excess sources engines research
19  we sun solar store vital every could constantly possibility
20  or jet homes needs which energy engines research adequately
```

Speed

```
21  used done heat ways fill than fuel save for run day out sun
22  rays kept find coal tank rely more ours jet its oil ray all
23  excess rather quiet store tank zero but sun and new are the
24  sources heat must from ways done used like ours jet for out
```

POSTTEST

Repeat the Pretest to see how much your skill has improved.

FORMATTING TEXT REFERENCES

In Lesson 47, you formatted reports with run-in references, which indicate to the reader the source of the statement cited. Run-in references were formatted in parentheses within the body of the report.

Another way to format references is to place the notes at the bottom (or the "foot") of the same page on which they occur. References formatted in this way are called footnotes.

To indicate the presence of a reference in the body of the report, type a superscript (raised) number immediately following the appropriate word, phrase, or sentence.

Practice typing a superscript number; use the example below. To type the raised number, turn the cylinder back slightly with one hand and type the number with the other.

```
    John Henry Abbott wrote the book.[1]  He frequently re-
ferred to the writings of Samuel Brooks Newhouse.[2]
```

JOB 91-1. TWO-PAGE REPORT WITH A TABLE
Double spacing. 5-space tab.

Dodge Skating Rink

By Chris Lee

The young people of Dodge have to drive to other towns for something to do. It is quite evident that the town needs to do something to attract people, rather than drive them away.

THE PROBLEM

The problem is to find out if the people of Dodge would support a skating rink. Four typing students were among the thirty students at Central High School who were asked to take part in a study to find out if a skating rink could survive as a major entertainment center for the people of Dodge. The four typing students typed the study that consisted of responses from 100 people chosen at random.

FINDINGS

The average age of those questioned was 18. Of those who took part in the study, 57 were female and 43 were male. Ninety percent felt Dodge entertainment could be better.

When asked if they knew how to skate, 79 knew how, and only 21 did not know how. Of those who did not know how to skate, 16 expressed an interest in learning how to skate.

Ninety percent believed that the rink should have game machines and pool tables. Another finding was that 89 percent believed there should be specific times for certain age groups to skate. Finally, the study revealed that most people wanted a variety of music played while they skated. Table 1, below, shows that 50 percent of the people wanted a variety of music played. The next most popular type of music was disco, with 22 percent preferring this type. The remaining 28 percent was divided among country and western, rock, and punk.

Table 1
Music Preferences

Type of Music	Percent
Variety	50
Disco	22
Country and western	12
Rock	10
Punk	6

RECOMMENDATIONS

Based upon the findings of this study, the city of Dodge should consider the construction of a skating rink for its residents.

LESSON 92

GOALS
- To use commas after introductory words and phrases while typing sentences.
- To type at least 37/5'/5e.
- To format an itinerary.

FORMAT
- Single spacing   60-space line   5-space tab

LAB 9

COMMAS AFTER INTRODUCTORY WORDS AND PHRASES

Type lines 1–4 once, providing the missing commas. Edit your copy as your teacher reads the answers. Then retype lines 1–4 from your edited copy.

1 In order to get there quickly Joan must leave immediately.
2 On the first day of each month call Ezra for my inventory.
3 Eventually computers will probably take over the business.
4 Actually David will not be able to fix these until Friday.

FORMATTING FOOTNOTES

To format footnotes:

1. Plan ahead to determine the number of lines you must "save" at the bottom of the page. As you type each superscript in the text, estimate the number of lines for that footnote, and mark lightly with a pencil the point at which you should stop typing the text.

2. Single-space after the last line of text, and type an underscore (20P or 24E strokes) beginning at the left margin. This line separates the footnotes from the text.

3. Double-space, indent 5 spaces, and type the footnote number (use a superscript) and the reference. Use single spacing for any continuation lines needed, and begin them at the left margin, as shown in the illustration below.

4. Double-space between footnotes.

5. Always format footnotes at the bottom of the page—even on the last page of a report that may have only a few lines of text. The bottom margin below the footnote should be a minimum of 6 lines or a maximum of 9 lines.

Note that April 1981 *(rather than* April, 1981,*) is the modern style for month/year dates. Also note that* p. *indicates one page;* pp., *more than one page.*

		Bottom lines
52	the year 1871.[1] This unique invention was not accepted until	15
53		14
54	the turn of the century, when Bobbsfield moved to England.[2]	13
55		12
56	_____	11
57	[1]Barbara Anne Hemsley, "The Distant Land," The National	10
58	Outlook, April 1981, pp. 215-216.	9
59		8
60	[2]Ibid., p. 217.	7
61		6
62		5
63		4
64		3
65		2
66		1

JOB 69/70-1. LONG REPORT WITH FOOTNOTES

Standard format. Change the run-in references to footnotes; use superscripts in the text.

THE HISTORY OF THE OLYMPICS
By Susan Lum Lin

Why did the Olympic Games begin? Why did they die after more than a thousand years of pomp and glory? And what forces caused them to begin again more than a thousand years later in a world that was not the same as the world in which they began?

THE LEGEND

Before you can answer these questions, you must know some facts about the history of the Olympic Games. In 490 B.C., the city-state of Athens sent a force of 9,000 to meet a great Persian army of 90,000.

On the plain of Marathon, where the armies clashed, the Greeks attacked, broke the foe, and won the day. ("The History of the Olympic Games," History of Sports, Randall Books, Chicago, 1982, p. 116.) As the Persians ran for their ships, the leader of the Greeks called for the great runner Pheidippides to carry the word to Athens, where the people longed for news of the battle.

Athens lay 40 kilometers, about 25 miles, south of Marathon. Pheidippides, who had fought in the war, put down his shield and began to run. He had to run uphill and over rough land, but he did not stop. Three hours later he reached

JOB 90-2. RESOLUTION

Standard format. Plain paper.

R E S O L U T I O N   WHEREAS Joyce   12
Renee Boynton is retiring from her position as   21
Chairperson of this board, having served it   30
and her associates for more than ten years;   39
and   40

WHEREAS she has devoted all of her skill   49
to the development of this board and the   57
growth of this firm, its products, and its staff,   67

to the end that today this firm is the most   76
successful in its field; and   82

WHEREAS she has given encouragement   90
to all those who worked with her during her   99
tenure on this board; therefore be it   106

RESOLVED, that the officers and mem-   114
bers of this board do, for her devotion to them   124
and for her loyalty, commend   130

JOYCE RENEE BOYNTON   145

LESSON 91

GOALS
- To identify when commas are used after introductory words and phrases while typing sentences.
- To format tables in reports.

FORMAT
- Single spacing   60-space line   10-space and center tabs

LAB 9

COMMAS AFTER INTRODUCTORY WORDS AND PHRASES

Type lines 1–4 once. Then repeat lines 1–4 or take a series of 1-minute timings.

1 On Friday evening, Joan Kim will go to the Noxzema Company.   12
2 During the spring, Veronica Buckley plans to visit Denmark.   12
3 No, Harris Quentin will not attend next Thursday's seminar.   12
4 At our next committee meeting, Ms. Rudi will discuss taxes.   12
   | 1 | 2 | 3 | 4 | 5 | 6 | 7 | 8 | 9 | 10 | 11 | 12

"OK" TIMINGS

Type as many 30-second "OK" (errorless) timings as possible out of three attempts on lines 5–7. Then repeat the attempt on lines 8–10.

5 Shelly acquired a prize for jumping over six feet backward.   12
6 Judy gave a quick jump as the zebra and lynx wildly fought.   24
7 Jacqueline was glad her family took five or six big prizes.   36

8 Max had a zest for quiet living and placed work before joy.   12
9 Zeke quietly placed five new jumping beans in the gray box.   24
10 Ken promptly requested five dozen jugs of wax for the club.   36
   | 1 | 2 | 3 | 4 | 5 | 6 | 7 | 8 | 9 | 10 | 11 | 12

FORMATTING TABLES IN REPORTS

Workbook 149–150.

When a report contains a great deal of statistical information, it is often easier to understand the information if it is arranged as a table. To format tables in reports:

1. Triple-space before and after the table.

2. Center a table number (if used) a double space above the table title.

3. a. Indent the table at least 5 spaces from either margin if possible.
   b. Do not extend the table beyond the line length in the report.
   c. Select intercolumnar spaces that will limit the table width.

4. Single-space the body of the table.

Athens, where a huge crowd waited. Pheidippides staggered toward the people and spoke these words: "Rejoice--we have won!" (Ibid., p. 119.) Then he fell to the ground and died.

ANCIENT OLYMPIC GAMES

The events of the Olympic Games in ancient Greece centered on the skills that were needed to stay alive; that is, good health and fitness. The athletes were not paid, so they had to pay for all their own expenses. The only prizes were wreaths of olive leaves. Later, though, prizes of money were given, and these prizes caused cheating to become common. (Harold Mark Kokoris, The Greeks, Spartan Press, New York, 1978, p. 79.)

MODERN OLYMPIC GAMES

From the fall of Rome until the late 1800s, nations were so busy fighting wars that they did not compete in sports. When the Olympics were started again in Athens in 1896 before 50,000 people, 12 countries played in the games. Track and field races were the main events, and the United States won first place in nine events. (Deborah and Grace Brumley, "A Man of Peace," Digest of History, April 1980, p. 31.)

Today athletes can score better than ever. They can study their form on slow-motion films. The surface on the track has been improved to give the runners better footing. Rules have changed--starting blocks can be used to give track stars that extra push, and springy poles help high jumpers soar much higher than jumpers in the early 1900s. (Kokoris, The Greeks, p. 88.)

In the Olympic Games, young men and women from many nations meet and compete. In this way, it is hoped that they will build friendships with people around the world so that the Olympics will lead the nations of the world to peace rather than to war.

LESSON 71

GOAL
- To format bibliographies, cover sheets, and endnotes.

FORMAT
- Single spacing   60-space line   5-space tab

KEYBOARDING SKILLS

Type lines 1–4 once. Then do what line 5 tells you to do. Repeat lines 1–4, or take a series of 1-minute timings.

Speed	1	When Lana and Nancy go to town, they may visit Ken and Pam.	12
Accuracy	2	Ask Jack Sworcz if he can quickly fix five machines for us.	12
Numbers	3	Betty ordered 10, 29, 38, 47, and 56 cartons, respectively.	12
Symbols	4	For $9 more (plus tax) she can get 32% more grain--only $9!	12
Technique	5	Retype line 3, underscoring each of the five numbers in the sentence.	

| 1 | 2 | 3 | 4 | 5 | 6 | 7 | 8 | 9 | 10 | 11 | 12 |

30-SECOND TIMINGS

Take two 30-second timings on lines 6–8, or type each line twice.

6   Six big Kansas jewelers have imported quartz for my clocks.   12

7   Alex A. Bishop may want foreign jade and zinc very quickly.   24

8   Six lively clowns quietly joked Fred about his dog, Grumpy.   36

| 1 | 2 | 3 | 4 | 5 | 6 | 7 | 8 | 9 | 10 | 11 | 12 |

PRACTICE

In the chart below, find the number of errors you made on the Pretest on page 152. Then type each of the designated drill lines four times.

Pretest errors	0–1	2–3	4–5	6+
Drill lines	24–28	23–27	22–26	21–25

Accuracy

21 some term every skills improve addition paragraph proofread
22 yet must ignored sentence spelling sometimes capitalization
23 have write paper errors chances retyped grammar punctuation
24 the most prepare projects mistakes completely typographical

Speed

25 classes closely person skills every able find want work all
26 lastly, correct create papers after hard page been word has
27 improve letters impact errors quite line look next read and
28 closely erased lastly phrase before find sure have been our

POSTTEST

Repeat the Pretest on page 152 to see how much your skill has improved.

FORMATTING RESOLUTIONS

A resolution is a formal statement of opinion or fact presented to an organized group. Study the illustration and follow these steps when formatting a resolution:

1. Use a 50-space line and double spacing on a full sheet of paper.
2. Spread-center the title *RESOLUTION* on line 13.
3. Indent each paragraph 10 spaces, and type the first word in each paragraph in all-capital letters.
4. Center the recipient's name in all-capital letters a triple space under the resolution.

JOB 90-1. RESOLUTION
Standard format. Plain paper.

```
                    R E S O L U T I O N                        12

        WHEREAS Philip Andrew Johnson will retire from the presi-  26
dency of The Students' Club of Maple High School, when he graduates 40
at the end of this year, having served as President with great    52
skill for the past nine months; and                               60
        WHEREAS he has devoted all of his abilities and much of   72
his time to the expansion of the services of the Club, with the re- 86
sult that under his leadership the Club has grown both in its ser- 99
vice to and its prestige in Maple High School; therefore be it    112
        RESOLVED, that the officers and members of The Students'  124
Club do commend him for his great devotion to them and do express 137
their deep gratitude to                                           142
                       ↓3

        PHILIP ANDREW JOHNSON                                     159
```

FORMATTING ENDNOTES

Endnotes are references gathered in a separate section at the end of a report. They are used instead of footnotes. To format endnotes:

1. Center the heading *Notes* in all-capital letters on line 13. Use a full sheet of paper.

2. Triple-space below the heading to begin typing the first note.

3. Use the same margins for the notes as used in the report.

4. Indent each note 5 spaces, and type the reference number followed by a period, 2 spaces, and the reference. (Do not use a superscript.)

5. Single-space notes that take more than one line, and begin contin-

uation lines at the left margin, as shown in the illustration.

6. Double-space between notes, to leave 1 blank line between them.

7. Number endnotes the same way you number the pages of a long report.

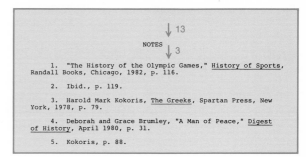

JOB 71-1. ENDNOTES

Prepare endnotes for the report on the Olympics. Use the run-in references in Job 69/70-1 on pages 121–122 as the copy for the endnotes. Standard format.

FORMATTING A BIBLIOGRAPHY

A bibliography is an alphabetic listing of all the books and articles consulted by the writer, including all references cited in footnotes.

To format a bibliography:

1. Center the heading BIBLIOG-RAPHY on a fresh sheet of paper, beginning on line 13.

2. Triple-space after the heading before typing the first entry in the bibliography.

3. Use the same margins as used in the report or term paper. Begin each entry at the left margin, and

indent any continuation lines 5 or 10 spaces.

4. Use single spacing for any continuation lines, but double-space between entries.

5. Do not number the entries.

6. List the entries in alphabetic order by the authors' *last* names. For an entry that has no author, alphabetize by the title of the article or book. (See below.)

7. Use six hyphens to avoid repeating an author's name after his or her first listing. (See below.)

When author is not known, put the book or article in alphabetic order by title. (Disregard the words The, A, *and* An.)

BIBLIOGRAPHY
↓ 13

↓ 3

Brumley, Deborah and Grace, "A Man of Peace," <u>Digest of History</u>,
    April 1980.

Drebrelis, Nichola, "In Search of Ancient Gods," <u>Modern Science
    Today</u>, November 1980.

"The History of the Olympic Games," <u>History of Sports</u>, Randall
    Books, Chicago, 1982.

Kokoris, Harold Mark, <u>The Beginning of the Olympics</u>, Dunne
    Publishing Company, Los Angeles, 1982.

------, <u>The Greeks</u>, Spartan Press, New York, 1978.

LESSON 90

LAB 9

COMMAS AFTER INTRODUCTORY WORDS AND PHRASES

GOALS
- To recognize when commas are used after introductory words and phrases while typing sentences.
- To format resolutions.

FORMAT
- Single spacing   60-space line   Tabs: 5, 10, center

Type lines 1–4 once. Then repeat lines 1–4, or take a series of 1-minute timings.

```
1   In case of fire, quickly close the door and leave the room.   12
2   In the meantime, I will wait to hear from you on this plan.   12
3   First, read all the materials you can find on this subject.   12
4   During Zeb's absence, you must attend six meetings for him.   12
    |  1  |  2  |  3  |  4  |  5  |  6  |  7  |  8  |  9  | 10  | 11  | 12
```

Place a comma after introductory words and phrases such as *first, in my opinion, for example*, and so on.

> *Yes*, she decided to cancel her order. (Word.)
> *Waiting for the next flight*, Fred reviewed his speech. (Phrase.)
> *In answer to the many requests*, we prepared a brochure. (Phrase.)

PRETEST

Take a 5-minute Pretest on lines 5–20. Then circle and count your errors. Use the chart on page 153 to determine which lines to type for practice.

```
5        The skill of proofreading is one of the most critical,    12
6   yet one of the most ignored, skills a person can have.  All    24
7   of us have chances to write a few letters.  In addition, we    36
8   sometimes must prepare term papers and do projects for some    48
9   classes.  If we find that we must write or type a paper, we    60
10  have to be able to find and correct every one of our errors    72
11  if our work is to create the impact we want.                  81
12       We must all try quite hard to improve our proofreading    93
13  skill.  Before taking a page out of the typewriter, we must  105
14  proofread it.  After a page has been typed, we must read it  117
15  word by word, phrase by phrase, and line by line.  Then, we  129
16  look closely for spelling, capitalization, or typographical  141
17  errors.  Next, the page has to be read sentence by sentence  153
18  in order to find punctuation and grammar mistakes.  Lastly,  165
19  a page is read paragraph by paragraph to be sure all errors  177
20  have been erased completely and retyped.                     185
    |  1  |  2  |  3  |  4  |  5  |  6  |  7  |  8  |  9  | 10  | 11  | 12   SI 1.36
```

FORMATTING A COVER PAGE

A cover page contains the title of the report, the name of the writer, the course title, the teacher's name for whom the report was prepared, and the date.

To format a cover page:

1. Center the report title and the writer's name in the upper 33 lines of the page.

2. Center the course title, the teacher's name, and the date in the lower 33 lines of the page.

```
THE HISTORY OF THE OLYMPICS

     By Susan Lum Lin


       TYPEWRITING

     Ms. Sue Champion

      March 1, 19--
```

JOB 71-2. BIBLIOGRAPHY AND COVER PAGE

Make a copy of the bibliography illustrated on page 123. Then prepare a cover page for a report entitled *The History of the Olympics*. Use your name as author and use *Typewriting* as the course title; use your teacher's name and today's date. Standard format.

LESSON 72

GOALS
- To identify how commas are used after introductory clauses while typing sentences.
- To type 35/3'/5e.
- To format a bound report.

FORMAT
- Single spacing   60-space line   5-space tab

LAB 6

INTRODUCTORY *IF, AS,* AND *WHEN* CLAUSES

Type lines 1–4 twice. Then take a series of 1-minute timings on each line.

```
1  When the jury was dismissed, everyone decided to celebrate.   12
2  As we walked along quickly, we spoke of their organization.   12
3  If I have time later this week, I'll check into the matter.   12
4  When you finish, let me know if the lock needs to be fixed.   12
   |  1  |  2  |  3  |  4  |  5  |  6  |  7  |  8  |  9  |  10  |  11  |  12
```

3-MINUTE TIMINGS

Take two 3-minute timings on lines 5–13.

```
5       Streets are as old as cities or towns, and some of the    12
6   oldest, like the Appian Way in Rome, are still in use.  The    24
7   whole growth of most towns followed the path where the road    36
8   was first made; so while the buildings in town changed, the    48
9   road remained just about the same.  Quite often one can get    60
10  a history of a city by exploring the names of some streets,    72
11  which were often named after local events or amazing people    84
12  of great deeds.  Are there any such streets in your city or    96
13  in your community that refer to famous citizens?            105
    |  1  |  2  |  3  |  4  |  5  |  6  |  7  |  8  |  9  |  10  |  11  |  12    SI 1.30
```

JOB 89-1. MAGAZINE ARTICLE
Standard format.

CREATURES FROM "DOWN UNDER"   16

By Sharon T. Cole   29

(lines of spaces)

The most curious creature that   38
lives on the other side of our globe is   46
none other than the kangaroo. Kanga-   53
roos are well known for their sturdy,   61
powerful hind legs and for their se-   68
cluded pouches in which they carry   75
their young. This report will reveal   83
some of the important facts about this   91
"rabbit-like" mammal.   95

PHYSICAL CHARACTERISTICS   102

Kangaroos have either gray or red   110
fur, stand close to 7 feet (2 meters)   117
tall when full grown, and weigh close   125
to 200 pounds (40 *91* kilograms). They   132
travel by jumping on their powerful   139
hind legs, sometimes leaping at the   147
rate of nearly 30 miles (48 kilometers)   155
per hour for short distances. *Their tails*   163
act as levers when they are running   170
at a fast pace and as stools on which   178
they may rest when they are stand-   185
ing still.   187

FAMILY LIFE   192

The male kangaroo accepts no re-   199
sponsibility for the newborn kangaroo.   207
It is the mother's responsibility to   214
feed and shelter the baby. The kanga-   222
roo's family life appears to be rather   230
casual, and there are seldom any long-   237
term commitments to any one group.   245
Kangaroos live 7 years, with a few of   252
them surviving until they are 20 years   260
old. *The greatest enemy of the kangaroo*   268
is drought, but some of the species are   276
killed by hunters and wild dogs.   283

CLOSING REMARKS   288

Kangaroos live both in tropical   296
forests and on the plains. They have   303
very sharp teeth that enable them to   311
eat the grasses much closer to the   318
ground than most other mammals can eat.   326
For this reason, they are a nuisance   333
to stock raisers because they eat the   341
grass that is needed for the raising of   349
livestock such as sheep and cattle.   356

JOB 89-2. MINUTES OF A MEETING
Standard format. 5-space and center tabs.

Staff Retreat Committee   14
MINUTES OF THE MARCH MEETING   32
[*Today's Date*]   45

ATTENDANCE   49

The March meeting of the Staff Retreat   58
Committee was held in the office of Mr. Doyle,   68
who presided at the meeting. The session   76
began at three o'clock and adjourned at five.   85
All members were present except Jean Crews   94
and John Mott.   97

UNFINISHED BUSINESS   103

The secretary read the minutes of the De-   112
cember meeting, and they were approved as   121
read.   122

Ms. Sanchez reported on the staff retreat   132
held last March at Clear Lake. Then it was   140
suggested that we return to Clear Lake for   149
next year's meeting.   153

NEW BUSINESS   158

Mr. Doyle then suggested a need for a theme   168
for this year's staff retreat meeting to be held   178
in June. A committee was organized to study   187
this problem and come up with a suitable   195
theme by next month's meeting. Ruth White   203
will chair this committee.   209

Respectfully submitted,   215

James Moore, Secretary   222

FORMATTING BOUND REPORTS

If a report is so thick or important that it needs a protective binder, the margins and tab stops should be moved 3 spaces to the right to provide space at the left for three-hole punching and notebook binding.

JOB 72-1. BOUND REPORT

Retype Job 69/70-1 on pages 121–122. Do not include footnotes in the report, but do type run-in references. Standard format.

LESSONS 73/74

GOALS
- To type sentences that use commas correctly following introductory clauses.
- To review formatting of personal-business letters, tables, memos, and reports.

FORMAT
- Single spacing   60-space line   5-space tab

LAB 6

Type lines 1–4 once, providing the missing commas. Edit your copy as your teacher reads the answers. Then retype lines 1–4 from your edited copy.

INTRODUCTORY IF, AS, AND WHEN CLAUSES

Workbook 105–106.

1 When it got very windy Joe had to call a halt to the game.   12
2 When you type a report be very sure that you erase neatly.   12
3 If I do not return in six hours please call my Azusa home.   12
4 As Pat started the car I realized that it was quite noisy.   12

PRACTICE

Type lines 5–12 on page 117 twice each.

3-MINUTE TIMINGS

Take two 3-minute timingson lines 7–15 on page 124.

TECHNICAL QUESTIONS

Type short answers to the following 15 questions:

1. What is the difference between a personal-business letter and a business letter.

2. On what line do you type the date in a business letter?

3. What is a salutation?

4. What items appear in the closing of a personal-business letter?

5. What is an enclosure?

6. What is a long report?

7. On what line should the page number of a report be typed?

8. What is a footnote?

9. How is a footnote separated from the body of a report?

10. How should you display the title of a table?

11. How should you display column heads?

12. What is the standard spacing between columns in tables?

13. What is an invoice?

14. Where do you type the words *Total amount due*?

15. On which side (left or right) should a column of numbers align?

LESSON 89

KEYBOARDING SKILLS

Type lines 1–5 once. In line 5, use your tabulator key to advance from one word to the next through the entire line. Repeat lines 1–4, or take a series of 1-minute timings.

Speed	1	They both wish to visit Japan and Turkey if they go by air.	12
Accuracy	2	Zachery joked about a group of wax squid from the carnival.	12
Numbers	3	In Chapter 10, we saw that 47 times 56 was less than 2,938.	12
Symbols	4	Please order 480# of #5 grade @ $17.69 before September 23.	12
Technique	5	by do go hi ha ho ma me no pa so to	

| 1 | 2 | 3 | 4 | 5 | 6 | 7 | 8 | 9 | 10 | 11 | 12

FORMATTING MAGAZINE ARTICLES

Workbook 147–148.

To format an article you wish to submit to a magazine for publication:

1. Use double spacing and standard 8½- by 11-inch (or metric A4) paper.

2. Use the top margins used in other reports—begin the title on line 13; begin page numbers (beginning with page 2) on line 7.

3. Under the by-line, indicate the line length used and number of lines in the article. (You will have to insert the number of lines after you have finished typing the article.)

4. Use a line length equal to the average line in the magazine (type 10 lines and average them); do not exceed that line by more than 2 spaces.

5. Follow the magazine's display style for headings and spacing.

6. Bottom margins should contain from 6 to 9 blank lines.

7. Except for page 1, type the writer's name before the page number, separating the two items with a diagonal—For example: Perez / 5

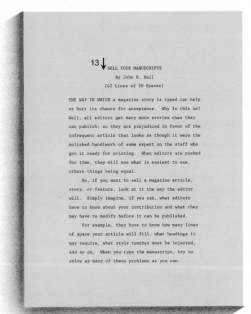

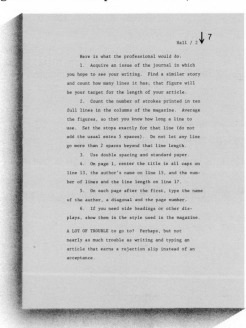

JOB 73/74-1. LONG REPORT

Standard format with side headings. Type run-in references as footnotes. Convert to capitals and insert commas as needed.

GOLD / By [*Your name*]

¶ What is it that gives gold its value? The only real value is that people want it! People everywhere in the world love gold. They trust it. It will not rust or rot. You can hide it--it is better than money. ¶ The first gold money was issued by the lydians in the sixth century B.C. (Charles Grunfeld, The History of Money, Able Press, New York, 1981, p. 65.) Soon the greeks began minting money in the shape of gold disks. Later, the romans notched the edge of each coin as a way to stop the practice of shaving off thin slices of gold. Although our coins today are not made of gold they are still notched in that way. ¶ Every country has had gold in its history. egypt ¶ Early egyptians linked gold to the sun--to life. The burial place of king tut was all of beaten gold. india ¶ In india every bride who has money wears gold trinkets in some form. She will never wear all that again; she will keep it as insurance against bad times. south africa ¶ Two-thirds of the world's production of gold is done here. The people of africa believe that the sight of gold keeps one in touch with powerful spirits. south america ¶ The spanish came here for spices and gold. When they saw the indians wearing gold they forgot about the spices and took all the gold home to spain. united states ¶ The main use of gold in this country is for jewelry. About half our gold reserve is stored in fort knox. The value of this gold is over $11 billion. (Ibid., p. 204.)

JOB 73/74-2. MEMORANDUM

Standard format. Workbook 107 top.

DATE: [*Today's date*] / TO: Sue Booth, President / Business Club, South Side High School / FROM: Tom Dunn, President, Business Club, Swissvale High School / SUBJECT: Joint Meeting.

¶ Sarah Klein and I will drive to South Side High on Wednesday, March 6, to greet you and show your drivers how to get to our school. We will be in your school parking lot at 2 p.m. to lead the way to Swissvale. ¶ If any of your members need a ride, we'll be happy to take three or four in our lead car. ¶ All of us are looking forward to March 6! / TD

JOB 73/74-3. TABLE

Standard format. Double spacing. Half sheet of paper.

Candidates for Club Officers
The Business Club

Office	Candidate	Grade
President	Alice Ann Blake	12
President	Charles B. Kaminsky	12
Secretary	Nancy Epstein	10
Secretary	Ted Woodward	11
Treasurer	Paul Montalvo	12
Treasurer	Virginia A. Petri	11

JOB 73/74-4. PERSONAL-BUSINESS LETTER

Standard format. Envelope: Workbook 107 bottom. Body 109 words.

[*Use your own address and today's date*] / Ms. Brenda Chan, Program Director / Keynote Studios / 50 Rockefeller Plaza / New York, NY 10020 / Dear Ms. Chan: I should like to add my cheers to those you must be receiving for your very fine "Stars of the Silver Screen" series of shows. They are wonderful. ¶ Is it possible to attend a broadcast? I plan to be in New York City on December 12 with three friends. The four of us would very much like to see the show while it is being taped or broadcast. We should be most grateful to you if we could obtain tickets. ¶ I hope that I may hear from you and learn that you can let us have four tickets for December 12. They would make our visit to New York complete. / Yours truly, / [*Your name*]

FORMATTING MINUTES OF A MEETING

Minutes of a meeting are usually saved in a three-ring binder. To format minutes:

1. Set margins for a bound report (60P/70E, shifted 3 spaces to the right).

2. Use a top margin of 6 blank lines.

3. Type the title on line 7 of page 1. Type page numbers on line 7 of additional pages.

4. Single-space.

5. Type side headings in all-capital letters. Double-space before and after side headings.

6. Begin closing lines at the center, a double space below the text. Leave 3 blank lines for the signature.

JOB 88-1. MINUTES OF A MEETING

Standard format. 5-space and center tabs.

New Products Committee

MINUTES OF THE MARCH MEETING

[Today's date]

ATTENDANCE

The March meeting of the New Products committee was held in the Boardroom of Sutton Publishing Company. Ms. Mae Lopez, Marketing Director, presided at the meeting. The following were present at the meeting.

Mr. Frank Swan
Mr. Wayne Hall
Ms. Donna Schultz
Ms. Cathy Cooper
Dr. A. R. Bloome
Mrs. Anne Krouse
Mr. E. G. Moore
Ms. Jan Bennett
Mr. Paul E. Scott
Ms. Mae Lopez

arrange alphabetically in two columns

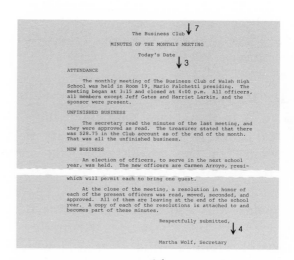

UNFINISHED BUSINESS

The secretary read the minutes of the February March meeting, and they were approved as read.

Ms. Moore reported on the progress of the new text on auto repair. Contracts for the text were drawn up and sent to the authors on March 1. First drafts of the text material are to be completed one year from the date of the contract.

New Business

Ms. Schultz suggested that the information processing texts be revised one year earlier than planned because of the rapid changes that have taken place in this area in the past 2 years. A committee was formed to study these changes and to come up with a recommendation at next month's meeting. Ms. Schultz will chair this committee.

Respectfully submitted,

Claire T. Stark, Secretary

COMPETENCY CHECK

GOALS
- To demonstrate competency by typing 35/3'/5e.
- To demonstrate competency by formatting and correctly typing a personal business letter, a memo, and a table.

FORMAT
- Single spacing   60-space line   5-space tab

PREVIEW PRACTICE

Type lines 1–2 twice as a preview to the 3-minute timings below.

Accuracy   1   art are barns signs noted cheap their native living rotting
Speed   2   examples antiques products through country symbol today era

3-MINUTE TIMINGS

Take two 3-minute timings on lines 3–11.

```
3       Have you ever driven through the country and noted the      12
4   number of barns painted with the same sign, all selling the    24
5   same product?  At the time farmers found it a cheap way for     36
6   them to have their barns painted.  Makers of products found     48
7   this to be an amazing idea to push their goods.  Today many     60
8   of the barn signs are thought to be good examples of living     72
9   native art.  They are a symbol of an era, and like antiques     84
10  and old things, some are being preserved; but most of these    96
11  barns are just rotting away or falling down.                   105
    |  1  |  2  |  3  |  4  |  5  |  6  |  7  |  8  |  9  | 10  | 11  | 12      SI 1.30
```

JOB 75-1. PERSONAL-BUSINESS LETTER
Standard format. Envelope: Workbook 109 top. Body 128 words. Use current date.

Ms. Ruth E. Gillis, Travel Agent / Western Worlds Agency / 294 Highland Parkway / Buffalo, NY 14223 / Dear Ms. Gillis: / Three of my friends and I want to spend one or two weeks of our next summer vacation at a dude ranch. We have heard from others that dude ranches can be great fun, and we would very much like to learn more about them. ¶ Would you please provide us with information on the activities available at dude ranches and, perhaps, some descriptive brochures? In addition, we would also appreciate your telling us the cost for each of us for two double rooms (with baths) and meals for both for a one-week stay and a two-week stay in the month of July. Can travel arrangements be made to and from our city--and if so, what is the cost of a round trip per person? ¶ We will appreciate hearing from you. / Sincerely yours, / [*Your name*]

JOB 75-2. MEMO
Standard format. Workbook 109 bottom.

[*To*] Mr. James Fetter, Principal, Swissvale High School / [*From*] Roberta Weinberg, Secretary of The Business Club / [*Subject*] Banquet Plans / [*Today's date*] / I am pleased to give you, as you requested, a progress report on the plans for our February banquet. I am enclosing copies of the last report from our treasurer and of the banquet program. ¶ So far we have sold 110 tickets, including those of the new members we plan to initiate just before the dinner. There will be 12 nonpaying guests at the head table. / RW / Enclosures

JOB 75-3. TABLE
Standard format. Half sheet of paper.

NEW ADVERTISERS FOR THE YEARBOOK
(Students Who Made the Sale)

Advertisers	Student's Name
Bailey Bottling	J. MacGill
Butler Coal Co.	S. Murray
Painters Resort	B. Chalkey
Rubicam Computer	A. Katzman

LESSON 88

GOALS
- To use commas correctly to separate adjectives while typing sentences.
- To improve accuracy on 30-second timings.
- To format minutes of a meeting.

FORMAT
- Single spacing   60-space line   5-space tab

LAB 8

COMMAS BETWEEN ADJECTIVES

Workbook 145–146.

Type lines 1–4 once, providing the missing commas. Edit your copy as your teacher reads the answers. Then retype lines 1–4 from your edited copy.

1 They will have to clean that dusty neglected cellar today.
2 Cool cloudy mornings often turn into beautiful afternoons.
3 That massive well-crafted desk weighs at least 500 pounds.
4 All students are released early on cold windy winter days.

30-SECOND TIMINGS

Take two 30-second timings on lines 5–7, or type each line twice.

5 Six jumbo elephants quickly moved the wagon from the blaze. 12
6 Jack found the gravel camp six below zero quite a few days. 24
7 Jo saw six big packs of cards and seized them very quickly. 36

1- AND 5-MINUTE TIMINGS

Take two 1-minute timings on each paragraph. Then take one 5-minute timing on the entire selection. Use single spacing for the 1-minute timings and double spacing for the 5-minute timing.

1'

8   We have heard in recent years that our nation needs to conserve its 15
9 energy. This is going to be quite a task, and all of us must contribute 29
10 in whatever ways possible to this task. 37

11   For energy conservation to work, please realize we are requiring 14
12 sacrifices. We may not be able to keep our homes as warm in the 27
13 winters or as cool in the summers as we have done. 37

14   Putting better insulation in our houses will also help in the 13
15 conservation program. By doing so, we let less heat escape through 27
16 the walls and ceilings. Yes, this will help a lot. 37

17   To help save energy, we should also turn off all those extra lights 15
18 in our homes while the rooms are not occupied. Over a period of 27
19 months, this effort will conserve a lot of fuel. 37

20   We might also save energy by car pooling when going to work. By 14
21 pooling, we will use only a fourth as much gas if just four of us ride 28
22 together in the morning to our various jobs. 37

| 1 | 2 | 3 | 4 | 5 | 6 | 7 | 8 | 9 | 10 | 11 | 12 | 13 | 14 | SI 1.37

LEVEL 3

BASIC BUSINESS FORMATTING

12   Jane gave my excited boy quite a prize for his clever work.   12

13   I was quickly penalized five or six times by Major Higgins.   24

14   The very next question emphasized the growing lack of jobs.   36

| 1 | 2 | 3 | 4 | 5 | 6 | 7 | 8 | 9 | 10 | 11 | 12

PRETEST

Take a 5-minute Pretest on lines 15–29. Then circle and count your errors. Use the chart below to determine which lines to type for practice.

15   Every once in a while you may come across a typewriter   12

16   with something very unique about it; the thing might simply   24

17   be a tray for a pencil or eraser, or just an extra key.   35

18   Or perhaps you might find a machine with small numbers   47

19   in the place of the symbols on the upper row; these are for   59

20   footnote annotations, for citations in the text, etc.   70

21   You might even find a machine that has a light instead   82

22   of a bell to signal the approach to the margin; the machine   94

23   is intended for somebody who's deaf or hard of hearing.   105

24   In a hospital you might find a typewriter mounted on a   117

25   special contraption that holds the keyboard where a patient   129

26   flat on his or her back is able to manipulate the keys.   140

27   But the most dazzling and unique of the surprise items   152

28   is the discovery that you have keys with accent marks--just   164

29   the thing for a project in typing in a foreign language.   175

| 1 | 2 | 3 | 4 | 5 | 6 | 7 | 8 | 9 | 10 | 11 | 12   SI 1.40

For Extra Speed

Tab-indent quickly, smoothly.

Return carriage or carrier quickly.

Release shift key instantly.

Get off space bar in a flash.

Keep eyes on copy so that you never lose your place.

PRACTICE

In the chart below, find the number of errors you made on the Pretest. Then type each of the designated drill lines four times.

Pretest errors	0–1	2–3	4–5	6+
Drill lines	33–37	32–36	31–35	30–34

Accuracy

30   every patient symbols foreign somebody discovery typewriter
31   thing instead eraser, example citation manipulate something
32   extra accents numbers machine language dazzling annotations
33   upper intends hearing project keyboard surprise contraption

Speed

34   might place these text, come back very just you may see the
35   who's light mount holds with tiny row; text are for the one
36   where would items marks even find that bell who can say you
37   bells trays notes while deaf able keys flat see and use key

POSTTEST

Repeat the Pretest to see how much your skill has improved.

Written business messages are the energy that moves the huge, complicated world of business. Level 3, "Basic Business Formatting," will introduce you to many essential business documents.

In Level 3 you will:

1. Demonstrate keyboarding accuracy and speed on straight copy with a goal of 38 words a minute or more for 5 minutes with no more than 5 errors.

2. Demonstrate production skills on basic formats for reports, tables, letters, and forms.

3. Correctly proofread copy for errors and edit copy for revision.

4. Apply more advanced techniques for formatting four categories of business documents from six input modes.

5. Apply rules for correct use of punctuation in communications.

LESSON 76

UNIT 13 KEYBOARDING SKILLS REVIEW

UNIT GOAL
35/5'/5e

GOALS
- To identify and practice the alphabetic keys on which more drill is needed.
- To build skill on the alphabetic keyboard.

FORMAT
- Single spacing   60-space line   Tabs every 7 spaces

KEYBOARDING SKILLS

Type lines 1–4 once. In line 5, use your tabulator key to advance from one number to the next through the entire line. Repeat lines 1–4, or take a series of 1-minute timings.

Speed	1	She may go to town for a pen, but she must come right back.	12
Accuracy	2	Five or six big jet planes zoomed quickly by the new tower.	12
Numbers	3	If 56 days are left, then 47, 29, 38, and 10 will not work.	12
Symbols	4	With our 4% raise we bought 17 lb of #38 & #29--what a buy!	12
Technique	5	102 293 384 475 561 102 293 384 475

```
| 1 | 2 | 3 | 4 | 5 | 6 | 7 | 8 | 9 | 10 | 11 | 12
```

PRETEST

Type lines 6–9 twice to find out which alphabetic keys are the most difficult for you. Force yourself to type rapidly—push yourself to your fastest rate. Circle each *letter* in which an error is made.

6   We amazed six judges by quietly giving back the four pages.
7   The expert quickly noted five bad jewels among the zircons.
8   Jack will exhibit very quaint games for Buzz's fall parade.
9   The exits were quickly filled by dozens of jumpy villagers.

PRACTICE

Type lines 10–22 once. Then repeat any of the lines that stress the letter errors you circled in the Pretest.

10   A aid apt ate aide aunt aisle B bus bit bad brag burn below
11   C cob cot cut cold crew cabin D dig dry dye dive dirt depth
12   E eye elf end each ease eight F fix fog fun fort foul fifth
13   G gap gun gem grip grow grant H hit hug hay hike hurt hoist

(Continued on next page)

JOB 86-2. INVOICE ON A FORM

Standard format. Workbook 143 bottom.

[*Today's date*] / Ramirez Home Improvements Inc. / 2320 Merrell Road
/ Dallas, TX 75229

11	Workbenches, Model 9109	69.00	759.00
26	20′ Aluminum drain gutters	27.36	711.36
4	Sure-Right 6″ electric saws, Model R78	47.00	188.00
8	6′ Steel storage cabinets	27.69	221.52
	Amount due		1,879.88
	Delivery charges		37.28
	Total amount due		1,917.16

LESSON 87

CLINIC

GOALS
- To improve accuracy on "OK" timings.
- To type 35/5'/5e.

FORMAT
- Single spacing   60-space line   5-space tab

KEYBOARDING SKILLS

Type lines 1–4 once. Then type line 5 using your return key or lever after each word. Repeat lines 1–4, or take a series of 1-minute timings.

Speed 1 Their big problem is half their profit is spent for enamel. 12
Accuracy 2 Have my six dozen quails joined two big flocks of sparrows? 12
Numbers 3 Shirley got Nos. 10 and 29; Chapin got Nos. 38, 47, and 56. 12
Symbols 4 Fox & Day ordered 25# of cheese (mellow) @ $3.09 per pound. 12
Technique 5 You should always operate the return key or lever by touch. 12

| 1 | 2 | 3 | 4 | 5 | 6 | 7 | 8 | 9 | 10 | 11 | 12

12-SECOND TIMINGS

Type each line four times, or take four 12-second timings on each line. For each timing, type with no more than one error.

6 It seemed to me that the birds got silent long before dark. 12
7 She put a stamp on it before she dropped it in the mailbox. 12
8 Six of us pitched in to give the car a push along the road. 12

25   30   35   40   45   50   55   60

"OK" TIMINGS

This version of a 30-second timing is used to build your accuracy on alphabetic copy. Try to type as many 30-second "OK" (errorless) timings as possible out of three attempts on lines 9–11. Then repeat the attempt on lines 12–14, page 147.

9 Five or six big jet planes zoomed quickly by the new tower. 12
10 Jars prevented the brown mixture from freezing too quickly. 24
11 Hal was quick to give us extra pizza and juice for my boss. 36

```
14  I ice ire imp inch itch ideas J joy jog jug joke just judge
15  K keg key kit kite kick knife L lip lie let land lark light
16  M mow map may mend myth minor N new nor nut nose none notch
17  O our own one oath ouch ought P pay peg pen pure prey probe
18  Q que qui quo quip quit quake R rot rob ran ripe rein ridge

19  S sap sob ski silk sang slide T try toy tip take tend there
20  U urn ups use urge used unite V van vie vow view vise vinyl
21  W way who wig wild wine wring X tax fix wax exam apex index
22  Y yes yet yam yard yawn yours Z zig zip zoo zero zany zebra
```

POSTTEST

Repeat the Pretest to see how much your skill has improved.

1- AND 5-MINUTE TIMINGS

Take two 1-minute timings on each paragraph. Then take one 5-minute timing on the entire selection. Use single spacing for the 1-minute timings and double spacing for the 5-minute timing. 5-space tab.

```
23      If you have ever had an opportunity to move to another    12
24  city or town, you realize that it might be quite a big job.   24
25  If you are like many others, you might move yourself.         35

26      The initial thing to do is to lease a truck or trailer    12
27  for loading all your household belongings.  Be very certain   24
28  to get a truck or trailer large enough for your needs.        35

29      Many large boxes and cartons must be packed and sealed    12
30  carefully.  Be sure to pack all your belongings tightly for   24
31  the move so that nothing will break inside the boxes.         35

32      Have some of your friends assist you in carrying heavy    12
33  items such as sofas, beds, desks, and television sets.  All   24
34  your larger items should be placed in the truck first.        35

35      As you cruise down a highway with a load of furniture,    12
36  watch carefully for any sudden stops in the traffic.  Drive   24
37  slowly so that you do not damage any of your furniture.       35
```
| 1 | 2 | 3 | 4 | 5 | 6 | 7 | 8 | 9 | 10 | 11 | 12 | SI 1.38

13   Raising dogs can be a combination of both fun and hard   12

14 work. Before you even begin, you have to decide what breed   24

15 will best adapt to your life-style and your residence.   35

16   If you need a dog to protect your house, a terrier may   47

17 not provide sufficient protection. If you are in an apart-   59

18 ment, a St. Bernard would certainly be just too large.   70

19   If you have decided upon the dog you want, be sure you   82

20 check its registration papers. Then, assuming that you now   94

21 purchase the puppy, you can expect to need to train it.   105

22   Of course, you know that most puppies have to be taken   117

23 outside quite frequently before they are housebroken. They   129

24 must be praised quickly when they respond to a command.   140

25   Ample care, plenty of good exercise, a solid diet, and   152

26 loads of love are all vital in the raising of an animal. A   164

27 zesty puppy should grow up to be a healthy, happy dog.   175

| 1 | 2 | 3 | 4 | 5 | 6 | 7 | 8 | 9 | 10 | 11 | 12 | SI 1.38

POSTTEST

Repeat the Pretest to see how much your skill has improved.

FORMATTING REVIEW
Workbook 142.

Before you type Jobs 86-1 and 86-2, review the typing of forms. Specifically, review alignment with guide words (page 59), memos on printed forms (page 107), and invoices on printed forms (pages 113–115).

JOB 86-1. INTEROFFICE MEMO ON A FORM
Standard format. Single-space. Workbook 143 top.

[*Today's date*] / [*To:*] James Bloom / District V Manager / [*From:*]   11
Ruth Lopez / Area Manager / [*Subject:*] Waterwheel Replacements   23

    We have had to place your order for 12 dozen #4216 waterwheel   37
sprinklers on back order. Your order will not be processed for at least   52
another two weeks.   56

    The whole district has suffered a long, hot drought that has caused   70
a drain on our supplies of those water sprinklers. The cooler weather   85
we are to have next week should bring you some relief until your   98
order can be filled.   102

                RL   105

[*Your initials*]   108

LESSON 77

GOALS
- To identify and practice the number keys on which more drill is needed.
- To build skill in typing numbers.

FORMAT
- Single spacing   60-space line   5-space tab

KEYBOARDING SKILLS

Type lines 1–4 once. In line 5, use the shift lock for each word in all-capital letters. Repeat lines 1–4, or take a series of 1-minute timings.

Speed   1   All of them might now work to make the new year a good one.   12
Accuracy   2   Vi kept it blazing sixty minutes with a quart jug of cider.   12
Numbers   3   We saw 10 fish, 29 rabbits, 38 birds, 47 dogs, and 56 cats.   12
Symbols   4   We paid 12% on a loan of $900; they (Ann and Joe) paid 13%.   12
Technique   5   The metals are COPPER and GOLD and IRON and NICKEL and TIN.
                | 1 | 2 | 3 | 4 | 5 | 6 | 7 | 8 | 9 | 10 | 11 | 12

PRETEST

Take a 2-minute timing on lines 6–8, or type them twice to find out which number keys are the most difficult for you to type. Keep your eyes on the copy as you type. Circle each digit in which an error is made.

6   2981 1073 5764 4711 5092 8920 3589 4056 8362 1594 2036 4637   12
7   5647 1525 8032 1337 6592 4094 6417 8867 5091 7723 8649 6052   24
8   6328 5049 1157 6924 8037 2480 9935 4062 8135 2766 9317 5048   36
    | 1 | 2 | 3 | 4 | 5 | 6 | 7 | 8 | 9 | 10 | 11 | 12

PRACTICE

Type lines 9–18 once. Then repeat any of the lines that stress the digit errors you circled in the Pretest.

9   We need 1 chair, 1 desk, 11 staplers, 11 pins, and 11 pens.
10   Player No. 22 ran 22 yards; then the score became 22 to 12.
11   Mel's ticket stub is for Seat 3, 13, 31, or 33--not for 43.
12   Through Gate No. 4 came Nos. 4, 14, 41, 44, 54, 48, and 74.
13   The scores were 65 to 55, 57 to 56,. 59 to 55, and 54 to 45.

14   State highways 16, 26, 66, 126, 166, and 186 are now paved.
15   On May 17 send $77 to reserve 17 seats for the June 7 game.
16   On 6/8, 7/8, and 8/8 we sold 8 quarts and 8 pints of pears.
17   They have 9 quarters, 19 dimes, 29 nickels, and 39 pennies.
18   We led by 10 points at 20 to 30 and by 10 more at 20 to 40.

POSTTEST

Repeat the Pretest to see how much your skill has improved.

PREVIEW PRACTICE

Type lines 19 and 20 twice as a preview to the 1- and 5-minute timing routine.

Accuracy   19   any sets heavy slowly realize carrying furniture belongings
Speed   20   have move city town that like many step load your must pack

1- AND 5-MINUTE TIMINGS

Repeat the 1- and 5-minute timing routine on page 130.

JOB 85-4. FOUR-COLUMN TABLE
Standard format. Double-space, full sheet of paper.

NATIONAL LEAGUE PENNANT WINNERS

Highest Won/Lost Percentages

Year	Club	Manager	Percentage
1880	Chicago	Anson	.798
1876	Chicago	Spalding	.788
1885	Chicago	Anson	.777
1906	Chicago	Chance	.763
1884	Providence	Bancroft	.750

LESSON 86

GOALS
- To apply the rule for commas between adjectives.
- To type at least 35/5'/5e.
- To review forms typing.

FORMAT
- Single spacing   60-space line   5-space tab

LAB 8

Type lines 1–4 once, providing the missing commas. Edit your copy as your teacher reads the answers. Then retype lines 1–4 from your edited copy.

COMMAS BETWEEN ADJECTIVES

1 It's dangerous to drive quickly on a wet slippery highway.
2 Soft soothing music plays in most restaurants and offices.
3 Six of us in Jan's building heard the loud strident voice.
4 A hazy summer morning often becomes a hot humid afternoon.

PRETEST

Take a 5-minute Pretest on lines 13–27 on page 145. Circle and count your errors. Use the chart below to find the number of errors you made on the Pretest. Then type each of the designated drill lines four times. Take a 5-minute Posttest on lines 13–27 on page 145 to see how much your skill has improved.

Pretest errors	0–1	2–3	4–5	6+
Drill lines	8–12	7–11	6–10	5–9

PRACTICE

Accuracy

5 would great quickly outside exercise dangerous registration
6 adapt papers puppies Bernard purchase residence housebroken
7 breed enough decide provide assuming life-style combination
8 begin before terrier raising apartment determine protection

Speed

9 praised raising course happy zesty both upon want sure just
10 command expect check train vital hard line part can fun and
11 healthy animal large taken ample work will your may not are
12 respond proper plenty times dogs even must what too its all

LESSON 78

GOALS
GOALS
- To recognize how commas are used in compound sentences while typing.
- To identify the symbol keys on which more drill is needed.
- To build skill in typing symbols.

FORMAT
- Single spacing   60-space line   5-space tab

LAB 7

COMMAS IN COMPOUND SENTENCES

Type lines 1–4 once. Then repeat lines 1–4 or take a series of 1-minute timings.

```
1  Sixteen pages were quite torn, and five dozen were missing.   12
2  Just pay the clerk by noon, or you will lose the last seat.   12
3  They will not accept your bid, nor will they allow another.   12
4  You must read a chapter, but you do not have to outline it.   12
   |  1  |  2  |  3  |  4  |  5  |  6  |  7  |  8  |  9  |  10  |  11  |  12
```

An "independent" clause is one that can stand alone as a sentence. Here are two examples: *Larry took the bus. Mary went by plane.* When two independent clauses are joined by the conjunction *and, but, or,* or *nor* into one compound sentence, place a comma before the conjunction:

Larry took the bus, *but* Mary went by plane.

We have an office in New York, *and* we will have one in Boston soon.

PRETEST

Type lines 5–9 twice to find out which symbol keys are the most difficult for you. Force yourself to keep your eyes on the copy, and type rapidly—push yourself to your fastest rate. Circle each symbol in which an error is made.

```
5  We sold 19 quarts @ $2, 17 quarts @ $3, and 16 quarts @ $4.
6  Our #4729 makes 10% profit; #3810 makes 8%; #5638 makes 7%.
7  Clay & Poe and Day & Ames predicted a 75¢ and an 82¢ climb.
8  Computers use asterisks to multiply:  2 * 3 (6); 4 * 2 (8).
9  In math, 6 − 2 = 4 and 9 − 4 = 5; 6 + 2 = 8 and 9 + 4 = 13.
```

PRACTICE

Type lines 10–19 once. Then repeat any of the lines that stress the symbol errors you circled in the Pretest.

```
@   10  They found 10 @ 29, 29 @ 38, 38 @ 47, 47 @ 56, and 56 @ 10.

¢   11  Soda is 56¢, candy is 47¢, gum is 29¢, and peanuts are 10¢.

*   12  Jones,* Hernandez,* Young,* Moletti,* and Gray* won prizes.

#   13  Our new scale shows #56 at 29#, #47 at 38#, and #29 at 10#.

$   14  Our show tickets should cost us $10, $29, $38, $47, or $56.

%   15  Your sales increased 10%, 29%, 38%, 47%, and 56% last year.

&   16  Day & Cole, Yung & Poe, and Lee & Madera are all attorneys.

( ) 17  Troy (Ohio), Leon (Iowa), and Lund (Utah) were represented.

−   18  Label the square cartons as 10-29, 38-47, 56-38, and 47-10.

+ = 19  We know that 56 + 47 = 103, 29 + 10 = 39, and 38 + 58 = 96.
```

LESSON 85

GOALS
- To type sentences that reinforce the rule for commas between adjectives.
- To review typing two-, three-, and four-column tables.

FORMAT
- Single spacing   60-space line   Tabs at center and as needed

LAB 8

COMMAS BETWEEN ADJECTIVES

Type lines 1–4 once. Then repeat lines 1–4 or take a series of 1-minute timings.

```
1  A dozen anxious, excited scouts began their overnight trip.   12
2  Last night four neighbors bought Joan a healthy, happy pup.   12
3  The scarecrow is wearing a long, loose coat and a silk hat.   12
4  The salesperson who waits on me is the quiet, helpful type.   12
   |  1  |  2  |  3  |  4  |  5  |  6  |  7  |  8  |  9  |  10  |  11  |  12
```

FORMATTING REVIEW

Workbook 141.

Review the typing of tables on pages 97 and 100 before completing Jobs 85-1 and 85-2. Review the typing of tables with column heads on pages 102 and 104 before completing Job 85-3 (below) and Job 85-4 (on page 144).

JOB 85-1. TWO-COLUMN TABLE

Standard format (see pages 97 and 100). Double-space, full sheet of paper.

```
            KVIX CONTEST WINNERS

            Week of April 10—14

    Monday        Sarah Wheeling
    Tuesday       Donald Riley
    Wednesday     Edward Bowman
    Thursday      Janice Barnes
    Friday        Sharon Larson
```

JOB 85-2. THREE-COLUMN TABLE

Standard format. Double-space, full sheet of paper.

BUSINESS EMPLOYEES
(Texas Branch Offices)

Accountants	Austin	28
Clerks	Austin	42
Clerks	Tyler	26
Secretaries	Dallas	37
Stenographers	El Paso	41
Typists	Houston	50
Typists	San Antonio	42

JOB 85-3. THREE-COLUMN TABLE

Standard format. Single-space, full sheet of paper.

```
            DISTANCES BETWEEN U.S. CITIES

                Expressed in Kilometers


    West Coast        East Coast        Distance

    Seattle           Boston            4,896
    Portland          Baltimore         4,481
    San Francisco     Philadelphia      4,753
    Los Angeles       Washington, D.C.  4,312
```

Repeat the Pretest on page 132 to see how much your skill has improved.

1- AND 5-MINUTE TIMINGS

Take two 1-minute timings on each paragraph. Then take one 5-minute timing on the entire selection. Use single spacing for the 1-minute timings and double spacing for the 5-minute timing.

```
20        Working with plants could be an exciting and fun hobby      12
21   for you.  If you have never waited, with expectation, for a      24
22   tiny sprig to grow into a plant, you have missed a joy.          35

23        Plants make ideal pets for apartment dwellers.  Plants     12
24   do not bark or meow, and the neighbors don't complain about      24
25   being kept awake or about being annoyed by a loud pet.           35

26        If you decide that plant growing will be an acceptable      12
27   hobby for you, you must be sure to purchase plants that you      24
28   know can survive in the environment of your residence.           35

29        Most plants require at least moderate light and warmth      12
30   to live.  Additionally, plants need to be watered, fed, and      24
31   misted on a regular basis so they will grow and thrive.          35

32        If you are like the many others who like their plants,      12
33   your zeal for growing them will increase rapidly.  You will     24
34   undoubtedly be urging your friends to grow plants too.           35
     |  1  |  2  |  3  |  4  |  5  |  6  |  7  |  8  |  9  |  10 |  11 |  12    SI 1.39
```

LESSON 79

GOALS
- To identify how commas are used in compound sentences while typing.
- To build your typing speed on 12-second timings and on 30-second timings.

FORMAT
- Single spacing   60-space line   5-space tab

LAB 7

COMMAS IN COMPOUND SENTENCES

Type lines 1–4 once. Then repeat lines 1–4 or take a series of 1-minute timings.

```
1  It is too cloudy to fly today, but tomorrow will be better.   12
2  On Tuesday the movie ends, and on Wednesday another begins.    12
3  Alex will take today's quiz, or he may just wait for Paula.    12
4  You should not send a check, nor should you send any money.    12
   |  1  |  2  |  3  |  4  |  5  |  6  |  7  |  8  |  9  |  10 |  11 |  12
```

5-MINUTE TIMINGS

Take a 5-minute timing on lines 5–19. Type six times each word on which you made an error, hesitated, or stopped during the 5-minute timing. Then take a 5-minute timing to see how much your skill has improved.

```
 5          Travel can provide you with exciting, fun experiences.    12
                              1                          2
 6      The skills you might gain from travel can make you a better    24
                     3                      4
 7      person when at work, at school, at home, or at leisure.        35
             5                  6                      7
 8          While at work, you will come into contact with men and    47
                              8                      9
 9      women from every walk of life.  The various people that you    59
                  10                          11
10      meet in traveling will prepare you for your employment.        70
             12                  13                      14
11          When you travel, you may sometimes find yourself among    82
                          15                      16
12      people who do not speak the same language as you.  The tact    94
                  17                          18
13      this situation demands may be very useful at home too.        105
             19                  20                      21
14          At school you can share many of your travels with your    117
                              22                      23
15      classmates and teachers.  You might tell them all about the   129
                  24                          25
16      colorful, historical sites that you were able to visit.       140
             26                  27                      28
17          It might be that the quality of your leisure time will   152
                              29                      30
18      improve.  Just think of the dozens of new, unique dances or   164
                     31                      32
19      other pastimes you can teach your friends and family.         175
             33                  34                      35
        |  1  |  2  |  3  |  4  |  5  |  6  |  7  |  8  |  9  |  10  |  11  |  12   SI 1.39
```

FORMATTING REVIEW

Review the typing of business letters on pages 92–93 before completing Job 84-1.

JOB 84-1. LETTER

Standard format. Workbook 139–140. Body 91 words.

[*Today's date*] / Mr. David R. Stone / 1738 13 Cecil Avenue / San Jose, CA 95128 / Dear Mr. 22 Stone: 24

You have always been a preferred customer 34 of ours, and we have appreciated your contin- 43 uous, faithful trust in our line of products. 52 You have made it a habit to pay your credit 61 card purchases on time, and this practice has 70 built for you a fine credit rating. 78

It has come to my attention, though, that 87 you have not used our credit card for the past 97 12 months. Have we done something to cause 106 you to stop buying our products? If our prompt, 115 reliable service has failed you, please let us 125 know. / Yours, / Ms. Elaine Burrow / 137 Customer Service / [*Your initials*] 143

12-SECOND TIMINGS

Type each line four times, or take four 12-second timings on each line. For each timing, type with no more than one error.

5 If the order is a big one, we will make a very good profit. 12
6 They may not go up there if they are to come up here first. 12
7 We will do all that we can to help them win the big prizes. 12

| 25 | 30 | 35 | 40 | 45 | 50 | 55 | 60 |

30-SECOND TIMINGS

Take two 30-second timings on lines 8–10, or type the paragraph twice.

8 One thing of which we are quite sure is never to expect our 12
9 speed to jump or zip higher for three minutes before we can 24
10 type with the same degree of skill for about half a minute. 36

| 1 | 2 | 3 | 4 | 5 | 6 | 7 | 8 | 9 | 10 | 11 | 12 |

PREVIEW PRACTICE

Type lines 11 and 12 twice as a preview to the 5-minute timing below.

Accuracy 11 you deck early dozing nothing relaxing afternoon facilities
Speed   12 what like days near your home want just rise they heat bike

1- AND 5-MINUTE TIMINGS

Take two 1-minute timings on each paragraph. Then take one 5-minute timing on the entire selection. Use single spacing for the 1-minute timings and double spacing for the 5-minute timing.

13   What kinds of activities do you like when summer comes 12
14 and brings along those sunny days? The kinds of things you 24
15 can do usually depend on the facilities near your home. 35

16   You may want to spend your days splashing in the water 12
17 or just dozing on the deck if there's a swimming pool near. 24
18 Whenever the temperature rises, just take a quick dip. 35

19   Or perhaps jogging is what you would rather do. A few 12
20 joggers rise early on hot days, and they run before sunrise 24
21 to avoid the heat that will arrive with the afternoon. 35

22   Playing volleyball on a beach, riding a bike through a 12
23 park, relaxing on a sailboat, playing tennis, and reading a 24
24 terrific book are things you might do on a summer day. 35

25   Whatever you choose to do with your summer, though, be 12
26 sure to set aside some time for doing nothing. During this 24
27 time you might plan ahead for next winter's activities. 35

| 1 | 2 | 3 | 4 | 5 | 6 | 7 | 8 | 9 | 10 | 11 | 12 | SI 1.39

**JOB 83-1
(Continued)**

      <u>Carbon Paper</u>. Many types of carbon paper--thick, colored,   ₃₁₅

soft--may be bought in different sizes and for almost any price   ₃₃₀

you are willing to pay.   ₃₃₅

      When you are ready to start typing your report, be certain   ₃₄₈

that the carbon pack (the carbon paper and the paper on which your   ₃₆₂

originals and copies will be typed) is inserted into the machine   ₃₇₅

correctly. To do this, you must: ₃₈₂

    1. Check to be sure that the printed side of the letterhead   ₃₉₅
        and the dull side of the carbon sheets are facing you.   ₄₀₇

    2. Be sure that the pack is straight in the machine.   ₄₁₉

    3. Operate the paper release to release the tension on the   ₄₃₂
        papers.[3]   ₄₃₇

                                                                       +7

[3]Ibid., p. 230.   +6

LESSON 84

GOALS
- To type sentences that use the rule for commas between adjectives.
- To review letter typing.

FORMAT
- Single spacing 60-space line 5-space tab

LAB 8

**COMMAS
BETWEEN
ADJECTIVES**

Type lines 1–4 once. Then repeat lines 1–4 or take a series of 1-minute timings.

1 The tall, silent stranger ran quickly down the narrow walk. ₁₂
2 Members of the strong, silent majority seldom speak loudly. ₁₂
3 Diaz is a member of our unbeatable, hard-working judo team. ₁₂
4 Inside Franklin's loose, ill-fitting vest were six tickets. ₁₂
   | 1 | 2 | 3 | 4 | 5 | 6 | 7 | 8 | 9 | 10 | 11 | 12

Adjectives describe or modify nouns. Note the adjectives in italics:

brief speeches   *interesting* speeches   *brief, interesting* speeches
effective ideas   *unique* ideas   *effective, unique* ideas

When two or more adjectives describe the *same* noun, place a comma between the adjectives. In all other cases, use no comma. To determine whether the adjectives do describe the same noun, use the following test:

Janice gave a *factual, detailed* account. (Say "An account that was factual AND detailed." Does it make sense? Yes, proving that each adjective describes *account* and that the comma is needed.)

She distributed a *new summer* schedule. (Say "A schedule that is new AND summer." Does it make sense? No, proving that each adjective does not describe the noun *schedule*. No comma is needed.)

LESSON 80

GOALS
- To use commas correctly while typing compound sentences.
- To review the use of and gain proficiency in operating the tab, the shift lock, the space bar, the return, and the backspace key.
- To type at least 35/5'/5e.

FORMAT
- Single spacing   60-space line   Tabs every 9 spaces

LAB 7

Type lines 1–4 once, providing the missing commas. Edit your copy as your teacher reads the answers. Then retype lines 1–4 from your edited copy.

COMMAS IN COMPOUND SENTENCES

1 We will save our money this year and we will go on a trip.
2 You can watch the rabbits but they will run when you move.
3 You should not run away nor must you ever leave your post.
4 You may buy the book now or you may wait until next month.

TECHNIQUE REVIEW

Type lines 5–22 once to determine the two groups that gave you the most difficulty. Then type each difficult group once.

Tabulator Review

5	if	or	up	at	be	an	to
6	one	nor	let	two	six	but	for
7	plus	last	nine	zero	four	five	sums
8	ninth	joker	minor	first	sixth	tenth	fewer

Shift Lock Review

9 On FRIDAY, MARY was in RENO; last MONDAY, she was in MIAMI.
10 We drove to HARBOR–DELANEY, INC., to visit PAUL and JANICE.
11 Is JAMES going to read EXODUS or TOPAZ or QB VII on FRIDAY?
12 Drive the HARBOR, the SAN DIEGO, and the PASADENA freeways.

Space Bar Review

13 The sun was high in the sky, but it was not hot in the car.
14 All of us must see it now if it is to be fun for all of us.
15 A big dog and a tiny cat ran down the road at a rapid pace.
16 If it is to be, then we will not have much to say about it.

Carriage/Carrier Return Review

Return carriage or carrier after each word. Type lines 17E and 18E if you have an electric machine or lines 17M and 18M if you have a manual machine.

17E hairy laugh prowl learn acorn churn cramp camel ivory weigh
17M focus robot slant spend cocoa elbow spent their whale endow

18E yearn cameo panel blink adorn clamp usual lapel mourn repel
18M bigot cubic flair rifle shale sight tight aisle civic giant

Backspace Key Review

Backspace and underscore each underlined word immediately after typing it.

19 ah _am_ an _as_ at _be_ by _do_ go _ha_ he _ho_ if _in_ is _it_ me _no_ so _to_
20 was _one_ the _you_ our _for_ per _off_ put _how_ but _nor_ rib _kit_ day
21 last _week_ what _plan_ that _told_ good _more_ seem _sort_ like _this_
22 audit _signs_ blame _slept_ tithe _shame_ visit _gowns_ title _burns_

FORMATTING REVIEW

Before you type Job 83-1, review the typing of reports. Specifically, review standard format (page 117), side headings (page 78), paragraph headings (page 80), footnotes (page 121), continuation pages (page 117), and enumerations in reports (page 84). Workbook 135.

Practice 1. Practice the start of a report: type in proper position on a page the heading lines and the first paragraph of the report shown below.

Practice 2. Practice the typing of footnotes: type the last paragraph (on page 141) and the footnote. Begin typing on line 30. Remember to place the footnote at the *bottom* of the page on which it is referenced.

JOB 83-1. LONG REPORT
Double spacing, 5-space tab. Workbook 137.

```
                  HOW TO TYPE A REPORT                       12

              A Review of Some Basic Guidelines             34

                Prepared by Jane T. Sloan                   51
                                   ↓3
     When you are typing a paper for final copy, you should be sure    68

that it is of the highest quality and that your best efforts have     81

been put into the project.  If your report is going to be dupli-      94

cated, you must use a high-quality paper.  This report will present   108

the steps you must follow when typing a paper.                        117
                                          ↓3
SELECTION OF A TYPEWRITER                                              124

     Either a pica or an elite typewriter may be used when typing a    138

report.  Whatever the choice, you must be sure that the element or     151

the keys are clean and that they provide a good impression.  The      164

platen and bail rollers must also be free of grease, carbon, and      177

dirt.                                                                 179
     ↓3
SELECTION OF SUPPLIES                                                 185

     Ribbon.  A good ribbon should be used when typing reports.       201

"Use a black ribbon so that the copy will be clear and permanent."¹   216

A carbon ribbon will give the best results, but cloth ribbons may     229

also be used.  A good cloth ribbon should give you a dark, even       242

print.                                                                244

     Paper.  "Only good-quality bond paper should be used when typ-   259

ing your report."²  Many believe that 20-pound paper should be used   273

for typing originals and that 16-pound paper should be used if car-   286

bons are typed.  The rag content of the paper should be 50 percent.   300
```

Watching for bottom margin? Remember that a footnote must go on the same page as the reference to it.

Separation line is 20P/24E long. Single-space before and double-space after typing it.

---

¹William A. Sabin, <u>The Gregg Reference Manual</u>, 5th ed., Gregg Division, McGraw-Hill Book Company, New York, 1977, p. 271. +7 +27 +12

²Ibid. +5

(Continued on next page)

Type lines 23 and 24 twice as a preview to the 5-minute timing below.

Accuracy
Speed

23 day your begin merely outside exercise squirrels beginnings
24 door open sign will just very even some seem then they into

**1- AND
5-MINUTE
TIMINGS**

Take two 1-minute timings on each paragraph. Then take one 5-minute timing on the entire selection. Use single spacing for the 1-minute timings and double spacing for the 5-minute timing.

1'

          1   2

25   The wonders of nature are waiting for you just outside   12
26 your door. The next time you wake up, just open your door,   24
27 and immediately dozens of morning signs will greet you.   35
28   Among the signs of the morning are the rising sun, the   12
29 setting moon, the dimming light of giant stars, the shining   24
30 dew of evening dampness, and the beginning of the day.   35
31   If you are watching and are very quiet, you might even   12
32 see some of nature's creatures begin to prepare for the day   24
33 to come. Rabbits, squirrels, and birds are just awake.   35
34   Listen to the quiet that seems to be all around you in   12
35 these early moments of the day. Listen just a little more,   24
36 and you can distinguish the sounds of nature awakening.   35
37   Rabbits hop through the grass taking their early morn-   12
38 ing exercise; squirrels scamper about looking for food; and   24
39 all the songbirds, young and old alike, start to chirp.   35

| 1 | 2 | 3 | 4 | 5 | 6 | 7 | 8 | 9 | 10 | 11 | 12   SI 1.39

LESSON 81

CLINIC

GOALS
- To review production techniques.
- To practice drills designed to strengthen production techniques.

FORMAT
- Single spacing 60-space line

**KEYBOARDING
SKILLS**

Type lines 1–4 once. Then, as you type line 5, do what line 5 tells you to do. Repeat lines 1–4, or take a series of 1-minute timings.

Speed
Accuracy
Numbers
Symbols
Technique

1 It is the right time for us to go to the fair and have fun.   12
2 Even Jacques may gaze up to find six crows in the blue sky.   12
3 Lee waited 10 days, 29 days, 38 days, 47 days, and 56 days.   12
4 Joyce* and David* invested $6.80 for 2 boards @ $3.40 each.   12
5 Your carriage/carrier will lock before finishing this line; use the margin release.

| 1 | 2 | 3 | 4 | 5 | 6 | 7 | 8 | 9 | 10 | 11 | 12

Accuracy	20	can time some living features dazzling possible responsible	
	21	fun life your friends sidewalk residing enjoyable apartment	
	22	you live that quickly business managers deciding appliances	
	23	mow edge have minimal carpeted families different commuting	
Speed	24	before offers quite might lawns paint areas works wide will	
	25	within courts house grass times close edges lives lawn home	
	26	latest tennis could since block place areas yours edge mows	
	27	modern choice found pools offer court often likes easy very	

POSTTEST

Repeat the Pretest on page 138 to see how much your skill has improved.

TABULATOR REVIEW

Review use of the tabulator on page 23. Then set tab stops at 10, 20, 30, 40, and 50 spaces from the left margin, and type by touch the following columns.

123	890	456	724	680
13	570	98	321	76
102	93	847	56	639

PRODUCTION WORD COUNT

The production word count (PWC) is used in production work to give you words-a-minute credit for operations such as using the tabulator, underscoring, and depressing the tab. In the practice exercises below, the PWC allows you additional credit for centering each line, for using the tabulator key, and for underscoring.

The production word count assumes that you have set all necessary margins and tab stops, and that your typewriter is in position to perform the first operation. In the example below, your carriage or carrier would be positioned at the center point, ready to backspace for the title.

CENTERING REVIEW

Practice 1. Review horizontal centering (page 25), vertical centering (page 29), and spread centering (page 31). Then center the display on the right. Add double spacing and use a full sheet of paper.

Practice 2. Repeat Practice 1 on a half sheet, using single spacing.

B U L L E T I N ↓3	9
	11
Homecoming Pep Rally	24
for St. James High School	41
Will Be Held On	51
WEDNESDAY, OCTOBER 1	64
at the <u>School Gym</u>	81

LESSON 83

GOALS
- To review report typing.
- To type a two-page report.

FORMAT
- Single spacing   60-space line   5-space and center tabs

KEYBOARDING SKILLS

Type lines 1–4 once. In line 5, use the shift lock for each word in all-capital letters. Repeat lines 1–4, or take a series of 1-minute timings.

Speed	1	They may take the bus for the day if it is not out of town.	12
Accuracy	2	By quietly giving back six tops, we amazed the four judges.	12
Numbers	3	Oh, 56 and 47 add up to 103; but 29 and 10 do not equal 38.	12
Symbols	4	Vi sold 2 @ $9 (6% profit), and Ed sold 3 @ $8 (5% profit).	12
Technique	5	The dates were MARCH 1, APRIL 2, MAY 3, JUNE 4, and JULY 5.	

| 1 | 2 | 3 | 4 | 5 | 6 | 7 | 8 | 9 | 10 | 11 | 12

PRINT ALIGNMENT REVIEW

Before doing Exercises 1, 2, and 3, review page 59.

Exercise 1. At various places and angles on a page, type three underscore lines 30 spaces long. Remove your paper. Reinsert it. Type your name on each line, blocking the first letter you type with the first underscore in the line.

Exercise 2. Type your first name on a page and then remove the paper. Reinsert the paper, align your first name with the aligning scale, and type your middle name. Once again

remove the paper. Reinsert the paper, align your first two names with the aligning scale, and type your last name. Note whether the names have been aligned correctly.

Exercise 3. Type an underscore line 20 spaces long. Remove your paper. Reinsert the paper; then continue the underscore for another 20 spaces. Check to see how straight your underscore is.

ERASER CORRECTIONS REVIEW

Before typing and correcting the lines in Exercise 4, review page 54.

Exercise 4. Type the even-numbered lines (6, 8, 10); then correct these lines so that they look like the odd-numbered lines (7, 9, 11).

6 The teacher said their are four exercises do type by seven.
7 The teacher said there are four exercises to type by seven.
8 Please place that vase on the cabinet; than close the door.
9 Please place that vase in the cabinet; then close the door.
10 The flower grow rapidly in the warm son and gentle breezes.
11 The flower grew rapidly in the warm sun and gentle breezes.

SPREADING CORRECTIONS REVIEW

Before typing and correcting the lines in Exercise 5, review page 56 for spreading a correction.

Exercise 5. Type the even-numbered lines. Then type the odd-numbered lines, leaving the exact number of blank spaces shown. Type the words listed in the margin into the blank spaces by spreading.

12   We will go too the fair. Four children went too the movie.
Insert *to.*   13   We will go   the fair. Four children went   the movie.
14   Please stay bye the car. We shall walk bye the wide river.
Insert *by.*   15   Please stay   the car. We shall walk   the wide river.
16   We want to sell that product. They will buy that red sofa.
Insert *the.*   17   We want to sell   product. They will buy   red sofa.

SQUEEZING CORRECTIONS REVIEW

Before typing and correcting the lines in Exercise 6, review page 55 for squeezing a correction.

Exercise 6. Type the even-numbered lines. Then type the odd-numbered lines, leaving the exact number of blank spaces shown. Type the words listed in the margin into the blank spaces by squeezing.

18   The to of them may drive. Would you to want to ride along?
Insert *two.*   19   The   of them may drive. Would you   want to ride along?
20   We want to buy two books. Do they want to buy two pencils?
Insert *four.*   21   We want to buy   books. Do they want to buy   pencils?
22   They want to sell the product. They will buy the red sofa.
Insert *that.*   23   They want to sell   product. They will buy   red sofa.

LESSON 82

GOALS
- To use commas correctly while typing compound sentences.
- To review use of the tabulator.
- To review horizontal/vertical centering.
- To review display typing.

FORMAT
- Single spacing 60-space line 5-space tab

LAB 7

COMMAS IN COMPOUND SENTENCES
Workbook 133–134.

Type lines 1–4 once, providing the missing commas. Edit your copy as your teacher reads the answers. Then retype lines 1–4 from your edited copy.

1 Jan plays on the tennis team but Ed is on the track squad.
2 The semester is now here but no one is quite ready for it.
3 Geese fly north in the spring and they wing south in fall.
4 Mt. Pleasant is in Texas but it is also found in Michigan.

PRETEST

Take a 5-minute Pretest on lines 5–19. Then circle and count your errors. Use the chart below to determine which lines to type for practice.

```
                                      1                                2
5        To some, living in an apartment is enjoyable.  At some      12
                   3                        4
6  time in your life, it is quite possible that you might live       24
          5                        6                              7
7  in an apartment complex before deciding to buy a home.            35
                              8                        9
8        When residing in an apartment complex, you do not have      47
                  10                            11
9  to mow lawns, paint a house, or edge the grass next to your       59
        12                          13                       14
10 sidewalk.  An apartment manager is supposed to do this.           70
                              15                         16
11       Very often an apartment is close to the business area,      82
                17                            18
12 and you will find that your commuting time to work is quite       94
        19                    20                          21
13 minimal.  You could take a bus and get to work quickly.          105
                          22                            23
14       You will find it easy to make friends in an apartment,     117
          24                          25
15 since so many different people live next door or very close      129
        26                        27                          28
16 to your place.  You may find this to be very enjoyable.          140
                          29                        30
17       Most apartments can be found with the latest in modern     152
              31                          32
18 appliances, they are carpeted, and they offer a wide choice      164
        33                        34                          35
19 of dazzling features like pools and new tennis courts.           175
   |  1  |  2  |  3  |  4  |  5  |  6  |  7  |  8  |  9  |  10  |  11  |  12  SI 1.39
```

PRACTICE

In the chart below, find the number of errors you made on the Pretest. Then type each of the designated drill lines on page 139 four times.

Pretest errors	0–1	2–3	4–5	6+
Drill lines	23–27	22–26	21–25	20–24